"What a rich feast of insight, knowledge, and information about eucharistic history and practice through the centuries! The liturgical tradition—in both its vibrant diversity and its lively engagement with material reality, the visual arts, music, and architecture—truly comes alive in this volume. *From Age to Age* is a must for anyone interested in how Christians have celebrated the sacrament of God's real presence in ever-changing contexts."

—Professor Teresa Berger
Yale ISM & Divinity School
New Haven, Connecticut

"This is an excellent historical survey of the development of the eucharistic celebration, with very helpful treatment of developments in architecture, music, books, vessels, and eucharistic theology in each major era. Running alongside the text are well-chosen quotations, photographs, diagrams, and musical examples. Each chapter ends with a delightful story suggesting what it must have been like for real people who celebrated the Eucharist. This second, revised edition is nearly twice as long as the original, and readers will welcome the addition of eucharistic theology to each chapter as well as the expansion of the quotations and accompanying material. This will be an indispensable text on the Eucharist for teachers and students. Congratulations to the author for this achievement. Very highly recommended!"

—Fr. Anthony Ruff, OSB
Associate Professor of Liturgy and Liturgical Music
Saint John's University and School of Theology•Seminary
Collegeville, Minnesota

From Age to Age

How Christians Have Celebrated the Eucharist

Revised and Expanded Edition

Edward Foley

LITURGICAL PRESS
Collegeville, Minnesota

www.litpress.org

Excerpts from documents of the Second Vatican Council are from *Vatican Council II: The Basic Sixteen Documents*, by Austin Flannery, OP © 1996 (Costello Publishing Company, Inc.). Used with permission.

Unless otherwise noted, all foreign translations in this volume are by the author.

Scripture texts in this work are taken from the *New Revised Standard Version Bible* © 1989, Division of Christian Education of the National Council of the Churches of Christ in the United States of America. Used by permission. All rights reserved.

1   2   3   4   5   6   7   8   9

Library of Congress Cataloging-in-Publication Data

Foley, Edward.
    From age to age : how Christians have celebrated the Eucharist / Edward
Foley. — Rev. and expanded ed.
        p.   cm.
    Includes bibliographical references and index.
    ISBN 978-0-8146-3078-5 (pbk.)
    1. Lord's Supper—Celebration—History.   I. Title.

BV825.5.F64 2008
264'.0203609—dc22

                                                                2008021298

Contents

Preface to the New Edition

In the sixteen years since the first edition of *From Age to Age* appeared, I have received a wealth of feedback on the book. Some came in the form of reviews that affirmed strengths and offered suggestions for improvements. These were very helpful. Most feedback, however, came from students and teachers, laypeople and professional liturgists, who commented on their own reading or use of the book. Because of the reviews, the feedback, and the apparent value of the format and approach—as well as my own more nuanced awareness of issues of culture, context, and the pluriformity of our tradition—it became increasingly clear to me over the past few years that a revision was in order.

One compelling reason for the particular shape and expansiveness of this revision is that, although it was not my original expectation, much to my surprise the book has been adopted in many places as a textbook for continuing education, undergraduate, and even graduate courses in liturgy, church history, and Eucharist. My original intent was to write an accessible book for laypeople that would introduce them to something of the richness of our eucharistic history. While wanting to respect that original and still very important audience, I have also tried to enhance the scope and content of the book so that it might be more useful as a textbook, even at the graduate level. Thus, in the current volume you will encounter more technical terms and words from languages other than English. I have striven to explain and translate all such words for the reader whenever they first occur in the text. There has also been a considerable expansion of the illustrations and quotations in order to provide a broader perspective on eucharistic history and practice. Admittedly, however, the book is still both focused on and bound by my own Western and Roman Catholic biases.

At the encouragement of many—and first prompted by a very insightful review by Mary Barbara Agnew—I have added a new section in each chapter to address more explicitly the eucharistic theology of each period under consideration. This has also necessitated an expansion of the introduction to each chapter so that the theological reflections in that final section might be grounded in a stronger contextual framework. This new edition does not purport to be a comprehensive overview of eucharistic liturgy in the West and, as the expanded bibliography attests, I rely on many other specialized and more comprehensive works to offer that vision. It is hoped, however, that the addition of this new section in each chapter might give the beginning student or nonspecialist a fuller vision of this complex of praxis and theory we call Eucharist.

Writing the first edition was a significant learning experience for me. This version has proven no less enriching, largely because of the many gifted colleagues who have assisted in the process. Gabe Huck initiated this revision project when he was at Liturgy Training Publications, and I remain grateful for his enduring insight and unflagging support for this project. Early in the revision process, seven colleagues each read an individual chapter or two from the original edition and were invited to offer any critiques or suggestions. Their analysis was a case study in collaborative learning, and I am very grateful to each of them for their serious work and collegial response in the revision process. These collegues are: chapter 1, Leslie Hoppe, OFM, Provincial Minister of the Assumption Province BVM; chapter 2, Carolyn Osiek, RSCJ, of Brite Divinity School; chapter 3, John Baldovin, SJ, of the Weston School of Theology; chapter 4, Richard McCarron of Catholic Theological Union; chapter 5, Kevin Madigan of Harvard University; chapter 6, James White (d. 2004), formerly of the University of Notre Dame where he was my teacher; and chapter 7, Keith Pecklers, SJ, of the Gregorian University and Sant Anselmo and, again, James White. I have also benefited from the careful reading of my Catholic Theological Union colleagues Amanda Quantz, who corrected early chapters of the revision, and Richard Fragomeni, who reviewed the new theological sections.

More generally, I am profoundly grateful to my colleagues in teaching and learning at Catholic Theological Union, students and faculty alike. They have left an indelible mark on the way I think and learn and teach and worship. The engagement of such a rich field of collaborators has helped me correct some mistakes, expand the vision of this eucharistic telling, and offer a richer exposition of eucharistic theory and practice. Whatever errors remain in no way reflect upon them, but belong solely to me.

Finally, as I am grateful to the original editorial and design team at Liturgy Training Publications who so effectively shaped words and graphics into an integrated whole, I have new gratitude and profound respect for my longtime friends at Liturgical Press who have so wholeheartedly taken up this revision project. I am particularly grateful to Peter Dwyer for his willingness to publish this new edition, to Susan Sink and Mary Stommes for their editorial wisdom, and to Colleen Stiller for the gracious way she guided the project through production. And I am grateful to Samantha Woodson who painstakingly crafted the new index.

The original edition of *From Age to Age* was dedicated to the memory of Niels Krogh Rasmussen, OP, and Ralph Keifer. Niels directed my doctoral dissertation, a work of medieval liturgical history, and previous to that Ralph had directed an MA thesis that I had written in liturgical history of the primitive church, both at the University of Notre Dame. In this year commemorating the twentieth anniversaries of their deaths, I gratefully recall their scholarship, direction, and friendship, and I reiterate the dedication of this ongoing work to their memories.

Edward Foley, Capuchin
13 December 2007
The Feast of St. Lucy

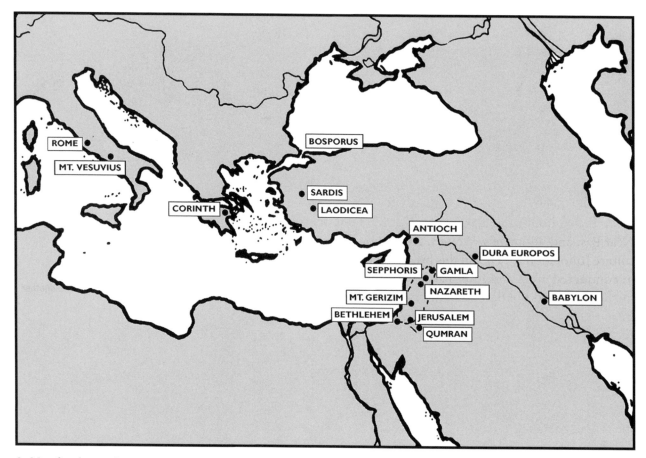

1. Map for chapter 1.

CHAPTER ONE

Emerging Christianity:
The First Century

Pope Pius XI (d. 1939) once commented that every Christian must become a spiritual Semite. While it might be possible to disagree with this formulation, it is less possible to dismiss the insight behind it. Christianity originated in a Jewish milieu and even today continues to be shaped by these Jewish beginnings. Christians believe that Jesus—as both human and divine—was unique in the history of salvation, establishing a new covenant [quotation 1] and revealing himself as God's fullest self-communication to humankind. Jesus was a Jew and his Jewishness unquestionably shaped his mission and ministry. Thus his unique message is linked to a specific time, place, and culture, although it is not confined by these. Jesus' message and the Christianity that emerged from those who accepted that message can be understood only in the context of the Jewish culture in which they originated.

It is not enough, however, to recognize that Christianity emerged in a Jewish setting. First-century Palestine was deeply influenced by Hellenistic culture. Almost four centuries before the birth of Christ, Alexander the Great (d. 323 B.C.E.) [illustration 2] conquered the whole of the eastern Mediterranean region, including Palestine. More than a brilliant military strategist, Alexander transformed the Near East and, ultimately, Western civilization by promoting Greek culture [quotation 2]. He did this by encouraging his troops to settle in conquered areas and intermarry with the local population. He further provided political and cultural incentives to those who acquainted themselves with Greek language and culture. Although Alexander's empire was divided among his generals after his death, the influence of his Hellenizing efforts continued for centuries.

Jewish and Greek cultures intertwined in Palestine through a long process of relatively peaceful integration. However, in 167 B.C.E. Antiochus IV (d. 164 B.C.E.), the Seleucid king of Syria, desecrated the temple, abolished Torah observance, and tried to establish the worship of Greek gods in Jerusalem. A revolt, led by Mattathias (d. ca. 166 B.C.E.) and his sons of the Maccabean or Hasmonean

2. Alexander the Great.

Quotation 1: *I give you a new commandment, that you love one another.* (John 13:34)

Quotation 2: *[Alexander's] career . . . spread Hellenism in a vast colonizing wave throughout the Near East and created, if not politically, at least economically and culturally, a single world stretching from Gibraltar to the Punjab . . . with a considerable overlay of common civilization and the Greek koinē as a lingua franca.* (Walbank, "Alexander," p. 473)

3. Coinage issued by the Hasmonean Hyrcanus, a sign of full political independence from the Seleucids.

Quotation 3: *The main west-east road through Galilee ran from Ptolemaïs on the Mediterranean cost through Sepphoris to Tiberias on the Sea of Galilee. Ptolemaïs itself was on the Via Maris, the coastal Way of the Sea, that most ancient Palestinian highway of international commerce and conquest that opened Sepphoris and its environs to cosmopolitan influence. Sepphoris was also the terminus of the north-south mountain road from Jerusalem. Two roads, therefore, and possibly carrying quite different types of influence, converged in Sepphoris so that the village or hamlet of Nazareth, while certainly off the beaten track, was not very far off a fairly well beaten track.*

To understand Nazareth, therefore, demands consideration not only of its rural aspects but also if its relationship to an urban provincial capital." (Crossan, The Historical Jesus, p. 18)

priestly dynasty, drove Antiochus from Jerusalem. The revolutionaries succeeded in recapturing Jerusalem and purifying the temple, while their successors eventually established an independent Jewish territory [illustration 3]. While the Jews attempted to assert their cultural independence from Hellenism in the midst of this political independence, the effort was short-lived and ultimately unsuccessful. Even before Rome conquered the Jewish monarchy in 63 B.C.E. and ended political independence, in an ironic twist the Hasmonean dynasty embraced the Hellenization that their forebears had rejected. The process of Hellenization was so successful that it is virtually impossible to speak of a non-Hellenized Jew in first-century Roman Palestine. Thus it was in a Hellenized Jewish milieu under the political and cultural influence of the Greco-Roman world that Christianity emerged.

The interplay of Jewish and Hellenizing influences on emerging Christianity converge in the historical Jesus. While from Nazareth—a small village of maybe four hundred people—Jesus was raised in the shadow of Sepphoris [quotation 3]. This was an urban center along a bustling trade route in Ancient Palestine, built by Herod Antipas (d. 39 C.E.) to serve as his capital. A city of approximately thirty thousand, Sepphoris was a provincial hub with many satellite villages in its ambit. Nazareth was one of them. While Jesus may have lived in a hamlet where Aramaic rather than Greek dominated the conversation, no Nazarean of his time could have escaped the pervasive Hellenizing influence of a great center like Sepphoris. Later in his life, Jesus did minister in small towns and traveled among the villages of Galilee. However, these were never far from large urban areas that dominated the region. Andrew Overman considers the lower Galilee one of the most densely populated regions of the entire Roman

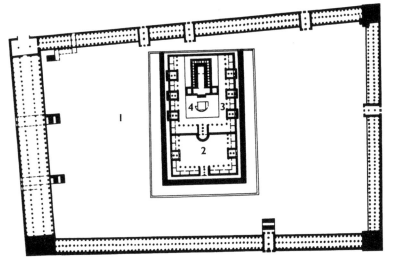

1. Court of the Gentiles
2. Court of the Women
3. Court of Israel
4. Court of the Priests

4. Plan of Herod's temple. (After Vincent-Steve as cited in Perrin-Duling, p. xx)

Empire, where life was as urbanized and urbane as anywhere else in the Greco-Roman world. It was in this context that the followers of Jesus of Nazareth were first called Christians [quotation 4].

Quotation 4: *It was in Antioch that the disciples were first called "Christians."* (Acts 11:26)

ARCHITECTURE

Jews at the time of Jesus did not confine their worship to a single location or type of building. A pious Jew was expected to pray not only in some specially designated room or structure but wherever he might be throughout the day [quotation 5]. No matter what the location, the believer was expected to bless God continuously throughout the day. Breaking bread, seeing lightning, purchasing a vessel, and watching the sun set were all occasions for blessing God. Although prayer was not confined to any specific location for Jews, certain types of prayer or ritual came to be identified with specific sites. The most important of these were the temple, the synagogue, and the home.

Quotation 5: *If he was riding an ass, he should dismount [to pray]. But if he cannot dismount, he should turn his face [toward the East]. And if he cannot turn his face, he should direct his heart toward the Chamber of the Holy of Holies. If he was traveling in a ship or on a raft he should direct his heart towards [sic] the Chamber of the Holy of Holies.* (Mishnah, Berakhot 4:5-6)

Temple

Following the instructions of his father King David (d. about 962 B.C.E.), Solomon (d. about 922 B.C.E.) built the first temple in Jerusalem [quotation 6]. This small but sumptuous structure became an important religious center for Israel, eventually overshadowing every other sanctuary in the country. Destroyed by the invading Babylonians in 587 B.C.E., the Jerusalem temple was rebuilt after the period

Quotation 6: *Then [David] called for his son Solomon and charged him to build a house for the LORD, the God of Israel. David said to Solomon: "My son, I had planned to build a house to the name of the LORD, my God. But the Word of the LORD came to me, saying 'You have shed much blood and have waged great wars; you shall not build a house to my name, because you have shed so much blood in my sight on the earth.'"* (1 Chr 22:6-8)

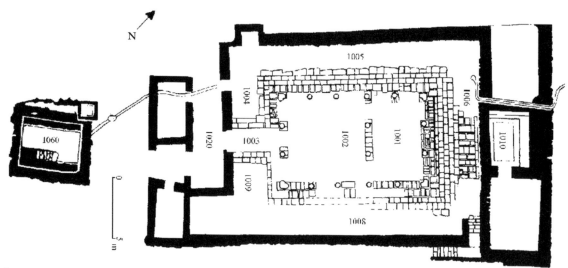

5. Gamla, first-century C.E. synagogue.

of captivity in about 515 B.C.E. By the first century B.C.E. this structure, ravaged by time and wars, was in considerable disrepair. Herod the Great (d. 4 B.C.E.) demolished this second temple and began building a magnificent replacement about the year 20 B.C.E. Construction was completed by 64 C.E.

The new temple, like the two before it, sat high on a hill overlooking the Kidron valley. This temple was about the same size as Solomon's building. It seemed more magnificent because it was set off by a series of walls and courtyards [illustration 4]: the outermost Court of the Gentiles, open to all; the Court of the Women, open to all Jews; the Court of Israel, open only to Jewish men; and the innermost Court of the Priests, open only to the priests. The altar for the daily sacrifices and an enormous water container for washing sacrifices, called the "Brazen Sea," as well as other smaller water basins on wagons stood within the Court of Israel.

Although sacrifices had once been offered throughout Israel, the temple in Jerusalem came to be the only place of sacrifice for the Jews, except for the Samaritans, who offered sacrifices in their temple on Mount Gerizim. The destruction of the Jerusalem temple during the Jewish revolt against the Romans in 70 C.E. marked the end of virtually all sacrifice among the Jews. To this day, however, the Samaritans sacrifice lambs on Mount Gerizim as part of their Passover celebration.

Jesus is remembered as having traveled to the temple in his childhood at Passover (Luke 2:41-50). It is especially the Gospel of John that remembers him frequenting the temple during his public ministry, while the Synoptic Gospels place him there only a few days before his death. The gospels do seem to agree, however, that Jesus

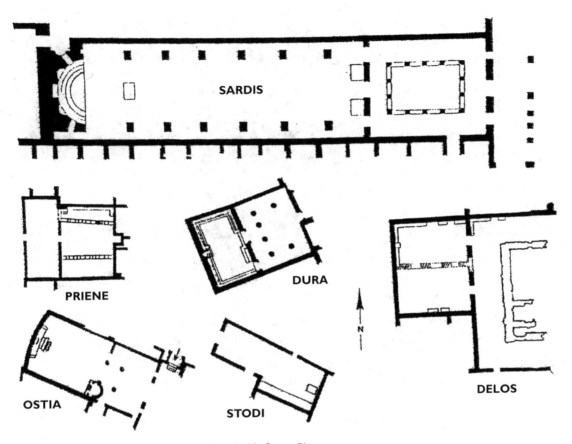

6. Synagogues in Diaspora. (L. Michael White, 1:63, figure 9)

prayed, taught, cured the sick, and challenged contemporary religious practice within the temple precincts [quotation 7]. After his resurrection, the disciples also continued to worship and evangelize in the temple precincts. As the early Jewish-Christians began to distinguish themselves from other Jews, the temple became a place of tension for them. Yet they never completely rejected the temple or its worship [quotation 8].

Synagogue

Unlike the temple, the origins of the Jewish synagogue are yet in doubt. Joseph Gutmann summarizes the three traditional theories for explaining the origins of this institution. Many believe that the synagogue emerged during the Babylonian exile (597–538 B.C.E.). Others favor the Deuteronomic origin of the synagogue during the reign of King Josiah (640–609 B.C.E.). Finally, a small group holds for a Hellenistic beginning of the synagogue (third century B.C.E.). The problem with these theories is a lack of hard evidence for each.

Quotation 11: *Then Jesus, filled with the power of the Spirit, returned to Galilee, and a report about him spread through all the surrounding country. He began to teach in their synagogues and was praised by everyone. When he came to Nazareth, where he had been brought up, he went to the synagogue on the sabbath day, as was his custom. He stood up to read.* (Luke 4:14-16)

Quotation 12: *For several days [Saul] was with the disciples in Damascus, and immediately he began to proclaim Jesus in the synagogues, saying, "He is the Son of God."* (Acts 9:19-20)

7. Niche in the wall facing Jerusalem in the Dura Europos synagogue (ca. 245 C.E.), believed to have been the repository for the Torah scrolls.

Firm literary evidence for the synagogue exists only from the first century C.E. [quotation 9]. There is archaeological evidence for only four structures from first-century Palestine that some are willing to identify as synagogues [illustration 5]. These factors led Gutmann to suggest that synagogue buildings only appeared in the second century B.C.E.

Like an early term for "church" (Greek, *ekkelsia*), the word synagogue (Greek, συναγόγ = "assembly"; Hebrew, *bet ha-keneset* = "house of meeting") can refer both to an assembly of people and to a building. In Christianity the assembly existed before it had any permanent housing; the same was true in Judaism. Given the variety of assembly needs, physical settings, and economic means among Jews, synagogues developed in various shapes and sizes. Thus it is difficult to generalize about the design of synagogues in the first century C.E. [illustration 6].

The earliest buildings that can actually be identified as synagogues were simple structures. This was due, in part, to the fact that such buildings served multiple purposes aside from worship. As synagogue ritual evolved, so did the buildings that housed it [quotation 10]. For example, as the reading of Scripture became an increasingly important element in synagogue worship, Torah shrines evolved. Originally portable, such shrines eventually became fixed and highly elaborated elements [illustration 7].

Jesus would have attended synagogue services while growing up in Nazareth. From early in his public ministry, he is remembered as having visited synagogues to pray. There he cast out demons, taught, and began his preaching ministry. In his hometown synagogue he is remembered as having read a prophecy from Isaiah and declaring himself to be the fulfillment of those words [quotation 11]. Following his example, the disciples continued to preach in the synagogues. Many times the Acts of the Apostles tell of Paul, Silas, Barnabas, and others preaching in the synagogues. Just as Jesus is remembered as first having preached his message in the synagogue, so is Paul remembered [quotation 12].

Synagogues, as both assemblies and buildings, were contexts in which Jesus and his disciples preached. So were they contexts in which many Jews came to believe in this new way. As the Jewish disciples did not reject Judaism initially, so they did not reject the practice of synagogue study and prayer. Consequently, for most of the first century, the Jewish followers of Jesus continued to frequent synagogues. Thus Raymond E. Brown, for example, believes that an early passage in the epistles of James assumes that the Christian addressees are assembling in a synagogue (Brown, *The Churches the Apostles Left Behind,* p. 26) [quotation 13]. Eventually, however,

Jesus' followers came to be identified more as a separate group than as a reforming agent within Judaism. About the year 80 C.E., a malediction against them was inserted into one of the central prayers of the daily Jewish service [quotation 14]. The appearance of this prayer at the heart of synagogue worship signals heightened tension between the Jewish followers of Jesus and other Jews, and the former's growing separation from the synagogue. While abandoning the Jewish synagogue context, the Jewish followers of Jesus did not abandon the synagogue ways of prayer. In places such as Jerusalem where there was a significant Jewish-Christian population, these followers probably had their own synagogues at least into the second century. Thus, as Hayim Perelmuter and others have suggested, it is possible to think of emerging Christianity and rabbinic Judaism as "siblings" [quotation 82, below], both born of the ferment that marked second temple Judaism. Furthermore, the separation between these siblings was a long and uneven process, so that even as late as the fourth century John Chrysostom (d. 407), Bishop of Constantinople, could chide Christians in Antioch for continuing to frequent synagogue services [quotation 15].

Home

If the temple was a place of sacrifice and the synagogue a place for study and gathering, then the home was a place for blessing, prayer, and ritual eating. Although certain prayers such as the *Shema* or "Hear, O Israel" came to be central elements in the synagogue service, they first were prayers offered in the home [quotation 16]. The home was particularly important for emerging Christianity as the center for that important familial and social institution, the meal. For Jews, every meal was a sacred act. In a singular way, the meal and its blessings recalled God's faithful generosity and became a living sign of the covenant that God had sealed with a meal. Festival meals had their own repertoire of prayers and ritual actions. Some of them, such as the Passover meal, developed into elaborate and treasured traditions.

Jesus certainly learned to pray as he ate with his family at home in Nazareth. At that table, he heard the accounts of God's wondrous deeds that confirmed and continued the covenant with Israel. There he must have learned the traditional prayer patterns of blessing before and after festival meals. It is commonly believed that the blessings surrounding such meals contributed to the development of Christian eucharistic prayers [quotation 17]. This pattern of table learning for the child became a pattern of table ministry for the adult. Time and again, Jesus is remembered as having entered the home of an outcast

Quotation 15: *Do you wish to see the temple? Don't run to the synagogue; be a temple yourself. God destroyed one temple in Jerusalem but he reared up temples beyond number, temples more august than that old one ever was. Paul said: "You are the temple of the living God. Make that temple beautiful, drive out every evil thought, so that you may be a precious member of Christ, a temple of the Spirit. And make others be temples such as you are yourselves. When you see the poor, you would not find it easy to pass them by. When any of you see some Christian running to the synagogue, do not look the other way. Find some argument you can use as a halter to bring him back to the Church. This kind of almsgiving is greater than giving to the poor, and the profit from it is worth more than ten thousand talents. (Eight Homilies against the Jews VI, 7.7, trans. C. Mervyn Maxwell)*

Quotation 16: *Hear, O Israel: The LORD is our God, the LORD alone. You shall love the LORD your God with all your heart, and with all your soul, and with all your might. Keep these words that I am commanding you today in your heart. Recite them to your children and talk about them when you are at home and when you are away, when you lie down and when you rise. . . . write them on the doorposts of your house and on your gates. (Deut 6:4-7, 9)*

Quotation 17: *And Isaac, too, sent by the hand of Jacob to Abraham a best thank-offering that he might eat and drink. And he ate and drank, and blessed the Most High God, who hath created heaven and earth, and given them to the children of men that they might eat and drink and bless their creator. (Charles, The Blessing after a Meal from The Book of Jubilees, [ca. 100 B.C.E.])*

8. Reconstruction of a multistory apartment block. (After Gardner, p. 186)

Quotation 18: *Then Levi gave a great banquet for [Jesus] in his house; and there was a large crowd of tax collectors and others sitting at the table with them.*
(Luke 5:29)

Quotation 19: *House patternings varied considerably across the empire: the Italian villa, the Greek peristyle, the Hellenistic-oriental multistoried insula, apartments, and others had their own local stylistic traditions. We must expect, then, that . . . there was considerable diversity from place to place depending on the local circumstances of each cell group.*
(L. Michael White, *Building God's House in the Roman World*, p. 107)

Quotation 20: *For, to begin with, when you come together as a church, I hear that there are divisions among you; and to some extent I believe it. . . . When you come together, it is not really to eat the Lord's supper. For when the time comes to eat, each of you goes ahead with your own supper, and one goes hungry and another becomes drunk. What! Do you not have homes to eat and drink in? Or do you show contempt for the church of God and humiliate those who have nothing?*
(1 Cor 11:18, 20-22)

or a dignitary and sharing a meal [quotation 18]. In these homes and in an upper room, Jesus continued the ministry that was manifest in the temple and the synagogue, where he prayed, taught, cured the sick, and reconciled sinners.

After Jesus' resurrection, the disciples continued to gather in believers' homes or apartment houses [illustration 8] as well as in borrowed rooms of public buildings. Jesus had celebrated his last ritual meal with the disciples in a borrowed room, and he appeared to them there after the resurrection. Borrowed rooms continued to serve the fledgling community through the first century. It is also possible that they gathered in caves, for example, in Bethlehem or Gethsemane, both of which give evidence of pre-Byzantine worship by Christians. Here the good news was announced, teaching was imparted, and reconciliation was offered. In these diverse places, the members of the early community also gathered for the breaking of the bread.

The spacious homes or villas of wealthy believers were key gathering places as the community expanded into the urban centers of the first-century empire. It is difficult to generalize about the types of homes that existed in the Roman Empire during the first centuries of the Common Era [quotation 19]. It was not uncommon to find members of the upper class living in large, four-sided structures that ordinarily included a large dining room well suited for Eucharist and a pool in the atrium adaptable for baptism [illustration 9]. This type of home well could have been the setting for Paul's famous admonishment about celebrating the Eucharist recorded in 1 Corinthians [quotation 20].

Jerome Murphy-O'Connor has suggested that a gathering for worship would have been confined to the two most public areas of such a home: the dining room and atrium. In the early history of these domestic gatherings one can imagine the worshiping community respecting the limitations of another family's dwelling. Any permanent changes would have been inappropriate, and the community likely rearranged furniture in order to accommodate its worship, using a table or tables for Eucharist and a chair for the host or bishop who led the worship. A recently excavated Roman house from Corinth, dating from the time of Paul, had a dining room that measured about eighteen feet by twenty-four feet, although the floor space was diminished by the couches that lined the walls. This space would have been too small for the projected forty or fifty members of the Corinthian Christian community. Consequently, the friends of the host or important guests would have been invited to recline in the dining room for the meal that was interwoven with the Eucharist. Those who were less well known to the host, or some of the poorer community members who arrived late because they had to work longer, were relegated to the open-air atrium. This space was not only more uncomfortable—especially if the weather was inclement—it was also farther from the food and drink. Apparently, some guests never received dinner. No wonder Paul suggested that people should eat at their own homes before gathering for Eucharist. Even after the Eucharist was separated from the meal, something that happened quite early in emerging Christian practice, private homes continued to be important settings for worship.

9. Roman villa excavated at Corinth, dating from the time of Paul. (After Murphy-O'Connor, p. 157)

Summary

The fledgling Christian community had no architecture of its own but, rather, continued to use the places of Jewish cult: the Jerusalem temple until its destruction in 70 C.E., synagogues, and homes. As this religious movement gravitated toward large Hellenized cities and evangelized large numbers of Gentiles, large homes of wealthy believers became important gathering places. Distinctive Christian rituals are clearly marked by such home environments.

The growing importance of the domestic setting for Christian worship raises an interesting gender question. The temple was clearly a male domain, and women were barred from the central court where sacrifices were offered. Synagogues reflected a more mixed picture regarding gender. Women appear more integrated into the central prayer events and even assumed leadership, though the latter seems more the exception than the rule. In the Greco-Roman world, however, the home could be considered "women's space," where the participation and even leadership of women was more common [quotation 21]. Women would eventually be muted in Christian worship, and Teresa Berger suggests that there is already evidence

Quotation 21: *The earliest ecclesial and therefore liturgical space was women's space. . . . It was a context genial to the active participation and leadership of women. Women formed new churches in their homes and functioned as heads of these house churches. (Berger, Women's Ways of Worship, p. 33)*

10. Shofar.

Quotation 22: *[L]ike living stones, let yourselves be built into a spiritual house, to be a holy priesthood, to offer spiritual sacrifices acceptable to God through Jesus Christ.* (1 Pet 2:5)

Quotation 23: *Examining the borders between music and other symbolic forms along a given continuum reveals that the semantic surface of the concept "music" is displaced from one culture to another. This is particularly clear in societies for which the word "music" does not exist.* (Nattiez, *Music and Discourse*, p. 54)

Quotation 24: *Hebrew and Greek have no separate word for music. The frontier between singing and speaking was far less precise. As soon as speech turned to poetry, or when public or ceremonial speaking was involved, rhythmic and melodic features were incorporated which today would be classified as musical, or at least premusical.* (Gelineau, "Music and Singing in the Liturgy," p. 448)

of this "liturgical muting" in the New Testament itself. Nonetheless, the domestic context of emerging Christian worship suggests a need to imagine the role of women in the shape and ethos of this worship that goes beyond patriarchal stereotypes.

Despite the growing preference for domestic settings, however, the first Christians seem imbued with that liberating perspective embedded in the Jewish imagination that God could not be confined to a single place. Prayer could and should be offered anywhere. Consequently, there existed little tendency in the beginning to develop distinctive designs or spatial arrangements for worship. Thus, borrowed spaces, the homes of the poor, and caves, virtually any sheltered place the believing community could gather around a table, nourished emerging eucharistic practice. The language of these first believers unquestionably stressed that the people were more important than the space. The assembly, not the building, is the true temple [quotation 22]. Similarly, the Greek work *ekklesia*, which often is translated as "church," did not refer to the structure but first to the believers. The only true Christian architecture of the first century was one of living stones and not of brick or mortar. This ideal accompanied the development of Christianity through its first centuries.

MUSIC

Ralph Martin once wrote that "the Christian Church was born in song." While this seems to be an apt characterization of emerging Christianity, it is also problematic. The problem stems from the fact that "music" and "song" are not univocal concepts shared by all peoples at all times. Most people living in Western industrialized countries make a clear distinction between singing and speaking. In some cultures like ancient Judaism, however, there were no such clear-cut boundaries [quotation 23]. This is particularly true when it came to public performance. Reading a sacred text for other worshipers, for example, presumed dynamic, rhythmic, and melodic features that fluidly migrated between the borders of speech and song. Public preaching and teaching also presumed a kind of chanting in cadence that cannot be adequately defined by modern Western categories but that exhibited what might be called degrees of musicality. Although many religions did have specially trained singers, dancers, and instrumentalists, the ritual music of the ancient world was not confined to their performance. In Judaism and emerging Christianity, to the extent that there was audible worship, that worship was lyrical [quotation 24]. Furthermore, liturgical leadership

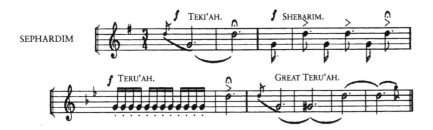

11. Shofar calls. (Werner, 2:12)

was not separate from musical leadership; every leader of public prayer in Israel would have rendered that prayer in a "musical" manner. Christian liturgy and its leadership clearly emerged in a heightened auditory environment.

Temple

The architectural splendor of Herod's temple certainly found a parallel in the temple's music. The temple at the time of Jesus had a large staff of professional musicians—possibly close to three hundred—drawn from the tribe of Levi. According to the Bible, the musician-king David appointed some of the Levites as musicians [quotation 25]. This account, however, was written centuries after the events it recounts; and the earliest biblical accounts of the temple (e.g., 2 Sam 6) do not mention professional musicians, which may have been a post-Davidic development. While Levites did have a definable role in the second temple period, their role in the temple of Solomon is unclear. Despite a lack of credible specifics, it seems plausible that David was deeply interested in things musical and that early on Levites were involved in temple music.

At the time of Jesus, rigorously trained professional instrumentalists and singers served in the temple. Instrumental music was an integral part of worship in Herod's temple. Of the various instruments mentioned in the Bible, some, like the trumpet and *shofar* [illustrations 10 and 11], were used primarily to signal ritual moments such as the entrance of the priests. Other wind and string instruments accompanied the singing of the choir [illustration 12]. Eric Werner believed that these instruments would have reproduced the vocal line of the singers with only slight ornamentation.

On certain occasions, a mixture of all the instruments with percussion joined with the voices of an expanded choir to offer a fitting song to the Lord [quotation 26]. The choir, which seems to have numbered at least twelve adult male singers, could be augmented

Quotation 25: *David and the officers of the army also set apart for the service the sons of Asaph, and of Heman, and of Jeduthun, who should prophesy with lyres, harps, and cymbals.* (1 Chr 25:1)

Quotation 26:
Praise him with trumpet sound;
  praise him with lute and harp!
Praise him with tambourine and dance;
  praise him with strings and pipe!
Praise him with clanging cymbals;
  praise him with loud clashing cymbals!
(Ps 150:3-5)

12. A kinnor, mentioned in Psalm 150:3 and often translated as "harp," as depicted on a coin (ca. 134 C.E.) at the time of the Bar Cochba revolution. The inscription reads, "For the freedom of Jerusalem."

with an unlimited number of adult males and male Levite children. The instrumentalists, for whom the number twelve also seems to have been an ideal, could have been joined by other instrumentalists according to need. On certain days, the combined forces of voices and instruments could have numbered more than fifty!

The psalms were one important part of the temple repertoire, and certain psalms came to be prescribed for specific events or festivals. Psalm 15, an examination of conscience for worshipers, probably was employed as a preparation for worship. Psalms 113 to 118 came to be sung at the three great pilgrim festivals of Passover, Pentecost, and Tabernacles. Besides the psalms, Levites also sang a variety of canticles and other poetic texts from the Bible. The Mishnah, for example, gives the impression that the Song of Moses (Exod 15:1-8) was employed in temple worship [quotation 27]. It is also possible that even nonbiblical texts were sung in temple worship.

While professional singers and instrumentalists became the primary musical forces early in the history of temple worship, the people were not completely excluded from ritual song there. Carroll Stuhlmueller's analysis of Psalm 44, for example, suggests how individual singers, a choir, and the larger assembly could have joined together in this hymn [illustration 13]. Psalm 136 was composed with a continuous refrain that probably was echoed by the assembly, while Psalms 146 to 150 may have been punctuated by a continuous "Alleluia" from the people. Although the assembly might have joined in singing a refrain or even a whole psalm known by heart, the musical landscape of temple worship was clearly dominated by professional musicians.

Synagogue

The great differences between the rituals of the temple and those of the synagogue produced divergent forms of music in these two institutions. Only one temple existed for the whole nation, while synagogues developed wherever there were Jews. The temple cult was sacrificial, while the synagogue was a gathering for study and prayer. Only adult Jewish males were allowed into the inner court of the temple, while synagogue gatherings were typically comprised of women, men, and children. The temple was staffed by a large body of professional ministers, while the synagogue and its worship were led by townspeople—both women and men—with no need or place for priests [quotation 28]. This was to change after the destruction of the Jerusalem temple in 70 C.E. The increasing need for stability in the synagogue, which bore a new responsibility for redefining Judaism after 70 C.E., as well as the influx of professional ministers

Quotation 27: *On that day did R. Aquiba expound as follows: "Then sang Moses and the children of Israel this song unto the Lord and spoke saying. Now Scripture hardly needs to add, saying. And why does Scripture state, saying? It thereby teaches that the Israelites responded word by word after Moses, as they do when they read the Hallel psalms. Therefore Saying is stated in this context."* (Mishnah, Sotah 5:4)

Quotation 28: *Seen in the larger context of women's participation in the life of the ancient synagogue, there is no reason not to take the [leadership] titles as functions, nor to assume that women heads or elders of synagogues had radically different functions than men heads or elders of synagogues.* (Brooten, Women Leaders in the Ancient Synagogue, p. 149)

Hymnic Introduction: vv. 1-8

vv. 1-2: Call to praise, sung by everyone
We have heard with our ears, O God,
    our ancestors have told us,
what deeds you performed in their days,
    in the days of old:
you with your own hand drove out the nations
    but them you planted;
you afflicted the peoples,
    but them you set free;

v. 3: Motivation by large choir
for not by their own sword did they win the land
    nor did their own arm give them victory;
but your right hand, and your arm,
    and the light of your countenance,
    for you delighted in them.

vv. 4, 6: individual cantor or special choir
You are my King and my God;
    you command victories for Jacob.
For not in my bow do I trust,
    nor can my sword save me.

v. 7: Confidence
For you have saved us from our foes,
    and have put to confusion those who hate us.

v. 8: refrain by everyone
In God we have boasted continually,
    and we will give thanks to your name forever.

Community Lament: vv. 9-22

v. 15: individual cantor or choir
All day long my disgrace is before me,
    and shame has covered my face

vv. 17-22: reflection in which different choirs speak:

to God (vv. 17-19)
All this has come upon us,
    yet we have not forgotten you,
    or been false to your covenant.
Our heart has not turned back,
    nor have our steps departed from your way,
yet you have broken us in the haunt of jackals,
    and covered us with deep darkness.

about God (vv. 20-21)
If we had forgotten the name of our God
    or spread our hands out to a strange god,
would not God discover this?
    For he knows the secrets of the heart.

to God (vv. 22)
Because of you we are being killed all day long,
    and accounted as sheep for the slaughter.

Prayer of Petition: vv. 23-26

Rouse yourself! Why do you sleep, O Lord?
    Awake, do not cast us off forever!
Why do you hide your face?
    Why do you forget our
        affliction and oppression?
For we sink down to the dust;
    our bodies cling to the ground.
Rise up, come to our help.
    Redeem us for the sake of your
        steadfast love.

13. Structural analysis of Psalm 44.

14. Some of the notational signs of ancient Jewish music, with their rendition according to Syrian practice. (Davidson and Apel, 1:8)

Quotation 29: *You are praised, O Lord our God and God of our fathers, God of Abraham, God of Isaac, and God of Jacob, the great, mighty and awe-inspiring God, God Supreme, Creator of heaven and earth, our Shield and Shield of our fathers, our trust in every generation. You are praised, O Lord, Shield of Abraham.* (The first of the Eighteen Benedictions, current Ashkenazi version of Babylonian provenance. Petuchowski and Brocke, *The Lord's Prayer and Jewish Liturgy,* pp. 30–31)

Quotation 30: *When he came to Nazareth, where he had been brought up, he entered the synagogue on the sabbath day, as was his custom. He stood up to read, and the scroll of the prophet Isaiah was given to him. He unrolled the scroll and found the place where it was written: "The Spirit of the Lord is upon me."* (Luke 4:16-18a)

from the temple, contributed to the development of more formal ministries in the synagogue.

It was in the synagogue that the distinction between music and public speech became especially blurred. The presence of choirs and orchestras make it easier to identify distinctive musical elements in temple worship. The synagogue, however, was never a place of instrumental music or choirs but a gathering of study, prayer, and proclamation. The performance of this word-centered worship continuously migrated back and forth between what today would be called speech and song.

Despite the pluriformity of practices and the lack of written records, at least two standard elements can be discerned as part of synagogue services of the first century. The oldest of these was the recitation of the *Shema* [quotation 16]. Centuries after the destruction of the temple in Jerusalem, various blessings that had developed around the *Shema* were standardized and became mandatory. A second element was the Eighteen Benedictions, also called the *Amidah* or "standing prayer" because it was prayed while standing [quotation 29]. The reading of Scripture was also an integral part of some synagogue services [quotation 30]. It is probable that in this era the Sabbath morning service included a reading from the Torah and another from the Haftorah or Prophets. It is also possible that the Torah was read in the synagogue on the market days, Monday and Thursday.

These various elements were rendered with a certain degree of musicality. Because every Jew knew the *Shema* by heart, it could have been chanted in unison by the whole assembly during the service. In some places, a prayer leader appears to have recited the first line, with the congregation responding with the second line, and so on through the entire prayer. Either style would require relatively simple musical settings for these congregational chants.

In contrast, the *Amidah* probably was not chanted by the whole assembly. This was due, in part, to the unfixed nature of these blessings in the first century. Although a general outline of the prayer had developed by the time of Jesus, the *Amidah* required further improvisation and expansion when it was prayed. This could be accom-

15. Intonation pattern used in reading from the Pentateuch, according to Syrian practice. (Davidson and Apel, 1:8)

plished only by a single voice, although the assembly might have added some phrases of blessings or affirmation in the midst of or at the end of the prayer.

While there is strong evidence that some psalms were sung in temple worship, no such evidence exists for the emerging synagogue service. The book of Psalms was not an early synagogue songbook. If it was used at all in the synagogue at this time, it was as a book of readings. Thus, it would have been chanted similarly to the other books of Scripture publicly declaimed in synagogue worship [quotation 31].

The musical building blocks for singing the *Shema* and the *Amidah* probably were derived from the repertoire of chants that had developed for cantillating Scripture. Cantillation is a way of chanting that consists of employing a series of set melodic formulas. The scrolls from which one chanted were marked with signs or accents that indicated the appropriate formula [illustration 14]. Although many variations existed in this practice, cantillation generally respects the structure and sense of the text being proclaimed, much like a contemporary psalm tone. Because such musical declamation is intended to serve the word and enable its clear proclamation, it ordinarily cannot be too florid or distracting in its artistry [illustration 15].

Quotation 31: *He who reads the Pentateuch without tune shows disregard for it. (Babylonian Talmud, Megilla 32a)*

Home

Temple worship certainly shaped the religious imaginations of the early followers of Jesus, virtually all of whom were Jewish. Temple practices, however, did not seem to exert any significant influence on the musical landscape of emerging Christian worship. Of more significance was synagogue worship, and even more so home rituals for shaping this auditory environment. It was particularly around the table that the lyrical quality of domestic prayer intensified. The Jewish influence for such lyricism stems from the various blessings chanted before and after meals, as well as psalms and other songs that would have been customary at festival meals. It is also possible that a broader Hellenistic influence was the symposium meal. Well known from such famous Greek literary works as Plato's *Symposium*, this was a well-orchestrated social event—usually for the rich—that consisted of a meal followed by discussion or entertainment. While the followers of Jesus would have rejected the more ribald aspects of this tradition, it is clear that the Hellenistic symposium did influence gospel narratives about meals with Jesus [quotation 32]. It is also probable that the musical presumptions of this Hellenistic social event contributed to the heightened auditory environment of emerging Christian Eucharist, especially when celebrated in the homes of wealthy Gentile converts. As the community began to reshape its prayer in the memory and example of Jesus, variations on Jewish and Hellenistic chants and odes developed. Variation gave way to distinctive musical texts, forms, and melodies, which were the antecedents of Christian music during the following centuries.

Although the New Testament does not record melodies, rhythms, or other such musical data, it does offer some information about the content and performance of emerging Christian music. For example, a number of short, lyrical praise formulas appear in the New Testament, such as the doxology sung by the angels at the birth of Jesus (Luke 2:14). While it is difficult to prove that any such musical fragment in the New Testament was actually used in worship, it is probable that some types of doxologies were employed to conclude vocal prayer or preaching. Based on Jewish models, such doxologies eventually gave way to the development of Christological doxologies [quotation 33]. The New Testament also contains a significant number of lyrical elements borrowed from Judaism but given a distinctively Christian treatment [quotation 34]. Hymns to Christ and other larger lyrical forms also were based on preexistent Jewish models [quotation 35]. Lyrical texts are not the same as musical settings, and their appearance in a literary medium like the New Testament does not prove that such texts were actually sung in worship. On the other hand, the consistent appearance of such texts throughout the New Testament seems to confirm that the followers of Jesus embraced the lyrical heritage of their Hellenized Jewish environment. Furthermore, their zeal for the good news could have translated into an auditory quality even more intense than that of their religious siblings.

Paul's words about public worship are helpful in understanding something of the lyrical forms and style of early Christian worship

Quotation 32: *Five of the meals in Luke's gospel reflect certain aspects of the Hellenistic symposium, namely, the banquet at the home of Levi (5:27-39), the three dinners taken at the home of a Pharisee (7:36-50; 11:37-54; 14:1-35), and the Last Supper. (LaVerdiere, Dining in the Kingdom of God, p. 18)*

Quotation 33: *To the only wise God, through Jesus Christ, to whom be the glory forever! Amen. (Rom 16:27)*

Quotation 34: *Amen. (Gal 6:18), Hallelujah. (Rev 19:1), Hosanna. (Mark 11:9), Marana tha. (1 Cor 16:22)*

Quotation 35: *[Jesus Christ] is the image of the invisible God, the firstborn of all creation; for in him all things in heaven and on earth were created, things visible and invisible, whether thrones or dominions or rulers or powers—all things have been created through him and for him. He himself is before all things, and in him all things hold together. He is the head of the body, the church; he is the beginning, the firstborn from the dead, so that he might come to have first place in everything. For in him all the fullness of God was pleased to dwell, and through him God was pleased to reconcile to himself all things, whether on earth or in heaven, by making peace through the blood of his cross. (Col 1:15-20)* [quotation 36]. Although Paul recognizes a place for solo expression in worship—such as the gift of tongues—his overriding concern is for the engagement and prayer of the whole community. His emphasis that all gifts should serve the common good would extend to the musical elements of worship as well. This suggests a preference for responsorial rather than solo forms, a leaning toward dialogue rather than monologue in worship, and a constant respect for the community's "Amen." Paul's instruction also implies a preference for a style of liturgical-musical leadership more akin to that which would be found in the synagogue than to that of the temple. Although

Quotation 36: *Therefore, one who speaks in a tongue should pray for the power to interpret. For if I pray in a tongue, my spirit prays but my mind is unproductive. What should I do then? I will pray with the spirit, but I will pray with the mind also; I will sing praise with the spirit, but I will sing praise with the mind also. Otherwise, if you say a blessing with the spirit, how can anyone in the position of an outsider say the "Amen" to your thanksgiving, since the outsider does not know what you are saying? For you may give thanks well enough, but the other person is not built up. I thank God that I speak in tongues more than all of you; nevertheless, in church I would rather speak five words with my mind, in order to instruct others also, than ten thousand words in a tongue. (1 Cor 14:13-19)*

16. Standard printed page of the Mishnah.

17. Standard printed page of the Talmud.

talented musicians undoubtedly graced the early community with their gifts, their solo singing did not dominate the lyrical landscape of first-century worship, which recognized the single-voiced praise of the community as the ideal.

Summary

Each place of Jewish worship made a distinctive contribution to the musical life of Israel and influenced Christian song, which at the beginning consisted of variations on borrowed material. The synagogue and home especially left their mark on the auditory environment of emerging Christianity. The liturgical-musical styles practiced there served the proclamation of the word and the full engagement of community members. This model was especially influential in shaping Christian music for the next three centuries.

BOOKS

Torah occupies a central place in the life of Judaism. "Torah" usually refers to the first five books of the Bible, which are also called "the Law." Ancient belief holds that on Mount Sinai, God revealed the Law to Moses, who wrote down this revelation in five books [quotation 37]. Already by the time of Jesus the belief further developed that God had communicated an oral revelation to Moses in addition to the written Law, which eventually became the special purview of the Pharisees [quotation 38]. This belief in an oral law is even the basis of some of Jesus' conflict with the Pharisees. While obeying the written Torah, Jesus did not abide by the oral law, which he dismissed as human tradition that can lead one to ignore the requirements of the written Law [quotation 39]. This oral law achieved its first written form in the Mishnah [illustration 16], codified around 200 C.E. The Mishnah and a series of Aramaic commentaries on the Mishnah, known as the Gemara, form the great compilations known as the Talmud [illustration 17], one version of which was redacted in Palestine around 400 C.E. and another in Babylonia around 500 C.E.

Christianity was born in this fluid Torah tradition. The influence of this rich heritage is significant and manifold. Christians, of course, accepted the Hebrew Scriptures and held it to be God's Word. Furthermore, Christians believed that reverencing, proclaiming, and even studying the Word of God are acts of worship. They continued the Jewish tradition of surrounding the public proclamation of God's Word with blessings and songs. Finally, they adopted the practice of embodying their own oral traditions in written texts and honoring them also as the Word of God.

Quotation 37: *Moses came and told the people all the words of the LORD and all the ordinances; and all the people answered with one voice, and said, "All the words that the LORD has spoken, we will do." And Moses wrote down all of the words of the LORD.* (Exod 24:3-4)

Quotation 38: *Moses received Torah at Sinai and handed it on to Joshua, Joshua to elders, and elders to prophets. And prophets handed it on to the men of the great assembly.* (Mishnah, Abot 1:1)

Quotation 39: *Pharisees and scribes came to Jesus from Jerusalem and said, "Why do your disciples break the tradition of the elders? For they do not wash their hands before they eat." He answered them, "And why do you break the commandment of God for the sake of your tradition? For God said, 'Honor your father and your mother,' and 'Whoever speaks evil of father or mother must surely die.' But you say that whoever tells father or mother, 'Whatever support you might have had from me is given to God,' then that person need not honor the father. So, for the sake of your tradition, you make void the word of God."* (Matt 15:1-6)

Temple

There is very little direct evidence to suggest that Scripture reading was an ordinary part of worship at the temple in Jerusalem. As previously noted, temple worship was oriented around various forms of sacrifice. At the same time, however, there is significant circumstantial evidence that makes it difficult to rule out completely public reading in temple worship.

Quotation 40:
*Then Deborah and Barak son of Abinoam
sang on that day, saying:
"When locks are long in Israel,
    when the people offer themselves
    willingly—
bless the LORD!
Hear, O kings; give ear, O Princes;
    to the LORD I will sing,
    I will make melody to the LORD, the
    God of Israel. (Judg 5:1-3)*

Quotation 41: *So the priests, the
Levites, the gatekeepers, the singers, some
of the people, the temple servants, and
all Israel settled in their towns. When
the seventh month came—the people of
Israel being settled in their towns—all the
people gathered together into the square
before the Water Gate. They told the
scribe Ezra to bring the book of the law
of Moses, which the LORD had given to
Israel. Accordingly, the priest Ezra brought
the law before the assembly, both men
and women and all who could hear with
understanding.* (Neh 7:73b–8:3)

Quotation 42: *[Ezra and the Levites]
read from the book, from the law of God,
with interpretation. They gave the sense,
so that the people understood the reading.*
(Neh 8:8)

Quotation 43: *It hardly seems
possible to imagine a situation in which
such significant and extended use was
made of scriptural texts without seeing
a concomitant recitation of these as
a regular feature of Jewish communal
activity. Whether such regularity can
be traced back as far as Ezra, as the
talmudic tradition would have it, is a
matter of some doubt; what seems
indubitable is that scriptural readings
were familiar to many Jews of the
Greek and Roman periods.*
(Reif, *Judaism and Hebrew Prayer*, p. 63)

Psalms have already been acknowledged as one important element of the musical repertoire in the Jerusalem temple. It also has been noted that, to the extent that psalms were employed in the synagogue, they were probably used like other scriptural books of the Hebrew Bible rather than a collection of song texts. These at least paradoxical if not contradictory uses—as song texts in the temple but not in the synagogue—demonstrate, again, the fluidity between categories of reading and singing. The "singing" of psalms in the Jerusalem temple could broadly be construed as a type of public declamation of God's Word. If psalms and some other lyric sections of the Hebrew Scriptures, such as the Canticle of Deborah [quotation 40], could find their way into temple worship, why not other great texts narrating God's covenant with the chosen people?

A second evidentiary fragment comes from the accounts of the restoration of worship in Jerusalem after the Babylonian Exile (587–516 B.C.E.). The temple had been rebuilt by 515 B.C.E., but the political and religious situation in Jerusalem seems to have been in serious disarray for at least another seventy years. The priest and scribe Ezra was a major figure in leading the religious reform of Jerusalem in the middle of the fifth century B.C.E. As part of that reform, Ezra is remembered as having publicly proclaimed the "law of Moses" to a large assembly [quotation 41]. Rather than simply recalling a single event, many scholars believe that Ezra was responsible for promoting the practice of proclaiming and interpreting the Torah to ordinary believers in an easily understood manner [quotation 42]. As there appear to have been no established synagogues in Jerusalem at this time, and given the prominence of the second temple in postexilic worship, it seems difficult to imagine that this Torah proclamation would not have taken place—at least some of the time—in the temple.

Finally, evidence suggests that the second temple period was a time of intensified Torah study. It was an era when innumerable scrolls were copied, exegeted, and, in the spirit of Ezra, communicated in an accessible manner to ordinary people. Stefan Reif contends that this attention to preserving and promoting traditional texts might have been prompted, in part, by the clash between Judaism and Hellenistic civilization. He also believes that this scriptural focus would necessarily presume some public recitation of these texts [quotation 43]. Given the centrality of the Jerusalem temple and the absence of synagogues in Palestine for most of the second temple period, it seems difficult to imagine that the Jerusalem temple would not be a site for the public reading of the Torah. On the other hand, it is not possible to discern any regular pattern using Scripture in second temple worship.

18. Piece of papyrus with a section of Psalm 50.

Synagogue

Over the centuries reverence for the Torah has been especially communicated through the synagogue. It is not clear, however, when the public reading of the Scriptures became a constitutive element of synagogue service. Even if the institution of the synagogue emerged in the second century B.C.E., it is not clear that publicly declaiming the Torah was an essential part of any synagogue worship from the beginning.

A well-known passage in the Gospel of Luke depicts Jesus publicly reading during a Sabbath synagogue service in Nazareth. Luke's narrative reflects a certain amount of choreography around this event, with Jesus 1) receiving the scroll, 2) opening it and finding a passage, 3) reading while standing, 4) rolling up the scroll, 5) handing it to an attendant, and 6) sitting down to preach [quotation 44]. Admittedly Luke's gospel was written after the destruction of the temple in Jerusalem—possibly between 80 and 85 C.E. As synagogues assumed a more central place in the Jewish cult after the temple destruction, their rituals were elaborated and eventually standardized. Luke's account, while probably reflecting some of these early developments, yet suggests that ritual patterns already surrounded the act of public reading in some synagogues. In his Acts of the Apostles, Luke further relates that, at least on one occasion in the synagogue in Antioch, there was a reading from both the Law and the Prophets, followed by preaching [quotation 45]. On another occasion he has

Quotation 44: *The scroll of the prophet Isaiah was given to [Jesus]. He unrolled the scroll and found the place where it was written: "The Spirit of the Lord is upon me. . . ." And he rolled up the scroll, gave it back to the attendant, and sat down. The eyes of all in the synagogue were fixed on him. Then he began to say to them, "Today this scripture has been fulfilled in your hearing." (Luke 4:17-21)*

Quotation 45: *And on the sabbath day [Paul and Barnabas] went into the synagogue and sat down. After the reading of the law and the prophets, the officials of the synagogue sent them a message, saying, "Brothers, if you have any word of exhortation for the people, give it." So Paul stood up. (Acts 13:14b-16a)*

19. An Essene manuscript from about the turn of the era (B.C.E. to C.E.) measuring 27 feet long, written on animal skin, containing at least 66 columns of text.

the Apostle James announcing that the Torah is read every Sabbath in all synagogues [quotation 46]. Despite such tantalizing hints about the ritual reading of Scripture in the synagogue, it is yet impossible to know with certainty what was read or even with what consistency reading marked synagogue gatherings at the time of Jesus [quotation 47]. This situation will change within a century. The Mishnah contains extensive instructions about who can read in public worship, the sequence of what is to be read on the various feasts and days, and also instruction for how the reading is to be done in order to fulfill one's obligation [quotation 48].

The written texts that were cantillated and studied in the synagogue were not in what today would be called book form. Originally, these texts were written on sheets of papyrus [illustration 18]—a kind of paper made from a river plant of the same name—or on animal skin. The papyrus sheets were glued together, or animal skins sewn, to form a scroll that could be rolled up. Scrolls would commonly be twenty-five or thirty feet long and about ten inches high. The text typically was written in five- or six-inch-wide columns, which were exposed as the scroll was unrolled from right to left [illustration 19]. Jesus is remembered as using such a scroll when he read from the prophet Isaiah in the Nazareth synagogue [quotation 44]. As the reading of Scripture became a more prominent feature of synagogue worship, so did the places for storing such scrolls. Thus a shelf or simple cupboard would give way to a special niche or highly elaborate shrine [illustration 7]. Some scrolls were beautifully decorated and became the treasures of the synagogue.

20. Fragment of *The Song of the Sabbath Sacrifice*.

Quotation 49:
The Song of the Sabbath Sacrifice

30. By the instructor. Song of the sacrifice of the seventh
Sabbath on the sixteenth of the month. Praise the God of
the lofty heights, O you lofty ones among all the

31. elim of knowledge. Let the holiest of the godlike ones
sanctify the King of glory who sanctifies by holiness
all His holy ones. O you chiefs of the praises of

32. all the godlike beings, praise the splendidly [pr]aiseworthy God. For in the splendor of praise
is the glory of His realm. From it (comes) the praises
of all

33. the godlike ones together with the splendor of all [His]
maj[esty. And] exalt his exaltedness to exalted heaven,
you most godlike ones of the lofty elim,
and (exalt) His glorious divinity above

34. all the lofty heights. For H[e is God of gods] of all
the chiefs of the heights of heaven and King of ki[ngs] of all the eternal councils.
(by the intention of)

35. (His knowledge) At the words of His mouth come into
being [all the lofty angels]; at the utterance of His lips all the eternal spirits; [by the in]tention
of His knowledge all His creatures

36. in their undertakings. Sing with joy, you who rejoice
[in His knowledge with] rejoicing among the wondrous
godlike beings. And chant His glory with the tongue of all who chant with knowledge;
and (chant) His wonderful songs of joy

37. with the mouth of all who chant [of Him. For He is]
God of all who rejoice {in knowledge}
forever and Judge in His power of all the spirits of understanding.

(transcription and translation by Carol Newsom, reprinted by permission of Harvard Semitic Museum)

Besides the various scrolls of the Law and the Prophets, ancient Israel had no other standardized books for prayer. It is true that in excavations at Qumran there were many fragments of psalm scrolls uncovered—the most scrolls devoted to any book of the Bible. It would be difficult to consider the Psalms a separate prayer book for Jews at this time, however, and better to classify it as a prophetic book and part of the Haftorah. The community of Qumran as well as others also produced poetic hymns in imitation of the psalms [quotation 49, illustration 20].

While some of these local compositions occasionally acquired currency outside their home area, none of them acquired "prayer book" status in emerging Judaism. The Mishnah and Talmud, as well as various other writings, also contained many examples of blessings and other prayers, but no other Jewish book for prayer or *siddur* (Hebrew, "prayer book") existed until that compiled by Amram Gaon (d. 871 C.E.).

The late development of the *siddur* reflects the Jewish community's reluctance to confine their prayer to written forms. Lawrence Hoffman also suggests that the slow evolution of a common book of prayer is testimony to the enormous variation that occurred in synagogue worship through much of the first millennium of the Common Era. Only the special genius of eighth- and ninth-century scholars called *geonim* made the emergence of the *siddur* possible. Unlike scholars of previous generations, the *geonim* were ready and able to answer liturgical questions in a clear and decisive manner. Their answers allowed for no variation in the ritual, which made a fixed prayer book finally possible. Until the time of the *geonim*, however, the Jewish community resisted creating written texts for their prayers and preferred to transmit orally prayer patterns that were improvised from generation to generation.

Emerging Christianity

The early followers of Jesus seem to have employed scrolls much like those used in the synagogue. The tradition of cantillating publicly the Law and the Prophets was probably continued by the Jewish followers of Jesus in their own gatherings. In the Christian synagogues of the late first and early second century, the ancient practice of lyrically proclaiming the word may also have been continued. Public readings from the Law and the Prophets may even have been part of the worship enacted by the Gentile Christian communities before 80 C.E.

The number of quotations from the Jewish Scriptures across the New Testament demonstrates that the ancient texts were both very familiar and highly valued by the emerging Christian community. Frederick Crowe has noted that after the resurrection, the early followers of Jesus began to believe that the Jewish Scriptures pointed to him in a special way. Paul's letter to the largely Gentile community at Rome, for example, declared that the Jewish Scriptures anticipated the new gospel of Jesus [quotation 50]. Luke, also writing for Gentiles, depicted Jesus sanctioning such a perspective [quotation 51]. The insights about the Law and the Prophets, reflected in Luke's gospel, probably emerged in the Jewish-Christian communities that continued the Jewish tradition of Scripture study. Through people such as Paul, this perspective spread to the Gentile communities, which learned to value and embrace this rich scriptural heritage. The First Letter to Timothy, written toward the end of the first century C.E., likely reflects the tradition of proclaiming the Jewish Scriptures in a Christian assembly composed of both Gentiles and Jews [quotation 52].

Aside from the ritual reading and study of the Jewish Scriptures, sections of what came to be called the New Testament also may have been read in the assemblies of the faithful [illustration 21]. This suggestion finds support in some sections of the New Testament

Quotation 50: *Paul, a servant of Jesus Christ, called to be an apostle, set apart for the gospel of God, which he promised beforehand through his prophets in the holy scriptures, the gospel concerning his Son.* (Rom 1:1-3)

Quotation 51: *Then beginning with Moses and all the prophets, [Jesus] interpreted to them the things about himself in all the scriptures.* (Luke 24:27)

Quotation 52: *Until I arrive, give attention to the public reading of scripture, to exhorting, to teaching.* (1 Tim 4:13)

Quotation 53: *We also constantly give thanks to God for this, that when you received the word of God that you heard from us, you accepted it not as a human word but as what it really is, God's word, which is also at work in you believers.* (1 Thess 2:13)

Quotation 54: *Give my greetings to the brothers and sisters at Laodicea, and to Nympha and the church in her house. And when this letter has been read among you, have it read also in the church of the Laodiceans; and see that you read also the letter from Laodicea.* (Col 4:15-16)

Quotation 55: *King Belshazzar made a great festival for a thousand of his lords, and he was drinking wine in the presence of the thousand. Under the influence of the wine, Belshazzar commanded that they bring in the vessels of gold and silver that his father Nebuchadnezzar had taken out of the temple in Jerusalem, so that the king and his lords, his wives, and his concubines might drink from them.* (Dan 5:1-2)

that equate the Christian message with the "word of God" [quotation 53]. If there existed a tradition for publicly reading the "Word of God" in any form in Christian assemblies, it would be difficult to imagine that the message of Jesus as the "Word of God" would not similarly be proclaimed. The proclamation of this Word, however, does not presume that it existed everywhere in written form. From the beginning, the good news was a preached event that required oral, rather than written, transmission. Although some collections of the sayings of Jesus and a few narratives existed earlier, only toward the end of the first century did written forms of the gospels appear.

One form of the Christian message that was written for the early community was the letter. Many of these letters, while intended only for a particular community such as the Galatians or Ephesians, were circulated among the various churches to be read at worship [quotation 54].

21. Fragment of the Gospel of John, third century.

Summary

The devotion of the Jewish community to the Word of God, particularly as it was embodied in the Law and the Prophets, greatly influenced Christianity. The emerging Christian community was born in this tradition; they also soon extended and adapted this tradition to the message of Jesus. This too came to be venerated as the Word of God, and some of this preached message eventually acquired a written form. Christian scrolls or books, however, did not materialize overnight. Even when they did appear, it is not evident that they immediately became the new Torah for the Christian community, displacing either the written Torah of the Jews or the preaching event in the new community. These written forms originally may have prepared communities to hear the good news of Jesus preached to them, or possibly even helped those who were to preach. Eventually, however, as the community moved further in time and space from the events of Jesus' life, the written forms took on more importance in the life and ritual of the community. At this formative stage, however, the "Word" was less a scroll or book than it was an auditory event resounding in the midst of believers.

VESSELS

Just as the temple was not the Jewish institution that most influenced the music, architecture, and books used in the earliest Christian worship, the same is true of ritual vessels. The temple did possess

Quotation 56: *It was also in the same document that the prophet, having received an oracle, ordered that the tent and the ark should follow with him, and that he went out to the mountain where Moses had gone up and had seen the inheritance of God. Jeremiah came and found a cave-dwelling, and he brought there the tent and the ark and the altar of incense; then he sealed up the entrance. Some of those who followed him came up intending to mark the way, but could not find it. When Jeremiah learned of it, he rebuked them and declared: "The place shall remain unknown until God gathers his people together again and shows his mercy." (2 Macc 2:4-8)*

22. Ark of the covenant.

exquisite cups and other utensils of precious metals, many of which were looted during the various campaigns against Israel and later replaced [quotation 55]. The most famous "vessel" in the temple was the ark of the covenant, which held the tablets of the law, Aaron's rod, and manna from the desert [illustration 22]. According to a late biblical tradition the ark was hidden in a cave at the time the Jerusalem temple was destroyed by the Babylonians in 587 B.C.E. [quotation 56]. None of the vessels of the temple were models for those used by the emerging Christian community in its rituals. It will be only after many centuries that Christianity will begin to embrace some of the grandeur of the temple in its arts. Nor did the synagogue influence the vessels used in Christian worship. As Leslie Hoppe points out, some synagogues served as hostels for Jewish travelers and even were the site of special meals, probably held in connection with the Sabbath and holidays. Synagogue worship, however, did not ordinarily include food or drink, and synagogues did not possess vessels for ritual eating or drinking.

It was in the home that Jews celebrated their ritual meals at the time of Jesus, and it is there that the types of vessels used by the first Christians for their ritual meals are found. The most important vessels were those that held bread and wine. Understanding the kinds of bread and wine common to the Jewish household will help in understanding the vessels in which these elements were served and stored.

Bread and Its Vessels

Daily bread in the Hellenistic world often was baked in round loves. Examples of such loaves were preserved in the ruins of Pompeii, destroyed by the eruption of Mount Vesuvius in 79 C.E., and are now displayed at the Archaeological Museum in Naples. These loaves, leavened and made of wheat, were approximately eight inches in diameter and weighed almost one pound [illustration 23]. Similar loaves are still made in the Mediterranean world today.

Barley was the most common grain used by the Jews for bread, but barley was not allowed to be used in the temple. Unleavened bread or *matzah* was prepared for religious services. Some rituals required a certain type of unleavened bread, known as a cereal offering, made of wheat ("choice") flour, oil, and frankincense [quotation 57]. The showbreads set out in the sanctuary of the temple every week and consumed by the priests were also unleavened [quotation 58].

Unleavened bread also played an important role in the yearly Feast of Unleavened Bread, which marked the beginning of the barley harvest. During this spring festival, it was traditional to eat bread prepared with only the new grain, without flour, leaven, or any ingredient from the previous year. These flat barley cakes were eaten during the seven days of the festival. The Passover celebration was the result of this ancient feast combining with an even earlier feast of nomadic origins, which included the sacrifice and consumption of a young lamb, possibly as a ritual offering for good pastures in the coming year. It is possible that the combined Passover feast may have marked the move of flocks from the marginal areas to the cultivated fields so that the animals could eat the stubble left after the barley harvest. The sharing of a lamb from the flocks at this stage may have been the shepherd's way of easing their way onto the farmer's land.

The New Testament writers agree that Jesus' Last Supper occurred within a Passover context: the synoptic writers place the supper on the first day of Passover [quotation 59], while John reports that the supper took place on the night before the Passover feast. Given the ritual requirements of this feast, and the tradition for ridding the household of all remnants of bread and starter from the previous year, it is probable that Jesus and his disciples ate the flat barley cakes of the Passover festival at their last meal together. The New Testament does not attach any significance to the use of unleavened bread, and little evidence exists that the early community continued to use such bread in their eucharistic gatherings. More probably, the barley bread eaten at daily meals became the staple for eucharistic meals as well.

Bread was customarily kept in baskets, both in the temple [quotation 60] and in Jewish homes [quotation 61]. Bronze bowls, used both for cooking and serving food, were also common in the Greco-Roman Empire [illustration 24]. Pottery plates were also quite commonly

23. Carbonized bread from Pompeii.

24. Bronze bowl from first to third century C.E.

25. Pottery plates from Qumran, first century B.C.E. to first century C.E.

Quotation 62: *And when the president has given thanks and all the people have assented, those whom we call deacons give to each one present a portion of the bread and wine and water over which thanks have been given, and take them to those who are not present.* (Justin Martyr, *First Apology*, 65.5, in Jasper and Cuming, *Prayers of the Eucharist*)

Quotation 63: *[If he said,] "Qonam be wine, because it is bad for the belly," [and] they told him, "but isn't old wine good for the belly?" he is permitted to drink old wine. And not old wine alone is permitted. But all wine [is permitted].* (*Mishnah*, Nedarim 9:8)

26. Terra cotta jug, first century C.E.

used for serving [illustration 25]. First-century sources give little evidence that fragments were saved after the eucharistic breaking of the bread; later sources indicate that bread from the celebration was sent to those not present [quotation 62]. It is probable that everything from a piece of cloth to various common household containers were employed for transporting the eucharistized bread to the absent believers.

Wine and Its Vessels

Although water was the usual drink of Jews at the time of Jesus, wine was served on many festive occasions, including the celebration of marriage, the Sabbath meals, Passover, and other festivals. Wine often was kept in the home for such occasions as well as for medicinal purposes [quotation 63]. Many kinds of wine were available in Palestine, although red wine seems to have been preferred. The wine usually was thinned with water because it was too strong to drink undiluted.

Wine was often stored in a covered pitcher or jar [illustration 26]. Smaller pitchers would rest on a table or shelf, while larger, more stationary vessels would sit on the floor. These containers were often earthenware, though some were made of stone and, less often, of metal. More portable containers made of goatskin [quotation 64], which came into use before the appearance of earthenware containers, still were in use at this time.

Individual drinking vessels were a familiar commodity in Jewish society, although it is not likely that individual cups were available to all the family members or guests at a meal. A communal cup frequently was used [illustration 27]. Vessels for drinking wine and other liquids were made from a variety of materials. A cup for ordinary use often was made of clay, though bronze or even precious materials were used to make drinking goblets for the wealthy. During the first century, glass was a common material for cups in the Hellenistic world. Simple glass beakers [illustration 28] and bowls with or without a base served as drinking vessels. Very seldom would a stem or node separate the base from the bowl.

A simple glass cup is probably the kind of vessel that Jesus commonly used during the various ritual meals in which he participated, including the Last Supper. These accounts also point out that Jesus passed his own cup to the disciples [quotation 65]. This consistent emphasis on the passing of Jesus' own cup seems to underscore the centrality of the action and suggests that other cups were at the table. Thus, the passing of Jesus' own cup seems an intentional and important action.

As already noted, the early community sometimes gathered for the breaking of the bread in domestic settings. These gatherings would have ordinarily included a meal with the Eucharist. Though various drinking vessels may have been used during the meal, the use of a single communal cup probably was typical of the Eucharist that accompanied the meal. Paul seems to imply the use of one cup in his discussions of Eucharist. A hallmark of the eucharistic discourses in Paul is his emphasis on unity and oneness in the breaking of the bread and the sharing of the cup [quotation 66].

27. Bronze cup from the Roman Period.

Summary

More than architecture, music, or books, an examination of vessels demonstrates the influence of domestic Judaism on first-century Christianity. In a very real sense, Christianity was born around the domestic table. The meal traditions of Israel and the instinct always to bless God at the breaking of bread is the context from which specific Christian rituals emerged. The borrowing and transformation of this table practice also reveals the Christian genius for borrowing and changing a tradition. As for specific vessels, Judaism had few that it would consider sacred to the domestic rites. Similarly, the ritual vessels of first-century Christianity were of a decidedly non-sacred nature. A cup, a pitcher, a basket, or bowl served the bread and wine which, in turn, served the unity of the community. In this era, it is not the things—not even the bread and wine—that are of central importance, but the actions of the community. The believers, more than any single food, are clearly the Body of Christ.

Quotation 64: *And no one puts new wine into old wineskins; otherwise, the wine will burst the skins, and the wine is lost, and so are the skins; but one puts new wine into fresh wineskins.* (Mark 2:22)

Quotation 65: *Then he took a cup, and after giving thanks he gave it to them, saying, "Drink from it, all of you; for this is my blood of the covenant, which is poured out for many for the forgiveness of sins."* (Matt 26:27-28)

Quotation 66: *The cup of blessing that we bless, is it not a sharing in the blood of Christ? The bread that we break, is it not a sharing in the body of Christ? Because there is one bread, we who are many are one body, for we all partake of the one bread.* (I Cor 10:16-17)

EUCHARISTIC THEOLOGY

It is somewhat problematic to speak of eucharistic theology in the New Testament. This is not to say that New Testament writers did not reflect theologically on their eucharistic practice. Paul's correspondence to the Corinthian community, for example, demonstrates that they did [quotation 66]. His writings also demonstrate, however, that this reflection is not narrowly focused on an isolated liturgy or ritual, as will happen in subsequent centuries. Rather, he is offering reflection on the Christian life and underscoring a fundamental New Testament perspective that does not separate the liturgy or Eucharist from the whole of Christian living. This continuity between living and worship is reflected in the language of the New Testament, which avoids cultic terminology for Christian worship. The Greek word for liturgy (*leitourgia*), for example, is not simply a term for

28. Cut glass cup.

Quotation 67: *The terminological evidence means not only that any cultic understanding of Christian worship is out of the question, but also that there is no longer any distinction in principle between assembly for worship and the service of Christians in the world.* (Hahn, *The Worship of the Early Church,* p. 38)

worship but can refer to evangelizing, taking up a collection, and even to the duties of state officials [quotation 67]. While there is no separate "eucharistic theology" in the New Testament, there are some key concepts there that can guide our thinking about emerging Christian Eucharist.

Sacrifice

The word "sacrifice" occurs often in the New Testament, especially in the letter to the Hebrews and in the book of Revelation. It is clear that the Lord's death, as well as the Last Supper preceding that death were both remembered in sacrificial terms. Besides these, however, other key New Testament passages contain much sacrificial imagery. For example, John's famous discourse on the "bread of life" contains many sacrificial allusions [quotation 68]. While comfortable with sacrificial language, the New Testament writers are not literalists and do not equate Jesus' dying with any temple or Passover sacrifice; nor do they give the impression that Christian table fellowship is in continuity with the practice of Jewish sacrifice. Rather, they evoke and build upon an authentic and *spiritual* understanding of sacrifice.

Quotation 68: *[T]he bread that I will give for the life of the world is my flesh.* (John 6:51)

The Old Testament provides very clear guidelines regarding the physical aspects of sacrifice, as this practice was at the heart of temple worship. Yet, it is clear in Jewish theology that the physical aspects alone, especially the destruction of the victim, were not the central point of sacrifice; rather, the interior disposition of the offerer was critical. The prophets, in particular, made this point. The prophet Amos, for example, mocks those who come to offer sacrifices but do not hear and obey God's word [quotation 69]. He, like the psalmist, recognized that the true sacrifice was not rubrical correctness but only a contrite heart (Ps 51:17). This "sacrificial spirituality" is most clearly embedded in the story of the sacrifice of Abraham, in which his son Isaac is never physically sacrificed—though Abraham is willing to sacrifice his son and Isaac is willing to be sacrificed. Robert Daly calls this the sacrifice par excellence of the Hebrew Scriptures and believes that the sacrificial imagery of the New Testament cannot be adequately understood apart from this key Old Testament image [quotation 70]. This emphasis on interiority became an important spiritual resource for sustaining the spirit of Jewish prayer when the Jerusalem temple was destroyed and physical sacrifice came to an end.

Quotation 69:
*Come to Bethel—and transgress;
  to Gilgal—and multiply transgression;
bring your sacrifices every morning,
  your tithes every three days.* (Amos 4:4)

Quotation 70: *The sacrifice to which the mature Isaac consented was looked upon as if actually consummated. It was God's remembering of [this sacrifice] that caused him to deliver and bless Israel at the first Passover and at the other moments of deliverance and blessing in its history. More specifically, the sacrificial cult was thought to be effective because it reminded God of [this sacrifice], the sacrifice par excellence.* (Daly, *The Origins of the Christian Doctrine of Sacrifice,* p. 52)

One of the theological lenses that the early Christian community employed to think about Eucharist was sacrifice. This sacrificial lens, however, in no way implied any literal or physical understanding of the Lord's Supper as a sacrifice. Rather, it betrayed an understanding of the Lord's life and death—and the summation of his life and death in meal sharing—as fundamentally self-giving. The table gatherings of the early community celebrated the complete self-giving attitude of the incarnate Word, and rehearsed a similar attitude in the follower of Jesus through the breaking of the bread and the sharing of a cup of wine. For Jesus' disciples the selfless obedience of Abraham's sacrifice found fulfillment in the sacrificial living and dying of the Lord.

Blessing

Previously we noted that a pious Jew was expected to bless God continuously through the day. Blessing (Hebrew, *berakah*) is a key concept in the Old Testament, one with more richness of meaning than often predicated in our English word "blessing." *Berakah* first refers to the blessings that God confers on all creation and every living thing. In a very real sense, all of creation is a blessing from God, dependent upon God's initiative alone [quotation 71]. As in all other things, God is the protagonist in the act of blessing, always acting first. It is only after admitting this divine initiative that one can talk about *berakah* as an appropriate name for people's response to God's action. *Berakah* in this second sense is more an attitude than a prayer form: a posture of gratitude in the face of God's unbounded generosity that bursts forth in blessing and praise. Eventually *berakah* prayer forms will emerge, first in the Old Testament, later on in the Mishnah, and finally the Talmud. The concept of *berakah* that shapes emerging Christian Eucharist, however, is not a prayer form. Rather, it is what could be called a "*berakah* spirituality."

To his early followers, Jesus could be considered the fulfillment of the Jewish *berakah*. Parallel to the original creation story, Jesus was also God's "good word" whom the Gospel of John proclaims to be the Word made flesh (John 1:14). Jesus was the gracious gift from God, the ultimate blessing on humankind [quotation 72]. The New Testament also reports that Jesus understood himself as one totally dependent upon his Father, who gave him every good thing. He lived and prayed out of a *berakah* spirituality, admitting God to be the source of revelation and sustenance to him [quotation 73].

This *berakah* attitude and intention is at the heart of Jesus' table ministry, so determinative for the emergence of Christian Eucharist. Time and time again the New Testament narrates that Jesus "speaks a blessing" or "give thanks" in a meal context. Both of these phrases are founded upon the language and spirituality of *berakah*. He also calls upon his disciples to do the same. This means not only that his

Quotation 71: *In the opening pages of the Bible, in the first chapter of the book of Genesis, we hear God pronouncing the creative words. At significant points of the creation account we hear the constant refrain: "And God said . . ." and the accompanying accomplishment of these words in the words of approval: "and it was good." When it was the creation of man and woman, God said: "it was very good." So the first words of God were words of blessing. The Latin language captures this sense in its translation of blessing as benediction, and its verb form bene-dicere literally means "to say a good word." (Malit, "From Berakah to Misa Ng Bayang Pilipino," p. 17)*

Quotation 72: *Blessed be the God and Father of our Lord Jesus Christ, who has blessed us in Christ with every spiritual blessing in the heavenly places. (Eph 1:3)*

Quotation 73: *I thank you, Father, Lord of heaven and earth, because you have hidden these things from the wise and the intelligent and have revealed them to infants; yes, Father, for such was your gracious will. All things have been handed over to me by my Father. (Luke 10:21-22a)*

followers were supposed to repeat his actions with bread and a cup of wine but they were also to continue living in the spirit of blessing. It was this spirit of gracious acceptance for God's initiative, especially in the death and resurrection of Jesus, that Christian Eucharist emerged and flourished.

Covenant Memorial

Related to this *berakah* spirituality is the abiding sense of memorial that pervades the Bible. This is an essential framework for understanding the table narratives of Jesus, especially his Last Supper. In trying to grasp this rich dynamic, it is important—as with "blessing"—to think beyond the ordinary English definition of memorial. The Jewish understanding of memorial or remembrance (Hebrew, *zikkaron*) is a dynamic one, which implies more than a fleeting recollection of past history. As with *berakah*, at the heart of the Jewish understanding of memorial is an insistence on God's initiative. In particular, God is remembered for time and time again calling Israel into covenant. Israel is invited to abide faithfully in that living memory. Thus, memorial is not simply about past events, but about present living and future hope because of God's previous interventions in human history.

In many respects, the Old Testament could be considered a textual enshrinement of this covenant memory. The book of Genesis, for example, holds the memory of God's covenant to Noah and his family (9:8-17) and that to Abraham and Sarah and their descendants (12:1-3). Exodus recounts the pivotal covenant with the Israelites at Mount Sinai and the determinative act by which God created them into a chosen people [quotation 74]. Various renewals of that covenant are recounted in the books of Joshua (24:1-28), Second Kings (23:1-3), and Nehemiah (8:1-11). Often the prophets chastise Israel for breaking the covenant, characterizing the chosen people as a faithless spouse (Ezek 16:15). Living the covenant is the promise and future of Israel.

If the Old Testament is a kind of textual enshrinement of this covenant memory, then the Passover meal is the central ritual enshrinement of this memory. In particular this ancient meal recalls the deliverance of the Israelites from Egypt, that unprecedented divine intervention that prepared the way for the Sinai covenant [quotation 75]. This ritual underscores that the remembering is not about past deeds or a covenant that was sealed once and for all in ancient history. Rather, this meal remembrance and its accompanying texts invite the community to make the experience of deliverance their own in the present day [quotation 76].

Quotation 74: *Then Moses went up to God; the LORD called to him from the mountain, saying, "Thus you shall say to the house of Jacob, and tell the Israelites: You have seen what I did to the Egyptians, and how I bore you on eagles' wings and brought you to myself. Now therefore, if you obey my voice and keep my covenant, you shall be my treasured possession out of all the peoples. Indeed, the whole earth is mine, but you shall be for me a priestly kingdom and a holy nation."*
(Exod 19:3-6)

Quotation 75: *You shall observe this rite as a perpetual ordinance for you and your children. . . . [W]hen your children ask you, "What do you mean by this observance?" you shall say, "It is the passover sacrifice to the LORD, for he passed over the houses of the Israelites in Egypt, when he struck down the Egyptians but spared our houses."*
(Exod 12:24, 26-27)

Quotation 76: *In every generation it is man's duty to regard himself as though he personally had come out of Egypt.*
(Birnbaum, *The Passover Haggadah*, p. 47)

Quotation 77: *The whole meal may be seen as a prophetic moment, when Jesus reshapes the memory and the promise of Passover and covenant in face of the tragedy of his own death and his abandonment by God. In fidelity to the covenant of Israel and in evoking its deepest meaning in the two commandments of love, he had preached the advent of God's kingdom. His word had been rejected and he was to be judged a blasphemer, given over to death by the one whom he addressed as Abba. Instead of leading to despair, in face of this rejection his words and actions*

Despite the different chronologies of the Synoptics and the Gospel of John, all the gospels recall that the Last Supper took place in a Passover context. The emerging Christian community interpreted Jesus' last meal and his death through the lens of this ancient memorial meal [quotation 77]. In this Passover matrix, images of God's initiative, deliverance, and living covenant provided a unique and compelling prism for interpreting the community's meals kept in the living memory of Jesus. Like their Jewish forebears, the followers of Jesus entered a ritual meal that invited them to collectively shape a living memory. They created this dynamic remembrance so that the new covenant, sealed in the passing over of Jesus from death to life, would be proclaimed in their lives.

Reconciling Love

While Jews had numerous cultic practices—some of them highly regulated—the covenant expressed and sustained through this cult was ultimately a matter of the heart. The external rituals were to be signs of an interior disposition of devotion to God. Thus, religion for the Israelites was not the keeping of certain practices but the sustaining of a relationship with God and with each other. In general, the Old Testament emphasizes the love of fellow Israelites, who share a covenantal relationship with God [quotation 78]. Besides this strong sense of solidarity with other Israelites, however, the Old Testament teaches care and respect for the stranger. Remembering that they had once been the outsiders living in a foreign land, Israelites are expected not only to be hospitable toward those outsiders who dwell with them but also to love them [quotation 79].

While the Israelites developed an idea of mutual love and emphasized it at the level of other commandments, Christianity placed the love of neighbor at the very center of the gospel, equating it with the love of God. This new covenant of love was symbolized in a memorable way by Jesus in his table ministry. Time and again he was remembered as not only eating and drinking with the ultimate outsiders—sinners—but also embracing them [quotation 80]. And this same Jesus who reached out to Samaritan women, tax collectors, and outcasts of every kind ultimately himself became an outsider, rejected by many of his own people and executed as a criminal. In an ironic twist, the Gospel of Luke presents the resurrected Jesus as a stranger to his own disciples on the road to Emmaus. One of the great surprises of that story is that if the disciples had not invited the unrecognized Jesus to walk with them and to dine with them, there would have been no recognition in the breaking of the bread: no Eucharist without the stranger.

reinterpret the meaning and the promise of salvation and locate them in the death itself. It is thus that it is to be remembered and it is in the act of this prophetic service that he himself is to be remembered. When the early Christians were filled with faith in his resurrection and celebrated the remembrance of his death, they could see the promise of the resurrection in the words about his forthcoming death. They could also see the anticipation of his coming anew, as this is evoked in Paul's version of the supper. Their own remembrance therefore would not only look back to the death and receive the self-gift of the risen Lord, but it would continue to interpret present history in the light of the eschatological expectation opened up by Jesus' Passover. (Power, *The Eucharistic Mystery*, p. 50)

Quotation 78: *You shall not hate in your heart anyone of your kin; you shall reprove your neighbor, or you will incur guilt yourself. You shall not take vengeance or bear a grudge against any of your people, but you shall love your neighbor as yourself: I am the LORD.* (Lev 19:17-18)

Quotation 79: *When an alien resides with you in your land, you shall not oppress the alien. The alien who resides with you shall be to you as the citizen among you; you shall love the alien as yourself, for you were aliens in the land of Egypt: I am the LORD your God.* (Lev 19:33-34)

Quotation 80: *The oriental . . . would immediately understand the acceptance of the outcasts into table fellowship with Jesus as an offer of salvation to guilty sinners and as the assurance of forgiveness. Hence the passionate objections of the pharisees who held that the pious could have table fellowship only with the righteous. They understood the intention of Jesus as being to accord the outcasts worth before God by eating with them, and they objected to his placing of the sinner on the same level as the righteous.* (Joachim Jeremias, *The Eucharistic Words of Jesus*, pp. 204–5)

Quotation 81: *I ask not only on behalf of these, but also on behalf of those who will believe in me through their word, that they may all be one. As you, Father, are in me and I am in you, may they also be in us, so that the world may believe that you have sent me. The glory that you have given me I have given them, so that they may be one, as we are one, I in them and you in me, that they may become completely one.* (John 17:20-23)

Jesus' table ministry revealed that the breaking of the bread—like the whole of the Jesus experience—was both an act of hospitality and an invitation to forgiveness. It also symbolized the reconciling openness that was to mark the life of every follower of Jesus. Harmony was to be a hallmark of table fellowship and the common life, with no division between liturgy and life. An ethics of love and reconciliation is essential to both. In the midst of his Last Supper with the disciples, Jesus is remembered as praying for the unity of his followers [quotation 81]. This paradox of unity and openness was not always easy for Jesus' followers, whose common meals sometimes mirrored their division rather than their love for each other [quotation 20]. When division erupted, a shared table in the name and memory of Jesus provided common ground for reconciliation.

Summary

The diversity of theological perspectives in the New Testament makes it difficult to provide any systematic theology of Eucharist from that source. Furthermore, the authors of the New Testament themselves were not interested in creating any separate or systematic eucharistic theology. The themes of sacrifice, *berakah*, covenant memorial, and reconciling love, however, provide a useful foundation for thinking theologically about Eucharist in the New Testament. In particular, they demonstrate that emerging eucharistic practice was intimately related to the way Jesus' followers were to live in the world. By God's initiative they had been given an astounding gift in Jesus, who never held back from his own self-giving. Jesus was the incarnate hospitality of God, who embraced every sinner willing to be forgiven. The table practice of Jesus' followers provided a living memory of this reconciling hospitality, which they were to live no matter what the personal cost.

JACOB AND RUBEN

Jacob splashed water on his face, shook the dust from his robes, and hurried to greet his guests. He had hoped to arrive home earlier, but camel trading was an unpredictable business. A dispute with one of his regular customers over the price of two small dromedaries delayed him. After finally arriving at an acceptable price—more acceptable to the customer than to Jacob, but that's what one does to keep good customers—Jacob excused himself, bolted out of the bazaar and raced through the back streets of Jericho, praying as he ran that he would arrive home before Ruben and the others.

Ruben was brother-in-law to the great preacher, Paul of Tarsus. Like Paul, Ruben traveled from city to city telling the stories of Jesus of Nazareth. He sometimes preached in the streets, but more often he would go to a local synagogue and there proclaim this "good news." It was at the synagogue in Jericho that Jacob first met him. Ruben had been asked by the president of the synagogue to say a few words after the reading from the scroll of Ezekiel. Ruben began by announcing that Jesus was the fulfillment of every prophecy and was the one true messiah. The synagogue immediately erupted into a holy brawl. Some were shouting to let Ruben speak, but most rushed forward to rebuff the heretic.

As the assembly turned into an angry mob, Jacob knew that he had better act quickly or Ruben, who stood his ground, could end up hurt or dead. A burly man who knew how to push his way through a crowd, Jacob soon reached the unwelcome prophet, grabbed him by the back of his tunic, and pulled him like a reluctant camel through the chaos. Once outside the synagogue, Jacob maneuvered Ruben through the back streets, finally dragging the prophet into his home.

Ruben was furious that he had been denied the opportunity to preach his message, to answer the objections of his detractors, and to suffer whatever fate would come to him through this witness. Partly to calm Ruben down—and partly to satisfy his own curiosity—Jacob invited Ruben to share the evening meal with his family and tell the stories to them.

As he prepared for dinner, Jacob mused that his children would be a formidable challenge for Ruben.

Although he loved them dearly, Jacob knew that they were a quarrelsome brood—especially the twins, whose penchant for misbehavior was only amplified by the presence of guests. Had Abraham experienced such difficulties with Isaac? To spare his guests the experience of his squabbling offspring, Jacob usually ate alone with his visitors. Tonight, however, he told his wife to bring all ten of his children to the table, hoping that they would keep Ruben occupied for the duration of the meal.

To Jacob's surprise, his lone guest mesmerized the children. How quiet they became as Ruben unfolded the stories of Jesus curing a boy with palsy, mending relationships between quarreling siblings, multiplying bread and fish for thousands, and sharing a final meal with his inner circle of friends. They sat transfixed as Ruben whispered the story of Jesus' trial, crucifixion, and burial. Then there were the events of the third day—most astonishing to them, but also quite believable. Jacob's own skepticism was muted by the simple assent of his own flesh and blood.

Then Ruben did something quite unexpected. He took a piece of bread and offered a blessing in the memory of Jesus. Then he shared the bread with the children, saying, "If you eat this, you too become part of the story, for this bread is the very body of Jesus." Jacob's youngest passed the bread wide-eyed to her father, who ate in silence. Then Ruben took his cup, spoke another longer blessing, and passed the cup to the children saying, "By drinking from this cup, you drink from the heart of Jesus who died that we might live, for this cup is an invitation to a new covenant sealed in his blood."

That was seventeen years ago. In the interim Jacob's camel trade has flourished, his children have given him grandchildren, and Ruben has become a frequent and welcome guest. In the early years, after the children had withdrawn, Ruben would spend long nights with Jacob exploring the Jesus story. Jacob began to invite a few selected friends for marathon dinners that often ended with the simple ritual of bread and wine. Over the years the company began to expand. Jacob's grown children often returned for dinner when Ruben came to town. Their children and friends now have become part of an ever-growing circle. Jacob never knows who will show up for dinners these nights. Even when Ruben is not present, these followers of the new way still gather around the table to hear Jacob repeat the stories, the invitations, and the rituals. Many times Jacob has broken the bread with his family and friends, repeating the blessings and evoking the memories that Ruben imparted to him. But for tonight, he will simply play the host, welcoming the old prophet and newfound friends who will again come to recognize Jesus in their midst through the breaking of the bread.

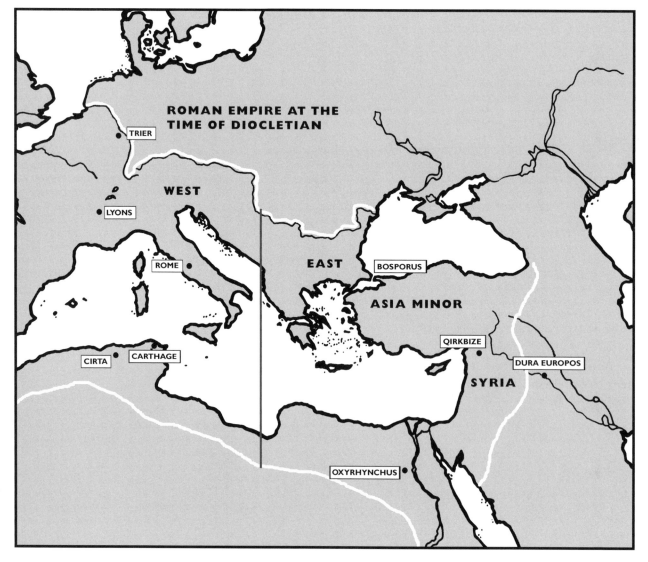

ROMAN EMPIRE AT THE
TIME OF DIOCLETIAN

TRIER

WEST

LYONS

ROME

EAST

BOSPORUS

ASIA MINOR

QIRKBIZE

DURA EUROPOS

SYRIA

CIRTA

CARTHAGE

OXYRHYNCHUS

29. Map for chapter 2.

CHAPTER TWO

The Domestic Church: 100–313

Christianity for much of the first century could be considered a movement within, rather than a religion distinct from, Judaism. One author has suggested the useful metaphor of emerging Christianity and Judaism after the destruction of the Jerusalem temple as siblings who eventually part company [quotation 82]. During the second and third centuries of the Common Era, however, Christianity established itself as a distinctive religion. This separation was gradual and did not occur at the same pace in every region. Edessa in East Syria, for example, was a city that remained outside the Roman Empire until 214 C.E. After the destruction of the Jerusalem temple, it became one destination for many Jewish exiles as well as a burgeoning center of Christianity. In such a place the "siblings" remained much closer than in a city such as Rome, where the followers of Jesus were under more pressure to distance themselves from Judaism. As noted previously, however, even in a city like Antioch, which the Romans employed as a provincial capital for Syria, some Christians were still frequenting synagogues as late as the fourth century [quotation 15]. Gradually, however, Christianity emerged as a separate religion within the empire. Marks of this independence were its own conflicts with the Roman authorities, the emergence of new governance structures, a distinctive theology (especially about Jesus), distinguishing cultic practices, and the development of a new body of sacred texts.

As noted in the previous chapter, some Jewish communities took steps to expel Christians from synagogues during the first century [quotation 14]. Eventually, the Christian community sought to distance itself from Judaism as well. The roots of this separation were the different views that these two groups held of Jesus: the former affirming that he was the Messiah and the latter denying this claim. This gradual but deliberate separation at the level of faith was concretely expressed in distinctive—sometimes competing—cultic practices. For example, early Christian writings indicate that Jewish fast days were intentionally abandoned by some Christians [quotation 83]. Similarly, Christians eventually came to observe Sunday, rather than the Sabbath, as the primary day for public worship [quotation 84].

Quotation 82: *I rejected the view of conventional wisdom that Judaism was the parent faith and Christianity the child. The Rabbinic Judaism that shaped the journey into history after the destruction of the Jewish State was in a real sense a mutation designed for survival. . . . Both Rabbinic Judaism and early Christianity received their basic form at the same time, each placing a different reading of the messianic force at work within Judaism and the Jewish people. Thus they can be viewed as siblings.* (Perelmuter, *Siblings,* p. 2)

Quotation 83: *Do not keep the same fast days as the hypocrites. Mondays and Thursdays are their fast days, but yours should be Wednesdays and Fridays.* (Audet, *La Didachè,* 8 [early second century])

Quotation 84: *. . . they who walked in ancient customs came to a new hope, no longer living for the Sabbath, but for the Lord's Day, on which also our life sprang up through him and his death—though some deny him—and by this mystery we received faith, and for this reason also we suffer, that we may be found disciples of Jesus Christ our only teacher.* (Ignatius of Antioch [d. 106], Letter to the Magnesians, 9.1, in *The Apostolic Fathers,* p. 205)

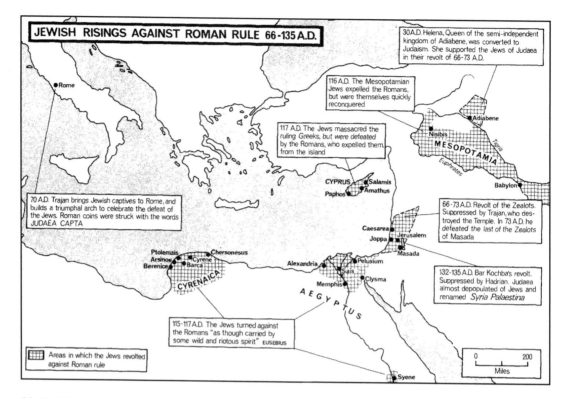

JEWISH RISINGS AGAINST ROMAN RULE 66-135 A.D.

30 A.D. Helena, Queen of the semi-independent kingdom of Adiabene, was converted to Judaism. She supported the Jews of Judaea in their revolt of 66-73 A.D.

116 A.D. The Mesopotamian Jews expelled the Romans, but were themselves quickly reconquered

117 A.D. The Jews massacred the *ruling Greeks, but were defeated* by the Romans, who expelled them from the island

70 A.D. Trajan brings Jewish captives to Rome, and builds a triumphal arch to celebrate the defeat of the Jews. Roman coins were struck with the words JUDAEA CAPTA

66-73 A.D. Revolt of the Zealots. Suppressed by Trajan, who destroyed the Temple. In 73 A.D. he *defeated the last of the Zealots* of Masada

132-135 A.D. Bar Kochba's revolt. Suppressed by Hadrian. Judaea almost depopulated of Jews and renamed *Syria Palaestina*

115-117 A.D. The Jews turned against the Romans "as though carried by some wild and riotous spirit" EUSEBIUS

Areas in which the Jews revolted against Roman rule

0   200
Miles

30. Jewish revolts.

Separation between Christians and Jews led, in some situations, to a growing adversarial relationship between the two. Anti-Semitism is clearly detectable in some Christian writings. It is possible that some of this may have been a survival tactic employed by Christians wanting to distinguish themselves from the Jews, who were becoming increasingly unpopular in the Roman Empire. The first and second Jewish revolts against Rome in the years 66–70 and 132–135 C.E. generated enormous contempt for Jews in the Roman Empire [illustration 30]. In view of these events, the followers of Jesus were motivated to distinguish themselves from their Jewish siblings as Christianity spread throughout the Mediterranean.

During the first century the disciples carried the gospel from Palestine into modern-day Syria, Turkey, Greece, and Italy. Paul is certainly the most celebrated of these missionaries [illustration 31], yet the spread of Christianity was the concerted effort of innumerable women and men, most of whose names are forever lost. The empire's network of roads connecting the various provinces and their key cities provided a useful system for the spread of Christianity [illustration 32]. By the second century, Christian communities could be found along the North African coast, scattered throughout Asia

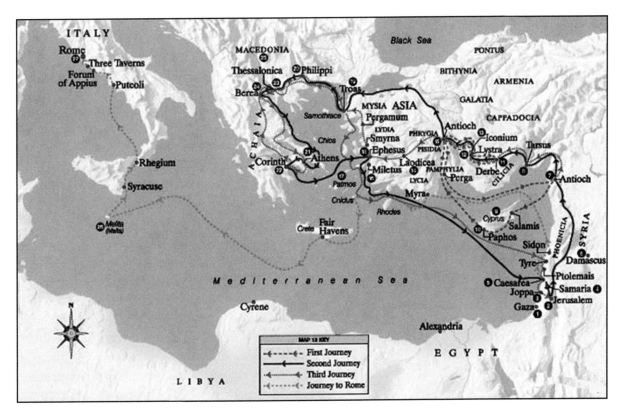

31. Paul's travels.

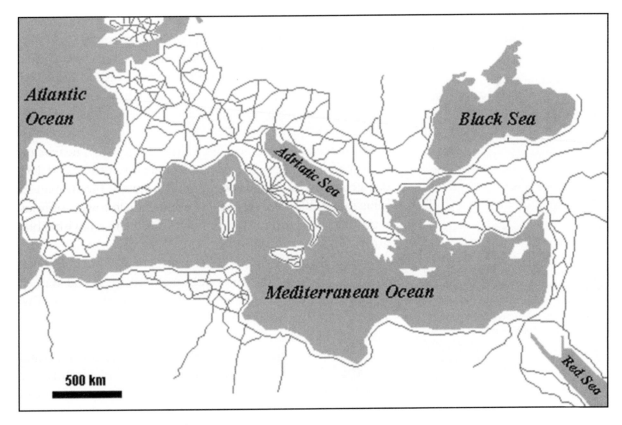

32. The roads of the Roman Empire.

Minor, and as far north and east as Trier and Lyons. By the following century, those borders stretched from India to the British Isles. From a handful of disciples, Christianity grew to almost twenty thousand adherents by the end of the first century, with five to seven million believers by the year 300. In an empire of fifty or sixty million inhabitants, this was a significant minority.

This expansion of Christianity set the stage for growing conflict with the Roman authorities. This conflict occasionally erupted into persecution. The first persecution of Christians by Roman authorities —limited to the city of Rome itself—occurred under the emperor Nero (d. 68) in the year 64. In his search for a scapegoat for the great fire of Rome—which many suspected Nero himself had set—the emperor blamed the Christians [quotation 85]. Other short-lived persecutions occurred under Domitian (d. 96) in Rome, Trajan (d. 117) in Asia Minor, and Marcus Aurelius (d. 180) in Lyons. Decius (d. 251) believed that Christianity was a threat to the state, and he persecuted Christians throughout the empire [quotation 86]. This brief but intense persecution was similar to the longer ones that occurred under Diocletian (d. 305). These persecutions—though sporadic, often confined to a specific geographic area and separated by long periods of peace—chart the progressive visibility of Christianity in the Roman Empire.

These external signs of growth were matched by internal developments within the church. The period between the year 100 and 313 saw the emergence of basic ecclesial structures, worship forms, and dogmas. During this period the roles of bishops, deacons, and many other ministries were delineated. Christians still follow an outline for Eucharist formed by the middle of the second century [quotation 87]. It was during this era that Greek philosophy was first employed in the service of a Christian theology, and the divinity of Christ was in the process of being defined. Although a definitive list of the New Testament canon was not to appear until the fourth century, these earlier centuries were critical for that canonization process. In short, this was a time when one could recognize a church: largely urban, increasingly Gentile and Hellenized, with a distinctive cult and a shared body of belief. This church, however, lacked any centralized government and might be better imagined as a series of local communities in communion with each other rather than the universal church of later centuries. Because of this "communion relationship" between the churches, there was significant pluriformity across the belief structures and worship practices of these communities. More familial than institutional in structure and practice, the years 100–313 have been appropriately called the era of the domestic church.

Quotation 85: *To eliminate the suspicion that he himself had set the fire, the emperor diverted it to the Christians, who were hated because of their misdeeds. (Tacitus [d. 120], Annals, 14.44)*

Quotation 86: *Philip, after a reign of seven years, was succeeded by Decius. Through hatred of Philip, he started a persecution against the churches, in which Fabian found fulfillment in martyrdom at Rome. (Eusebius of Caesarea [d. ca. 340], The History of the Church, 6.39.1)*

Quotation 87: *The records of the apostles or writings of the prophets are read for as long as time allows. Then, when the reader has finished, the president in a discourse admonishes [us] to imitate these good things. Then we all stand up together and offer prayers; and as we said before, when we have finished praying, bread and wine and water are brought up, and the president likewise offers prayers and thanksgiving to the best of his ability, and the people assent, saying the Amen; and there is a distribution, and everyone participates in [the elements] over which thanks have been given; and they are sent through the deacons to those who are not present. (Justin Martyr [d. ca. 165], First Apology, 67:3-5, in Jasper and Cuming, Prayers of the Eucharist)*

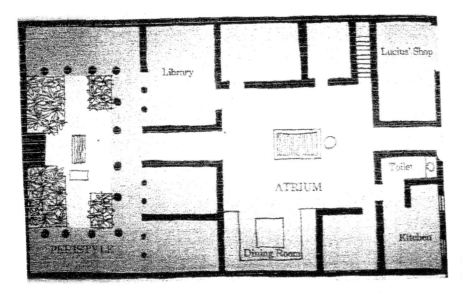

33. Floor plan of a Roman home.
(Macaulay, p. 66)

ARCHITECTURE

During the early part of this era, the community gathered in borrowed spaces, the most important of which were homes of believers, though other types of borrowed spaces were also employed at this time [quotation 88]. It is also during this period, however, that Christian communities began to acquire domestic spaces designated for worship. This evolution will be reflected in changes in language. The catacombs in which Christians buried their dead also were significant places for the evolution of Christian worship. There is some evidence that believers also had "Christian synagogues" but as there was no standard architecture to synagogues, these were not architecturally influential; rather, it was the synagogue service that was ritually influential on emerging Christianity. Finally, aside from borrowed spaces or renovated homes, there is evidence at the end of this era that the community began constructing substantial rectangular edifices, which L. Michael White labels *aula ecclesiae* (Latin, "hall of the church"). These will be succeeded by Christian basilicas, which are usually thought to have emerged only after the ascent of Constantine and so will be dealt with in the next chapter.

The House Church

As noted previously, borrowed rooms and believers' houses were important gathering places for the Christian community during the first century of the Common Era. The destruction of the temple in Jerusalem and the growing separation of the Christian community

Quotation 88: *Now Luke [having come] from Gaul and Titus from Dalmatia had been waiting for Paul at Rome. When he saw them Paul rejoiced so that he hired a storehouse [horreum] outside the city [of Rome], where with the brethren he taught the word of truth.* (The Acts of Paul 11:1, ca. 190, in L. Michael White, II:48)

from the synagogue in most of the empire contributed to the emergence of the house church as the primary place for community worship. This more familial setting also held a special connection with the table ministry of Jesus that so characterized his public life. Thus, this domestic setting was at once practical and at the same time symbolic, theologically charged, and even traditional. While there was no "mother church" in Christianity, the domestic table was unquestionably an important wellspring of the faith.

In the Roman Empire at this time, the building of homes was an important architecture concern. We have already noted how difficult it is to generalize about the types of homes that existed in the empire during these centuries [quotation 19]. One common form was the four-sided structures for the wealthy found in many urban centers of the empire [illustration 33]. The resulting walled-off interior provided shelter from the commotion of the street. Such settings also could have provided the community privacy for their rituals, if they were concerned about the disapproving gaze of neighbors or authorities. There is some evidence, however, that during this era the front doors of important houses stood open, especially while dining was going on. This practice challenges some of the mythology that has grown up around the idea of *disciplina arcani* (Latin, "discipline of the secret"), which supposed that early Christians imitated the secrecy of certain ancient mystery religions by not revealing key information about their teachings or ritual practices.

Besides large one-story homes, there were multiple-story single-family dwellings that could also have served to house the eucharistic gatherings of the early community. According to Richard Krautheimer, these structures were common in the eastern provinces of the empire. The only large room in such an edifice was the dining room on the top floor. Krautheimer imagines that it was such a dwelling, with the community crowed into the upper dining room, that served as the setting for the incident at Troas reported in the Acts of the Apostles in which a young man fell asleep during Paul's preaching and fell out a window [quotation 89].

Since the first house churches were family dwellings, this would have set certain spatial limitations on the worshiping community. Permanent structural changes in a home might have disrupted the family's life, so the community probably limited its modifications to rearranging the little furniture it needed in order to accommodate worship. In the dining room, for example, the host or presider would have led the worship from the triclinium [illustration 34], with others seated outside the dining room proper in the adjoining atrium or peristyle, depending on the design of the house. As the size of the community increased and the limits of ordinary rooms were strained,

Quotation 89: *On the first day of the week, when we met to break bread, Paul was holding a discussion with them; since he intended to leave the next day, he continued speaking until midnight. There were many lamps in the room upstairs where we were meeting. A young man named Eutychus, who was sitting in the window, began to sink off into a deep sleep while Paul talked still longer. Overcome by sleep, he fell to the ground three floors below and was picked up dead. But Paul went down, and bending over him took him in his arms, and said, "Do not be alarmed, for his life is in him." Then Paul went upstairs, and after he had broken bread and eaten, he continued to converse with them until dawn; then he left. Meanwhile they had taken the boy away alive and were not a little comforted.* (Acts 20:7-12)

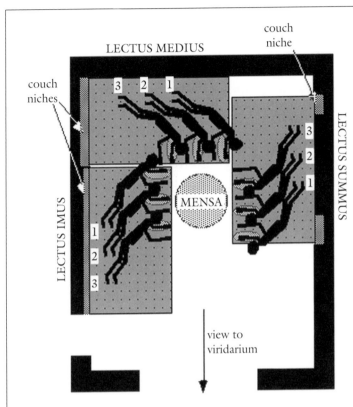

couch niche

LECTUS MEDIUS

couch niches

LECTUS IMUS

MENSA

LECTUS SUMMUS

view to viridarium

**POMPEII IX.1.7, room(e)
Casa di Paccius Alexander**

Reconstruction of triclinium and the arrangement of the diners, couches, and table, based on the size and the placement of couch niches.

key to couch position:
1: *locus summus*
2: *locus medius*
3: *locus imus*

Lectus imus #1 is the place of the master of the house.

Lectus medius #3 is the *locus consularis*, or place of honor.

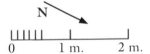

N

0   1 m.   2 m.

Fig. 1.27: Reconstruction of the Standard Order of Reclining Diners in Triclinium(e) of the Casa di Paccius Alexander, IX.1.7. Diners (stick figures in black) are shown three to a couch, supporting themselves on their left elbows, which rest on ovals that signify cushions.

34. Triclinium.

a community might have looked for a larger home in which to gather or, with increased frequency, acquired permanent places for worship.

L. Michael White convincingly argues that the first steps toward architectural adaptation of a building took place in an edifice where Christians were already accustomed to meet. He believes that the gradual or partial renovation of such house churches is already detectable in places like Rome by the third century (I:114). White distinguishes the earlier unrenovated "house church" from permanently renovated spaces by the new designation "house of the church" or *domus ecclesiae*—a term of White's own invention that does not appear in early Christian literature.

Several sources—a number of which are secular—document the ownership of such *domus ecclesiae* by Christian communities. A court history from East Syria, for example, reports of a flood that ravaged the capital city of Edessa in 201 C.E. Listed among the damages was

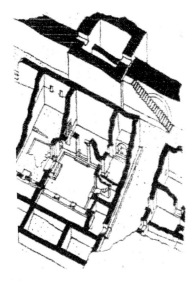

35. *Domus ecclesiae.*

"the holy place of the congregation of the Christians," which White thinks indicates a building that had become publicly identifiable as the regular meeting place of the Christians, or a renovated *domus ecclesiae* (I:118). Another account from a secular historian even records that the Roman emperor sold a house for use as a place of Christian worship rather than allow it to be converted into a tavern [quotation 90].

The most famous architectural evidence of a renovated *domus ecclesiae* comes from the ancient fortress town of Dura Europos in eastern Syria. This domestic dwelling, built about 200 C.E. as a four-sided structure around an open courtyard, underwent significant renovation in about 232 C.E. [illustration 35]. A wall was torn down between adjoining rooms, creating one large space—about 16 ½ feet by 43 feet—which was large enough for the community's Eucharist. A basin with a canopy was built in another room; frescoes in that room—for example, Christ walking on the water—suggest that the space was used for baptisms. Although few other examples from this era are as well preserved as the house in Dura Europos, its arrangement is not considered extraordinary. White surmises that the renovation that transformed this building into a *domus ecclesiae* came about through the donation of a benefactor. He further surmises that, generally speaking, access to property through patronage and donation was an essential element in the transition from the temporary use of unrenovated "house churches" to the acquisition and transformation of "houses of the church" (I:148).

The Hall of the Church

There is general agreement that the basilica was adopted for worship by Christians after the ascent of Constantine to power (313–337 C.E.). Thus, we will consider the basilica in the next chapter. Given the architectural distance between a *domus ecclesiae* like Dura Europos and a basilica like Old St. Peter's [illustration 68], however, we need to consider what developments might have intervened between these two forms of Christian architecture.

There is both textual and archaeological evidence that, even before the reign of Constantine, Christians were building large and impressive buildings. The philosopher Porphyry (d. ca. 304), for example, wrote a treatise against Christianity (*Adversus Christianos*) in the second half of the third century. While only fragments of the work remain, one extant passage chastises Christians for erecting great buildings [quotation 91]. Christian writers also provide evidence that new types of worship spaces were emerging for Christians at the end of the third century. The church historian Eusebius of Caesarea, for example, not only notes that many churches were built during the peace after the reign of the emperor Gallienus (253–268) and before the persecution of Diocletian (284–305) but also comments on the spaciousness of such buildings [quotation 92].

L. Michael White believes that such documentary evidence points to an important link between the permanently renovated house of the church (*domus ecclesiae*) of the mid-third century, and the basilica-style church that emerges in the fourth century. The name he invents for one of these interim structures is the "hall of the church" (*aula ecclesiae*). White believes that the "hall of the church" naturally evolved from the *domus ecclesiae*. This evolution could occur either through continuous renovation of a domestic space or through new construction. What marks these as "hall[s] of the church" is not so much their size but their rectangular shape, without apse or side aisle construction. Some of these could have been relatively large edifices, while others would have been quite modest.

White believes that one example of a modest structure, newly constructed and not evolving from a previous building, was a church at Qirqbize in Syria [illustration 36]. Built in the first third of the fourth century, the building was approximately 48½ feet long, 21 feet wide and 21½ feet tall. While it went through a series of subsequent renovations that rendered it more recognizable as a worship space, it appears that at its earliest stage this was a simple hall church—devoid of apse and aisle characteristic of basilicas. While from the outside it resembled the architecture of the villa just a few feet away, its interior was not house-like but a single hall for assembly with no internal divisions or specially marked areas except the raised platform across the east end (White I:129).

Shifts in Language

Parallel to these architectural changes were changes in language about the community's gathering spaces. In the previous era the Greek word *ekklesia* or "assembly" was commonly used to designate the followers of Jesus, whether that be a specific community gathered in a single locale (e.g., 1 Cor 11:18) or his followers more universally considered (e.g., Matt 16:18). Already at the beginning of the third century, however, there is evidence that the place where the community gathers is beginning to assume the name of the assembly and, by extension, reflect something of the community's holiness. Clement of Alexandria (d. ca. 215), for example, while arguing that he would rather call the elect a "church" than apply that name to the place where they gather, yet gives evidence that the latter is already occurring [quotation 93]. Clement does not seem to be

Quotation 92: *How could one describe those mass meetings, the enormous gatherings in every city, and the remarkable congregations in places of worship? No longer satisfied with the old buildings, they raised from the foundations in all the cities churches spacious in plan. These things went forward with the times and expanded at a daily increasing rate, so that no envy stopped them nor could any evil spirit bewitch them or check them by means of human schemes, as long as the divine and heavenly hand sheltered and protected its own people, as being worthy.* (Eusebius [d. ca. 340], *The History of the Church,* 8.1)

Quotation 93: *But if "the sacred" is understood in two ways—both as God himself and as the structure built in his honor—how shall we not rightly call the church, made through knowledge for the honor of God, sacred to God—of greater value, neither constructed by mechanical skill nor embellished by the hand of a vagabond priest, but by the will of God made into a temple! For I call not the place but the assembly of the elect the church [ekklesia]. This is the better temple for receiving the great dignities of God.* (Clement of Alexandria, *Stromata* 7.5, in L. Michael White, II:52)

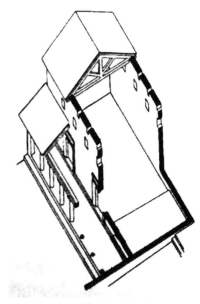

36. Church at Qirqbize, Syria.
(L. Michael White, 2:137)

37. Catacomb of Saint Callistus.

38. Small chapel, sometimes called the Crypt of the Popes, in the Roman catacomb of Callistus, as it appeared at the time of its discovery in 1854.

originating this language change, but reflects an evolution already underway in his own community.

By the middle of the third century other texts—both Christian and non-Christian—substantiate this linguistic evolution. Thus, Bishop Cyprian of Carthage (d. 258) makes an architectural reference to "pulpit or tribunal *of the church*" [quotation 112, emphasis added]. Later a municipal survey from the city of Oxyrhynchus, written ca. 295 C.E., notes the existence of two streets known as "North-Church street" and "South-Church street" (White, II:166), so designated because of the most notable edifices on those streets.

Besides variations on the Greek word for assembly (*ekklesia*), the use of other Greek and Latin terms demonstrates that the Christian community of the third century was crafting language for speaking about spaces permanently designated for worship. One of the more influential of these was the Greek word *kuriakón*. Literally it can be translated as "[thing] belonging to the Lord." Already in the writings of Clement of Alexandria the term is used, but it could be referring more generally to a bishop's "household." Yet, since some bishops were among those whom White believes donated property to the Christian community for permanent renovation into a *domus ecclesiae*, it is possible that such a "household" was also a place for worship. A secular document from the early fourth century recounts the marriage dispute in which a Christian wife reports that her husband had locked her out of their home because she had gone to the church building [*kuriakón*] [quotation 94]. It is from this Greek word that we derive the English word "church" (Scottish, *kirk*; German, *Kirche*), while *ekklesia* is the basis of modern French (*église*), Italian (*chiesa*), and Spanish (*iglesia*) words for church.

While a clear evolution in language is occurring for the communities of this era who are developing terms for permanently renovated or even newly constructed places for worship, believers understood that these buildings were important or even sacred only by extension. It was the community that was yet considered to be the first and primary expression of the Body of Christ and the true *ekklesia*.

Catacombs

Few places of the ancient Christian world have captured the imagination as much as the catacombs. They are often depicted in epic movies and historical novels as subterranean hideouts where Christians gathered for worship during constant persecutions. This scenario is more fanciful than truthful. We previously noted that persecutions were a sporadic occurrence; thus, they did not have a lasting effect

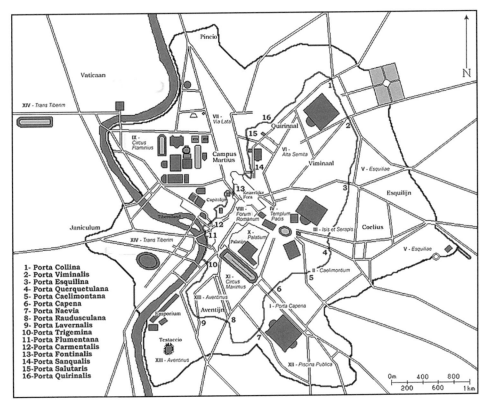

39. Walled city of Rome.

1- Porta Collina
2- Porta Viminalis
3- Porta Esquilina
4- Porta Querquetulana
5- Porta Caelimontana
6- Porta Capena
7- Porta Naevia
8- Porta Raudusculana
9- Porta Lavernalis
10-Porta Trigemina
11-Porta Flumentana
12-Porta Carmentalis
13-Porta Fontinalis
14-Porta Sanqualis
15-Porta Salutaris
16-Porta Quirinalis

on the worship spaces of the early community. Christian places of worship not only were above ground but often were well known [quotation 90]. When there were persecutions, the authorities often knew exactly what buildings the Christians were using for their worship [quotation 95].

The catacombs were a network of subterranean cemeteries that existed in many cities of the empire from as early as the second century. This was not exclusively a Christian phenomenon, and Jews as well as other groups also had their own catacombs. More than forty such cemeteries were dug outside the walls of Rome, where the law required all burials to take place. Often consisting of three or four stories of passageways, the narrow corridors of the catacombs stretched for miles; in Rome there are over 350 miles of catacombs. Niches were cut from the floor to the ceiling to receive the bodies of the dead [illustration 37]. Occasionally, these passageways opened into small chapels or burial chambers for the more notable deceased [illustration 38]. These chapels, however, were never intended to accommodate large groups of worshipers, demonstrating again that catacombs were not ordinary gathering places for Christian Eucharist.

The catacombs of Rome were the site of tens of thousands of Christian burials. Some of the more important catacombs were those of Saints Callistus, Domitilla, Pancras, and Priscilla. After the period

Quotation 94: *Yet after this agreement and these oaths, he again hid the keys from me. And when I had gone to the church building on the Sabbath Day he had the outsides doors locked against me saying "Why did you go to the church building?"* (L. Michael White, II:171)

Quotation 95: *When he came to the house in which the Christians gathered [for worship], Felix the high priest and supervisor [of the colony of Cirta] said to bishop Paul, "Give me the scriptures of the law and whatever else you have here as ordered so that you may be able to comply with [this] order." Paul said, "The lectors have the scriptures, but what we have here we give . . . two chalices of gold, six chalices of silver, six silver jars, a silver dish, seven silver lamps, two torches, seven short bronze candlesticks with their candles, eleven bronze lamps with their chains. . . . Afterwards the book chests [armaria] in the library were found to be empty.* (from the *Acts of Munatus Felix* [19 May 303] as cited in *Gesta apud Zenophilim* [*Acts of Zenophilus*])

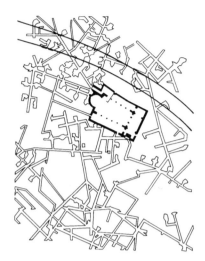

40. Rome, the catacomb of Domitilla (off the Via Ardeatina, south of the city), in use as a Christian cemetery since ca. 200 C.E.; plan of the section under the modern street called Via delle sette chiese. A small chapel was raised over the tombs of Saints Nereus and Achilleus by Pope Damasus (d. 384). A larger church was built in 524. (After Kostof, p. 249)

Quotation 96: *In your assemblies, in the holy churches, after all good patterns form your gatherings, and arrange all the places for the brethren carefully with all sobriety. Let a place be reserved for the presbyters in the midst of the eastern part of the house, and let the throne of the bishop be placed amongst them; let the presbyters sit with him; but also at the other eastern side of the house let the laymen sit; for this it is required that the presbyters should sit at the eastern side of the house with the bishops, and afterwards the laymen, and next the women: that when ye stand to pray the rulers may stand first, afterwards the laymen, and then the women also, for towards the East it is required that ye should pray as ye know that it is written, "give praise to God who rideth on the heavens of heavens towards the East." (Connolly, Didascalia Apostolorum [early third century], 12)*

of persecutions in Rome these and others became favored places of burial for Christians who wish to be interred near the saints. This honor could be afforded to many because the same niche or alcove often was used for a series of burials over the centuries as the bodies of those previously buried there decayed.

After the collapse of the eastern part of the empire in the fifth century, the inhabitants of Rome retreated within the old city walls for refuge [illustration 39]. Christian citizens, now in the majority, took the bodies of many saints from the catacombs and placed them in churches within the city. Because the bodies of many saints were removed, the catacombs were abandoned as burial cites in the sixth century and forgotten altogether by the Middle Ages. The catacombs were rediscovered accidentally in 1578.

Although the architecture of the catacombs did not influence the development of Christian worship, the cult surrounding the bodies of the saints did. The cemeteries became places of great reverence and veneration. They became centers of pilgrimage, which prompted the building of above-ground churches over them; these churches were much frequented before Christians were forced to retreat within the city walls [illustration 40]. Eventually this cult of the saints became disconnected from the original place of burial, and relics were divided and dispersed throughout Christendom. As we will see, the proliferation and enormous interest in relics in the Middle Ages will have a profound impact on Christian cult, eucharistic theology, and the very shape of our churches. Originally, however, there was virtually no concern for the possession of relics, and the catacombs were unspoiled places for burial and veneration of the dead.

Summary

The house church was the primary architectural symbol of the second- and third-century church. Although the worship in some communities of this period and some worship spaces were very well regulated [quotation 96], the spaces themselves ordinarily symbolized a church that was more an extended family than an international organization. As these homes—increasingly renovated for Christian worship—became more prominent in the community, they took on new significance in the Christian consciousness. One of the results of moving from borrowed rooms to renovated and permanent worship structures was the transference of the name traditionally given to the community—*ekklesia*—to the building itself. While this change in terminology did not indicate that the community no longer considered itself the true *ekklesia* or foundation of living stones, it did anticipate a time when such consciousness would be lost among the baptized. Eventually, it would be more the building than the community that would be recognized by the vast majority of believers as "the church."

Another, more subtle change in this era regards the diminished influence of women symbolized in the move from temporary to permanent spaces. In chapter 1 we noted that in the Greco-Roman world the home could be considered "women's space," and worship in that space would have been marked by the more equal participation of women and even their leadership. As Christian worship moves from domestic settings to more public buildings, however, the influence of women is going to diminish [quotation 97]. While the change of space is not the only factor in the marginalization of women that will take centuries to be complete, the seeds have already been planted in this era in which separate, more public buildings were acquired by Christians for worship.

Quotation 97: *Christianity and its liturgy . . . initially grew in the sphere dominated by women, that is, houses. When Christianity went "public" on a large scale in the fourth century, it entered a sphere where, in varying degrees in the larger culture, women were marginalized. A public liturgy, therefore, almost inescapably entailed some measure of marginalization for women in Christian worship. (Berger, Women's Ways of Worship, p. 47)*

MUSIC

As a distinctive Christian cult emerged within the setting of the house church, so did a distinctive Christian song emerge. The fragmentary information about worship in this period allows only the broadest sketch of what ritual elements might have been sung, how they were sung, and who did the singing. One thing that can be said with some certainty is that Christian song of this era was ordinarily unaccompanied. In the first century of the Common Era the only worship instruments the followers of Jesus would have accepted—aside from the *shofar*—would have been those that accompanied temple services. With the destruction of the temple, however, instrumental music within Judaism was silenced and the Christian sibling would not take up the sound for centuries.

The reasons for this embrace of vocal rather than instrumental music are complex. One reason was certainly the centrality of the word-event in Christianity in both evangelization and worship. Jesus was the incarnate Word, and his followers were commissioned to live and proclaim that unadorned Word. Thus preaching and storytelling are foundational for the birth of Christianity. In the minds of Jesus' first followers, instrumental music was also closely associated with the Jerusalem temple. As the community intentionally distanced itself from the type of leadership and cult practiced at the temple, so was it necessary to avoid its professional and instrumental musical practices. Yet, there had to be something more, for even when Gentiles came to dominate Christianity, they did not import the use of instruments

41. An ancient Roman fresco depicting a tambourine.

that were so widely employed throughout the empire [illustration 41]. It is also probable that the close association of instruments with certain pagan cults dissuaded Gentiles from introducing them into Christian worship. Foundational, however, must have been the connection between vocal music of Christian worship and the unity of the community. Eucharistic practice in the primitive community was both a celebration of and a call to unity. Musically, this unity was symbolized in the uniting of many voices into a single hymn of praise. Johannes Quasten has pointed out how the performance style of instrumental music stood in sharp contrast to the primitive Christian ideas of unity and communion. Thus, it was especially vocal music that embodied this eucharistic ideal and served as a kind of "auditory ecclesiology" [quotation 98].

Prayer and Readings

It is virtually impossible to distinguish clearly between song and speech in the worship of this period. Public prayers and even readings had a certain tunefulness about them. While there were differing degrees of lyricism in the worship of this period, all public declamation migrated toward what today in the West would be called musical.

All prayers, including the early eucharistic prayers, were at least to some degree improvised by the leader ordinarily according to established patterns. Like improvised synagogue prayer, these were offered in such a way that the community members could make them their own by adding their "Amen" [quotation 87]. These prayers probably were cantillated; the Jewish forms of chanting employed for grace after meals may have provided early models for singing this great thanksgiving. As Christian prayer developed a separate identity from its Jewish precedents, the chanting most likely did the same.

The tradition of public reading is already detectable in first-century sources. Allusions to this function appear in the new Testament [quotation 99]. By the second century public reading has become a constitutive element of Christian worship. Justin Martyr notes the central role of the readings in the Christian assembly [quotation 87]. The great North African Latin author Tertullian (d. ca. 225) further notes the existence of what could be called the "order" of lector in a work against the Gnostic heretics, whom he derides for the capricious way their ministers exchange places [quotation 100]. There is also a famous passage in the *Apostolic Tradition*, long attributed to Hippolytus (d. ca. 236), offering information about the appointment and installation of readers for Christian worship [quotation 101]. Recent scholarship, however, has raised so many questions

Quotation 98: *Therefore by your concord and harmonious love Jesus Christ is being sung. Now do each of you join in this choir, that being harmoniously in concord you may receive the key of God in unison, and sing with one voice through Jesus Christ to the Father, that he may both hear you and may recognize, through your good works, that you are members of his son. It is therefore profitable for you to be in blameless unity, in order that you may always commune with God.* (Ignatius, "Letter to the Ephesians" 4:1 in *The Apostolic Fathers*, p. 177)

Quotation 99: *Blessed is the one who reads aloud the words of the prophecy, and blessed are those who hear and who keep what is written in it; for the time is near.* (Rev 1:3)

Quotation 100: *And so, today one man is a bishop, tomorrow another. Today one is a deacon who tomorrow will be a lector. The presbyter today is a layman tomorrow. Even the laity are charged with priestly duties.* (Tertullian [d. ca. 225], *The Prescription against Heretics,* 41:6)

about the provenance, date, and authorship of this document, that it is difficult to accept it as reliable testimony for third-century Roman practice. On the other hand, we do have reliable reporting of a letter from Cornelius that lists lectors among the clergy who served at Rome while he was bishop [quotation 102]. Thus, although we may not know for sure how they were appointed, it is clear that lectors were a recognized Roman ministry during this period.

At first the readings probably were cantillated in a manner similar to that found in the synagogue [illustration 42]. As Gentile influence arose and Christianity distanced itself from Judaism, the lyrical rendering of the readings developed in different and distinctive styles, undoubtedly influenced by the music of the local culture.

Biblical and Nonbiblical Psalms

Although it is traditional to speak of the Psalter as the Christian prayer book, there is little evidence that Christians sang psalms in first-century worship. The Pauline admonition to sing psalms [quotation 103]. cannot be taken as proof that the psalms of David were an ordinary part of early Christian worship. "Psalms" in this context simply means a Christian song, and no precise differentiation is possible between the three genres of songs that he mentions. As noted

Quotation 101: *A reader is appointed by the bishop giving him the book, for he does not have hands laid on him.* (Hippolytus [d. ca. 236], *Apostolic Tradition*, 11, in Jasper and Cuming, *Prayers of the Eucharist*)

Quotation 102: *There are 46 presbyters, 7 deacons, 7 subdeacons, 42 acolytes, 52 exorcists, readers and doorkeepers.* (Letter of Cornelius of Rome [251], in Eusebius, *The History of the Church*, 6:43)

Quotation 103: *[W]ith gratitude in your hearts sing psalms, hymns, and spiritual songs to God.* (Col 3:16)

42. Cantillation of Exodus 18:1-2, according to the style of the Babylonian Jews. (As transcribed by A. Z. Idelsohn, p. 40)

Quotation 104: *And each shared in the bread and they feasted . . . to the sound of David's psalms and hymns.* (Acta Pauli [Acts of Paul] 7.10)

Quotation 105: *The scriptures are read and psalms are sung, sermons are delivered and prayers offered.* (Tertullian [d. ca. 225], On the Soul, 9.4)

Quotation 106: *After the ritual washing and the lights, each one is invited to stand and sing to God as he is able: either something from the holy Scriptures or of his own making.* (Tertullian [d. ca. 225], Apologeticum 38.18)

1. I extend my hands
   And hallowed my Lord,

2. For the expansion of my hands
   Is his sign.

3. And my extension
   Is the upright cross.
   Hallelujah.

43. Syriac text and James Charlesworth's translation of Ode 27, *Odes of Solomon.*

in chapter 1, to the extent the biblical psalms were used, they were probably treated more as readings than as discreet pieces of music or songs.

The first certain reference to the singing of the Davidic psalms in Christian worship appears in the apocryphal *Acts of Paul*, written about the year 190 [quotation 104]. Soon after this Tertullian notes that psalms were sung as part of the liturgy of the word [quotation 105]. However, since Tertullian made this observation when he belonged to a heretical sect (the Montanists) that emphasized personal and ecstatic prophecy, it is possible that this is not a reference to a Davidic psalm but a personally composed one. Thus, James McKinnon concludes that the use of the David psalms in this period is best understood under the rubric of a biblical reading rather than an independent act of liturgical music.

Besides biblical psalms, many pieces were created in imitation of the psalms. In some communities—both orthodox or heretical like the Montanists—such imitation psalms or *psalmi idiotici* were improvised in the worship event [quotation 106]. Some communities collected these new songs to the Lord and wrote them down. One such collection is the *Odes of Solomon*, written in the first or second century [illustration 43]. Scholars such as James Charlesworth believe that this collection is the earliest Christian hymnbook.

As in today's worship, prayers and readings in the ancient church were ordinarily rendered by a single voice. There were several ways, however, of rendering nonbiblical psalms. Even the Davidic psalms, employed as readings, could have been performed in varying fashion [quotation 107]. Like the other readings, a psalm could have been cantillated in its entirety by a soloist [quotation 103]. It is also possible that a psalm as a liturgical reading could have been divided between a lector and the congregation [quotation 108]. A preference for the responsorial form is detectable in the constant concern that the community would be able to join their "Amen" to the prayer. Paul was even concerned that the outside visitor should be able to do this [quotation 36]. The underlying message through the second and third centuries about the centrality of the assembly and the call to accommodate all ministries to the needs of the community further underscore this empathy for responsorial forms.

Hymnody

The development of a distinctive Christian hymnody was anticipated in the New Testament, with "hymns" to God and to Christ [quotation 35]. One illustrative text from the early second century acknowledges that the Christian community continued to sing hymns to

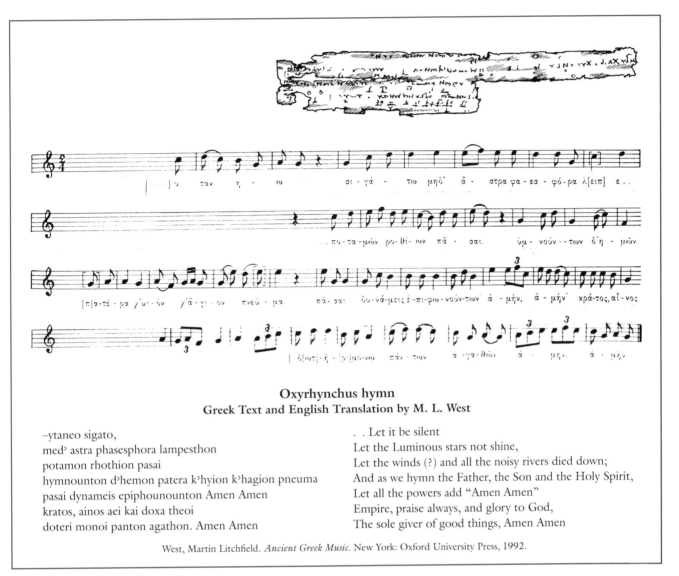

Oxyrhynchus hymn
Greek Text and English Translation by M. L. West

–ytaneo sigato,
medʾ astra phasesphora lampesthon
potamon rhothion pasai
hymnounton dʾhemon patera kʾhyion kʾhagion pneuma
pasai dynameis epiphounounton Amen Amen
kratos, ainos aei kai doxa theoi
doteri monoi panton agathon. Amen Amen

. . Let it be silent
Let the Luminous stars not shine,
Let the winds (?) and all the noisy rivers died down;
And as we hymn the Father, the Son and the Holy Spirit,
Let all the powers add "Amen Amen"
Empire, praise always, and glory to God,
The sole giver of good things, Amen Amen

West, Martin Litchfield. *Ancient Greek Music.* New York: Oxford University Press, 1992.

44. The Oxyrhynchus paprus 1786, from the end of the third century, showing the end of a hymn written in Greek vocal notation. (*New Groves Dictionary of Music and Musicians,* 4:368. Modern musical transcription by H. Stuart Jones as found in *Musik in Geschichte und Gegenwart,* s.v. "Fruehchristliche Musik.")

Christ [quotation 109]. It is only from the mid-second century on, however, that it is possible to find compositions that can be accurately described as hymns. Two distinguishing features allow this definition: one textual, the other musical. Textually these first Christian hymns are new works of metric poetry that are based on models of poetry from the Greco-Roman world, and not imitations of biblical prose. The texts are shaped into stanzas of two or more lines. Each stanza employs the same meter, rhyme scheme, and number of lines. Music is composed for the first stanza, and each succeeding stanza is sung to the same music. These are true hymns. In contrast, psalms are not

Quotation 107: *We can well imagine that "readings" from the Psalter might vary widely in their mode of execution from something indistinguishable from the reading of any other biblical passage to something that responds with full musicality to the latent lyricism of the Psalms. This would depend upon the aptitude of the lector and liturgical personality of the congregation.* (McKinnon, *The Advent Project,* pp. 33–34)

Quotation 108: *When they recite psalms, all shall say, "Alleluia."* (Hippolytus [d. c. 236], *Apostolic Tradition*, 25, in Jasper and Cuming, *Prayers of the Eucharist*)

Quotation 109: *They were accustomed to meet on a fixed day before dawn and sing alternately among themselves a hymn to Christ as to a god, and bound themselves by a solemn oath (Lat., sacramento), not to any wicked deeds, but never to commit any fraud, theft or adultery, never to falsify their word, nor deny a trust when they should be called upon to deliver it up; after which it was their custom to separate, and then reassemble to partake of food—but food of an ordinary and innocent kind.* (Pliny, "Letter to the Emperor Trajan," [ca. 112])

Quotation 110: *King of Saints, almighty Word of the Father, Highest Lord. Wisdom's head and chief, Assuagement of all grief; Lord of all time and space Jesus, Savior of our race.* (Clement of Alexandria [d. ca. 215], *Hymn to Christ*, in *Ante-Nicene Fathers*, p. 296)

structured in stanzas or similar meter, rhyme, and length. In psalms, the music changes, however slightly, from line to line to accommodate the varying meters and accents of the text. This is also true of new pieces of Christian prose written in imitation of the psalms, like the *Odes of Solomon*. Thus, the *Odes of Solomon* and other such imitation psalms are more properly understood as "hymnodic psalmody" rather than as "hymns."

The first Christian metrical hymns were apparently composed by second-century Gnostic writers who borrowed a style of classical Greek poetry as a vehicle for their unorthodox theology. In order to counter these false claims it appears that Clement of Alexandria (d. ca. 215) used the same style of metrical poetry for composing his hymn to Christ the Savior [quotation 110]. While there was some opposition to using this "pagan" form to promote the gospel, eventually the poetry of the Greco-Roman world provided the foundation for the flowering of Christian hymnody in the fourth century.

One musical fragment survives from this period. The "Oxyrhynchus hymn" takes its name from an archaeological site in Egypt where thousands of documents were discovered at the end of the nineteenth century. Papyrus 1786 in this collection contains the closing words and music of a Christian hymn in Greek and notated in ancient Greek notation [illustration 44]. It is difficult to draw any conclusions, however, from this tantalizing but isolated example, incuding whether it was ever employed in worship.

Hymns could have been performed by soloists or even small groups. It is also possible that they were performed responsorially, with the leader singing each line and the assembly repeating it. It is probable, however, that once these hymns became familiar to a community they were sung in their entirety by the assembly. This style of performance was made possible by the structure of the hymn, which presumes the repetition of poetic and melodic units. It is also consonant with the previously noted concern for unity in the community. Unity for Christians referred to the bond that existed not only between Christians and Christ but also among Christians themselves. Singing with one voice is a privileged way of expressing and creating this unity [quotation 98].

Summary

During the second and third centuries, identifiable Christian music developed. Increasingly distinctive in text and tone, this music still was closely related to the lyrical environment of the first century. This was true not only in music's contribution to the unity of the community but also in its integration into the ritual. Thus it was difficult to consider music as a separate element in the Christian cult of this time; rather, it was the aural aspect of that cult. The intimate relationship between prayer and song is further reflected in the absence of references to special singers, psalmists, or cantors in this period. There is no separate liturgical musician. The whole of the worship was musical: to the extent that the worship belonged to the entire assembly, so did the music belong to them as well.

BOOKS

Although it eventually became possible to condense all of the official rites of the church into a few bound volumes, the worship of the second and third centuries was not prayer by the book. Worship was, rather, a largely improvised and auditory event, similar to the worship of the synagogue. Improvisation does not mean haphazard, and there developed clearly established patterns for eucharistic worship at this time [quotation 87]. Prayer leaders as well as the community knew and followed these patterns, employing them as frameworks for weaving the worship, which often continued to exhibit a marked degree of spontaneity and informality.

The Gospel of the Nazaraeans
The Gospel of the Ebionites
The Gospel of the Hebrews
The Gospel of the Egyptians
The Gospel of Peter
The Gospel of the Four Heavenly Regions
The Gospel of Perfection
The Gospel of Truth
The Sophia Jesu Christi
The Dialogue of the Redeemer
The Pistis Sophia
The Two Books of Jeu
The Gospel of the Twelve Apostles
The Gospel of the Twelve
The Memoria Apostolorum
The (Manichean) Gospel of the Twelve Apostles
The Gospel of the Seventy
The Gospel of Philip
The Gospel of Thomas

The Book of Thomas the Athlete
The Gospel according to Matthias
The Gospel of Judas
The Apocryphon of John
The Apocryphon of James
The Gospel of Bartholomew
The Questions of Mary
The Gospel according to Mary
The Genna Marias
The Gospel of Cerinthus
The Gospel of Basilides
The Gospel of Marcion
The Gospel of the Apelles
The Gospel of Bardesanes
The Gospel of Mani
The Protoevangelium of James
The Infancy Story of Thomas
The Gospel of Nicodemus

45. Partial listing of New Testament Apocrypha according to Hennecke and Schneemelcher.

46. Codex Sinaiticus.

Just as Christians began to develop distinctive architectural and musical forms appropriate to their worship, they also began to develop their own books. The first of these was the New Testament, which was combined with the Hebrew Scriptures to form the Christian Bible. Besides this book, which was read in worship, there also appeared books that were used to prepare for worship. These auxiliary liturgical books reemerge in various forms throughout the history of Christian worship. Early examples are sometimes called church orders. Because Christianity contributed to the transition in Western civilization from the scroll to the codex, the physical appearance of these books as well as their use in worship and their content will be considered.

The New Testament

The Scriptures were an integral part of early Christian worship: the Jewish Law and the prophetic books first, and then increasingly the letters of Paul. To these were joined what have come to be known as the gospels, and other letters and narratives. Originally, there were many more than the twenty-seven books that the Christian churches today consider part of the New Testament. Many works now considered apocryphal were publicly read and revered in Christian communities [illustration 45]. Others that are now considered "Apostolic Fathers"—a collection of orthodox early Christian texts—were also reverenced as Scripture. The Shepherd of Hermas, for example, was included in the first full manuscript of the New Testament from the mid-fourth century known as the Codex Sinaiticus [illustration 46].

During the middle of the second century a move was underway to define the authentic books of the new religion. The four gospels and the thirteen epistles attributed to Paul were central; other letters and books eventually were added to this group. A fragmentary list from the late second century—called the Muratorian canon after its discoverer, Ludovico A. Muratori (d. 1750)—represents the widespread consensus of the orthodox churches regarding the New Testament canon. This list is similar to that promulgated by the Council of Trent in 1546. Although the first complete list of the books eventually accepted by the church appeared in the writings of Athanasius (d. 373), the second and third centuries were pivotal for the establishment of the New Testament canon.

We have already noted how the act of public reading and eventually the ministry of reader or lector grew in importance during this period. This ministerial development is itself a testimony to the importance of the Scriptures for the fledgling Christian community. Even when they were not being read, the Scriptures came to be venerated by Christians. There is a precedent for this in Judaism, for when the Torah scrolls were not in use, they came to be stored in a place of honor in the synagogue [illustration 7] and were cared for by specially appointed people [quotation 111]. Similarly, Christians often designated special places for holding their books of Scripture. For example, in one of his letters from about the year 250, Cyprian, Bishop of Carthage, speaks of ordaining someone to the office of reader and mentions a raised "pulpit" for reading the Scriptures [quotation 112]. The previously cited report of a church under persecution in North Africa [quotation 95] noted that the Scriptures were kept in special book chests (*armaria*) in the house church library. In this instance the books had been removed from these chests and transported to safety before the officials arrived. The account further confirms that particular people were entrusted with the care of the Scriptures. Many stories are told about lectors who were martyred because they refused to surrender the Scriptures to pagan officials. Such stories also underscore the fact that the Scriptures of the Christians had become one of their most tangible symbols and thus were often designated for destruction by their persecutors [quotation 113].

Quotation 111: *And [Jesus] rolled up the scroll, gave it back to the attendant, and sat down.* (Luke 4:20)

Quotation 112: *When this man [Celerinus] came to us, beloved brethren, with such honor of the Lord, being honored even with the testimony and amazement of the very men by whom he had been persecuted, what else was there to do than to place him upon the pulpit, that is, upon the tribunal of the church, so that, propped up in the place of highest elevation and conspicuous to the entire congregation for the fame of his honor, he may read the precepts and gospels of the Lord which he follows with such courage and faith?* (Epistle 39, 4.1, in L. Michael White, II:69)

Quotation 113: *It was the nineteenth year of Diocletian's reign and the month Dystrus, called March by the Romans, and the festival of the Saviour's Passion was approaching, when an imperial degree was published everywhere, ordering the churches to be razed to the ground and the scriptures destroyed by fire.* (Eusebius, The History of the Church, 8.2.3)

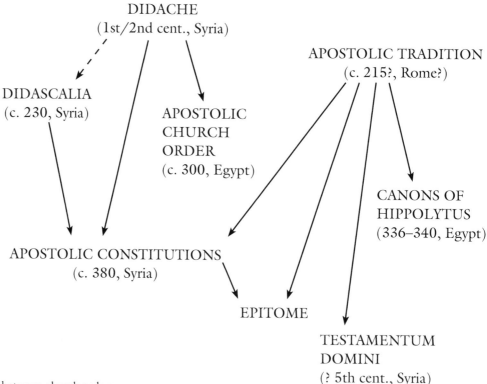

47. Chart of relationship between church orders.
(Bradshaw, "Ancient Church Orders," p. 7)

Church Orders

During this period, auxiliary books for worship also appeared. A handful of these pastoral handbooks survive from this era. Although not exclusively concerned with worship, they often contained instructions about various aspects of the community's prayer. The *Didache* or "Teaching of the Lord to the Gentiles through the Twelve Apostles" was a compendium of instructions and regulations, probably dating from the early second century. It included information about fasting [quotation 83], baptism, the Lord's Prayer, and possibly one of the earliest examples of a eucharistic prayer. The *Didascalia Apostolorum* or the "Catholic Teaching of the Twelve Apostles and Holy Disciples of Our Redeemer" is from the early part of the third century. More developed than the *Didache*, this church order included liturgical instructions about the consecration of bishops, the celebration of baptism, and the place and manner of gathering for prayer [quotation 96].

The *Didache* and the *Didascalia Apostolorum* were but two examples of various handbooks, guides, and church orders that circulated throughout the early church. While originating in a particular community, most were shared with others—not unlike the letters of Paul written for a specific church but circulated to other local churches. Some church orders were more influential than others—especially

Didache and *Apostolic Tradition*—not only providing direction for worship but also serving as the inspiration and foundation for other pastoral handbooks [illustration 47]. While these texts were not used everywhere and are only a few pieces of the puzzle for early Christian worship, they do demonstrate how common patterns of worship were spreading.

Church orders were the forerunners of important auxiliary liturgical books containing instructions and rubrical details that would appear in the Middle Ages. Eventually these books of instructions would merge with collections of prayers to produce the mixture of prayers and rubrics typical of today's liturgical books. This combination would reflect and produce a style of worship that was increasingly regulated and tied to a text. During the period of the domestic church, however, Christian worship—like its Jewish sibling—was more improvised according to accepted patterns. Auxiliary books like church orders were never intended to eliminate improvisation, but only to safeguard the traditional patterns of such improvisation.

The Codex

Until the dawn of Christianity, the ordinary form of the book in the empire was the scroll. A scroll was composed of papyrus sheets glued together or animal skins sewn end to end so that they could be rolled together into a bundle [illustration 19]. Since papyrus was expensive, it was also common to use wax writing tablets for texts that did not need to be preserved for extended periods of time [illustration 48].

48. Roman stylus and reconstructed wax writing tablets.

49. Depiction of the evangelist Matthew with a codex, writing tools, and a box filled with scrolls, from the bema San Vitale in Ravenna (547).

Eventually the Romans replaced the wax tablets with similarly shaped pieces of parchment. This innovation was the forerunner of the codex. A codex could also be composed of papyrus sheets or animal skins, bound together on one side so that a single sheet of information could be exposed more easily [illustration 49]. Christians did not invent the codex, but they certainly took advantage of its development. The majority of Christian manuscripts from the second and third centuries were codices, while most other manuscripts from that time are scrolls.

Jews began to use codices for many purposes by the fifth century of the Common Era, although they continue to use scrolls for the Torah to this day. Christianity's preference for the codex may have been purely functional: having more than one book of Scripture on a scroll may have become too unwieldy. Some books of the Hebrew Scriptures, such as the book of Kings, were divided into two books because they could not fit on a single scroll. Some scholars speculate that Christians may have employed the codex to bind the four gospels together. Others do not overlook the possibility that Christians adopted the codex in order to distinguish their sacred books from those of Jews and even from the secular literature of the Greco-Roman Empire. Whatever the complex of reasons, Christians adopted a form for preserving writings that would become the standard for the empire by the fourth century and one that would have an unforeseen yet significant impact on the development of Christian worship [illustration 50].

Summary

Despite the emergence of some written liturgical documents in this period, Christian worship of the second and third centuries was not dominated by books. Rather, this was a period of improvisation, experimentation, and significant freedom. As Christianity grew, the natural tendency to regulate and record traditions, teachings, and worship developed. Thus a New Testament canon took shape, models for eucharistic prayers emerged, and pastoral handbooks for community life and worship appeared.

As with the architecture of this period, these textual and material changes contributed to shifting perceptions. Just as both the community and the building came to be called "church," so not only the spoken word but also the written word began to be identified as "gospel." During persecutions, not only were Christians martyred but their buildings were destroyed and their sacred books burned. These objects and buildings served the community in prayer, but they also began to take on identities of their own.

VESSELS

The development of distinctive spaces, music, and books for an increasingly defined Christian cult found a parallel in the development of specific Christian vessels. Of particular importance were those employed in Eucharist, the central and distinguishing ritual of Christianity. From this period there appears both documentary and iconographic evidence for distinctive Christian vessels for both bread and wine. This evidence, however, is meager and fragmentary. As Christian worship in this era was generally situated in a domestic setting, so were the vessels employed in that worship generally of a type found in any large home of the area.

Bread and Its Vessels

Throughout Eastern and Western Christianity during this period, people used the same kind of bread for Eucharist that they baked and consumed at home. Although the tradition recalled that Jesus shared unleavened bread with his disciples during the Last Supper, this detail had no apparent impact on primitive Christian Eucharist. The memory of Jesus sharing himself through bread and wine, rather than a memory about any specific kind of bread and wine, shaped this unfolding ritual. It is likely that, as the rites of Christian Eucharist developed, there was a natural concern to use quality materials for this defining ritual. Decisions about the quality of something like bread and its vessels, however, were determined by local taste and usage, and often meant selecting from the best that was available rather than crafting something completely new.

Vessels for Use During the Eucharist   As in the first century, homemade baskets were likely containers for bread for the Lord's Supper [illustration 51]. Pottery plates or bowls were also probably vessels for holding the bread [illustration 52]. Surprisingly, glass plates or shallow glass bowls were in all likelihood used as well [illustration 53]. As previously noted, glass was a very common commodity around the Mediterranean. When the two great centers for glassmaking in the ancient world (Syro-Palestine and Egypt) came under the control of the Roman Empire (62 and 30 B.C.E. respectively), glass products and production spread throughout the empire and into the West, where there was no previous history of glass production. A sixth-century source reports that a third-century bishop of Rome named Zephyrinus (d. 217) issued a directive about glass vessels for the eucharistic bread [quotation 114]. The same sources notes that another bishop of Rome, Urban I (d. 230), donated silver patens to various churches [quotation 115]. Although the historical

50. Image of a young man with a book, from the Cemetery of Saints Peter and Marcellinus, possibly from the late third century C.E.

51. Baskets excavated from Karanis in Egypt from the Roman period. (Kelsey Museum of Archaeology, University of Michigan.)

52. Roman pottery from the first to second century C.E.

53. Roman glassware.

accuracy of such passages is uncertain, it is unquestionable that a wide variety of materials including glass, precious metals, wood, pottery, and possibly even bone were used to make vessels for the eucharistic bread.

Vessels for Use Outside the Eucharist   From very early on, bread from the community's celebration of the Eucharist was sent to members who could not be present. As already seen in the writings of Justin Martyr, the Eucharist was sent through the deacons to those who could not share in the Sunday celebration [quotation 87]. This second-century practice is corroborated in a letter from Irenaeus of Lyon (flourished ca. 170) to Victor, bishop of Rome (d. 198), which reports how Eucharist was shared between churches in Rome, even though they all did not keep the same date for the annual commemoration of the resurrection [quotation 116]. Frescoes in the catacombs of Callistus, dating from the second century, show wicker baskets that may have been used for this purpose [illustration 54]. A third-century fresco from the catacombs of Peter and Marcellinus in Rome depicts a small box, possibly used for the same purpose. These little boxes—sometimes called *arcae* [Latin, "boxes"] or *pyxis* [Greek, "boxes]—were worn around the neck or kept in people's homes. Often designed for holding cosmetics, jewelry, or some other valuable item, they could have easily served as containers for the eucharistized bread as it was carried to those who were prevented from gathering with the Sunday assembly [illustration 55]. Cyprian, bishop of Carthage, tells of the shocking results of a woman who attempted to open her own *arca* after she had denied her faith during a persecution [quotation 117]. There is evidence from the sixth century that the Eucharist was carried by acolytes in linen bags. It is quite possible that this practice reaches back to the earliest Christian centuries.

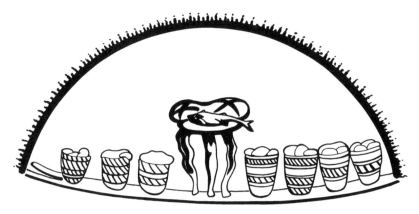

54. Baskets holding eucharistic bread from the Catacomb of Callistus, second to third century.

55. First-century bone pyx.

On some occasions during this period and in some places the eucharistized bread was preserved after Sunday Eucharist in house churches or people's homes. More permanent places of reservation may have included cupboards, closets, and chests. The Eucharist often would be wrapped in a cloth or placed in an *arca* before being stored in a cupboard or closet.

Wine and Its Vessels

Since the time of Jesus Christians have commonly celebrated the Eucharist with bread and a cup of wine. There is also evidence that some groups celebrated Eucharist with bread and water. These "aquarians" (Latin, *aqua* = water) may have followed this practice because of their poverty or for ascetic purposes. Andrew McGowan believes that "ascetic" celebrations of the Eucharist were early and quite widespread, with a strong tradition in places like Carthage. Increasingly, however, this ritual practice was branded as unorthodox and was condemned, along with the groups who practiced it. Cyprian, bishop of Carthage, was quite familiar with the "aquarian" tradition and argued against it [quotation 118].

There is also evidence, especially from apocryphal sources [illustration 45], that Eucharist was celebrated with bread alone without any drink. While this has often been dismissed as simply a Gnostic practice, David Power suggests otherwise (pp. 87–88). It could be, for example, that Palestinian Christians—living and praying in a strong Semitic context where the ritual accent was on the bread blessing—gave great importance to a blessing over bread, which

Quotation 116: *. . . the presbyters before you, even though they did not keep it* [i.e., the 14th of Nisan as the annual celebration] *used to send the Eucharist to Christians from dioceses which did.* (Eusebius, *The History of the Church,* 5.24.18)

Quotation 117: *When a certain woman with unclean hands attempted to open her arca, in which the body of the Lord was contained, she was prevented by a flame which flared up from it.* (Cyprian [d. 258], *Concerning the Lapsed,* 26)

Quotation 118: *You know, however, that we have been warned. In offering the chalice, the dominical tradition is to be observed so that nothing may be done for us other than what the Lord first did for us. The chalice which is offered in commemoration of him is offered mixed with wine. For when Christ says, "I am the true vine," the blood of Christ is, indeed, not water but wine.* (Cyprian, *Letter 63 to Caecilius* [253])

Quotation 119: *And then let the offering be brought up by the deacons to the bishop: and he shall give thanks over the . . . cup mixed with wine for the antitype . . . of the blood which was shed for all who have believed in him; and over milk and honey mixed together in fulfillment of the promise which was made to our fathers in which he said "a land flowing with milk and honey" . . . and over water as an offering to signify the washing that the inner man also, which is the soul, may receive the same things as the body.*
(Hippolytus, *Apostolic Tradition*, 21, in Jasper and Cuming, *Prayers of the Eucharist*)

56. Good Shepherd statue.

served as the medium of the gifts of redemption. Finally, some ritual situations called for a cup of water and a cup of milk and honey to be present along with the cup of wine, most notably the Eucharist following baptism [quotation 119]. While the text from the *Apostolic Tradition* supplies some of the most famous pieces of evidence for this practice, further legislative teachings from the era condemning this practice confirm that at least this aspect of the *Apostolic Tradition* reflects actual practice [quotation 120]. By the end of the period of the domestic church the orthodox presumption was that Eucharist was only properly celebrated with bread and wine.

While many literary sources speak about wine being used in Eucharist, Tertullian is one of the first writers after the New Testament to mention the cup or chalice in connection with this ritual. He also notes that at least one chalice was decorated with an image of the "Good Shepherd" [quotation 121]. This does not mean that the chalice in question was fabricated for Christian worship, for the image of a young shepherd was a popular one in both pastoral and agricultural societies around the Mediterranean [illustration 56]. The cup may have been fashioned without Christian intent, and appropriated by believers for use in worship.

Although Tertullian says nothing about the material or shape of the cup in question, other sources confirm that glass, precious metals, wood, bone, and certain stones such as onyx were used in the fashioning of these cups. Irenaeus of Lyons is remembered as having criticized the heretic Marcus, who celebrated an unacceptable Eucharist with a glass chalice [quotation 122]. It does not seem, however, that the use of glass had anything to do with the unacceptability of the Eucharist.

Precious metals were used for Christian ritual vessels with increasing frequency over the centuries. The testimony about Urban I bestowing a gift of silver vessels and patens on the church at Rome [quotation 115] and the inventory of vessels in the account of the fourth-century persecution of the church in North Africa [quotation 95] bear this out. At first vessels fabricated for other purposes were adopted for use in Christian worship [illustration 57]. Eventually, cups specifically intended for Christian Eucharist were fashioned out of precious materials, although glass, stone, wood, and bone chalices continued to be used well into the Middle Ages.

Because the use of a single cup during Eucharist was highly valued at this time [quotation 123], the size of such a cup would have been proportional to the number of believers who gathered for worship. Chalices large enough to serve seventy-five people or more would have been needed in some of the larger house churches, while some of the smaller gatherings could have used a simple, stemless cup or even a bowl. Joseph Braun believes that double-handled cups probably were used for Eucharist during this period. Although no examples of this type of eucharistic cup survive from this era, Braun offers this conjecture based on examples of double-handled chalices from a later period and on surviving examples from households from the pre-Constantinian period [illustration 58]. Braun also notes the practically of this form of cup for communal use.

57. Roman glassware, first to third century.

Summary

In this era of the domestic church the vessels for Eucharist originated as domestic elements. A wicker basket and a wooden bowl would have sufficed in many situations. Because the large homes of the wealthy also were settings for Christian Eucharist during this time the precious goblets, trays, glass bowls, and other vessels of these households undoubtedly also were used in worship. The acquisition of buildings specifically set aside for the work and worship of the community, with special storage places for materials employed in worship, parallels a development in the vessels themselves. In a specially renovated or, eventually, constructed building for worship, it would not be surprising to find vessels fabricated especially for Eucharist, sometimes of the finest materials. These vessels would reflect the size, means, and needs of the community that they served.

58. Example of a secular, two-handled drinking cup from the pre-Constantinian Roman Empire.

EUCHARISTIC THEOLOGY

The domestic period was one of enormous growth and increasing diversification for the young church. It is possible to recognize both continuity and discontinuity between this era and that of the New Testament in such things as the structures of ministry, the practices of worship, and the emerging theologies of Eucharist.

Continuity with the eucharistic thinking of the previous era, for example, is evident in the continued and widespread use of sacrificial language for reflecting on the Lord's Supper. Irenaeus of Lyons is one of many church leaders who continually speaks of the Eucharist in sacrificial terms [quotation 124]. While the manifold ways in which early Christian writers employed the language and image of sacrifice differ in some respects from the New Testament, there is a general tendency to continue speaking of sacrifice as primarily a "spiritualized sacrifice." This approach emphasizes the importance of the disposition of the worshiper and stresses that the Christian life itself is to be a living sacrifice of praise, in imitation of the life of Christ. There

Quotation 120: *If any bishop or presbyter used any other things in the sacrifice at the altar except what the Lord ordained, that is, either honey or milk or a strong beer instead of wine . . . let him be deposed.* (Apostolic Canons [fourth century], canon 3, in Funk I:564)

Quotation 121: *Perhaps that shepherd whom you picture on the chalice will favor you.* (Tertullian, *On Purity*, 10.2)

Quotation 122: *Sources report that three chalices of glass are prepared with white vinegar to which white wine is added. (Epiphanius [d. 403], The Panarion, 34.1, drawing on a report from Irenaeus of Lyons)*

Quotation 123: *Be careful therefore to use one Eucharist (for there is one flesh of our Lord Jesus Christ, and one cup for union with his blood, one altar, as there is one bishop with the presbytery and the deacons my fellow servants), in order that whatever you do you may do it according unto God. (Ignatius of Antioch, Letter to the Philadelphians, 4, in The Apostolic Fathers, p. 243)*

Quotation 124: *The oblation of the Church, therefore, which the Lord gave instructions to be offered throughout all the world, is accounted with God a pure sacrifice, and is acceptable to Him; not that He stands in need of a sacrifice from us, but that he who offers is himself glorified in what he does offer, if his gift be accepted. (Irenaeus, Against Heresies, 4.18.1)*

Quotation 125: *[In Hippolytus] The idea of Christian sacrifice . . . had begun to shift away from the practical living of the Christian life toward the church's public liturgical celebration of the Eucharist. The dominant New Testament idea, that the life and activity of Christian people are themselves the sacrifice which they offer, does not seem even to be mentioned in Hippolytus. It seems to be wholly replaced by the idea of the Eucharist as sacrifice in which the central sacrificial act is the divine Logos offering his incarnate (and eucharistic) body and blood to the Father. (Daly, The Origins of the Christian Doctrine of Sacrifice, pp. 133–34)*

is also a distinctive shift in sacrificial thinking in this period, however, especially apparent in the writings of Hippolytus. For Hippolytus, sacrifice is less a metaphor for Christian living—a dominant metaphor in the previous era—than the proper framework for understanding the Eucharist [quotation 125]. While not a dominant trend in the early centuries, this development hints at a later stage in Christianity when it will be possible to discourse extensively about the Eucharist without making reference to the eucharistic implications for Christian living.

One can also chart the continuity and discontinuity between this period and the previous one regarding the other key concepts explored at the end of the last chapter. For example, remnants of a "*berakah* spirituality" are yet detectable in the community's continued posture of gratitude for God's generous initiative in Jesus. At the same time, however, there is a growing Christian preference for language of "thanksgiving" rather than "blessing." In centuries to come this will contribute to an approach to blessing that is predominantly intercessory, more focused on asking God to make something holy rather than a grateful admission of the implicit holiness of all God's creation.

Theological reflection during this period also continued to emphasize that the Eucharist is a living memorial of God's unsurpassable covenant revealed in the death and resurrection of the Lord. One of the ways this memorial begins to evolve through the second and third centuries is a lessening of emphasis on the whole of Jesus' table ministry or the multiplication stories as key symbols of this covenant and more emphasis on the Last Supper as the ritual touchstone for this memorial. Ritually this will become manifest with the introduction of the institution narrative into the eucharistic prayer, explicitly recalling Jesus' final meal as the primary warrant for the community's continued eucharistic practice. It appears, however, that this ritual development will come to fruition only after the ascendancy of Constantine, for there is apparently no eucharistic prayer in existence before the fourth century that contains an institution narrative as an original and integral part of that prayer [quotation 126].

The understanding of Eucharist as a ritual encounter in reconciling love also develops in new ways during these centuries. In particular, the Eucharist becomes focal for reconciling believers who have committed serious sin, which in this era ordinarily meant having done something to rupture seriously the unity of the community, such as denying fundamental teachings about Christ. In such cases the person wishing to be reconciled was temporarily excluded from table fellowship, thus the later word "excommunication" or the act of being cut off from communion. After an appropriate period of penance, the believer was invited back into eucharistic sharing, which effectively established their renewed communion. Thus, long before any distinctive sacrament of penance developed, Eucharist emerged as the church's original sacrament of ongoing reconciliation.

Besides considering "what" Christians said about Eucharist and eucharistic practice during this era, it is also instructive to examine "how" people attempted to reflect upon or teach about the Eucharist. Of particular interest are three different approaches to explaining this mystery. While there was some continuity with the styles of theological reflection or catechesis that can be detected in the New Testament, the second and third centuries were times of great innovation in eucharistic thinking.

Typology and Analogy

Among the various approaches employed to unfold the meanings of Eucharist in the early church, the most common was the typological approach. In Greek the word *tupos* meant a visible impression or mark left by a blow or by the application of pressure; thus, the mark left by a sculptor's chisel would be a *tupos*. By extension the word came to mean an image, figure, pattern or model. An early form of Christian theologizing involved selecting patterns or models from the Hebrew Scriptures and applying or contrasting them to Christ, the church, or Christian worship. Thus, for example, Christ is imaged as the "paschal lamb" (1 Cor 5:7), the followers of Jesus are called into a "new covenant" (Heb 8:13), and "the bread of life" (John 6:35) is distinguished from "manna in the wilderness" (John 6:31).

This style of theologizing, which already existed in the Hebrew Scriptures, is quite prominent during the period of the domestic church. While not a terribly exacting type of theology—sometimes, as David Power notes, reduced to nothing more than proof-texting— this imaginative and symbolic way of thinking was a powerful tool for the early community. It enabled them to maintain links with their Jewish roots and remain grounded in the Hebrew Scriptures while at the same time allowing the followers of Jesus to distinguish and define themselves in Christ. It can become problematic only when one takes the "type" too literally. Thus "similarity in difference" is both a hallmark and inherent tension in typological explanations. For example, one of the most commonly evoked "types" or images of the Eucharist from the Hebrew Scriptures is the offering that Melchizedek made after Abram's victory over Chedorlaomer [quotation 127]. Cyprian of Carthage employs the image of Melchizedek in one of his epistles, where he both draws parallels between the offering of Melchizedek and the offering of Christ and at the same

Quotation 126: *There is not a single extant pre-Nicene eucharistic prayer that one can prove contained the Words of Institution, and today many scholars maintain that the most primitive, original eucharistic prayers were short, self-contained benedictions without Institution Narrative or Epiclesis.* (Taft, p. 493)

Quotation 127:
And King Melchizedek of Salem brought out bread and wine; he was a priest of God Most High. He blessed [Abram] and said, "Blessed be Abram by God Most High, maker of heaven and earth; and blessed be God Most High, who has delivered your enemies into your hand." (Gen 14:18-20)

59. The sacrifice of Abel, Melchizedek and Abraham, and Saint Apollinare in Classe, Ravenna (sixth century).

Quotation 128: *Also in the priest Melchizedek we see prefigured the sacrament of the sacrifice of the Lord, according to what divine Scripture testifies, and says, "And Melchizedek, king of Salem, brought forth bread and wine." Now he was a priest of the most high God, and blessed Abraham. And that Melchizedek bore a type of Christ, the Holy Spirit declares in the Psalms. . . . For who is more a priest of the most high God than our Lord Jesus Christ, who offered a sacrifice to God the Father, and offered that very same thing which Melchizedek had offered, that is, bread and wine, which is to say, His body and blood? . . . In Genesis, therefore, that the benediction, in respect of Abraham by Melchizedek the priest, might be duly celebrated, the figure of Christ's sacrifice precedes, namely, as ordained in bread and wine; which thing the Lord, completing and fulfilling, offered bread and the cup mixed with wine, and so He who is the fullness of truth fulfilled the truth of the image prefigured.* (Cyprian, *Letter 63 to Caecilius* [253])

time emphasizes the distinctive and unique nature of Christ's priesthood and his offering [quotation 128].

Closely related to typological reflection was theologizing through images or metaphors that were not borrowed from the Hebrew Scriptures. This reflection through analogy, quite common through this period, employed everyday images as metaphors for the Eucharist. Thus Eucharist was imagined as a kind of medicine, antidote to sin, food for the journey, and divine gift. This unsophisticated yet effective approach could be considered a kind of folk theologizing that was very accessible to ordinary believers. It was also quite appropriate for believers who instinctively thought symbolically and did not manifest much need for detailed or tightly argued explanations. Eventually this symbolic, metaphorical style of theologizing fell out of favor with theologians in the West but continued to capture the imagination of ordinary believers. Thus the iconography and plastic arts in Christianity, which from their inception are highly symbolic, continue to draw upon beloved images for introducing people to the eucharistic mystery [illustration 59].

A Turn to Philosophy

While Christians of the second and third centuries continued to theologize out of the Hebrew Scriptures and images of everyday life, there was also a very different development in Christian theology at this time. That was the turn to the prominent philosophies of the day as resources for explaining and exploring Christianity. This movement within Christianity paralleled a trend detectable throughout the Roman Empire. As Gary Macy summarizes, educated people in this period were more and more turning from the classical religions of Greece and Rome, and adopting as their personal beliefs the teachings of the great philosophers of ancient Greece. Yet, while many were making the move from classical religions to the philosophies of the time, others like Justin Martyr found such philosophies wanting and turned to Christianity instead for the answers to life [quotation 129]. Justin not only turned to Christianity but was one of the first Christians to be remembered as consciously building a bridge between the philosophies of the day and Christian belief.

While there were a number of prominent philosophies in the Greco-Roman Empire of this period, it was increasingly the thought associated with Plato (d. 347 B.C.E.) that influenced Christian thinkers like Justin. Although Platonism goes through a series of developments—and scholars distinguish between Platonism, Middle

Quotation 129: *. . . a flame was kindled in my soul; and a love of the prophets, and of those men who are friends of Christ, possessed me; and whilst revolving his words in my mind, I found this philosophy alone to be safe and profitable. Thus, and for this reason, I am a philosopher and would wish that all were of the same mind as myself, not to turn from the teachings of the Savior.* (Justin Martyr, *First Apology,* 8, in Jasper and Cuming, *Prayers of the Eucharist*)

60. Detail of Raphael's fresco *The School of Athens* (the Vatican, 1510–1511); Plato, on the left, and Aristotle, on the right. Plato is pointing toward the heavens, indicating his belief in the truth of the forms or ideals "above" or outside the realm of the senses, while Aristotle is gesturing toward the earth, indicating his concern for the world around us that could be apprehended through the senses.

Platonism and neo-Platonism—over the centuries, certain enduring features of this philosophical strand made it quite amenable to emerging Christian thought. One of the most attractive aspects of Platonic philosophy for Christian thinkers was Plato's theory of knowledge. Plato draws a sharp contrast between the world of the senses and the higher world of the "ideas" or forms. He believed that knowledge acquired through the senses was faulty and untrustworthy. True knowledge, according to Plato, comes through the intellect, for it is only the mind that can grasp what is essentially real [illustration 60].

Plato's emphasis on true perception as more a matter of the mind than a matter of the senses offered a ready-made framework for expounding the spiritual realities of the Christian faith to nonbelievers. In terms of Eucharist, for example, it provided a credible philosophical construct for explaining how the eucharistic elements could actually be Christ's body and blood, when to the senses they appeared only to be bread and wine. In general, therefore, the various forms of Platonic philosophy were helpful to Christians in their attempt to negotiate a plausible and accessible relationship between the physical and spiritual world, and for affirming the importance of an interior or spiritual disposition rather than the exterior and material. This was not a new struggle in Judeao-Christianity. Earlier, for example, we considered how the Hebrew prophets stressed that what was essential about sacrifice was not its physical aspects but the interior disposition that ideally accompanied such sacrifice [quotation 69]. Now, Christians had a vehicle for extending this understanding through a philosophy broadly accepted across the empire and not rooted in Judaism.

Plato's philosophy even affected the way Christian theologians used typology. In the theological center of Alexandria, for example, Clement of Alexandria and his student Origen (d. ca. 254) developed a more philosophical and decidedly Platonic approach to typology. As David Power summarizes, this approach gives primacy to life of the spirit and sees the spirit limited and impeded by the body; thus, the historical events recounted in the Scriptures do not count for much in themselves. Though Scriptures have a literal sense and tell true stories, it is their spiritual sense that will be counted most important.

The innovative move to employ secular philosophies of the day was an effective and, ultimately, seismic shift for Christian theology in the West. These philosophies would provide a platform for eucharistic theology, for example, that was no longer anchored in biblical texts, folk wisdom, or human practice. Rather, the underpinning for such theology would be a series of abstractions and systems of ideas, eventually far removed from the thought processes of ordinary believers. Philosophy would become the "handmaiden" of theology, and in many stages of Christian thought, constructing any eucharistic theology would be impossible without it. Even in our own day, the legacy of Justin and the other "philosophical theologians" of his era endure. In the United States, for example, no candidate can move toward presbyteral ordination without mandatory philosophical training equivalent to a bachelor's degree in philosophy.

Latin and *Sacramentum*

Another significant development in this period was the emergence of Latin as a language for Christian worship and theology. While Jesus probably spoke some Greek, the first language of Jesus and his close circle of disciples was Aramaic, a Semitic language closely related to Hebrew that had become the common language of Jews in Palestine. The language of currency in the empire, however, was Greek, which also became the dominant language of emerging Christianity. Every book of the New Testament was written in Greek. Christian worship, of course, was not confined to Greek, Aramaic, or Hebrew and was conducted in whatever language served the local community. Luke's Pentecost image from the Acts of the Apostles provides a metaphoric image of the multiculturality of emerging Christianity [quotation 130]. Surprising to some, cross-cultural theology and multicultural worship are not late twentieth-century developments but the bedrock of the emerging Christian experience.

Latin was an ancient language brought to the Italian peninsula by people from the North. It became the language of ancient Rome, and as the influence of the Roman Empire expanded, it would become the dominant language of western Europe. In the first century of Christianity, however, it had not achieved this dominance. It is true that Latin was the first language of Roman administrators even in Palestine, as evidenced by the passage in John's gospel that reports how Pilate affixed a sign in Hebrew, Latin, and Greek to Jesus' cross [quotation 131]. While Latin was not a dominant language of emerging Christianity, it did rise in prominence during the period of the house church. The noted Latinist Christine Mohrmann (d. 1988) believes that this happened, in part, because Christians increasingly considered themselves a "third race," distinct from Gentiles and Jews. The use of Latin was an important way for Christians to distinguish themselves (Mohrmann, p. 32). The turn to Latin as an increasingly distinctive vehicle for Western Christianity was to have a clear and lasting effect on Christian theology in general and eucharistic theology in particular.

Quotation 130: *Now there were devout Jews from every nation under heaven living in Jerusalem. And at this sound the crowd gathered and was bewildered, because each one heard them speaking in the native language of each. Amazed and astonished, they asked, "Are not all these who are speaking Galileans? And how is it that we hear, each of us, in our own native language? Parthians, Medes, Elamites, and residents of Mesopotamia, Judea and Cappadocia, Pontus and Asia, Phrygia and Pamphylia, Egypt and the parts of Libya belonging to Cyrene, and visitors from Rome, both Jews and proselytes, Cretans and Arabs—in our own languages we hear them speaking about God's deeds of power."* (Acts 2:5-11)

Quotation 131: *Pilate also had an inscription written and put on the cross. It read, "Jesus of Nazareth, the King of the Jews." Many of the Jews read this inscription, because the place where Jesus was crucified was near the city; and it was written in Hebrew, in Latin, and in Greek.* (John 19:19-20)

Just as one cannot borrow a philosophical framework without that framework influencing the ideas being communicated, so one cannot employ a language without the language itself having a similar influence. One of the ways this "Latinizing" process will affect Christian thought is through the translation and adaptation of Greek texts, like the New Testament. For example, the Greek New Testament does not speak about "sacrament" but about *musterion*. *Musterion*, which occurs twenty-seven times in the New Testament, is a difficult word to translate. It was a term that was employed in Greek philosophy and ancient mystery cults to designate rites in which devotees of a god celebrated and participated in the god's fate. In the Greek translation of the Hebrew Scriptures known as the Septuagint the word appears nine times, and it takes on the sense of a divine mystery in the process of being fully revealed in the future [quotation 132]. In the New Testament the term occurs when Jesus explains the purpose of the parables (e.g., Mark 4:11) or when Paul speaks of Christ as the "mystery of God" (Col 2:2), but it is never used to describe or explain worship.

One of the more common translations of the Greek *musterion* was the Latin *sacramentum*. As used by Romans, the word *sacramentum* had numerous legal meanings. For example, it could designate a sum of money that the parties to a lawsuit had to deposit with a magistrate before the suit would go forward. The "sacred" connotation of the word (Latin *sacra* = holy) comes from the practice of turning the money of the losing party over to the state for religious purposes. Another common meaning of the word was an oath [quotation 109], particularly one taken by newly enlisted troops to the emperor. According to Edward Malone, newly initiated soldiers were also provided with some sort of identification mark (e.g., a branding or tattoo) and often given a new name by the army. These three acts (the oath, identification mark, and registration of the new name) were called the *sacramenta militiae* (literally, "military sacraments"). Eventually these acts would find clear analogies in the initiation of Christians who would profess a creed, receive an "indelible mark" on the soul, and receive a Christian name. More important for the history of Christian sacramentality, however, was the borrowing of the word *sacramentum* by Latin writers like Tertullian —the son of a soldier who understood the range of legal and political meanings of this word. By borrowing such a word, Tertullian inadvertently introduces legal connotations into a Christian understanding of worship that did not exist with the Greek *musterion*. The long-term result of this and many parallel developments would be the emergence of an enormous body of canonical literature addressing sacramental issues. This is but one example where the turn to Latin

Quotation 132: *Daniel answered the king, "No wise men, enchanters, magicians, or diviners can show to the king the mystery that the king is asking, but there is a God in heaven who reveals mysteries, and he has disclosed to King Nebuchadnezzar what will happen at the end of days. Your dream and the visions of your head as you lay in bed were these."* (Dan 2:27-28)

Quotation 133: *Priests had no sacred space to safeguard or to guide into and out of by means of rites of passage. Therefore, their role and importance changed. Even more importantly, the entire land of Babylon, wherein the Israelites lived, was unclean according to their laws of purity. This meant that the religious status of all of the people had to be determined in a new way. . . . It was most likely at this time that personal integrity and loyalty to the covenant, which were always important elements in the religion of Israel, took on heightened meaning. These became the criteria for determining the religious purity necessary for entrance into the presence of God. Conformity to these standards flowed from a decision freely made by the individual rather than from a fixed pattern imposed by the group. Thus the meaningful yet restrictive standards of cultic purity gave way to the more encompassing demands of covenant fidelity.* (Bergant, "Come Let Us Go up to the Mountain of the Lord," p. 24)

and the borrowing of secular terms would significantly shape eucharistic and sacramental theology.

Spiritualization

Another theological trend in this early period is what could be called spiritualization. We previously noted this trend when discussing the developing concept of sacrifice during this period. The spiritualization of the concept of sacrifice in regards to Eucharist meant an emphasis on the disposition of the worshiper rather than on the physical aspects of the rite. In this sense Eucharist could continue to be understood as a sacrifice even though there was little if any recognizable ritual continuity between Eucharist and the sacrifices of Judaism.

This trend toward spiritualization was not a distinctively Christian development and was certainly apparent in Judaism. In this regard, the period after the destruction of the Jerusalem temple in 70 c.e. was somewhat analogous to that previous moment in Jewish history (587 b.c.e.) when Jerusalem was captured, the temple defiled, and the sacrificial cult suspended [quotation 133]. In both situations Jewish leaders were forced to rethink the cult. One way this happened was through increased emphasis on the internal attitudes and personal integrity of believers rather than on legal or rubrical correctness in worship. This emphasis on the proper spirit or disposition was an important resource for Judaism in the Common Era, as its cultic center moved from temple to synagogue, and physical sacrifice was replaced by spoken prayer [quotation 134].

In a parallel way, the emerging Christian theologies of worship put distinctive emphasis on the spiritual rather than physical aspects of the rite. The correct intention rather than the proper execution of rubrics is what marks Christian Eucharist from its inception [quotation 20]. Even though there emerge physical requirements for Christian Eucharist like bread and a cup of wine, early Christian texts underscore that these are spiritual food and drink meant to nourish believers to live eternally [quotation 135].

Summary

Christian worship and emerging Christian theologies emphasize the importance of the reign of God and living not for this world but the next. In its origins Christianity is what James Russell calls a "world-rejecting" and salvation-orientated religion, whose adherents are seriously focused on transcending their earthly existence. Believers in this faith stance would eagerly embrace martyrdom, so common

Quotation 134: *The spiritual attitude of both rabbis and the masses could be described in the following way: "We are absolutely worthless, and are now deprived even of the former ways of finding favor with You. Once there was a Temple, and we could offer sacrifice there, but now it is no more, so we must give the sacrifice of our flesh and blood. . . . We are sanctified in all which we do out of love and loyalty to you." (Neusner, There We Sat Down, pp. 88–89)*

Quotation 135: *The 10th Chapter of the Didache provides the following prayer which may have been used for Eucharist: We thank you, holy Father, for your holy name, which you have caused to dwell in our hearts, and for the knowledge and faith and immortality which you have made known unto us through Jesus your Son; to you be the glory for ever. You, Almighty Master, did create all things for the sake of your name, and have given both meat and drink for men to enjoy, that we might give thanks to you, but to us you have given spiritual food and drink, and life everlasting, through your Son. Above all we thank you that you are able to save; to you be glory forever. Remember, Lord, your church, to redeem it from every evil, and to perfect it in your love, and gather it together from the four winds, even that which has been sanctified for your kingdom which you have prepared for it; for yours is the kingdom and the glory for ever. (Audet, La Didachè)*

in the first centuries of Christianity. Such a community would similarly be empathetic to a dialogue with Platonism, which also marked this period. In terms of eucharistic theology and practice, this spiritual, world-rejecting approach underscored issues of ethics and personal integrity in eucharistic practice. While there was some attention to the norms for procedures and materials for use in worship, these were clearly secondary to the emphasis on spiritual nourishment and the continuity between Christian prayer and Christian living.

Even in the early centuries, Christianity initiated believers and encountered cultures that were more "world-accepting" than "world-rejecting." Sustained encounters with these cultures would ultimately transform Christianity and its worship. Thus, in the coming centuries there will be increased attention to and regulation of the tangible aspects of the cult. There will even be teachings about Christ's presence in the Eucharist that stress the presence of his earthly body under the appearances of bread and wine. Such developments will be distant from the early Christian instincts to emphasize the spiritual, otherworldly, and ethical nature of Christian worship and Christian life.

JULIA

Voices from the atrium woke Julia from a sound sleep. At first, she was confused by the commotion outside her window. Then she remembered that it was Sunday. This morning there was to be another gathering at her parents' villa in Antioch.

Julia was used to large crowds at the villa. When she was very young, her parents often hosted elaborate parties that lasted long into the night. Her father's important friends, visiting dignitaries, and sometimes a famous charioteer would dine for hours, debating issues unresolved in the city council or listening to the odes of Antioch's newest poet. Julia had often watched the crowds from her room overlooking the atrium, wishing that they would all go home so she could go to sleep. But ever since she was eight years old, no noisy night gatherings have been held at the villa. That was the year she and her parents were baptized. Now large crowds come to the villa only on Sunday mornings.

Julia would like to have stayed in bed a little longer this morning, but now that she was twelve years old, her parents thought it was important for her to greet the guests. As Julia combed her hair, she wondered who might join them today. There were always old friends to greet and strangers to welcome. Some were from important and wealthy families, while others were very poor. Julia's mother had taught her that it was important to treat everyone the same, even their servants.

The ritual this morning would be a familiar one. After friends and strangers have been welcomed, the community will gather in the garden with Anicetus, their bishop. The meeting begins with news of other communities of believers from around the provinces. Sometimes there is sad news about some who have been arrested or even put to death because of their belief. Other times there are stories of wonderful conversions or healings. After these stories of faith, Anicetus calls the community to prayer. Then they sit on the ground and listen to the prophetess Cara.

Julia knows well the story of how Cara met the apostle Peter when she was a little girl. She had been blind from birth, and many thought that Peter would restore her sight. But Peter told Cara that it was not her eyes but her voice that would give glory to God. From that day forward, Cara listened to the stories about Jesus and to the letters of instructions written by his followers. By the time she was Julia's age, Cara had memorized all the stories and letters. Julia's favorite letter is the one from Peter. She especially likes the part in the middle about baptism that Cara always sings.

After Cara's message, Anicetus asks if there are any in the community who, having heard the instruction, would like to be baptized. If there are, the bishop takes them to the pool in the garden and asks about their faith. If enough people testify about the faith and virtue of these people, Anicetus baptizes them right there. Others are not ready for baptism. The bishop embraces them and assures them that they are always welcome to return, but they are not allowed to remain for the rest of the gathering.

After all the unbaptized are escorted out of the garden and the gate is locked, the community prays for those in need. After these prayers, everyone shares the kiss of peace. Some men bring a table into the garden, and Julia's mother places bread and wine on the table. Anicetus steps forward and prays over the community and their gifts. Julia's father and mother assist at the table and help Anicetus break the bread and share the wine with all present.

After the holy banquet, the bishop inquires about those who are missing from the assembly. Philip and his wife Romana record the names of those who are absent and see to it that the sanctified bread is brought to them and that their other needs are also taken care of. Often, at the end of the service, Cara breaks out into song that the community takes up until all are dispersed.

Sunday is certainly Julia's favorite day of the week.

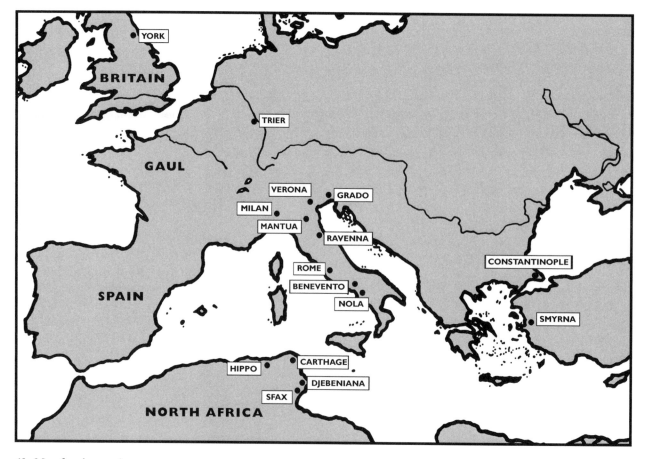

61. Map for chapter 3.

CHAPTER THREE

The Rise of the Roman Church:

313–750

Few individuals loom as large in early church history as the Roman emperor Constantine (d. 337) [illustration 62]. Son of the emperor Constantinius (d. 306), Constantine became one of the two rulers of the West when his father died. Previously (in 293) the emperor Diocletian (d. 313) had divided the empire into East and West [illustration 29] to increase the stability of his government. In each division of the empire he appointed a primary emperor, or "Augustus," and also an assistant emperor, or "Caesar." Constantine became the sole emperor of the West by defeating Maxentius, his Caesar, in 312. History records [quotation 136] that before the battle with Maxentius, Constantine was instructed in a dream to place a Christian symbol [illustration 63] on his soldiers' shields. The ensuing victory purportedly sealed his commitment to Christianity, though there has been continuing debate about the motivations for this commitment. While some believe his primary motivation was faith in Christ, others think that he valued Christianity for its political potential and the moral contributions it could make to his empire.

62. Sculpture of Constantine.

With his co-emperor Lincinius, who was serving as Augustus of the East, Constantine recognized in 313 the right of all religions to exist. The "Edict of Milan" that they issued, however, only explicitly names the Christian religion and extends toleration to other religions by virtue of the fact that Christians are hereafter tolerated and protected [quotation 137]. This important gesture was at the beginning of a reign that would see an increasing number of privileges extended to Christianity. Over the next twenty-five years Constantine would become more involved in ecclesial affairs, intervene in various doctrinal controversies, and even convoke and preside over the Council of Nicea in 325, despite the fact that he was yet unbaptized. His baptism finally occurred at the end of his life, after Easter in the year 337. The emperor died a few weeks later on Pentecost of the same year.

Although the depth of Constantine's conversion may be debated, the effects of his turn to Christianity are significant. Under his reign

Quotation 136: *Constantine was instructed in a dream that he should mark the shields [of his solders] with the heavenly sign of God and so enter into battle. He did as he was ordered and placed a symbol for Christ [on the shields] by bending the upper part of a transverse letter x.* (Lactantius [d. ca. 320], *The Death of the Persecutors*, 44)

the church of the martyrs gave way to a process of Christianization that would sweep through the empire. An illegal sect was transformed into the preferred religion of the empire that was politically advantageous to profess. Christian initiation, which had previously been a somewhat perilous commitment made by a believing adult, evolved into a familiar act of christening infants. Over time, Christian identity for many became more an accident of birth than a result of conversion.

One by-product of the expansion of the church and its heightened status in society was the gradual acquisition of external trappings of this new imperial favor. Bishops were granted various honors and wore the insignia of civil magistrates. This caused some people to criticize the bishops for their new positions of privilege [quotation 138]. Impressive buildings for Christian worship were constructed, and the expectations for liturgical ministers in such surroundings evolved. During this era corps of specialists began emerging to take responsibility for the more imperial form of worship that developed in Rome. This was fitting for what would become the official state religion under the emperor Theodosius (d. 395) in 380.

Constantine also exerted a long-range influence on Western civilization in general, and Christianity in particular, by moving the center of his government from Rome to the ancient city of Byzantium on the Bosporus. There he dramatically rebuilt the old town, which he renamed Constantinople [illustration 61]. By doing so, Constantine gave the eastern empire a fitting capital, one that was geographically well situated for controlling the eastern part of his empire. The rise of the city of Constantinople foreshadowed the political collapse of Rome during the following century.

While Constantine's influence on church history is undeniable, it also should not be exaggerated. He did have a profound direct and indirect influence on the development of Christianity, and during his reign there were many obvious changes in the church and its worship. Paul Bradshaw reminds us, however, that every development that happened at the time was not necessarily a result of Constantinian leadership. Rather, many developments in the fourth century had their roots in the third century and even earlier [quotation 139].

After Constantine's death in 337, the empire was divided among his three sons (Constantine II, Constans I, and Constantius II). Though briefly reunited under Emperor Theodosius, the eastern and western parts of the empire eventually separated permanently. As the eastern empire grew, the western declined: Barbarian tribes invaded from the North, overrunning Britain, Gaul, Spain, and North Africa [illustration 64]. When the Visigoths invaded Italy, the western emperor Honorius moved his capital in desperation from Rome to

63. Roman coin (c. 350 C.E.) depicting Emperor Magnentius, a successor of Constantine, and the Chi Rho symbol of Christianity.

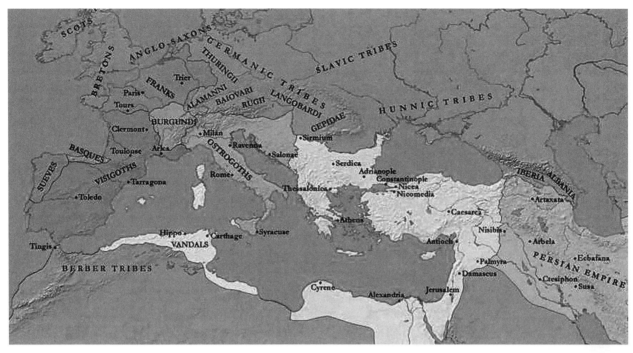

64. The Roman empire and Barbarian Europe, 500.

the more secure city of Ravenna in 404. Rome was plundered by the Visigoths in 410 and again by the Vandals in 455. The last Roman emperor, Romulus Augustulus, was deposed in 476 and the Germanic chieftain, Odoacer, became the first barbarian ruler of what today we call Italy.

Throughout this time of increasing instability in the western empire, the church grew and established itself as one of the few reliable institutions in Rome during the barbarian invasions. This was true not only socially and spiritually but also politically. Thus, it was not the Roman emperor Valentinian II, but Pope Leo the Great (d. 461) who is remembered as having met Attila the Hun in 452 at Attila's camp in Mantua and persuading him to accept a payment of tribute and spare Rome. This story highlights the growing influence of the church and its leadership in the wake of the collapse of the Roman Empire.

ARCHITECTURE

Parallel to the evolution of the church of the martyrs into the official church of the Roman Empire was the dramatic transition in the settings for Christian worship. A variety of venues continued to be

Quotation 137: *When I, Constantine Augustus, as well as I Licinius Augustus fortunately met near Mediolanurn [Milan] . . . we thought . . . those regulations pertaining to the reverence of the Divinity ought certainly to be made first, so that we might grant to the Christians and others full authority to observe that religion which each preferred; whence . . . we thought to arrange that no one whatsoever should be denied the opportunity to give his heart to the observance of the Christian religion, of that religion which he should think best for himself, so that the Supreme Deity, to whose worship we freely yield our hearts, may show in all things His usual favor and benevolence. (Lactantius, The Death of the Persecutors, 48)*

Quotation 138: *[The bishops] are well off, for they grow rich on the gifts of noble ladies. They ride in carriages, dressed in exquisite robes. They give such sumptuous dinners that their banquets rival those of kings. (Ammianus Marcellinus [born ca. 330], History, 27.3.14-15, in van der Meer and Mohrmann, Atlas of the Early Christian World)*

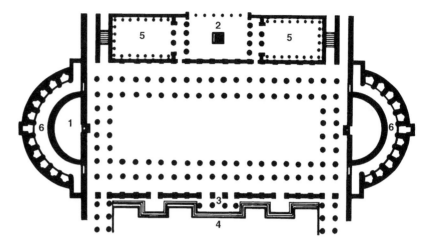

1. Altar
2. Column of Trajan
3. Entrance from forum
4. Forum of Trajan
5. Library
6. Tribunal for judges and assessors

65. Basilica Ulpia. (After Gardner, p. 190)

employed by Christians for their worship in this era. Many permanently renovated house churches undoubtedly continued to flourish around the Mediterranean. Christianity's growth in membership and stature, however, increasingly called for a new type of worship space, especially in the larger cities of the empire. In the previous era we already saw that preexisting buildings were being reshaped into large halls, or what L. Michael White called the *aula ecclesiae*. Some of these were also built in this era. After the ascent of Constantine, however, this preference for large, rectangular spaces led Christians to adopt the basilica as the new paradigm for worship spaces. Separate buildings for baptism and honoring martyrs also came into being during this period.

66. Artist's reconstruction of the interior of the Basilica Ulpia.

67. Trier Basilica.

Basilica

The word "basilica" is derived from the Greek word for king (*basileus*). It eventually came to mean "hall of the king." The Romans built these rectangular structures as meeting halls. What architecturally distinguishes a basilica from other rectangular structures is the existence of at least one apse, and often the presence of side aisles separated from the main space by a series of columns. Often used for law courts, they were also used for a wide variety of business, administrative, and civic purposes. Some basilicas were quite modest in size and, for example, could be incorporated into the home of an affluent citizen who used it for conducting business affairs. Others were gigantic public structures, created as monuments to the power of the Roman Empire and designed to impress, if not overwhelm, visitors. The Basilica Ulpia was one such building [illustration 65]. Constructed around 112 C.E., it dominated the northwest quadrant of the Roman Forum. This imposing structure was 426 feet long and 138 feet wide, with a spectacular enclosed space under a huge vaulted ceiling [illustration 66]. Each of the two shorter sides of the building included an apse. This multifunctional building housed law courts, administrative bureaus, and business offices. It was also the site of various official events. Creating a structure like this was possible because the Romans had perfected an unusually strong form of concrete by adding fine volcanic sand to the mix that enabled them to construct such huge enclosed spaces.

Quotation 139: *[In some instances] the so-called Constantinian revolution did not so much inaugurate new liturgical practices and attitudes as create conditions in which some preexistent customs could achieve a greater measure of preeminence than others which were no longer considered appropriate to the changed situation of the Church.* (Bradshaw, *The Search for the Origins of Christian Worship*, p. 67)

As Christians had borrowed homes and other smaller spaces for worship in earlier centuries, so did they borrow architecturally from the culture of imperial Rome. Because of their new and more publicly acceptable status at this time, they turned to the basilica. After the triumph of Constantine and the legalization of Christianity, the basilica became a preferred model for Christian churches. Rather than employing the double-apse basilica style, like the Basilica Ulpia and others, Christians adopted the single-apse style. Smaller versions of this design had been employed in some home constructions, and this design was also employed for some larger audience halls like the imperial building in Trier [illustration 67]. In this design, one of the apses was removed and ordinarily replaced by a main entrance. The result was a dramatic, longitudinal path, sometimes flanked by columns, leading to the apse, which was the focal point of the building. In writing about Christians' adaptation of this building, Richard Krautheimer notes that "the Christian basilica, both in function and design, was a new creation within an accustomed framework."

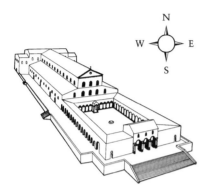

68. Old Saint Peter's. (After Gardner, p. 217)

One of the first great Christian buildings was Old St. Peter's [illustration 68], constructed over what was believed to be the burial place of the apostle Peter. Begun possibly as early as 319, the building was finished in the 340s. Of immense proportions, the inner length of the building was over 390 feet in length and over 200 feet wide. In addition to the rectangular design, similar to that of the imperial audience hall, Old St. Peter's included a large atrium outside the church for the gathering of the people. While such enclosed atriums have largely disappeared, one still exists today in front of the basilica of St. Ambrose in Milan [illustration 69]. Also notable about Old St. Peter's was the double colonnade on either side of the nave and short transepts, resulting in a rudimentary cross shape. Christian Norberg-Schulz hypothesizes that this cross shape is a hallmark of churches dedicated to the apostles, and its design recalls that the apostles were the first to take up the cross of Christ. This architectural design also distinguished these churches from secular basilicas, which did not have transepts.

69. Basilica of Saint Ambrose, Milan.

The basilica functioned as a kind of enclosed path. Originally there was little in the body of these churches that interrupted the movement from the atrium to the apse; benches or pews in the nave were a much later addition. The bishop's throne often was placed in the center of the apse, where the civic official would have sat if it was a secular basilica. The episcopal throne was surrounded by the college of presbyters who sat on a long, low bench [illustration 70]. The congregation usually stood in the nave—though some sources indicated that the faithful sat in the nave—often with the men separated from the women [quotation 140]. The altar was a freestanding

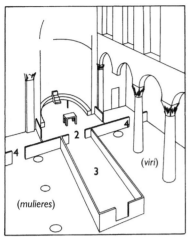

1. Presbyterium: place in the apse for the throne of the bishops and benches for presbyters

2. Sanctuarium (sanctuary): site of the altar, set off by a low barrier from the body of the church

3. Solea-scholas: processional area set off by a pair of low walls. This area was used principally in the ceremonies of pontifical entrance and exit but was also used for the reading of Scripture.

4. Senatoreum and Matroneum: areas set off by barriers and used for the presentation of the gifts in the offertory procession and for the reception of Eucharist by the laity: men (*viri*) and women (*mulieres*).

70. An early Roman chancel arrangement.
(After Thomas Mathews)

structure—sometimes fabricated from wood but more often of stone in the great basilicas—situated in front of the apse so that people could gather around it [quotation 141]. As the centuries progressed, the altars were moved farther away from the people, into the apse, which came to be called the "sanctuary" (Latin = *sanctuarium*, "sacred place or shrine"). By the fourth century, women were excluded from the sanctuary in some places [quotation 142]. Further evidence shows that in some churches in Rome, at least by the fifth century, the sanctuary and the pathway that led to it were open only to the clergy and to the choir that participated in the procession [illustration 70].

Given the Mediterranean context for the emergence of Christianity, it is not surprising that light and sun imagery were important for Christian liturgy and affected the architecture. One of the major religions of the Roman Empire was the cult of Mithra, the ancient Persian god of light and wisdom. Constantine was a known sun worshiper, and there is some evidence that his decision in 321 to close the law courts on Sundays was as much rooted in his leanings toward Mithraism as to Christianity. Temples of various religions built in this context were often designed with a clear relationship to the sun, for example, so that worshipers could pray toward the rising sun. There is widespread evidence already in the third century that Christians were not only praying toward the East but encouraged to do so. By the fourth century there are clear directives that Christian church buildings should be orientated toward the East. While there is substantial evidence that churches in both the East and West

Quotation 140: *First of all the building should be oblong, directed toward the rising sun, with sacristies on each side toward the east, so that it resembles a ship. Let the throne of the bishop be placed in the middle, the presbytery to sit on either side of him, and the deacons to stand nearby, neatly dressed in their full garments, resembling the sailors and officers of a ship. Relative to them the laymen are to sit toward the other end in complete quiet and good order, and the women are to sit alone, and they too are to maintain silence. In the middle the reader is to stand upon something high and read the books of Moses.* (Apostolic Constitutions [late fourth century], 2.57.3-7, in McKinnon, 108–9)

Quotation 141: *Consequently, the table, like the fountain, lies in the middle in order that the flocks may surround the fountain on every side and enjoy the benefits of the saving waters.* (John Chrysostom [d. 407], *Second Baptismal Instruction,* 2)

Quotation 142: *Women should not approach the altar.* (Council of Laodicea [ca. 363] canon 44, in Mansi, *Sacrorum Conciliorum*)

71. Artist's conception of the baldachino erected by Constantine. (Bergere, p. 21)

Quotation 143: *Even some Christians think it is so proper [to worship the sun] that, before, entering the blessed Apostle Peter's basilica, which is dedicated to the one living and true God, when they have mounted the steps which lead to the raised platform, they turn round and bow themselves toward the rising sun and with bent neck do homage to its brilliant orb.* (Leo the Great [d. 421], Sermon 22)

Quotation 144: *Rising on the chord of the apse, [this] monument was set off by a bronze railing. A baldacchino, resting on four spiral vine scroll columns, rose above it; two more architraved columns linked the baldacchino to the corners of the apse, the openings into the apse being closed by curtains.* (Krautheimer, *Early Christian and Byzantine Architecture*, p. 56)

were orientated with their apse toward the sun, this is not true of the earliest basilicas in Rome, some of which—like St. John Lateran and Old St. Peter's—have their apses facing west. Leo the Great (d. 461) provides evidence for the ongoing sun cult in Rome and further substantiates the fact that some churches have their apses facing west. In a sermon delivered when he was bishop of Rome, he chastises some Christians for worshiping the sun on their way to church [quotation 143].

Old St. Peter's, constructed by Constantine, was a martyrial church rather than the bishop's church. Consequently, it did not hold the bishops chair or *cathedra*—which was at St. John Lateran—but the *confessio* (Latin, literally a "confession"; by extension, "an announcement of faith") or what was thought to be the tomb of St. Peter [quotation 144]. While we cannot be certain about the construction or placement of the altar in the early Constantinian basilica, it is probable that it was a portable structure. Toynbee and Perkins suggest that on special festivals this altar would have been placed within the bronze railing, in front of the shrine of St. Peter and under the baldacchino [illustration 71]. At other times, the focus of worship was probably away from the shrine and more toward the nave. For these ceremonies it is likely that the portable altar was

72. Reconstruction of the transept of Old Saint Peter's, with the *confessio* on the left and the back of the great arch on the right.

positioned near the great arch that separated the nave from the apse [illustration 72].

One architectural innovation that took place during the papacy of Gregory the Great (d. 604) had the unintended effect of further distancing people from the altar. It appears that Gregory wanted to make it possible to celebrate Eucharist "over" the body of St. Peter. To accomplish this, Toynbee and Perkins calculate that the old Constantinian apse was raised almost six feet above the old pavement level to form a new, raised presbytery (216). In order to construct a large enough crypt that would allow access to the tomb-shrine now beneath the presbyter, the floor was sunk two feet below the level of the Constantinian church. In order to construct steps up to the presbytery and down into the crypt, the platform was extended almost twenty feet into the transept toward the nave. This destroyed most of the old shrine except for the central part of the *confessio*, one side of which was visible between the two sets of stairs. The upper part of the ancient shrine was incorporated into the new altar, placed directly over what was thought to be the apostle's tomb [illustration 73]. The ambo, which probably originated as a wooden platform, was also moved into the sanctuary. While designed to provide a stronger connection between Eucharist and the tomb of the martyr,

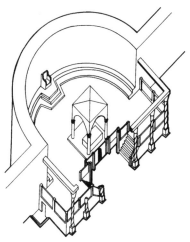

73. Saint Peter's in Rome, ca. 600, with altar raised over tomb of Saint Peter. (After J. B. Ward-Perkins as cited in Jones, p. 483)

this reconstruction moved the altar and the presider further away from and above the faithful. Consequently, the altar at this central Christian shrine was no longer one that the people could gather around but was more like a stage that people watched from below.

Baptistries and Martyria

Quotation 145: *"First of all [the Emperor] adorned the holy Cave where the bright angels once announced good news of a new birth for all men, revealed through the Saviour. This principal feature the munificent Emperor adorned with choice columns and much ornament, sparing no art to make it beautiful."* (Eusebius [d. ca. 340], *Life of Constantine* 3.28, in *The History of the Church*)

Besides the emergence of Christian basilicas, there also arose during this period what Spiro Kostof calls "occasional buildings." Especially important were the places for baptism and those that memorialized martyrs. Although the longitudinal layout of the basilica could have been used for these structures—as it was in the martyrium of Old St. Peter's in Rome—occasional buildings generally employed a central-plan construction. From an architectural perspective, this central-plan design was effective for celebrating a particular object like a tomb or baptismal font. "To do so, the architect raised a canopy directly above the object, a symbolic dome of heaven that would mark the object as hallowed." (Kostof, p. 258). The Roman tradition for building round burial mausoleums [illustration 74] was certainly one important influence on the Christian preference for shaping occasional buildings in this symbolic form, with its many overtones of perfection and eternal life.

74. Hadrian's Mausoleum, now more commonly known as Castel Sant' Angelo, is an enormous circular structure begun by Hadrian (d. 138) as a sepulcher for himself and his family, completed in 139 C.E.

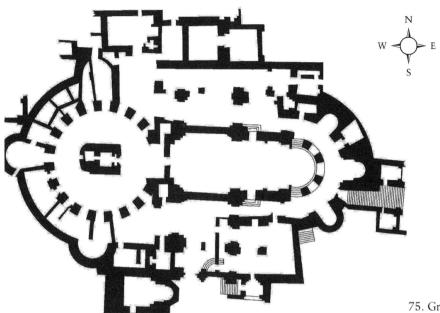

75. Ground plan of Holy Sepulchre, Jerusalem.

The Anastasis (Greek for "Resurrection") in Jerusalem is one of Christianity's most famous central-plan buildings. Still standing today, it has been rebuilt many times over the centuries. It was originally constructed during the middle of the fourth century—sometime between 348 and 381 [illustration 75]. At its center is what was thought to be the tomb of Christ. Constantine's architects leveled out the area around this cave-like structure on Golgatha and created a ring of columns around it [quotation 145]. Martyrs, who were venerated for imitating the death of Christ, often were honored with similar central-plan buildings over their tombs that were called martyria. A forecourt and a large basilica were also constructed on the site in Jerusalem, and eventually the Anastasis occupied the western end of a long complex of buildings and courtyards on Golgatha. While the building expansion eventually obscured the original design, at the heart of the Anastasis is a central-plan structure.

The Christian belief in baptism as a participation in the death and resurrection of Christ [quotation 146] contributed to the architectural resonance between martyria and baptistries. This is particularly apparent in the tendency to shape separately constructed baptistries as central-plan buildings. One historic example of this influence can be seen in a baptistery located in the ancient town of Grado in Northeast Italy [illustration 76]. The eight-sided building, dating from the fifth century and restored in 1925, stands adjacent to a sixth-century cathedral. The octagonal shape is a reminder of the "eighth day," a symbol of resurrection and eternity in Christian thought. Inside the eight-sided building is a six-sided font, symbolizing among other things the sixth day of the week (Friday), when Jesus was martyred.

76. Interior of fifth-century baptistery at Grado, an eight-sided building, showing a six-sided font inside.

Quotation 146: *Just as Christ was truly crucified, buried, and raised again . . . you are considered worthy to be crucified, buried and raised with him in likeness by baptism.* (Cyril of Jerusalem [d. ca. 386], *Catechetical Sermon,* 3.2, in Yarnold, *The Awe-Inspiring Rites of Initiation*)

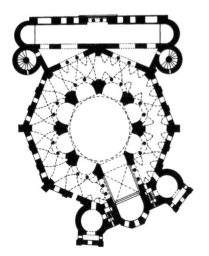

77. San Vitale in Ravenna.
(After Gardner, p. 235)

Longitudinal Versus Central Plan

Although central-plan buildings continued to be constructed for worship by Christians in the West, the longitudinal shape of the basilica was preferred. This was due, in part, to the ability of a basilica design to support liturgical processions—such as the entrance, gospel, and communion processions—which became increasingly important in the worship of this period [quotation 147]. In later centuries a central plan was often integrated into a basilica-style building in the West. This was accomplished by adding a central dome to a cruciform or other basilica-shaped building [illustration 177] or by connecting a central plan structure to the apse end of a basilica.

As the Christian builders in the West demonstrated a clear preference for the rectangular design of the basilica, Christians in the East embraced the central-plan, domed church [quotation 148]. While there are many cultural and historical reasons that contributed to this growing architectural distinction between Eastern and Western Christianity, there are also spiritual and theological reasons. Some hold that central plan churches embody a more communal ecclesiology, while the basilica form reflects a more hierarchical image of the church. Robert Taft is probably closer to the mark, however, when he suggests that Byzantine architecture and iconography contribute to a sense that in such spaces one experiences worship as a participation in the heavenly liturgy. That is certainly a feeling one gets, for example, when entering San Vitale in Ravenna, Italy. This church was completed about the year 548 after this former capital of the Ostrogothic Kingdom was captured from the Ostrogoths and united to Justinian's Byzantine Empire. San Vitale consists of two concentric octagons with a dome surmounting the inner one [illustration 77]. San Vitale was not the first central-plan Byzantine Church—a distinction that belongs to Ss. Sergius and Bacchus in Constantinople, whose construction began in 527. As an important monument in the new seat of the Byzantine government in Italy, however, San Vitale greatly influenced church design in much of the Byzantine Empire. This is due, in no small measure, to the breathtaking mosaics that mark San Vitale as one of Christianity's great treasures.

Summary

Great diversity is evident in the development of Christian architecture during this period. One can also detect a pervasive flexibility that allowed the community to shape its spaces according to evolving needs. Within such diversity and flexibility, however, a few trends can be detected.

Shortly after Constantine's ascent as sole ruler of the West, Christian worship migrated to the public forum. Simple rooms or reno-

78. Christ depicted in the apse of San Vitale, Ravenna.

vated houses that could accommodate twenty-five, fifty, or even one hundred people slowly gave way to enormous enclosed spaces that, in some instances, could actually accommodate thousands. Worship spaces were increasingly constructed in the style of audience-hall basilicas, whose long internal path led to the apse, where the throne of the emperor or other state authority was replaced by the bishop's chair. Auxiliary buildings, on the other hand, generally were designed on a central plan; this shape became the preference for churches in the East by the sixth century.

While there appear to have been some hall-like churches in existence before the time of Constantine, what marks the worship architecture after Constantine is both the size and the public nature of the new buildings. While it is true that the spaces used for worship previous to this period were often well known to non-Christians [quotations 90 and 95], they were not designed to allow public observation of the rituals, and sometimes shielded the worshiping community from public view. As Christianity evolved as the official religion of the empire, however, it began to adapt its worship and the architectural settings for such worship so the rituals could be observed by believers, inquirers, the curious, or even its critics.

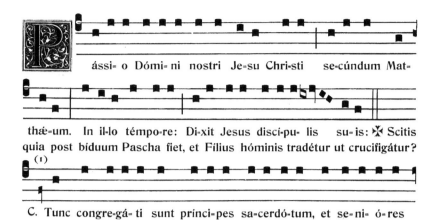

79. Traditional chant or cantillation for the Passion from the Gospel of Matthew, sung on Palm Sunday.

As the buildings and the rituals they housed became more public, so did they more obviously reflect the cultural contexts in which they were situated. In great imperial cities like Rome, this meant that presiders began to look and act more and more like court officials. Similarly, the iconography [illustration 78] that adorned such buildings began to depict Christ more as an emperor, philosopher, magician, or competitor to the ancient gods rather than as Good Shepherd [quotation 149]. The buildings were internally configured to correspond to these developments. One result was the eventual restriction of certain parts of the buildings to clergy and other officials. Eventually all laity would be excluded from the sanctuary, which became the privileged domain of the clergy.

In this context the Christian community's language for themselves and the worship spaces they designed continued to evolve. We have already seen that in the previous era the Greek term *ekklesia* ("assembly") began to be used to designate both the community and the permanently renovated edifice in which the community gathered. Christine Mohrmann believed that the Latin equivalent *ecclesia* makes a parallel transition by the early fourth century. She also believed that the Greek term *kuriakón*, which also appeared in the previous era, became an important technical term in the fourth century, more popular than *ekklesia* for naming the places where Christians gathered to pray. The Latin equivalent, *dominicum*, also became a popular term in the fourth century [quotation 150], although it will disappear in the course of the fifth century. Finally, in the fourth century Christians adopted the word *basilica* in the sense of a church building. While some will argue that the Christian basilica only appears after the ascent of Constantine, Mohrmann notes that the word already appeared as a designation for a church building a decade before Constantine became emperor. She also held that this was a somewhat neutral term for Christians in the beginning and did not indicate any determined or fixed architectural style.

MUSIC

James White once commented that each church building is a musical instrument. This maxim helps us understand that—like every musical instrument—a worship space both affects and is affected by the music. The buildings we employ for worship are not only visual spaces but acoustic spaces as well. The evolution of worship venues for the Christian community—from borrowed spaces to permanently renovated house churches to halls and then to basilicas—was a significant factor in shaping the worship music of this period. Not surprisingly, like the spaces that housed it, the liturgical music at the end of this period will be significantly different from that at the beginning of this period.

Prayers and Readings

In the arena of public proclamation, Christian practice in the fourth century was similar to that of previous centuries in that there was little public speech that was not musical to some degree. This was especially true for the proclamation of key texts such as readings, orations, and eucharistic prayers. To the extent that presiders proclaimed orations and prayers—particularly in the increasingly spacious basilicas of the era—such texts migrated more toward song than what we would call speech. The same could be said of the readings. The tradition of cantillating readings, which the followers of Jesus had experienced in the synagogue, continued uninterrupted.

The exact style of cantillation in these centuries is difficult to ascertain. Because musical notation did not develop until a later period, cantillation patterns—like all melodies—had to be memorized [quotation 151]. Though the living memory of the chant from this era has been lost, later examples of psalm tones might suggest how some readings were cantillated in this time period [illustration 79].

Various nonmusical developments also offer hints about the chanting of the readings at this time. For example, previously we noted that the ministry of the lector—and not just the act of public reading—is well documented in the third century. By the fourth century this is a relatively fixed ministry in Christianity. Some served as lectors for many years [quotation 152], which could have enabled them to develop distinctive cantillation patterns. These patterns may

Quotation 150: *On your left is the hillock Golgatha where the Lord was crucified and about a stone's throw from it the vault where they laid his body, and he rose again on the third day. By order of the emperor Constantine there has now been built there a "basilica"—I mean a "place for the Lord" [dominicum]—which has beside it cisterns of remarkable beauty, and beside them a bath where children are baptized."* (The Pilgrim of Bordeaux [333], in Wilkinson, *Egeria's Travels,* p. 158)

Quotation 151: *Unless sounds are remembered, they perish because they cannot be written down.* (Isidore of Seville [Isidori Hispalensis Episcopi, d. 636], *Etymologies,* 3.15)

Quotation 152: *At times a child was already designated a lector, and only when he reached the age of thirty was he entrusted with the task of acolyte or subdeacon. . . . If one began as an adult, the first ministry was often that of lector or exorcist. After two years . . . he was eligible to be an acolyte or subdeacon.* (Osborne, *Priesthood,* p. 197)

80. Ambo of Beyazit Basilica, sixth century. (From Mathews, *Early Churches of Constantinople*, figure 56)

Quotation 153: *Lector chant is both more individual and more ephemeral, some might say more free, relating it to the charisma and spontaneity of early Christian worship, as opposed to the quest for order and uniformity that characterizes medieval liturgy.* (McKinnon, *The Advent Project*, p. 63)

Quotation 154: *No one shall sing in the assembly except the canonical singers who ascend to the ambo and chant from parchment.* (Council of Laodicea [ca. 363], canon 15, in Mansi, *Sacrorum Conciliorum*)

have been handed on from one generation of lectors to the next within a particular community. On the other hand, James McKinnon recalls the distinction made by Dom Jean Claire between "*schola* chant" (*schola* = Latin, "a place or system for learning," "a school") and "lector chant." In McKinnon's view, the former is marked by a developed repertoire and a significant organization to maintain that repertoire. The latter he characterizes as individual and resonant with the spontaneity of early Christian worship [quotation 153]. Thus, it could be problematic to talk about any body of lector chant and best to think more of a style of cantillation whose primary purpose was to enable believers to hear and comprehend the proclaimed Word.

Architectural developments underscore the importance of proclaiming the Word in worship and provide supporting evidence about the importance of lectors in the liturgy. The earliest permanent worship spaces allowed for a cleared space in the midst of the assembly that could have been employed for the proclamation of the Word. Later churches provided a special structure, the ambo, for this action. As we have already seen, documentary evidence for a pulpit or ambo already exists in the third century [quotation 112]. Archaeological evidence for ambos is in evidence by the fourth century and multiplies exponentially in the following centuries [illustration 80].

Further literary evidence from the fourth century connects not only the lector but also the newly emerging psalmist or cantor with the ambo [quotation 154]. This distinction between psalmist and lector is based on the different texts each of these ministers proclaim from the ambo, with only psalmists or cantors proclaiming the psalm.

In the previous chapter we noted that the David psalms were probably treated like other readings in early Christian worship and could have been performed in a way that was indistinguishable from the reading of other biblical passages [quotation 107]. In some places by the mid-fourth century, however, a pattern developed for performing psalms in a markedly different way from other biblical readings. It is probably that this performance encompassed both an increased attention to the latent lyricism of the psalmody as well as a growing preference for a responsorial form rather than the direct approach of reading a psalm directly through from beginning to end. This distinction between lector and psalmist might suggest not only the existence of "lector chant" and "*schola* chant" but also "psalmist chant," which would share the freedom of lector chant but with a more marked level of musicality.

Biblical and Nonbiblical Liturgical Chants

During the period 313 to 750, the eucharistic liturgy acquired many of the musical elements that are familiar today. The biblical psalms were central. They were chanted at the entrance, with an alleluia refrain before the gospel, and at what we formerly called the offertory, and at communion. The traditional view is that these biblical psalms—eventually known as the "proper of the Mass"—developed

81. Advent Introit, *Graduale Romanum* (1979).

slowly over many centuries. Recently James McKinnon has challenged that view and proposed a very different scenario for the development of the Roman Mass proper. His historical reconstruction presumes the emergence of "schola chant" as distinctive from the more individualistic, free and ephemeral "lector chant" [quotation 153]. According to McKinnon, *schola* chant is distinguished by repertoire and organization and involved both the creation of a large body of chant and the maintenance of that repertoire year after year. These two related tasks could be accomplished only by an established group of quasi-professional musicians (McKinnon, *Advent Project*, p. 63).

The Roman *schola cantorum* (Latin, "school of singers") was such a group, and McKinnon believes that they decided to produce a complete cycle of Mass propers for every date in the church year, beginning with Advent. Work commenced at the end of the seventh century with introits, graduals, offertories, and communions, resulting in a near-perfect set of these "propers" for the Advent-Christmas season [illustration 81]. It was not possible, however, for members of the *schola* to complete this ambitious design for the rest of the church year, and they only managed to compose the introits and communions. They could not compose new graduals and offertories for every day and often used the same chant for different days. Composition of alleluias, which were latecomers to the Mass propers, were barely begun before this creative period came to a close around 720 C.E.

The Emerging "Ordinary" of the Mass

Besides the "proper" of the Mass, this era also saw the emergence and standardization of what a later period will call the "ordinary" of the Mass, composed of biblical and nonbiblical texts. The *Kyrie* originated as an acclamation in Roman imperial cult and first appears in Christian litanies in the East in the fourth century. It is part of the Mass by at least the eighth century. While originally a key response of the people, by the eighth century it is already being sung by the choir alone at papal Masses. Eventually the laity will be eliminated from joining in singing the *Kyrie* during the Eucharist.

The *Gloria* (Latin, "Glory") was written in imitation of the psalms of David, and an early form of it appeared in the East in the late fourth century [quotation 155]. Originally employed in the East as part of morning prayer, the *Gloria* became part of the Roman Eucharist possibly by the sixth century. At first used at Christmas, then on Sundays and feasts of martyrs when the bishop presided, priests were allowed to include the *Gloria* at Mass only during Easter night and on the day of their ordination. By the early 700s in the Frankish kingdoms, however, the *Gloria* was employed on Sundays and feasts regardless of who presided. While there is some evidence that the people joined in singing the *Gloria*—even outside of Mass—it was decreasingly a hymn that included the voices of the assembly.

A primitive form of the *Sanctus* (Latin, "Holy") is already quoted in Clement's *Epistle to the Corinthians* (ca. 96 C.E.) [quotation 156], although there is no evidence that this text dictates any particular or fixed liturgical usage. By the third century there is a relatively clear reference to the use of the *Sanctus* in the Eucharist by Origen (d. ca. 254), and there are many more references from the East in the fourth century. The first evidence that the *Sanctus* was part of the Mass in the West, however, does not appear until around the year 400 from the north of Italy. From its first introduction into the Eucharist, it appears that the *Sanctus* was sung by all the people. The *Sanctus* maintained its position as the people's acclamation in the West longer than any other element of this emerging "ordinary." In some places, evidence as late as the twelfth century indicates that people were still singing the *Sanctus* at Mass.

A final element of the emerging ordinary that was introduced during this period was the *Agnus Dei* (Latin, "Lamb of God"). There is general agreement that this litany was introduced into the Roman liturgy by Pope Sergius I (d. 701) [illustration 82] who was born at Palermo of a Syrian family from Antioch. It is difficult to find an exact precedent for the *Agnus Dei* in the churches of the East. Nonetheless, the liturgical practices and symbolism of these churches, familiar to Sergius, provided him with the background either to import directly this element or to more creatively fashion it for the Roman church. One example of such symbology was the tradition in numerous Eastern sources to refer to the sanctified bread as the "lamb." The earliest Roman documents to mention the *Agnus Dei* indicate that the litany was repeated until the breaking of the bread was finished [quotation 157]. The continued repetition of the short phrases that make up the liturgy suggest that, from its introduction into the liturgy, the assembly joined in singing the *Agnus Dei*.

Hymns

During the years of peace that followed Constantine's recognition of the church, Christian hymnody flowered. This was due, at least in part, to the way that the hymnody of the day was cued to congregational engagement and employed a relatively popular compositional style. Hilary of Poitiers (d. 367) was instrumental in introducing metrical hymnody into the West from the East where it had been developing for over a century. Ambrose of Milan (d. 387)

82. Pope Sergius I.

Quotation 156: *Let Him be our boast and the ground of our confidence; let us be subject to His will; let us consider the vast multitude of His angels, and see how they stand in readiness to minister to His will. For the Scripture says, "Ten thousand times ten thousand stood ready before Him, and thousands times one thousand ministered to Him, and cried out: 'Holy, Holy, Holy is the Lord of Hosts; the whole creation is replete with His splendor.'"* (I Clement 34:5-6, in The Epistles of St. Clement of Rome and St. Ignatius of Antioch)

Quotation 157: *While the deacons were breaking bread onto the patens, the archdeacon nodded to the schola, indicating that they should begin the Agnus Dei, which they continued to sing until the breaking is complete.* (Roman Ordo, 3:2 [ca. 700 C.E.], in Andrieu, Les Ordines Romani)

Ae-ter-ne re-rum con-ditor, Noctem di-em-que qui re-gis, Et tempo-rum das tem-po-ra, Ut al-le-ves fa-sti-di-um.

83. Three melodies for the hymn *Aeterne rerum conditor* (Latin, "Eternal Creator of All Things") by Ambrose of Milan.

popularized the form in Latin and is sometimes called the father of Western hymnody. Ambrose understood the attraction and accessibility of this kind of music [quotation 158]. He divided his hymn texts into short stanzas, each following the same pattern (e.g., number of lines, meter, and rhyme scheme) as the previous stanza [illustration 83]. In so doing, Ambrose canonized basic principles for hymn writing that have endured for centuries. Although the music for Ambrose's hymns has not survived to the present day, Richard Hoppin suggests that these early hymns may have been sung to well-known secular tunes. Whether or not this is true, the music was probably as accessible and engaging as the texts, qualifying it as an authentic form of "folk" music.

Popular Latin hymnody was born at a time when the assembly in the West was intimately engaged in the worship event and understood the language of the liturgy. The flourishing of Latin hymnody over the next few centuries, however, paralleled a slow but steady decline in the direct engagement of the assembly in the eucharistic action. Thus, even though some hymns were sung at Mass by worshipers, such hymns never made an impact on the structure of the Mass or became a constitutive part of it. The more Latin hymnody developed, the more peripheral it became to the Eucharist, just as the actions of the baptized were to become peripheral to the actions of the priests and other ministers. Official attempts to ban nonbiblical hymns from the liturgy [quotation 159] had little effect on their popularity. Many Latin hymns eventually were incorporated into the Liturgy of the Hours or employed in popular devotions.

Musicians and Their Music

Musical specialists, or what might be considered ancient parallels to today's "professional musicians," increased in number and kind during this era. The first evidence of a specially appointed singer who alone led the chants comes from the East in the latter part of the fourth century [quotation 154]. Also from this time we find the first clear distinctions between liturgical readers and singers, similarly from the East [quotation 160]. There is testimony regarding the existence of choirs in both East and West in these centuries, although there is little evidence to support the popular legend that Pope Gregory the Great (d. 604) founded a choir school (*schola cantorum*) at Rome. Gregory, however, did restrict the ministry of chanting psalms and other readings to subdeacons or others in minor orders [quotation 161].

This growing number of specialists exercised their musical leadership especially in the liturgies where the bishop presided. It is important to note, however, that there was worship in this era in which presbyters presided, which would have had a different style and tone than episcopal worship. Rome was an unusual city because of its size

1. S. Sisto
2. SS. Giovanni e Paolo
3. SS. Quattro Coronati
4. S. Clemente
5. SS. Marcello e Pieto
6. S. Pietro in Vincoli
7. S. Martino ai Monti
8. S. Praesseda
9. S. Eusebio
10. S. Pudenzia
11. S. Vitale
12. S. Sussana
13. Cyriaci
14. S. Marcello
15. S. Lorenzo in Lucina
16. S. Lorenzo in Damaso
17. S. Marco
18. S. Anastasia
19. SS. Nerei et Achillei
20. S. Balbina
21. S. Sabina
22. S. Prisca
23. S. Maria in Trastevere
24. S. Cecilia
25. S. Chrysogono

TITULAR CHURCHES OF ROME

0 ——— 500

84. Map of titular churches of Rome.
© 2001 Katherine W. Rinne.

and imperial import. While estimates vary, it is possible that at the height of the empire—often thought to have occurred under the emperor Trajan (d. 117 C.E.)—Rome could have had close to one million inhabitants. Because of the size and cultural diversity of the population, Rome was a city that saw the emergence of many house churches, which served the needs of specific neighborhoods and often particular cultural groups. The establishment of permanent places of worship in Rome resulted in a system of neighborhood churches or *tituli* (Latin, literally "titles")—twenty-five of them by the fifth century [illustration 84]—as well as a series of large basilicas like the shrine church of Old St. Peter's and the bishop's church of St. John Lateran (early fourth century). There is already evidence from the fifth century that the bishop of Rome regularly moved from church to church (Latin = *statio*, "station") to celebrate Eucharist. Special singers would have joined him in these "stational" liturgies. While the people would have joined in many responses and refrains, in Masses with the bishop the musical specialists would have played a more prominent role and the people's voice would have been more muted. On the other hand, when presbyters led worship in the *tituli* it is probable that the people's vocal role was more prominent.

As the Roman liturgy—especially that celebrated by the bishop—assumed prominence as a model for worship in Western Christianity, there was a parallel diminishment of the voice of the people in the midst of the eucharistic celebration. This was especially true when the Roman liturgy was exported to places where Latin was not the language of ordinary believers. As this was a gradual process, in some places the people maintained a more central and audible role. Eventually, however, just as people in virtually every geographic context were more and more distanced physically from the center of the liturgical action, they were also distanced musically. Notable in this era are the growing number of restrictions on women and girls in worship. Just as they were the first to be prohibited from entering the sanctuary, so were they similarly prohibited from assuming leadership roles in music. These prohibitions originated in the East [quotation 162] and spread to the West.

Quotation 162: *Women are ordered not to speak in church, not even softly, nor may they sing along or take part in the responses, but they should only be silent and pray to God.* (The Teaching of the Three Hundred Eighteen Fathers [ca. 375], in Quasten, *Music and Worship in Pagan and Christian Antiquity*, p. 81)

Families of Chant

It is difficult to know precisely how the music of this period sounded. During these centuries many liturgical centers in the East and West—including Milan, Constantinople, and Benevento—developed their own styles of chant. Some of these repertoires, like Beneventan chant of South Central Italy, are no longer the living repertoire of a worshiping people. They are even difficult to reconstruct, given the disappearance of manuscripts or the process by which some of these bodies of chant were overwhelmed by other musical trends of the era.

The body of Latin chant most widely recognized—at least in name—is Gregorian chant. The mythical origin of this chant is imbedded in one of the many legends about Pope Gregory the Great, who purportedly penned this body of chant for the Roman church at the end of the sixth century [illustration 85]. The true history of this repertoire, however, is much more complex and still being debated. Interwoven with the history of Gregorian chant is that of another repertoire called "Old Roman Chant."

James McKinnon offers an insightful summary of the relationship between these two bodies of chant in his book *The Advent Project* (pp. 375–403). He notes that in the second half of the twentieth century a number of scholars were convinced that there were two distinct chant "dialects" that existed together in the city of Rome. One common expression of this theory held that the original Roman chant is what is today called "Old Roman chant," which was sung in the basilicas of Rome from the time of Gregory the Great but was not written down until the end of the eleventh century. A second body of chant was what we call "Gregorian chant." This repertoire was not developed until the time of Pope Vitalian (d. 672) and was the work of the *schola cantorum*. This chant was thought to be much more closely associated with papal liturgy and was conceived as a style of music worthy of the papacy. It was also thought to be "a chant of universal musical appeal as opposed to the parochial urban chant" (McKinnon, p. 375). According to this theory Gregorian chant was conveyed north to the Carolingian Empire during the papacy of Pope Stephen II (d. 757) and was notated in that realm around the year 900.

McKinnon believes this "two-chant" theory is implausible for a variety of reasons. Instead, he proposes a variation on another theory, which held that there was only one original form of Roman chant that went through a series of changes both in the process of its transmission to the Carolingian Empire and during its long period of oral transmission in Rome. McKinnon's reconstruction relies on the previously noted distinction between lector chant and *schola* chant [quotation 153]. In his chronology, "lector chant" was the original style of chant in Rome. While such singing may have differed significantly from church to church, McKinnon suggests that the churches of Rome shared a goodly measure of what he calls "pan-Roman melodic substance." As noted above, McKinnon believes that members of the *schola cantorum* decided to produce a complete cycle of Mass propers for every date in the church year, beginning

85. Gregory the Great depicted with the Holy Spirit in the form of a dove on his right shoulder, "dictating" the chant melodies which he writes down.

with Advent. This work of *schola* chant commenced at the end of the seventh century and the project came to a close around 720.

According to McKinnon, "graduates" of the *schola* went on to serve as singers in the urban churches (*tituli*) and thereby transmitted this newly developed chant to the city. Members of the *schola* also carried it to other regions like the Carolingian Empire. McKinnon believes that there was a gap of less than a century between the *schola*'s creation of this new chant and its definitive recording by the Franks. In Rome, however, this *schola* chant did not get written down for almost four hundred years. This is how McKinnon distinguishes between "Gregorian" (written down within a century of its transmission) and "Old Roman" (written down almost four hundred years after its development) chant.

Whether McKinnon's reconstruction will stand the test of time is yet to be determined. In the interim, it is a cogent and useful framework for negotiating the relationship between "Gregorian" and "Old Roman" chant and, more important, for imagining how music for Christian liturgy might have developed in the West.

Summary

The developments in worship music that mark this period are both notable and dramatic. Prior to the fourth century it would be difficult to speak of distinctive styles of Christian music, just as it would be difficult to speak of distinctive styles of Christian architecture. Both musical and architectural styles were borrowed from the surrounding culture and slowly adapted for liturgical use. With the maturing of Christianity to the point that it was deemed a suitable public venue for the emperor of Rome, however, the degree of borrowing was met with an equal and increasing degree of adaptation and innovation. Thus, at the end of this era there is distinctive Christian architecture and music, though yet culturally tied to its local contexts, especially that of Rome.

It appears that Christian worship of this era yet occurs in what we have noted to be a "heightened auditory environment," so that all public liturgical discourse had a level of musicality to it. At the same time, there begin to develop distinctions between the more musical and the less musical, between readers and cantors, between what Jean Claire deemed lector chant and *schola* chant. These distinctions will eventually become separations, especially in the churches of the West. For now, however, Christian liturgy is yet what we might call "musical liturgy." The growing number of musical specialists are yet sharing the acoustic environment with other ministers and assembly. Movements like that which McKinnon christened the "Advent Project," however, point to the increasing prominence of trained musicians who will come to dominate the musical landscape of official and especially episcopal liturgy. As a balance to this change, people cultivated popular forms of religious music that were not essential to the celebration of the Eucharist, such as hymns. In all of these developments, the emphasis was still on vocal, unaccompanied music. Instruments were yet to find a place in Christian worship.

BOOKS

The Eucharist of the post-Constantinian period becomes markedly more complex than that of the previous era. This complexification is the result of a number of factors. One is the remarkable growth of Christianity. As noted in chapter 2, some calculate that Christians comprised at least 10 percent of an empire of fifty or sixty million people by the dawn of the fourth century. This percentage will dramatically increase during the reign of Constantine (d. 337) and the following centuries. This growth in the number of worshipers will require not only new and larger venues but levels of planning and organization unnecessary in a house church. Besides expanding numbers, the alliance between the emperor and the church influences the quality and style of worship. Imperial etiquette will contribute to the elaboration of vesture, personnel, and gesture appropriate to a basilical setting for what will become the empire's official religion. Finally, the many doctrinal controversies and theological developments of this era demanded new levels of precision in public prayer. Thus, the era of improvisation gave way to one of approved texts. These new dogmatic, imperial, and numeric pressures required new books to outline the increasingly complex rituals and to assist those who directed them. Besides new genres and quantities of books, the quality of manuscripts produced in this period also begins to change. Some liturgical books from this era are true works of art and are valued as much for their appearance as for their content.

Types of Liturgical Books

The categories that contemporary scholars use for cataloging medieval books did not exist in the Middle Ages. Consequently, ancient books assumed a variety of forms and were called by many different names. This section will employ standard identifications for these books and describe them in their purest forms, while acknowledging that manuscripts of the era did not always exist in such pure states.

Antiphonaries and Cantatories   In Rome, a series of books developed that contained the chant texts for the Mass propers, or those

Quotation 163: *St. Gregory ordered the English churches to celebrate the summer ember days as it is set forth in his antiphonary and missal during the week after Pentecost. Such observances were not only present in our antiphony, but I also saw them with my own eyes in the Roman books in the churches of Peter and Paul themselves. (Egret of York [d. 766], On the Catholic Foundation, 16, in Patrologia Latina 89:441)*

changing texts sung at the entrance, between the readings, during the procession of the gifts, and at communion. The Mass antiphonary (Latin = *antiphonarium* or *liber antiphonarius* or *antiphonale*, terms also employed for the "office antiphonary") contained the texts of the antiphons, that is, those sentences ordinarily drawn from the Bible that were sung between the verses of the psalms during the entrance and communion processions. There is some evidence to suggest that such collections circulated outside of Rome by the early eighth century [quotation 163].

The cantatory (Latin = *cantatorium*) contained the chants sung by a soloist between the readings (the gradual, tract, and alleluia verses), and sometimes it contained the verses for the offertory. The Frankish name for the cantatory was the gradual (Latin = *gradale* or *graduale*). Derived from the word *gradus* (Latin, "step"), or the step of the ambo where the cantor stood to sing the chants between the readings, the *graduale* will eventually become the name for the book that contains all of the chants for the Mass.

Even medievals were sometimes confused by the various names for these books, and the renowned scholar Amalarius of Metz (d. ca. 850) devotes some time in one of his works to explaining some of these differences in nomenclature [quotation 164].

Bibles, Gospel Books, Epistle Books, and Lectionaries   By this stage in the development of the liturgy, reading from the Old Testament, the epistles, and the gospels could be considered a traditional element in the celebration of the Eucharist. Originally it is probable that the readings were proclaimed from the codex of a complete Bible. This has led some to conclude that the practice of *lectio continua* (Latin, "continued reading"), or the sequential reading through books of the Bible at the eucharistic liturgy, was common. This does not seem to be the case, however [quotation 165], and instead it appears that from the earliest times readings were chosen to harmonize with the feast or day being celebrated. As to what sections were read from the Scriptures on ancient feasts like Easter, customs certainly developed early on, but there were no firm directives before the fifth or sixth centuries. Improvisation was still widespread, under the watchful eye of the local bishop. There was also significant diversity as to how many readings were proclaimed, and scattered evidence that what we would consider nonbiblical readings still appeared during the Eucharist in this period. Common practice in the West was the use of three readings, for example, one from the Old Testament, a second from an epistle, and the third from a gospel. There is some debate whether the Roman church used three readings, however, and evidence suggests that Rome only used two: an epistle and gospel.

Ebdomada III die dominica ad scum Laurentium. Scd. Luc. cap. CXXVI. Erat Iesus eiciens daemonium usque Beati qui audiunt verbum Dei et custodiunt illud.

The third week [of Lent] on Sunday at St. Lawrence [outside the walls]. According to Luke chapter 126 [according to the division by Eusebius]. "Jesus was casting out a demon" [Luke 11:14] until "Blessed are those who hear the word of God and keep it" [Luke 11:28].

86. A capitular.

Constantine reportedly commissioned fifty manuscripts of the Bible for liturgical use [quotation 166]. Originally liturgical Bibles were marked with signs or notes in the margins of each page, indicating where a reading began and sometimes where it ended. This was a relatively effective tool for specifying readings in Bibles of this era, which were not divided into chapters and verses—something that does not happen until the late Middle Ages.

Besides these marginal indicators, a second tool for designating readings was a separate list called a capitular (Latin = *capitulum*, "a chapter"), which often included the date, the liturgical feast, the place where the worship was to take place, the biblical book from which the reading(s) was drawn, and the beginning or *incipit* (Latin, "it begins") and ending or *explicit* (Latin, "it ends") for each reading [illustration 86].

Eric Palazzo provides a helpful guide in distinguishing between three types of these lists or capitulars. One capitular enumerates the epistles to be read, which will eventually give rise to the book of epistles called an epistolary (Latin = *epistula*, "letter"). A second type of capitular prescribes the gospel readings, which will give rise to the evangeliary (Latin = *evangelium*, "good news"). A third genre of capitular combines the two previous types and will be foundational for the origin of the Mass lectionary (Latin = *lectio*, a "reading"). Capitular lists for epistles and gospels are extant from the sixth century and probably existed in the fifth.

Besides marginal notes and independent lists, a third method for supplying readings for eucharistic liturgy was the crafting of a specific book that contained only one type of reading. Such a book, for example, would contain the complete texts of the four gospels and would be accompanied by marginal notations or a gospel capitular to indicate which part of the gospel was to be read on what day. This would not, however, be a true evangeliary (with the gospel texts arranged according to how they were to be proclaimed liturgically) but, instead, what is more properly called a Book of the Gospels. Examples of such books exist already in the fifth century [illustration 87].

When all of the readings for a liturgical day are collected together in the same book—combining evangeliaries and epistolaries—the result is a "Mass lectionary" (there were also lectionaries for the Divine Office). The first documentary evidence of a Mass lectionary comes from the end of the fifth century [quotation 167] and manuscripts survive from the sixth century. While lectionaries are clearly later developments than marginal notes or lists, they did not automatically supersede these other two means for indicating Mass readings, especially because producing lectionaries would have been considerably more labor intensive and expensive. All methods of

87. Panel of a binding for a copy of the gospels from the early fifth century.

Quotation 164: *The volume that we call an Antiphonary, the Romans call by three names: that which we call Gradale they call Cantatorium which, according to their ancient custom is still bound in a single volume in some of their churches. That which remains they divide with two names: the part which contains the responsories is called the Responsoriale, and the part which contains antiphons they call the Antiphonarius.* (Amalarius of Metz [d. 850/1], *Liber de Ordine Antiphonarii, Prologus* 17, in *Amalarii episcopi Opera*)

Quotation 165: *No testimony allows us to affirm that even in the most ancient time lectio continua was the practice at Mass.* (Martimort, *Les Lectures liturgiques et leurs livres*, p. 19)

Quotation 166: *It seems appropriate to request from your excellency that you make 50 codices of the sacred scriptures—which you know are very necessary for the church—elegantly written on magnificent parchments by experts thoroughly versed in the ancient arts.* (Letter of Constantine [d. 337] to Eusebius [d. ca. 340], cited in Eusebius's *Life of Constantine*, 36, in *The History of the Church*) indicating readings for the eucharistic liturgy were in use to varying degrees during much of this period.

Calendars and Maryrologies   Commemorating the dead has always been an essential element of Christian worship, especially the Eucharist. There is evidence that, from the earliest years, the followers of Jesus kept an annual feast according to the Jewish calendar commemorating his death. Christian calendars eventually developed as aids for remembering and venerating the dead, especially martyrs who where honored as images of the crucified. Polycarp of Smyrna was one of the first to be widely venerated after his martyrdom on February 23, in the year 55. Lists noting the dates and places of the deaths of martyrs began to develop after this time. One of the earliest lists, the *depositio martyrum* (Latin, "burial [list] of martyrs") [illustration 88], dates from 354. As these early liturgical calendars expanded, they became true martyrologies, which included not only the anniversary day of the martyr's death and the place of martyrdom or burial but also a short "history" (Latin = *historia*) summarizing the martyr's life, virtues, and manner of death. Eventually they listed not only martyrs but many other categories of saints.

One of the earliest martyrologies was that attributed to Jerome (d. 420), known as the Hieronymian (Latin = *Hieronymus*, "Jerome") martyrology. Composed in fifth century Italy, the work contains few biographical details concerning the saints it lists, and the attribution to Jerome is apocryphal. The first "historical" martyrology, containing more ample reporting on its saints, can be attributed to the English scholar Bede (d. 735).

While calendars will continue to be important for the celebration of Eucharist, designating which feast is to be celebrated, martyrologies will eventually play more of a role in the Liturgy of the Hours.

Libelli Missarum and Sacramentaries   As worship became more complicated and formalized, the practice of improvising public prayer decreased, and books containing previously composed prayers for presiders appeared. Another influence here was the rapid doctrinal development in Christianity during this period and the growing concern about right theology. Major church councils in the fourth and fifth centuries were defining central Christological and other doctrines. Since public prayers are by their very nature theological, it was and is essential that the theology in those prayers be orthodox. While writing a prayer down did not assure its orthodoxy, written prayers could be reviewed and approved by bishops, councils, or other learned teachers [quotation 168].

The first liturgical books were not actually books but more like small, handwritten pamphlets. Initially these *libelli missarum* (Latin,

| December 25 | VIII Kal. Ianu. | Natus Christus in Bethleem Iudeae. |

—————————————— Mense Ianuario ——————————————

| January 20 | XIII Kal. Feb. | Fabiani in Calisti et Sebastiani in Catacumbas. |
| January 21 | XII Kal. Feb. | Agnetis in Nomentana. |

—————————————— Mense Februario ——————————————

| February 22 | VIII Kal. Mart. | Natale Petri de catedra. |

—————————————— Mense Martio ——————————————

| March 7 | Non. Mart. | Perpetuae et Felicitatis, Africae. |

—————————————— Mense Maio ——————————————

| May 19 | XIIII Kal. Iun. | Partheni et Caloceri in Calisti, Diocletiano VIIII et Maximiano VIII cons. [304]. |

—————————————— Mense Iunio ——————————————

| June 29 | III Kal Iul. | Petri in Catacumbas et Pauli Ostense, Tusco et Basso cons. [258]. |

—————————————— Mense Iulio ——————————————

| July 10 | VI Id. | Felicis et Filippi in Priscillae; et in Iordanorum Martialis, Vitalis, Alexandri; et in Maximi, Silani; hunc Silanum martyrem Novati furati sunt; et in Praetextati, Ianuari. |
| July 30 | III Kal Aug. | Abdos et Sennes in Pontiani, quod est ad Ursum piliatum. |

—————————————— Mense Augusto ——————————————

August 6	VIII Id. Aug.	Xysti in Calisti, et in Praetextati, Agapiti et Felicissimi.
August 8	VI Id. Aug.	Secundi, Carpophori, Victorini et Severiani in Albano; et Ostense VII ballistaria, Cyriaci, Largi, Crescentiani, Memmiae, Iulianae et Smaragdi.
August 9	III Id. Aug.	Laurenti in Tiburtina.
August 13	Id. Aug.	Ypoliti in Tiburtina et Pontiani in Calisti.
August 22	XI Kal. Sept.	Timotei, Ostense.
August 28	V Kal. Sept.	Hermetis in Bassillae, Salaria vetere.

—————————————— Mense Septembre ——————————————

September 5	Non. Sept.	Aconti in Porto, et Nonni et Herculani et Taurini.
September 9	V Id. Sept.	Gorgoni in Labicana.
September 11	III Id. Sept.	Proti et Iacinti in Bassillae.
September 14	XVIII Kal. Octob.	Cypriani Africae, Romae celebratur in Calisti.
September 22	X Kal. Octob.	Bassillae, Salaria vetere, Diocletiano XIIII et Maximiano VIII cons. [304].

—————————————— Mense Octobre ——————————————

| October 14 | prid. Id. Octob. | Calisti in Via Aurelia, miliario III. |

—————————————— Mense Novembre ——————————————

| November 9 | V Id. Nov. | Clementis, Semproniani, Claudi, Nicostrati in comitatum. |
| November 29 | III Kal. Dec. | Saturnini in Trasonis. |

88. *Depositio Martyrum.* (Denis-Boulet, pp. 53–54)

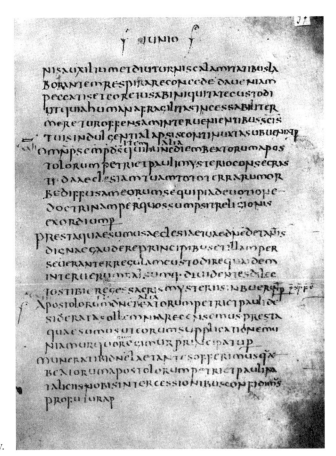

89. A page from the Verona Sacramentary.

"little books of Masses") contained the orations and the preface for one or more Masses for a particular church. Sometimes several *libelli* were gathered together in a collection of often unrelated materials. Collections of these booklets existed in certain parts of Christianity by the end of the fourth century. Although individual *libelli* from this era do not survive, a collection of them from the end of the sixth century does. The collection is sometimes called the *Leonine Sacramentary*, though in actuality it is neither a sacramentary nor a work of Leo the Great (d. 461). Rather, it is a private collection of formularies and prayers, adapting materials from the papal liturgies for use by presbyters in the Roman *tituli*, falsely ascribed to Leo in the 1735 edition of the work by Giovanni Bianchini. It is now more properly considered *The Verona Collection of Libelli Missarum*, named after the city that houses the only known manuscript of the text [illustration 89].

A sacramentary is a book that contains texts that a presider needs at Eucharist or in another liturgical rite. The first authentic sacramentary that survives is the *Old Gelasian Sacramentary*, a title based on an unprovable hypothesis that the work was attributable to Pope

Gelasius (d. 496). This work was originally compiled in Rome between 628 and 715. There were two types of sacramentaries employed in Rome during this period: one for papal liturgies and another for worship presided over by presbyters in the *tituli*. The *Old Gelasian* appears to have originated as the latter, though papal elements are interwoven through the book. This mixing can be explained, in part, by the fact that the only version of this sacramentary in our possession is a manuscript copied in a monastery near Paris around 750, where the scribe introduced materials from a papal sacramentary (or "Gregorian" sacramentary) into this presbyteral (or "Gelasian") sacramentary.

Ordos   Increasingly complex Christian worship required written directions for its smooth enactment. These directions were ordinarily not included in the books of prayers or music but collected in a separate volume known as an *ordo* (Latin, "order" or "arrangement"). In the previous chapter we noted that church orders already supplied some instructions about how worship was to proceed. Such church orders, however, were conceived for a church whose worship was

---

A-2	APRIL	103

20 ✠ FIFTH SUNDAY OF EASTER
Wh HOURS*   **Pss I** Seasonal prop
    MASS   Prop Gl Cr Easter Pf I-V
    RDGS   52: Acts 6:1-7 Ps 33:1-2,4-5,18-19
                1 Pt 2:4-9 Jn 14:1-12
We are "a chosen race, a royal priesthood" (2) called to place our faith (3) and trust (Ps) in the Spirit of Jesus who guides the community of faith (1).

21 Monday: Easter Weekday [5]; *Anselm, bishop, doctor*
m HOURS   **Pss I** Seasonal wkdy *Sanctoral*
Wh   *Common of pastors or of doctors*
Wh MASS   Prop Easter Pf I-V
V²R² RDGS   285: Acts 14:5-18 Ps 115:1-4,15-16
                Jn 14:21-26
Barnabas and Paul attempt to reveal (2) to the Gentiles the true nature of the living God (1,Ps).

Anselm, † 1109; abbot of Bec in Normandy; later (1093) archbishop of Canterbury; twice exiled for defending the rights of the Church; theologian and philosopher: *fides quaerens intellectum*; authored *Proslogion, Cur Deus Homo*, and *The Procession of the Holy Spirit*; known as the "Father of Scholasticism."

22 Tuesday: Easter Weekday [5]
Wh HOURS   **Pss I** Seasonal wkdy
V²R² MASS   Prop Easter Pf I-V
     RDGS   286: Acts 14:19-28 Ps 145:10-13b,21
                Jn 14:27-31a
Paul and Barnabas recount their blessings (Ps) to the church in Antioch (1), and the peace they experienced in the Lord's service (2).

90. A page from a contemporary ordo.

more domestic and improvisatory. With the growing complexity of worship, its official status in the empire, and concerns about orthodoxy and right order, these early forerunners proved inadequate and were superseded by the ordo. Ordos were particularly important when Roman worship was exported to Christians outside of Rome, who were unfamiliar with some of the patterns of the Roman liturgy.

Like *libelli missarum*, ordos originally were small booklets or sometimes even a single page of instruction. Eventually, many of these were gathered into collections. The earliest known collection is the "Roman Ordos" (Latin = *Ordines Romani*) from the seventh century [quotation 169]. Like the Gelasian sacramentary, Roman Ordos reflect Roman usage, though the collection was compiled outside of Rome and thus containing many non-Roman elements.

Ordos were auxiliary liturgical books, used in preparation for worship but ordinarily not employed during the liturgy itself. Eventually these and other books would merge with sacramentaries to produce the mixture of prayers and rubrics typical of today's missals. Ordos do exist today [illustration 90] and are produced by many dioceses, religious orders, and even national churches. The contemporary ordo has more in common with ancient calendars, however, than with collections like the Roman Ordos.

Reverence for the Book

Gestures of respect were common for the first liturgical book, the Bible, which people guarded with their lives during times of persecution. During the post-Constantinian era, signs of reverence for liturgical books increased. Architecturally this meant providing not only special places for proclaiming the word, such as the ambo [illustration 80], but also special cabinets (Latin = *armaria*) for storing the Scriptures when they were not in use [illustration 91]. Only specially designated people were allowed to read and care for ritual books. Lectors, who from ancient times were guardians of the Scriptures, eventually were replaced by higher ranking clergy, with deacons responsible for proclaiming the gospel [quotation 161] and subdeacons for reading the epistle. A description of a seventh-century papal Mass notes that after the proclamation of the gospel, the gospel book was kissed by all the clergy in the sanctuary [quotation 169]. Moreover, when the book was carried by anyone of lesser rank than a deacon, that person's hands were covered.

91. Example of a cabinet (*armarium*) with the four gospels. These cabinets stood in the sacristy adjoining the apse of the basilica. Based on a detail from a mosaic in the so-called mausoleum of Galla Placidia, Ravenna, ca. 450 C.E.

The ritual books came to be great works of art. Although this was especially true for the Scriptures, it became increasingly true for other books as well. Vellum (calfskin) and parchment (lambskin) became preferred materials. These were better than papyrus for writing and also for illustration or illumination. The earliest illuminated

92. Four bishops, each carrying a rich jeweled gospel codex, from the apse of Saint Apollinare in Classe, Ravenna, sixth century.

books of the gospels date from the sixth century. On rare occasions, the parchment was dyed purple, and gold or silver was used as ink. Many book coverings were also magnificent works of art [illustration 87]. Besides those few books that have survived from this time, various mosaics from the period attest to the priceless codices owned by the church [illustration 92]. During this period there even began the custom of giving liturgical books as gifts.

Standardization of Content and Language

The post-Constantinian period was a time of transition from improvised prayer to more standardized liturgical texts. Although the content of the Bible was relatively fixed by about 200 C.E., liturgical prayers were still evolving. The first written example of a eucharistic prayer did not appear until the third century. Bishops, who were the only presiders at fourth-century Eucharist, retained their right to improvise prayer. Because of the growing complexity of worship as well as the many theological controversies of the time, a new concern for orthodoxy in public prayer developed. A synod in Hippo, attended by Augustine, required that prayers at the altar should be directed to the Father and that prayers borrowed from other places could not be used until they had first been examined [quotation 170]. We have previously seen that Augustine himself was concerned about the unorthodox nature of some prayers. In the early fifth century one North African council tried to impose a collection of prayers that had been prepared with hierarchical approval [quotation 171].

Quotation 170: *When one serves at the altar, prayer is always directed to the Father. Whoever borrows prayers for himself from another place must not use them unless he first submits them to the more learned brothers [of his own church].* (Council of Hippo [393], canon 21, in Mansi, *Sacrorum Conciliorum*)

Quotation 171: *It is decided that the prayers, orations, Masses, prefaces, commendations and imposition of hands which were examined in council may be celebrated by all. No others whatsoever may be used in church—neither those strongly against the faith, nor though composed by the ignorant, nor those written by the less zealous. Exceptions to this rule are those employed by the more skilled or those sanctioned in synod.* (Council of Carthage [407], canon 10, in Mansi, *Sacrorum Conciliorum*)

Quotation 172: *Bread should not be placed on the altar to be consecrated if it is not complete, proper and especially made.* (Council of Toledo [693], canon 6, in Galavaris, *Bread and the Liturgy*, p. 45)

Quotation 173: *Perhaps you say: "My bread is ordinary bread." In fact before the sacramental words are spoken this bread is simply bread. But when the consecration occurs it changes from bread to the body of Christ.* (Ambrose, *Des Sacrements* [About the Sacraments], 4.14)

Although examples of such legislation are few in this period, they bear witness to a growing concern for controlling the content of liturgical books. This move toward standardization eventually spread throughout the church.

Another type of standardization that developed during this period is that toward Latin as the liturgical language for the Western churches. As noted at the end of chapter 2, Christianity was born in cultural diversity, and Eucharist was celebrated in whatever language was spoken by the local community. In Rome, Greek was the dominant language both in the city and for the growing Christian population. As Cyril Vogel notes, it was the African rather than the Roman church that first gravitated toward Latin, and it was a cadre of North African theologians like Tertullian (d. 225) and Augustine who created both the juridical and liturgical vocabulary for the Latin Church of the West. The Latinization of the Roman church was a gradual process, and Greek coexisted with Latin as a liturgical language for centuries. By the end of this period, however, the tide had clearly shifted, and the Western Church was on a path that would make Latin the exclusive language for worship in the Roman Rite until the twentieth century.

93. One of the oldest extant examples of a stamp for eucharistic bread, measuring about 6¼ inches in diameter, from Djebeniana (on the coast of present-day Tunisia). It shows a stag among the trees with the inscription, "Ego sum panis vivus qui de celo descendi" (Latin: "I am the living bread come down from heaven"). Dating from the sixth century. (After Righetti 3:483–84)

94. Detail of the "Sacrifices of Abel and Melchizedek" showing bread shaped as a crown or *corona*.

Summary

Generally speaking, at the beginning of this period the only liturgical book was the Bible. After the conversion of Constantine, a whole library of liturgical books emerged. These confirm both the growing complexity of worship and an increased concern about the theological content of public prayer at a time when the church was shaping basic tenets of the faith. New attention to the content and etiquette of ritual meant new restrictions concerning both the books and the people who used them. Care for a book's content was beginning to be matched by concern for the appearance of books, which increasingly became magnificent works of art. The growing reverence for liturgical books—initially dictated by their content, later by their artistic value as well—prepared the way for a later time when objects such as liturgical books would be treated with the same reverence that was originally reserved for the baptized.

VESSELS

The Eucharist was always central to the life of the Christian community, but to a certain extent this became even more true after Constantine. Initially celebrated only on Sunday, Eucharist soon came to be celebrated on the other days of the week. Communal worship such as morning and evening prayer diminished in importance for ordinary people and increasingly became the domain of the numerous monastic communities that developed during this time. Although many devotional practices evolved, none became

Quotation 174: *The priest said, "It is not customary for me to appear ungrateful to the man who was so helpful to me. It is necessary for me to bring him a gift. Thus he brought with him two crowns of bread [Latin = coronas] as an offering. . . . The man sighed with distress and said, "why do you give this to me, Father? This bread is holy and I am not able to eat it."* (Gregory the Great [Grégoire le Grand], *Dialogues,* 4.55)

Quotation 175: *Nothing costly for the one who carries the body of the Lord in a wicker basket.* (Jerome [d. 420], *Epistle to Rusticus,* 20, in *Patrologia Latina* 22:1086)

Quotation 176: *[After the gospel] The regional subdeacon receives the offerings from the pontiff and presents them to the next subdeacon, who places them in the linen bag, which two acolytes hold. . . . [Before communion] the subdeacons, with the acolytes who are carrying the sacks, come to the right and the left of the altar while the acolytes extend their arms with the sacks. The subdeacons step forward so that they may prepare the open sacks for the archdeacon to put in the offerings, first in the right one and then in the left one.* (Roman Ordo I.71, 101, in Andrieu, *Les Ordines Romani*)

more important than the Eucharist, which dominated Christian piety. In the wake of this expanding eucharistic focus, a variety of vessels developed, especially for the bread.

Bread and Its Vessels

The tradition of employing ordinary leavened bread for the Eucharist continued during this period. One documentary piece of evidence for this is the Council of Toledo (693), which forbids using bread for Eucharist that is not made for this purpose [quotation 172]. It is a well-accepted principle that if a church law forbids something, whatever being prohibited is actually occurring. Thus, according to George Galavaris, this canon is indicating that until the end of the seventh century, Christians were still using ordinary loaves of bread for Eucharist in some parts of the empire. Ambrose appears to be aware of this practice in late fourth century Milan, for he had to explain to the newly baptized that although Eucharist looked like ordinary bread, it really was the Body of Christ [quotation 173].

Various texts and artistic renderings as well as many surviving bread stamps from the period show that eucharistic bread took various forms at this time. Sometimes the bread was a flat disk [illustration 93]. There is also literary evidence that a loaf of bread was sometimes braided into a circle called a crown [quotation 174]. This type of bread is depicted in a sixth-century mosaic in the church of San Vitale in Ravenna, with the central hole of the crown filled in with a cross at the center of each disk [illustration 94]. Often the bread was a small round loaf marked with a cross. This was a common form of Roman bread, with two crossed lines that divided the bread into four parts (Latin = *panis quadratus*). Galavaris believes that before Constantine's Edict of Milan this bread offered Christians the advantage of having what they could interpret as "the sign of the cross" on their bread without arousing suspicion from the authorities because it was sold publicly in the markets. Even after Christianity became legal, however, there is evidence that Christians continued to use this form of bread, conveniently scored for breaking, for Eucharist [illustration 95].

Baskets   Given the varying shapes and sometimes substantial size of the bread of the day, baskets continued to be useful containers for eucharistic bread [illustration 96]. Jerome noted the appropriateness of baskets for this purpose [quotation 175]. Besides baskets, other common containers crafted from ordinary materials were used to hold the eucharistic bread. A description of the papal Mass at Rome in the seventh century, for example, notes the ancient custom of people

95. Detail of loaves from the side of a sarcophagus (350–80 C.E.) in Arles, in a presentation of loaves and fishes prefiguring the Eucharist.

bringing bread and wine from home to be used in the Eucharist, with the surplus distributed to the poor. The bread collected from the faithful was put into linen sacks; later in the ceremony the consecrated bread was carried in linen sacks back to the people for communion [quotation 176].

Patens   We have already seen that while ordinary bread, bought off the street, was used for the Eucharist, there is also a growing concern to have specially made bread for the eucharistic liturgy [quotation 172]. Similarly, although common household vessels had been employed in Christian liturgy from the beginning, during this era special flat dishes or patens (Latin = *patena*, "pan") were produced for holding the eucharistic bread. With increasing frequency, these were made of precious metals. Patens could be relatively large vessels used to hold the small loaves, crowns, or disks of leavened bread needed to accommodate worshipers who filled the basilicas of the era [back cover illustration, Justinian (d. 565) carrying a large gold paten]. According to a sixth-century source, Constantine donated many

96. Christ depicted with seven jars of wine and seven baskets of bread. Panel from the door of Santa Sabina, Rome, 422–30.

97. Sixth-century paten of silver gilt from Riha in Syria, 9½ inches in diameter.

98. The so-called Berlin pyx from the fourth century, made of ivory and measuring approximately 4¾ inches in height and 5⅛ inches in diameter. (After Righetti, 1:451)

gold and silver patens to the Lateran Basilica in Rome, each weighing at least thirty pounds [quotation 177]. Extant patens from the sixth century measure almost twenty-four inches in diameter. A description of the papal Mass at Rome at the end of the seventh century noted that one paten was carried by two acolytes, indicating its substantial size. Even the smaller examples from this period suggest that ordinary leavened bread was still being used [illustration 97].

Pyxes Besides vessels for bread during the Eucharist, vessels for holding the consecrated bread outside of Mass continued to develop. A variety of names were employed: *arca* (Latin, "box"), chrismal (from Greek, *chrisma*, "unction"), and pyx (Greek, "box") were some of the most common. Because the term "pyx" is the most familiar of these, it will be used here. The pyx was usually a small, cylindrical vessel, shaped so that it could hold a small round loaf or quadrant of bread [illustration 98]. Examples exist from the fourth century. These small, portable cases were sometimes employed for carrying communion to the sick [quotation 178]. Literary evidence also exists that people carried the Eucharist with them in small cases or sacks around their necks as talismans against evil, for giving themselves communion, and for offering viaticum to the dying. Irish writings about the saints from this era are filled with stories of monks who carry the Eucharist with them in this manner [quotation 179].

Tabernacles Besides portable containers, there is limited evidence in this period indicating that more permanent containers also were used for the consecrated bread. Although these were known by a variety of names, here they will be gathered under the general heading of "tabernacle" (Latin = *tabernaculum*, "tent"). The fourth-century Syrian church order *Apostolic Constitutions* and the great doctor of the church Jerome both speak about a special place where the Eucharist is kept, called a *pastophorion* (Greek = *pastos*, "bridal chamber") [quotation 180]. These *pastophoria* could have been niches made in side walls of the church or in the rear of the apse near the altar. Francis Schaefer thinks that there is evidence for such eucharistic niches in a poem of Bishop Paulinus of Nola (d. 431) describing the basilica of St. Felix of Nola, in which he notes that in the apse there were two small chambers in one of which was kept the "sacred food."

Besides *pastophoria* or niches, Basil (d. 379) purportedly attests to another form for reserving the Eucharist. There is apocryphal evidence that he commissioned a vessel, shaped like a dove, that was used for eucharistic reservation [quotation 181]. Although the text could be from as late as the eighth century, it appears as one of the

Quotation 177: *In his time the emperor Constantine built these churches and adorned them: the Constantinian basilica [St. John Lateran] . . . 7 gold patens each weighing 30 lb; 16 silver patens each weighing 30 lbs; 7 scyphi of finest gold each weighing 10 lbs; a special scyphus of hard coral, adorned on all sides with prase and jacinth jewels, inlaid with gold, weighing in all its parts 20 lb 3 oz; 20 silver scyphi each weighing 15 lb; 2 amae of finest gold each weighing 50 lb, capacity 3 medimni each; 20 silver amae each weighing 10 lb, capacity 1 midimnus each; 40 smaller chalices of finest gold each weighing 1 lb; 50 smaller service chalices each weighing 2 lb.* (Book of Pontiffs [ca. 540], 34.9)

Quotation 178: *Nothing may be placed upon the altar except the capsa with the remnants of the sancta . . . or the pyx with the Body of the Lord for viaticum for the sick.* (Leo IV [d. 855], On Pastoral Care)

earliest testimonies of the use of "eucharistic doves," which becomes both common and widespread throughout Eastern and Western Christianity [illustration 99].

John Chrysostom (d. 407), in his baptismal instruction, speaks of a wooden chest holding the Eucharist [quotation 182]. In his hymn to Lawrence the deacon, Prudentius (d. after 405) speaks of the deacon having keys to what some have construed to be a container for the Eucharist [quotation 183].

During this period the Eucharist was also reserved in receptacles shaped like small towers (Latin = *turris*, "tower"; or *turricula*, "little tower"). References to such vessels ordinarily appear in Western rather than Eastern sources. The sixth-century *Book of the Popes*, for example, lists such a tower among the gifts that Constantine bestowed upon Old St. Peter's Basilica [quotation 184]. Given the late dating of this source, it is probable that these eucharistic towers were more a vessel of the sixth century than of the fourth. Schaefer believes that while these eucharistic towers were of varying sizes, at least in Gaul, they were small enough to be kept in the sacristy and carried to the altar when Eucharist was celebrated. Such *turricula* were probably best understood as pyxes with a conical rather than a flat lid. Other times it appears that larger eucharistic towers, such as the previously mentioned gift of Constantine that weighed thirty pounds, were more stationary. Sometimes such vessels were used in combinations, for example, a eucharistic dove placed inside a tower, or a pyx placed in a special container in or near the sacristy. Such a combination of containers is noted in the seventh-century papal Mass: as the pope enters he is presented with a container (Latin = *capsa*, "box") from which he selects some reserved Eucharist for use in the current liturgy, while the rest was returned in the *capsa* to the *conditorium* (Latin, "repository"). This could have been something like an *armarium* [illustration 91] used for storing books.

Wine and Its Vessels

While we have previously noted some exceptions, the dominant tradition for eucharistic use throughout early Christianity was grape wine—a common commodity throughout the Mediterranean countries—diluted with water. Red wine seems to have been preferred, at least in part because it symbolized blood. Like bread, wine for the Eucharist was brought by the people from their homes.

Chalices   The large number of people that filled the Christian basilicas after the conversion of Constantine dictated that large vessels were required for communion; sometimes multiple vessels were

99. Twelfth-century eucharistic dove from Limoges, made of gold-plated copper and enamel.

Quotation 179: *"One day, when St. Comgall was working alone outside in the fields, he put his chrismal on his cloak. That day, a band of foreign robbers fell upon the village with the intent of seizing everything there—both men and beasts. When the foreigners came upon St. Comgall working outside, and when they saw the chrismal on his cloak, they assumed that the chrismal was Comgall's god. And because they feared his god, the robbers dared not touch him." (Life of St. Comgall [d. ca. 602], in Mitchell, Cult and Controversy, pp. 272–73)*

Quotation 180: *The sacred place where the body of Christ is kept, who is the true bridegroom of the church and of our soul, is called the thalamus or pastophorion. (Jerome [d. 420], Commentary on Ezechiel, n. 40, in Schaefer, "The Tabernacle")*

Quotation 181: *Basil, having called upon a goldsmith, asked him to make a dove of pure gold in which he placed a portion of the body of Christ. He suspended it over the holy table as a figure of the sacred dove that appeared at the Jordan over the Lord during his baptism. (Apocryphal Life of St. Basil, no. 32, attributed to Amphilochius of Iconium [d. after 394], in Acta Santorum)*

Quotation 182: *I would have shown you the holy of holies and all therein, a vessel holding not manna but the body of the Master, the bread of heaven. I would have shown you not a wooden chest holding the stone tablets of the law but one holding the blameless and holy flesh of the lawgiver.*
(John Chrysostom [d. 407], "Second Baptismal Instruction" 10.2)

Quotation 183:
*He guarded well the sacred rites
And kept in trust with faithful keys
The precious treasure of the Church,
Dispensing riches vowed to God.*

(Prudentius [d. after 405], *Hymn in Honor of the Passion of the Blessed Martyr Lawrence,* in *The Poems of Prudentius*)

employed. Since earliest times, the symbolism of one bread and one cup [quotation 123] underscored the ideal that a single cup sufficiently large to hold wine for the whole community would be used. Sometimes these chalices (Latin = *calix,* "cup") were large, vase-shaped vessels attached to a round base, often with handles attached to the side to aid in drinking [illustration 94; see vessel on altar]. Examples of much smaller chalices from this period exist as well [illustration 100]. The material for these vessels—large or small—was more often a precious metal than glass, wood, or bone. Examples in amber, onyx, and ivory also survive from this time.

The size of a chalice generally indicated the size of the community that used it, because everyone who stayed for the celebration of the Eucharist—catechumens and penitents would have been dis-

100. Late fifth- or sixth-century chalice from Syria, measuring 7½ inches in height and 6 inches in diameter.

missed after the liturgy of the word—would ordinarily have drunk from the chalice. Evidence from the papal Masses in Rome at the end of the seventh century shows that chalices of different sizes were used at the same Mass: a large chalice (Latin, *calix maior*) used for collecting the offerings of wine from the people, and a more sizable container (Latin, *sciffus*) into which the large chalice was emptied so more gifts of wine could be collected [quotation 185]. Later on in the papal Mass chalices would be refilled from the scyphus for the communion of the people. Though unique to the church of Rome, this distinction in vessels is further testimony that communion under both forms was presumed for the assembly during this period and vessels were crafted to meet that need.

Cruets   The evidence from this period indicates that increasingly special vessels were employed for carrying the wine and water before they were poured into the chalice at Eucharist. Undoubtedly, people originally brought their gifts of wine to the church in ordinary containers of the day. The inventory of the church of Cirta, dating from the early fourth century, however, noted that six silver jars (Latin = *urceolum*, [quotation 95]) had been confiscated during persecution. This may be the first literary evidence of a special vessel for wine before it was poured into a chalice for consecration. With the elaboration of the offertory and its processions in the post-Constantinian church, evidence for these special vessels increases. In a late fifth-century document from Gaul, *urceola* are mentioned as part of the "ordination rite" of an acolyte [quotation 186]. In the papal Mass of the seventh century, the wealthy, at least, seem to have brought their gifts of wine in a special vessel (Latin = *ama* or *amula*, "small vessel," [quotation 185]). Such vessels were seldom large [illustration 101], but when multiplied by the number of the laity bringing a gift of wine to church, would have produced a significant amount of wine. Since this would have been too much to consume, even at a papal liturgy, the surplus would have been distributed to the poor.

Summary

Significant changes occurred in the number, size, and quality of vessels for the bread and wine after the ascendancy of Constantine. What is most striking is the transition from household utensils to liturgical vessels. The ordinary wicker, pottery, wood, and glass vessels that had long been used to hold the bread and wine before and after their consecration became less and less common. Gold and silver became the preferred materials, the hand of the artisan was more evident, and the sacredness of the vessel itself was emphasized.

101. Example of an early Christian *amula*. (After Kraus, 1:517)

Quotation 184: *[Constantine] also provided . . . a gold paten with a tower [turris] of finest gold and a dove adorned with prase and jacinth jewels and with pearls, 215 in number, weighing 30 lbs.* (Book of Pontiffs [ca. 540], 34.18)

Quotation 185: *The pope goes down to the senatorium and . . . accepts the offering of the noblemen in order of their rank. After him the archdeacon accepts the flasks of wine [amulas] and pours them into the larger chalice [calice maiore] held for him by the regional subdeacon, whom the acolyte follows with the scyphus held outside the vestment in which the full chalice is emptied.* (Roman Ordo I [ca. 700], 69–70)

Thus the *Book of the Popes* (18.2) will describe Urban I (d. 230?) as making all "sacred vessels" (Latin = *ministeria sacrata*) of silver. While unlikely language for the third century, such language seems entirely appropriate for the sixth century when the earliest portions of this book were compiled. Thus, as seen previously with liturgical architecture, the vessels for worship begin to acquire their own sacrality, particularly by association with the eucharistic species.

EUCHARISTIC THEOLOGY

Attempting to summarize the range of thinking about the Eucharist in this period of the church's history is daunting. Gary Macy implicitly seems to acknowledge this when he titles his chapter on the eucharistic theology of this era "The Origins of Diversity." Theological diversity abounds in this era of astounding growth in Christianity's population, structures, and doctrine. There is also much continuity with what earlier Christians had understood about the Eucharist. This continuity, however, is not simply a static continuance of ideas but a pastoral and theological evolution that would prepare the way for even more startling changes in future periods.

Continuity is detectable in some of the central themes that preachers and writers draw upon as they seek to draw believers deeper into this mystery. For example, the image of sacrifice flowers in this era, and there continues to be a strong connection between considering the Eucharist in sacrificial terms and considering Christian living as a living sacrifice [quotation 187]. According to Robert Daly, however, there is a notable shift in the balance of Christian thinking about sacrifice in this period. In the previous era Tertullian would seem to be breaking ground when he spoke of the eucharistic prayer and by extension the whole of the eucharistic celebration as the *sacrificiorum orationibus* (Latin = "sacrificial prayers"). Increasingly in this period, however, it is the eucharistic celebration more than Christian living that is cast in sacrificial terms. Even a writer like Augustine will reveal a growing stress on the eucharistic liturgy [quotation 187] rather than ethical living as the primary symbol of Christian sacrifice. Increasingly, as well, the trajectory initiated in Tertullian of seeing the eucharistic prayer as sacrificial will develop to the point that the prayer itself will be understood as a sacrifice offered by the priest. The Roman Canon, which first appears in this era and by the middle of the sixth century is deemed the "canonical prayer" (Latin = *prex canonica*), is filled with language of sacrifice and offering and will contribute significantly to Western thinking about Eucharist as primarily the "Sacrifice of the Mass" [quotation 188].

Another display of continuity and discontinuity concerns the use of typology in explaining the meaning of the Eucharist. As noted previously, the typological approach relied upon images from the Hebrew Scriptures for interpreting the Eucharist. This form of theologizing continues to be prominent throughout the fourth and fifth centuries in both the East and the West. Enrico Mazza notes, however, that during the fourth century a second form of theologizing about the Eucharist develops that does not rely on biblical images or on philosophical categories such as those derived from the works of Plato. Instead, Mazza characterizes this new kind of theologizing as one that "restricts itself to asserting the realism of the sacrament in a naive and decidedly rudimentary way, ending in the assertion of a complete physical identity between the bread and the Body of Christ and between the wine and the Blood of Christ" [Mazza, p. 148]. As one example of what he considers a widespread trend, Mazza cites an instruction by Ambrose (d. 397) [quotation 189], who is accomplished at typological explanations but seems compelled to employ this more rudimentary form of theologizing. This and similar explanations seem to give new focus to the change of the eucharistic elements, whose transformation is of the order of a miracle.

Quotation 189: *You may say, "I see something different. How can you claim that I am receiving the body of Christ?" This is what we must still show. How great are the examples we use to show that this reality [the bread] is not what nature has formed but what the blessing has consecrated, and that the power of the blessing is greater than that of nature, since the blessing changes the very nature itself.* (Ambrose [d. 397], *On the Mysteries 50*, in Mazza, *The Celebration of the Eucharist*, p. 152)

Spirit and Word

Increasingly through this period, various writers speak of the "change" that takes place in the eucharistic elements and, by consequence, how that change comes about. Trying to underscore that the eucharistic elements are different from ordinary food is nothing new at this stage of Christianity. One evolution in eucharistic theology, however, is moving from a stage of asserting "that" the bread and wine become the Body and Blood of Christ, to "how" or "when" that change takes place. It is clear from the birth of Christianity that Eucharist was celebrated in memory of Jesus, with pride of place in that memory belonging to the Lord's passion, death, resurrection, and to that final meal of Jesus with his disciples that anticipated this paschal mystery. At its origin, Christian Eucharist was not imagined in any way to be a reenactment of that Last Supper—thus, the literal meal could fade away from Christian Eucharist with little argument. Rather, Eucharist was and is a participation in a life-giving memorial of Jesus' dying and rising, which does not simply recall a historical past but realizes and makes present the continuing power of those events through the Holy Spirit.

By the end of the fourth century, theologians like Cyril of Jerusalem (d. ca. 386) and Theodore of Mopsuestia (d. 427) were beginning to indicate in a new way a particular role for the Holy Spirit in

Quotation 190: *Once we have been sanctified through these spiritual hymns, we call upon the merciful God to send the Holy Spirit on our offerings, so that he may make the bread Christ's body, and the wine Christ's blood; for clearly whatever the Holy Spirit touches is sanctified and transformed.* (Cyril of Jerusalem, *Mystagogical Catechesis* [ca. 348], 5.7, in Yarnold, *The Awe-Inspiring Rites of Initiation*)

Quotation 191: *How can something which is bread be the body of Christ? Well, by what words is the consecration effected, and whose words are they? The words of the Lord Jesus. All that is said before are the words of the priest . . . but when the moment comes for bringing the most holy sacrament into being, the priest does not use his own words any longer: he uses the words of Christ. Therefore, it is Christ's word that brings this sacrament into being.* (Ambrose, *On the Sacraments* [ca. 391], 5.14, in Yarnold, *The Awe-Inspiring Rites of Initiation*)

Quotation 192: *The priest says: "Make this offering for us approved, spiritual, pleasing; it is the figure [quod est figura] of the body and blood of our Lord Jesus Christ. The day before he suffered, he took bread in his holy hands, looked up to heaven to you, Holy Father, almighty, eternal God, and giving thanks blessed it and broke it, and gave what was broken to his apostles and disciples, saying: take and eat of this all of you, for this is my body which shall be broken for many. . . . In the same way, after supper on the day before he suffered, he took the chalice, and looked up to heaven to you, holy Father, almighty, eternal God, and giving thanks he blessed it and gave it to his apostles and disciples, saying: take and drink of this, all of you, for this is my blood.* (Ambrose, On the Sacraments [ca. 391], 5.21-22, in Yarnold, *The Awe-Inspiring Rites of Initiation*)

the transformation of the elements. These theological and liturgical developments parallel doctrinal reflections on the Holy Spirit that culminated in the Council of Constantinople (381), which authoritatively defined the divinity of the Holy Spirit and the consubstantiality of the Spirit with the Father and the Son. According to Cyril, it is through the invocation of the Holy Spirit—what we now call the epiclesis (Greek, "invocation")—that the elements become the Body and Blood of Christ [quotation 190].

A different approach, also apparent at the end of the fourth century, can be found in Ambrose's teaching to the newly baptized in Milan. In his mystagogical catechesis, Ambrose is explaining to the newly baptized about the bread and wine at the Eucharist that appear to be ordinary food but are actually the Body and Blood of Christ. When it comes to explaining how this takes place, while Cyril and other writers from the East will stress the role of the Holy Spirit, Ambrose will emphasize the pivotal role of the words of Jesus from the Last Supper, which are a part of the eucharistic liturgy in Milan at this time [quotation 191]. Even more than addressing the issue of "how" this consecration takes place, Ambrose will provide the first extant evidence for noting "when" the change in the elements takes place, noting that before the priest repeats the words of Jesus it is "not the body of Christ, but after the consecration [Latin = *consecrationem*] I tell you that it is now the body of Christ" (*On the Mysteries*, 54, in Mazza, *The Celebration of the Eucharist*).

Ironically, Ambrose seems to contradict the liturgical text that he cites in the midst of this baptismal instruction. The bishop of Milan is our earliest source for sections of the eucharistic prayer that will come to be known as the Roman Canon. The text that he quotes, which includes the words of Jesus, does not appear to allow for such a "moment of consecration," despite Ambrose's commentary. In that text, even before the recitation of the institution narrative, the elements are announced to already be the "figure" of the Body and Blood of Christ [quotation 192]. As we noted in the previous chapter, figure and prefigurement are some of the typological tools writers use to draw connections between Old Testament "types" and Christian realties. The eucharistic text that Ambrose cites still employs such typological imagery, but Ambrose's explanation here is anything but typological. Thus, as Mazza summarizes, "he feels compelled to leave aside that method of interpretation and develop another that is patterned on the Old Testament miracles, which show the power of God's word. It is the heavenly words, that is, the words which Christ speaks as God, that works the miracle of consecration" (Mazza, p. 154).

Ambrose was not the sole originator here, for already in the writings of people like Justin Martyr (d. 165) [quotation 193] the role of the "words that come from him" are recalled in explaining how the elements become the Body and Blood of Christ. Yet Ambrose's distinctive promotion and development of these ideas were highly influential. His views on the role of the institution narrative are repeated by his most famous student, Augustine (d. 430), and eventually became the standard view in the West. Another contributing factor to this development is the continuing evolution of the Roman Canon, which as a literary construct eventually places the institution narrative at the structural center of a carefully constructed prayer, highlighting its central transformative role in that prayer in the West [illustration 102]. The East, however, will continue to honor the role of the Holy Spirit in the sanctification of the eucharistic elements, both in its theologies and the structures of its prayers. Eventually these strands of Word and Spirit will be rewoven for the West through the reforms of the Second Vatican Council (1962–65). Considerable unraveling of these theological strands, however, will occur before any reweaving commences.

Quotation 193: *For we do not receive these things as though they were ordinary food and drink. Just as Jesus Christ our Savior was made flesh through the word of God and took on flesh and blood for our salvation, so too through the word of prayer that comes from him the food over which the thanksgiving has been spoken becomes the flesh and blood of the incarnate Jesus.* (First Apology 66.2, in Sheerin, *The Eucharist*)

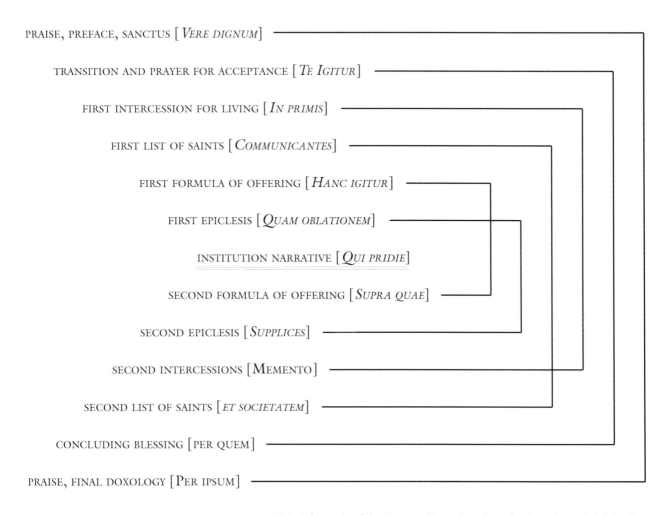

102. Schematic of the Roman Canon based on the thought of Ralph Keifer.

From Mystagogy to Infant Baptism

A frequently cited set of sources in our discussion of the Eucharist of this era is what is known as the mystagogical (Greek = *mustes*, "one initiated into the mysteries" + *agogos*, "leader") catechesis. These are instructions ordinarily given to the newly enlightened by their bishop in the days following their initiation. There is also a tradition for offering such reflections before candidates experience the sacraments of initiation [quotation 194]. It is thus not the chronology that renders such instructions "mystagogical" but the fact that these instructions are rooted in the "mysteries," what today we would call the liturgy.

We have already drawn from the teachings of four of the great mystagogues of this era: Cyril of Jerusalem, Ambrose of Milan, John Chrysostom, and Theodore of Mopsuestia. The very existence, not to mention importance, of their instructions teaches us much about eucharistic thinking of the era. First of all, Eucharist was not considered apart from the initiation process and was the culmination of those central incorporating rites that today we call baptism and confirmation. This explains, in part, why there are virtually no individual treatises on Eucharist in this era, attempting to set forth some systematic teaching about this central sacrament. Those will have to wait for centuries to appear. The reflections and teachings about the Eucharist were pastorally driven by the liturgical needs or challenges of a local church rather than by some speculative reality. This is why so much of our material of this era is from working bishops, who were concerned with pressing pastoral realities. Consequently, it is appropriate to consider the eucharistic theologies of the age as both expressions of local theology and a form of practical theology, rooted in a very particular ecclesial practice.

Another eucharistic insight that finds great resonance with this mystagogical tradition is the intimate link between reflections on the Eucharist and what it means to be church. Augustine, in particular, expends significant energy and notable eloquence drawing parallels between the Eucharist and the church. Mazza considers Augustine the most important heir to Paul's thinking of Eucharist as a sacrament of unity. Paul was also a pastoral theologian, particularly concerned about the unity of the Corinthian community. His very brief treatment of the Last Supper arises out of concerns for divisions in this community [quotation 20], and he takes great pains to stress that the community itself is the Body of Christ and that there are ecclesial and ethical consequences to that identity. Augustine resonates with Paul's concern about unity and advances the idea even further. Through the principle of "participation," Augustine teaches that the church as the Body of Christ participates in the eucharistic Body of Christ, so that they are both identical and different (Mazza,

158). For Augustine, like Paul, this identity comes about not by mere physical participation in the Eucharist but by authentic Christian living [quotation 195].

While a rich and treasured part of our tradition, this golden age of mystagogy was relatively short lived. In part this was due to the successful expansion of Christianity. As more and more Christians in the empire were baptized, the number of adult baptisms eventually waned. By the beginning of the seventh century, infant baptism became the norm in many places. As a consequence, the linkage between Eucharist and initiation will largely disappear, and rather than a sacrament of "unity," increased attention will be given to the role Eucharist plays in individual holiness and salvation.

Unworthiness and the Sacred

There are other developments in this era that, though they may not appear to be directly concerned with the Eucharist, will nonetheless contribute to dramatic changes in the thinking about the Eucharist and, particularly, in how people approach the Eucharist. Generally speaking, we can suggest that from the beginning of the fourth century to the middle of the eighth century there is a significant shift in the theological anthropology of Christians. If anthropology is the study of what it means to be human, theological anthropology can be considered the study of what it means to be a human being before God. It is a fair generalization—recognizing the many exceptions—that the baptized at the beginning of this era shared a common image of themselves as blessed and gifted with the Holy Spirit. In the words of the eucharistic prayer from the *Apostolic Tradition* (third–fourth century), they considered themselves "worthy to stand in your presence and serve you." Because of many factors, by the end of this era a very different view of the baptized will be reflected in the Roman Canon: not so much one of *circumstantes* (Latin, "those standing around") but of sinners [quotation 196]. While many factors contributed to this shift, we will here highlight three of them: the Arian heresy, the doctrine of original sin, and the rise of penitential practices.

Arius (d. 336) was a priest in Alexandria who had a reputation as a gifted preacher and astute student of the Bible. Around 320, while serving in one of the most important churches in Alexandria, he began to teach a particular view of the Trinity which held that the Son was not equal to the Father. According to Arius, while the Son was divine, he was yet a creation of the Father and inferior to him. He used pointed scriptural passages to prove his point [quotation 197]. His teaching falls under the umbrella of what is called "subordinationism," or teaching that one member of the Trinity is

Quotation 195: *If, then, you wish to understand the body of Christ, listen to the Apostle [Paul] as he says to the faithful "You are the body of Christ, and his members." If, therefore, you are the body of Christ and His members, your mystery has been placed on the Lord's table, you receive your mystery. You reply "Amen" to that which you are, and by replying you consent. For you hear "The Body of Christ," and you reply "Amen." Be a member of the body of Christ so that your "amen" may be true.* (Augustine, Sermon 272 [ca. 405–411], in Sheerin, *The Eucharist*)

Quotation 196: *To us sinners your servants also, who trust in the multitude of your mercies, deign to grant some part and fellowship with your holy apostles and martyrs . . .* (Roman Canon [ca. 700])

Quotation 197:
*I will tell of the decree of the LORD:
He said to me, "You are my son;
today I have begotten you."* (Ps 2:7)

subordinate to another. There were many people before Arius who held subordinationist views, including such revered church teachers as Justin and Irenaeus, both of whom the church venerates as saints. Arius is different from these two luminaries and others, because subordinationism was not simply an aspect of his teaching but was the linchpin of his theological contribution. He was also different because of the philosophical support he could muster.

Arius became a proponent of this particular mode of subordinationism at a distinctive moment in the development of Western philosophy. We have already noted the influence of Plato on emerging Christian thought. Philosophies based on Plato's foundational insights continued to develop in many and distinctive ways. One major development in Platonic philosophy was due to the work of Plotinus (d. 270), considered the founder of the stage of Platonic philosophy known as neo-Platonism. A key concept that Plotinus emphasized was the nature of the "one." The "one," in his view, was the source of all reality. Arius, relying upon this very influential philosophical force, had difficulty with a Trinity that appeared "many" when his philosophical background prompted him to believe that, behind all else, there was only "one." Arius's preaching gift coupled with this new philosophical tool provided amazing impetus to a particular form subordinationism, forever known as Arianism.

Arius was denounced by the many and the influential. At the Council of Nicea (325), called by Constantine, he was condemned. Yet his views—well reasoned, scripturally based, and grounded in the philosophy of Plato whom so many Christian thinkers honored—did not die. Emperors and large numbers of bishops continued to be persuaded by Arius's reasoning, most important the Roman emperor Constantius (361). Even after repeated condemnations, Arianism flourished among the Germanic tribes north of the Alps well into the sixth century.

While Arius's views would eventually fade, the reaction to his views continued. If he would deny that the Son was equal to the Father, those who held the opposite view (the "orthodox" view) expended untold energy promoting an equal divinity of the Son with the Father. In the process, the humanity of the Son—also asserted by council after council—began to fade from the religious imagination of the time. Jesus the Christ, truly God and truly human, was eventually celebrated only for the former. The humanity of Jesus, so foundational for a theological anthropology honoring other humans questing for the divine, began to evaporate. In the process, ordinary humans no longer found a resonance in the Trinity that decreasingly reflected a human dimension, and the ordinary baptized found less and less basis for identifying themselves with the Christ. Thus, those who dared to broach communion no longer found an ally; they no longer encountered a God who reveled in his humanity. Rather, they encountered a God—in preaching, prayers, and iconography—who was so different from them that they questioned whether they could have a relationship with him, much less accept him on their tongue.

Another contributor to this shift in theological anthropology among Christians of this era was the emergence of the doctrine of original sin. The scriptural basis of this teaching is found in the writings of Paul. In drawing comparisons between Christ and Adam, Paul reflects on how sin came into the world through Adam and spread to everyone [quotation 198]. This idea found resonance with numerous early Christian writers. In the middle of the second century, for example, Melito of Sardis crafted a famous sermon (Greek: *Peri Pascha*, "On the Pascha") in which he notes how sin was "stamped" on every soul. Already Cyprian of Carthage (d. 258) has linked baptism with this sin, arguing that children should not be kept from baptism because, as Adam's heirs, they have "contracted the contagion of the ancient death" (*Epistle* 58.5). Many other Western writers reflected upon this unwelcome inheritance from Adam, and by the end of the fourth century there was widespread belief that all human beings inherited not only the consequences of Adam's sin but also the sin itself.

One of the events that galvanized Christian thinking about original sin was the teaching of Pelagius (d. ca. 435), an influential thinker from Britain who taught in Rome. Pelagius and his followers were ascetics who were concerned about the declining morality of their time. As an antidote to such declining morals, "Pelagians" stressed people's personal responsibility for the moral life. They also held that human beings could achieve some level of spiritual perfection on their own initiative, which appeared to allow no room for God's grace in people's lives. While Pelagius himself did not appear to be interested in the teaching of original sin, some of his followers were. It was especially Celestius (d. early fifth century) who argued emphatically against this teaching. The teachings of Celestius, and by extension Pelagius, were condemned at the Council of Carthage in 411.

Prior to the Council of Carthage Augustine had written about original sin and taught that because of such sin one could consider the human race a "condemned mass" of sin (Latin = *massa damnata*, *To Simplicianus* 1.2.16), a phrase he will repeat at the end of his life in his *City of God* (12.12). In 415 Augustine writes a letter to Jerome about the origin of the soul. In that letter he considers the case of an infant who dies without baptism and concludes that the unbaptized

Quotation 198: . . . *sin came into the world through one man, and death came through sin, and so death spread to all because all sinned.* (Rom 5:12)

Quotation 199: *Every soul, even the soul of an infant, requires to be delivered from the binding guilt of sin, and . . . there is no deliverance except through Jesus Christ and Him crucified. (Letter 166, 7, in The Confessions and Letters of Augustine)*

infant will not be saved [quotation 199]. In condemning the Pelagians, Augustine's teaching is very influential and becomes central to the church's understanding of original sin.

Such anti-Pelagian teaching about the essentially sinful nature of humanity, combined with the anti-Arian tendency to emphasize the divinity of Christ, contributed to a significant shift in the theological anthropology of the age. By the beginning of the early Middle Ages ordinary Christians considered themselves more sinful than graced, more unlike than like God, and unworthy for something as sacred as communion. Already in the late fourth century bishops like Ambrose and John Chrysostom are complaining about the infrequent reception of the Eucharist by some Christians.

Summary

The theological developments of this era match the breadth of changes that we have seen in the eucharistic ritual of these centuries. There are many strands of continuity with the theology of the early church. On the other hand, the increased theological sophistication of the pastoral bishops of the era and the dogmatic teachings of great ecumenical councils in the face of new heresies not only produced new understandings of the Eucharist but also influenced the attitudes of the baptized toward this central Christian sacrament. Furthermore, with the growth of the church throughout the empire, more and more infants were born into the faith rather than making an adult decision toward baptism. As a consequence, eucharistic reception was delayed for an increasing number of the newly baptized, the bond between baptism and Eucharist was lessened, and the latter became decreasingly understood as the culmination of Christian initiation.

FELIX

Felix is convinced that he has the best grandfather in all of Rome. Felix never knew his father, and he hardly remembers his mother, who died when he was three. Felix's grandfather has been his whole family for almost as long as he can remember. They do everything together. When grandpa gets up, Felix gets up. When grandpa goes to the market, Felix goes to the market. And when grandpa goes to work making sandals in his little shop on the slope of the Esquiline Hill, Felix goes to work and makes sandals. When he was younger, Felix just pretended to make sandals, playing with scraps of leather and a wooden knife. But now that he is eight, he is learning how to measure a foot with chalk on the stone floor of the shop and how to choose the right leather for the different parts of the sandals. Soon his grandfather is going to teach him how to cut the leather. In the meantime, Felix is in charge of dyeing the straps for the sandals and setting them in the sun to dry.

But today there is no work. Today is Sunday and there is going to be a great worship service at the Church of St. Mary on the hill. Felix remembers the stories he has heard about the old days when Sunday was a workday. But then the emperor who believed in Jesus closed the law courts on Sunday. Pretty soon, everyone who believed in Jesus took Sunday as a free day. Felix thinks that Constantine must have been a very great man.

Although they are not going to work today, Felix and his grandfather rise before dawn because they want to get a good spot inside the church before the service begins. They pass the bread sellers along the streets that lead to St. Mary's but know that breakfast will have to wait until they first feast on the heavenly bread. A crowd already is streaming into the church when they arrive. There also are many people inside, singing hymns and responding to the litanies, but Felix and his grandfather manage to work their way through the crowd and arrive at the barrier that creates a passageway to the altar. Felix likes this spot because the barrier is low enough that he can rest his arms and chin on it and hold himself up during the long service. If he stands on his toes and cranes his neck, Felix can look down the open passageway to watch the movement around the altar. Right now, the area behind the altar is filled with bishops and presbyters singing and praying with the people, while deacons scurry everywhere.

The crowd behind Felix and his grandfather is so thick that they cannot see the back of church, but grandpa always seems to know when something is about to happen. He has been going to the bishop's liturgy for almost fifty years now, and he knows the worship inside and out. Grandpa whispers that all of the bustle in the back and the movement in the sanctuary must mean that the saintly Bishop Leo has arrived.

Sure enough, in a few minutes one of the sub-deacons, accompanied by an acolyte, winds his way though the crowd. The acolyte is carrying a beautiful book in front of him on a white cloth. As they pass, Felix can almost reach out and touch the book, its gold cover and precious stones gleaming. Felix stretches himself over the barrier to watch them carry the book into the sanctuary and place it on the altar and then return back through the crowd. A few minutes later, the singers who were standing at the side of the altar leave the sanctuary. Grandpa says they are going to join the procession that now is forming in the back of the church. When the singers leave, the singing of the assembly dies down as people sense that the procession is about to begin.

A song erupts from the back of the church, "Introibo ad altare Dei"—"I will go to the altar of God." First intoned by a few strong voices, the refrain soon is picked up by the whole congregation, whose voices echo throughout the vast hall. The choir of men, accompanied by boys not much older than Felix, sings alternating texts as they make their way through the crowd to form an honor guard inside the barrier. Felix squirms along the railing, trying to see through the choir members who stand in two rows inside the passageway, men on the outside and boys on the inside. Finally, Felix finds a spot about ten feet away from grandpa, right on the end of the barrier, where he has an unobstructed view of the passageway—and just in time. A cloud of incense announces that the main procession is reaching the front of the church.

After the man with the incense passes, seven torch-bearers follow, their faces all red from the blazing torches. Then come the subdeacons and the deacons. One of them, Marcus, lives down the street from Felix and his grandfather. At the end of the procession is the bishop.

Although he is an old man with a long beard, the bishop moves steadily through the crowd, greeting the people and often leaving behind the archdeacon, who walks to his right. Felix is transfixed as the old man approaches. As the crowd parts to let him into the passageway, the bishop spies Felix leaning on the edge of the barrier, reaches out and gently pats him on the head as he passes.

It was a long service, but Felix doesn't remember any of it. He doesn't remember the splendid singing of the gospel, the collection of gifts by the deacons, or the solemn prayers. He doesn't even remember drinking from the gold chalice. What Felix does remember, and one day will tell his own grandson, was the moment when the saintly Bishop Leo reached out and blessed him.

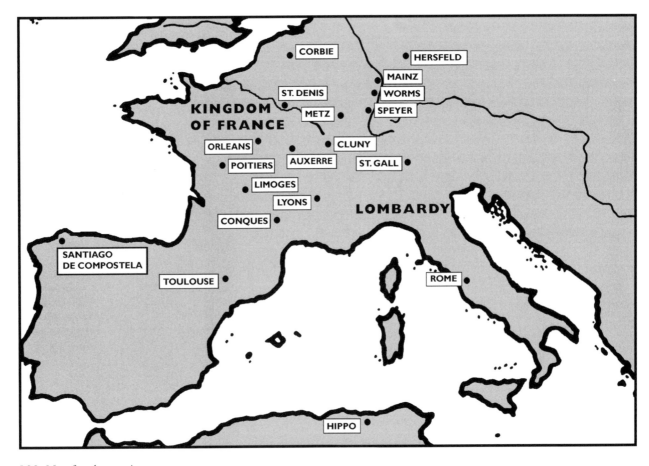

103. Map for chapter 4.

CHAPTER FOUR

The Germanization of the Liturgy:
750–1073

By founding Constantinople in the year 330, Constantine was able to establish a geographically central capital for the empire [illustration 61]. He also was able to construct a Christian center and first capital for the Greco-Roman world that was devoid of pagan temples and put under the protection of the Mother of God. According to Baldovin, the city itself could be considered a *domus dei* (Latin, "house of God") [quotation 200]. This geographic shift of political power to the East prepared for the dissolution of the Roman Empire in the West and the ultimate division between the churches of East and West. Distanced from the strongholds of the eastern portion of the empire, weakened by internal corruption, and overwhelmed by the migration of the German tribes [illustration 104], the Roman civil government collapsed by the end of the fifth century. Though

Quotation 200: *Worship within the context of the late antique and early medieval world was not merely a pious curiosity, nor was it a discreet activity, one among many cultural or social events in the life of the city. Rather, it was an expression of the very heart of urban life, of the very meaning of the civitas as a holy place. The domus ecclesiae of the pre-Constantinian period may have become a domus dei in subsequent centuries, but the city itself became a house for the Christian assembly. It could even be conceived of as a domus dei.* (Baldovin, *The Urban Character of Christian Worship*, p. 268)

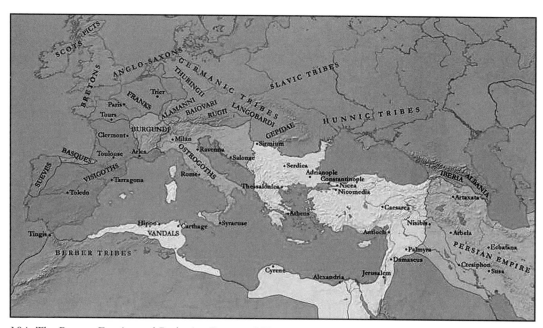

104. The Roman Empire and Barbarian Europe, 500.

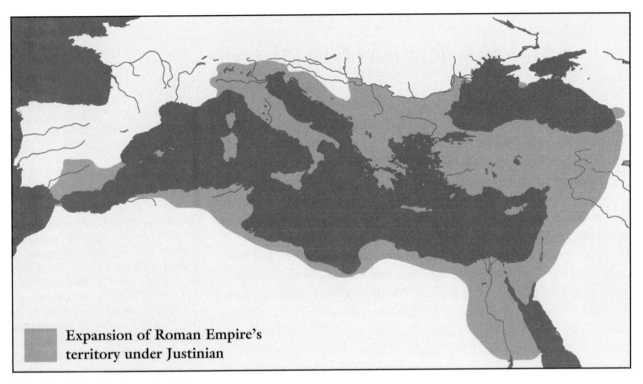

**Expansion of Roman Empire's
territory under Justinian**

105. Map of Justinian's empire, 565.

ecclesiastical structures remained intact, ties with the emperor and the church in the East began to wane.

It is true that Emperor Justinian (d. 565) reconquered the western portion of the empire [illustration 105] and sustained ecclesiastical ties between the imperial see of Constantinople and the Roman church. For example, the papal elections held in Rome required the ratification of the Byzantine emperor. Famous in this regard is the correspondence of Gregory the Great (d. 604) to the Emperor Maurice (d. 602), asking the latter not to approve his election. This practice will end by the eighth century, however, as the two worlds and churches drift apart.

Another significant religious and political change at this time was the spread of Islam. After the death of the prophet Mohammed (d. 632), Islam quickly spread throughout Arabia, into Persia, across Syria, Egypt, Tunis, Tripoli, Algeria, Morocco, and into Spain [illustration 106]. In a decisive battle at Tours in 732, Frankish forces led by Charles Martel (d. 741) stopped the expansion of the Islamic Emirate of Cordoba beyond the Iberian Peninsula. This event catapulted Martel and his offspring into leadership that would be foundational for the emergence of the Holy Roman emperor.

James Russell offers an enlightening introduction to the new alliance between the church and the Franks, which leads to the "Germanization of early Medieval Christianity." According to Russell, Christianity had come in contact with Germanic society in the late fourth century. It was Arian Christianity (see above, pp. 125–26), however, that was accepted by many Visigoths and then transmitted to other Germanic peoples. The Franks and a few other German groups remained pagan until the end of the fifth century. Then an astute young Frankish king by the name of Clovis (d. 511) was baptized in union with the Church in Rome in 498, possibly as a way to consolidate his political position. According to Russell, however, Clovis was not a Christian in any real sense, and the Franks remained largely pagan during this period. To the extent that Christianity did spread among the Franks, it seems to have been "a fundamental folk-religious interpretation of Christianity, and maybe more properly described as a syncretic development" (Russell, p. 179). This process of "Germanization" will have an enormous impact on liturgy and its theology, something we will explore throughout this chapter.

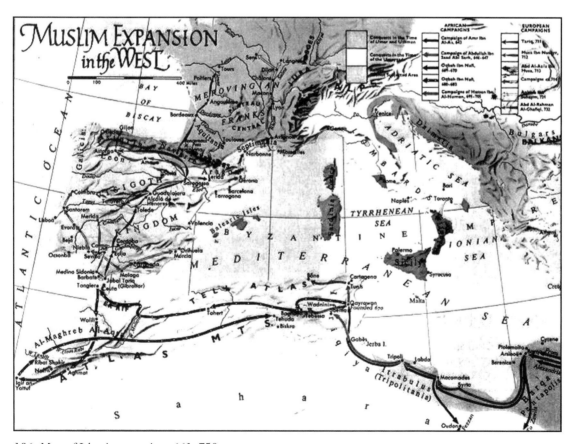

106. Map of Islamic expansion, 661–750.

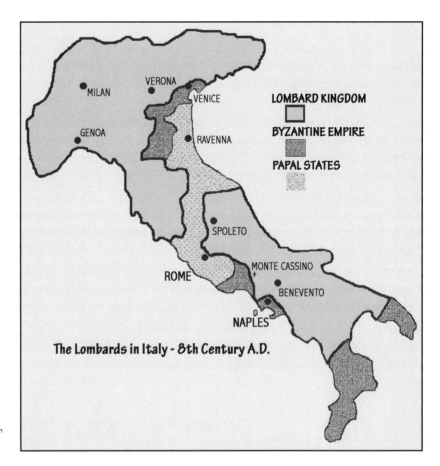

The Lombards in Italy - 8th Century A.D.

107. The Lombard Kingdom,
eighth century.

The Merovingian kingdom, named for Clovis's grandfather Merowig, was severely weakened during the seventh century through a series of internal power struggles, and Christianity there was in disarray. With the dawn of the eighth century, however, things began to turn for the Franks. The change in political fortunes is symbolized in the victory of Charles Martel. Religiously, there was a new wave of Anglo-Saxon missionaries, the most important of whom was St. Boniface (d. 754). According to Russell, the relationship between Boniface and Charles Martel was a mutually beneficial one. Charles and his descendants were challengers of the Merovingian kingdom, and affiliation with the church of Rome provided an alternative source of sacred legitimation. Boniface was in need of a local protector for his missionary efforts, and Rome was in need of someone to defend against the Lombards, who had invaded Italy in the late sixth century and now were a threatening presence [illustration 107].

In 751 Pope Zachary recognized Charles's son Pepin III (d. 768, and also sometimes referred to as Pippin) as king of the Franks. In July of 753, shortly after Pepin promised to defend the church, he and his sons Carloman (d. 771) and Charlemagne (d. 814) were consecrated at St.-Denis. In 774 Charlemagne defeated the Lombards and took to himself the title "King of the Lombards." A more important title was the one conferred upon him in 800, when he journeyed to Rome and on Christmas Day was crowned emperor by Pope Leo III (d. 816).

Besides responding to external military and political threats, another major challenge to this newfound dynasty was the internal unification and reform of the Frankish kingdom. To no small degree, this was achieved by first reforming the church that had experienced significant decline in the seventh century and then employing it as an agent of unification for the realm. One important step in this reunification process was the establishment of a unified liturgy. To that end Pepin and Charlemagne attempted to impose the Roman liturgy on the Frankish church. Previous to this, the style of worship among the Frankish people could be called "Gallican," though it was by no means a unified rite like that from Rome. Some characteristics of Gallican worship were: 1) its penchant for addressing prayers to Christ rather than to the Father, 2) significant variations in the prayers according to the church year—including the eucharistic prayer, 3) the use of the Trisagion and the "Canticle of the Three Young Men" (Dan 3:35-66) during the Liturgy of the Word, and 4) the placement of the sign of peace before the eucharistic prayer.

In order to promulgate the Roman liturgy through the kingdom, liturgical books and personnel were imported from Rome. Anglo-Saxon missionaries who had strong ties to Rome assisted in this venture. The incompleteness of the Roman books [quotation 201], combined with the significant differences between Roman and Frankish temperaments, resulted not so much in the imposition of the Roman liturgy as in the emergence of a new genre of worship. This hybrid form of worship, mixing the sobriety of the Roman style with dramatic elements, is sometimes called the "Franco-Roman" or "Roman-Franco-Germanic" liturgy. This form will eventually be adopted throughout Europe, even by Rome, and will come to be the predominant liturgy of the Latin church during the late Middle Ages. The result is truly a Germanization of medieval Christianity and its worship.

108a. Saint-Jean at Poitiers, reconstructed north view of the original fourth-century building (ca. 40 x 27 feet).

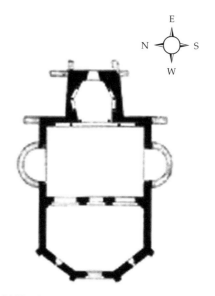

108b. Ground plan of Merovingian expansion, showing five-sided narthex to the west of the original fourth-century building and the pentagonal apse to the east of the original building.

ARCHITECTURE

In the centuries following the legalization of their religion, Christians used various types of buildings for their worship. As noted in the previous chapter, however, the basilica form rose to prominence as a preferred shape for Christian worship spaces in the West. This was true, as well, in the Merovingian era, though there are few extant

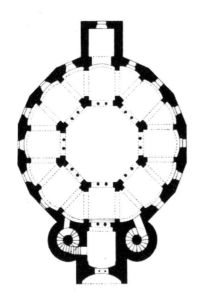

109. Ground plan of San Vitale, 526–47.

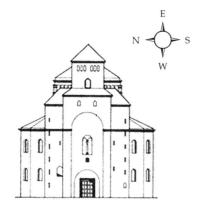

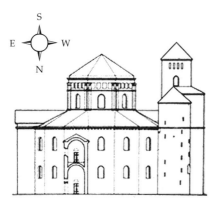

110. Reconstruction of Aachen chapel.

monuments from this time, as architecture from this period was largely impermanent. One exception is the baptistery of Saint-Jean at Poitiers. Constructed on Roman foundations, this small basilica was further enlarged with a narthex and apse in the sixth to seventh centuries [illustration 108]. Remnants of other Merovingian basilica can today be found, for example, in Paris's Saint Germain des Pres and beneath the Church of St. Piat in Tournai.

The burgeoning of the Carolingian kingdom was also a period of an architectural renaissance. Reflecting the confidence of new leadership and influence, builders abandoned the smaller scale of the Merovingian period and began to build large, expansive structures. One important inspiration was the legend of Rome. Even though the Roman Empire was long collapsed and the city only a shadow of its previous splendor, the myth of ancient Rome—sometimes called *Romanitas* (Latin, "Roman-ness")—and especially of that first Christian emperor Constantine, continued to inspire. Drawing upon legendary precedents of imperial Rome, many buildings constructed under Charlemagne and his heirs were monumental in size and geometrical in design. Charlemagne's architectural projects enhanced his attempts at liturgical reform. As his concern was to replace local, "Gallican" forms of worship with "official" Roman worship, so did he help to replace local architectural forms with an idealized version of the architecture of Constantine's empire.

While there was emulation of a Roman ideal, Carolingian churches—like the liturgy that coursed through them—were quite different from that of Constantine's Rome. Whereas the first Christian basilicas were large open spaces with few architectural divisions, the churches of this era were shaped to respect the increased separation between clergy and laity. They also had to address new ritual requirements, such as the development of private Mass, and shifts in baptismal practice that dictated the construction of fonts suited for infants rather than adults. One architectural solution to these liturgical shifts was the subdivision of the building into various sections, each with a different ritual focus. Later on we will consider these various subdivisions more closely.

Charlemagne's most important ecclesial building was the palace chapel at Aachen. Designed by Odo of Metz—one of the first times we actually have the name of a church architect in the West—the building was modeled after Ravenna's church of San Vitale built during the reign of Emperor Justinian [illustration 109]. The Aachen chapel, which later became the cathedral of that city, prefigures another important Carolingian architectural development: the expansion of the "westwork" of church buildings. In many churches, the sanctuary was located in the east end of the building. The west face

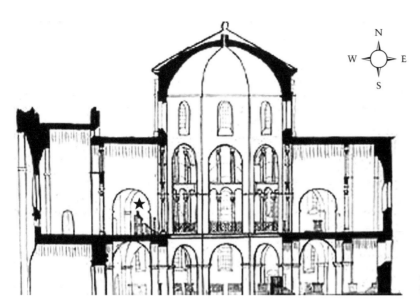

111. South view of Aachen chapel. Charlemagne's throne (★) would have been in front of the westwork.

of churches in previous eras were usually simple and unadorned. At Aachen, however, the west end developed into a massive vertical structure of multiple levels culminating in two imposing towers [illustration 110]—a concept emulated in many subsequent churches. The significance of this westwork is debated, and its functions were probably multiple. Some think a principal purpose was to provide bell towers. Bells were of increasing importance for Christian churches and by the eighth century could be cast in bronze and other metals, rather than being riveted together from forged iron plates. Others hold that the westwork provided an architectural balance to the well-articulated east end, which often held the sanctuary. Still others believe that the west end served as an architectural and political counterpoint, symbolizing the emperor's claim to authority within the church [quotation 202]. This last interpretation finds resonance in the Aachen chapel, in which Charlemagne's throne occupied the upper gallery on the west side of the building, with the imposing westwork to his back [illustration 111].

In 843 the Carolingian Empire was divided between Charlemagne's three grandsons and then further reapportioned in 870, foreshadowing the emergence of modern Germany and France. In the early tenth century strong leadership in the "German" kingdom blossomed under Otto I, who first became king in 936 and then reigned as Holy Roman Emperor (962–973). The architecture of the Ottonian Empire (936–1024) developed and refined the Carolingian style and could be characterized as "imperial." One outstanding building program from this period is St. Michael in Hildesheim, originally the abbey church for a Benedictine community. This basilical

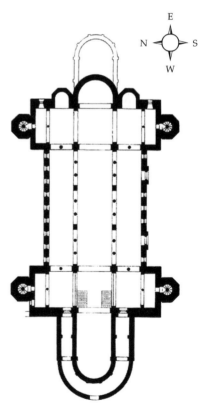

112. Ground plan of Saint Michael in Hildesheim.

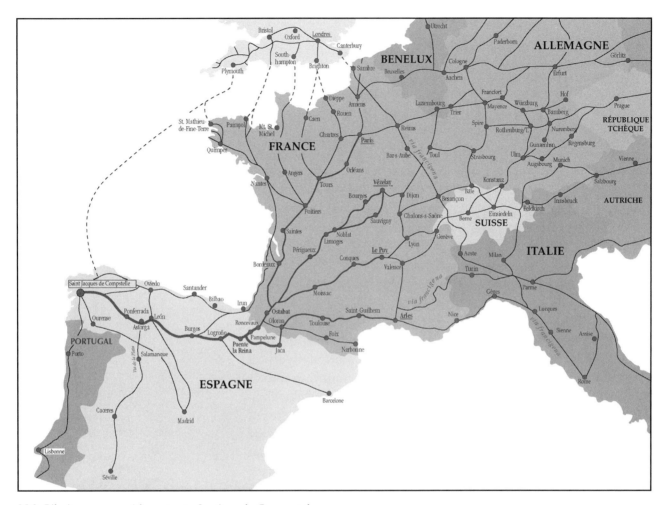

113. Pilgrimage map with routes to Santiago de Compostela.

plan has an east as well as a west apse, but rather than symbolizing the realms of priest and king, the east apse is the location of the altar and the focus for Eucharist, and the west apse is the place of the monastic choir where the Liturgy of the Hours were celebrated [illustration 112].

Romanesque architecture, properly speaking, is an eleventh- and twelfth-century phenomenon, though the term itself was not coined until 1818 by the French archaeologist Charles-Alexis-Adrien de Gerville (d. 1853). Unlike Carolingian and Ottonian architecture, it is not linked to a specific empire or dynasty and is more a popular phenomenon reflecting the spirit of the age—what some have called a "pan-European" rather than regional style of building. The influence of Benedictine monasticism in this period, which showed a

114a. Saint Foy, Conques, France.

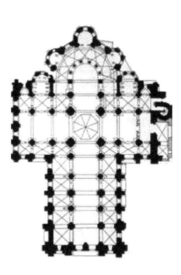

114b. Ground plan of Saint Foy.

marked preference for this style of architecture, is not to be under-estimated in the spread of this form. Other factors were the ascendancy of the middle class, a new economic promise, and relative political stability, all of which contributed to a more positive outlook in the eleventh century. In this optimistic age, Christians were on the move, crisscrossing Europe on pilgrimage [illustration 113]. One of the most famous medieval pilgrimage destinations was Santiago de Compostela in northwestern Spain. The relics of St. James (in the Spanish dialect of Galacian = *Santiago*) were "discovered" in 813, and from the tenth century to the present day, millions have trekked more than eight hundred kilometers (480 miles) along *el camino de Santiago* (Spanish, "the way of Saint James"). The pilgrimage centers were beneficiaries of booming economies that developed around the relics that were the focus of these pilgrimages. It was around such relics that many of the great Romanesque churches of Europe were built. One notable example of such a Romanesque pilgrimage church is the abbey church of St. Foy at Conques in France [illustration 114].

As Spiro Kostof notes, no "typical" Romanesque church exists; though a "pan-European style," Romanesque varied according to region and the needs of the community. It is possible, however, to enumerate some basic characteristics of this style, many of which were anticipated in Carolingian and Ottonian buildings. These included the use of basic geometric shapes, especially the round arch, to achieve a sense of overall proportion and harmony. The addition of towers and higher vaulting gave these buildings a new sense of verticality. Because of the fire danger posed by wooden roofs of pre-Romanesque churches (e.g., that of St. Michael in Hildesheim), stone and masonry vaults were perfected. Often the walls just below the vault known as the clerestory (from Old French *cler* = "bright") were pierced with windows. The increased weight of this vaulting [quotation 203] required massive walls, columns, and piers. This served to subdivide the walls of the nave into uniform sections or bays. On the one hand, this regular subdivision of the building re-sulted in a kind of rhythmic undulation through the nave, but it also contributed to the feeling of a building subdivided into discreet units rather than the large open hall that marked earlier basilica.

Quotation 203: *The interior vault of Worms Cathedral (dedicated in 1018) is 89 feet; that of Mainz Cathedral (975–1037) is over 95 feet; that Speyer Cathedral (1030–1061) is over 108 feet.*

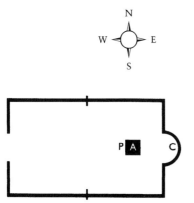

115a. Arrangement of presider (P), chair (C), and altar (A) in basilica with apse facing east.

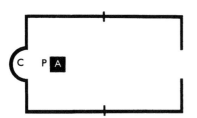

115b. Arrangement of presider (P), chair (C), and altar (A) in basilica with entrance facing east.

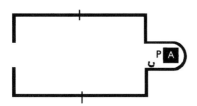

115c. Arrangement with the altar (A) against the back wall of the apse, with presider (P) and people both facing the altar; chair (C) at side.

Main Altar

As previously noted, a basilica is a type of enclosed path. As every path leads someplace, that place in the post-Constantinian Christian basilica was the apse. As the architectural focal point, it naturally became a liturgical point. Initially, the apse was the place for the bishop's throne, with the altar out in the nave. A variety of theo-logical and cultural factors, however, shifted these placements.

Originally the altar was a wooden table, often moveable, usually placed in the body of the church so that the community could gather around at least three sides of it. The presider stood on whichever side of the altar allowed him to face East, the place of the rising sun, a symbol of the resurrection, and an important metaphor for Chris-tians living in the sun-drenched Mediterranean. If the apse pointed toward the East, then the presider stood on the same side of the altar as the community and faced the same direction as they did. If the entrance to the basilica pointed toward the East, then the presider faced across the altar [illustration 115]. The second arrangement was more common in the West after the time of Constantine until the period of Frankish ascendancy. During the eighth century the first arrangement, with the priest facing away from the people, be-came more common. Over time, the altar was pushed farther into the apse until it ended up close to or against the back wall, with the presider and community facing the altar, whether it pointed toward the East or not. Eventually, more emphasis was placed on the back embellishment, called the reredos, than on the altar table itself.

There are many contributing factors that led to the movement of the altar out of the body of the church to up against the back wall. For instance, we have already seen [illustration 73] that under Gregory the Great the altar was moved from the body of the church into the apse over the tomb of St. Peter. This Roman practice was idealized and repeated in some Frankish churches, even though they did not possess such relics. Culturally, the people north of the Alps did not understand the Latin language. This architectural move of altar into the apse, therefore, was symbolic of a linguistic separation that was already occurring between the baptized and presider in the central eucharistic action. We have also noted Russell's theory of Germanization, that the Franks and other Germanic people had a different religious imagination than that of Christians of other places or earlier times. One of those characteristics, according to Russell, is a more magico-religious interpretation of Christianity, rather than what he considers to be a more original ethical and doctrinal interpretation of Christianity. Russell believes this more "magical" Germanic outlook can help explain certain well-recognized liturgical developments among the Germanic peoples, including great physical and spiritual distance between the people and presider, who took responsibility for performing the sacred acts, and increased focus on the objects employed in the holy mysteries (Russell, p. 191).

Another change was in the material used for altars. Stone altars, already mentioned by John Chrysostom in the fourth century, were mandated in some places by the sixth century [quotation 204] and for the whole Frankish kingdom by Charlemagne in 769. The practice of building altars over the tombs of saints eventually gave way to the imbedding of the relics of saints within the altar itself. Previously, the only essential act for dedicating a church or an altar was the celebration of Eucharist. By the end of the eighth century Roman Ordos describe depositing relics in the altar as a central part of consecrating a church. One of these even prescribes the enclosure of relics along with three particles of consecrated bread when consecrating an altar [quotation 205]. As altars were moved into the sanctuary, no longer allowing the faithful to gather around them, and were increasingly associated with relics, they began to look less and less like tables and more like sarcophagi.

Secondary Altars

One significant difference between Western churches of this period and those of the pervious era was the impulse to include more than one altar within a church. Although some evidence suggests the existence of secondary altars before the seventh century [quotation 206], it was after the seventh century in Gaul that the number of altars within churches generally increased. There were several factors that contributed to this trend. Of great significance was the increased demand for Masses.

Since the period of the domestic church, the Eucharist was originally only celebrated on Sundays and only once on that day in a given community. Increasingly, Saturday also became a liturgical day. In

Quotation 204: *Altars may not be consecrated unless they are made of stone.* (Council of Epaon, Gaul [517], canon 26, in Mansi, *Sacrorum Conciliorum*)

Quotation 205: *Then he places three portions of the body of the Lord within the confessio and three of incense, and the relics are closed up within the confessio.* (Roman Ordo 42:11 [ca. 720–750], in Andrieu, *Les Ordines Romani*)

Quotation 206: *The presbyter Leuparicus who brought us your fraternal greetings, informed us of your church constructed in honor of the blessed apostles Peter and Paul and also the martyrs Lawrence and Pancratius. We have learned that in that church there are 13 altars, four of which are yet to be dedicated.* (Gregory the Great, *Letter to Bishop Palladius of Santes* [ca. 590], VI:50)

North Africa Cyprian gives evidence that there was a daily celebration of Eucharist, something that over a century later Augustine also acknowledged. Augustine also knew, however, places where Mass was celebrated only on Saturdays and Sundays, and in some places—like Rome—only on Sundays. According to Daniel Callam there is little evidence for daily Mass in Gaul even during the sixth century, but soon this began to change. By the seventh century daily Mass was common in the West. Callam believes that this development was, in part, the product of monastic communities that were led by bishops. In these contexts the ascetic practice of receiving communion—common enough in the early church outside of Mass—migrated toward a full celebration of the Eucharist.

It was not the impulse for daily Mass by itself, however, that generated the need for multiple altars in a single space. More influential was the growing request for Masses offered for the dead. Prayer for the dead is an ancient Christian tradition. As early as the Apocryphal Acts of John (ca. 170 C.E.) there is evidence that Eucharist was celebrated for the dead. Tertullian (d. 225) documents that, at least in his North African Montanist community, there was a practice of celebrating Eucharist on the anniversary of one's death [quotation 207]. Growing concern over the state of the dead led to sometimes bizarre practices, and there were strong condemnations from various synods (Hippo in 393, Auxerre in 578, Trullan in 692), concerning the practice of giving the eucharistic bread to corpses.

Richard Rutherford believes that Augustine, more than any other figure, was responsible for providing the direction that medieval Western Christianity would take in praying for the dead. Especially influential was his insistence that prayer, almsgiving, and particularly the Eucharist were efficacious for the dead (Rutherford, p. 18). Consonant with Augustine's teaching was an influential story from Gregory the Great. One of his monks died in disgrace, and Gregory strongly condemned him. Because of the intervention of other monks, Gregory ordered that Mass be celebrated for thirty consecutive days; after the final Eucharist the dead monk appeared to Gregory, confirming that he had been freed from purgation by the eucharistic celebrations. This new approach to the role of Eucharist in changing the state of dead Christians [quotation 208] inevitably contributed to increased demand on behalf of the faithful for celebrations of the Eucharist for their beloved dead. Eventually some would leave money for Masses to be celebrated for themselves after their own demise; those with extraordinary means would even establish monasteries whose founding purpose was the offering of Masses and prayers for the souls of the founding donor and his family.

Another source of requests for the celebration of Eucharist was from a new form of penance that had appeared on the continent in

Quotation 207: *We make offerings for the dead on the anniversary day of their death.* (Tertullian, *The Crown* [211 C.E.], n. 3, in Corpus Christianorum)

Quotation 208: *With the advent of severe penitential discipline, being Christian became more and more a preoccupation with sin; care for the dead Christian became in turn a preoccupation with the wages of sin. Thus, for Gregory and his contemporaries even the faithful Christian was presumed a sinner whose immediate lot after death was at least one of purification. . . . It was here that the prayers of the church, and especially the Mass, were believed to benefit the dead. Implicit in Gregory's teaching is a new sense of something approaching the automatic, if by "performing" so many prayers and Masses the release of a soul from the purifying fire would be achieved provided the deceased had earned the right to such help during life.* (Rutherford, *The Death of a Christian*, pp. 26–27)

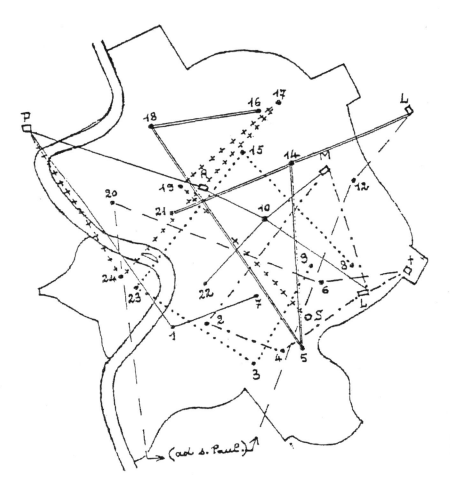

116. Map of the eighth-century Lenten stational liturgies crisscrossing the city of Rome. (Chavasse, p. 30)

the seventh century. The Irish monks introduced this new form of penance known as "tariff" penance. Similar to the form of individual reconciliation familiar to Roman Catholics today, this ritual required the confessor to impose a particular tariff or penance on the penitent, commensurate with the seriousness of the sin confessed. Many of these tariffs were gathered together in collections known as penitentials. Some of the penances were quite severe but could be "commuted," often through monetary donations. In a related development, the Carolingian period also witnessed the development of Mass stipends. This was a monetary gift given to a priest that required him to celebrate Mass for the particular intention of the donor. Sometimes, a stipend was required for the celebration of one or more Masses, which served as commutations for the tariff imposed as a penance [quotation 209]. As a consequence, the growth of stipends, and particularly the growing demand for Masses as commutations of penances, were a further factor contributing to the need for more altars within a single church building.

A final factor contributing to the multiplication of altars in this period was the attempt by churches north of the Alps to imitate the

Quotation 209: *He who is willing to confess his sins ought to confess with tears, since tears do not ask pardon but deserve it; he shall ask a presbyter to sing Mass for him . . . the singing of one Mass is enough to make redemption for twelve days; ten Masses, for four months; twenty Masses for eight months; thirty Masses, for twelve month—if the confessors so determine.* (Penitential of Bede [8th cent.] in McNeill and Gamer, *Medieval Handbooks of Penance,* p. 233)

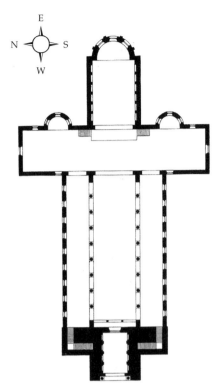

117. Ground plan of Hersfeld Abbey church, ca. 1037.

stational liturgy of Rome. As noted in the previous chapter, stational liturgy is the name given to the practice by the bishop of Rome of regularly celebrating Eucharist at the different churches or "stations" throughout the city. These roving papal Masses, which included separate processions by the faithful to the designated stational church, served a pastoral purpose in cosmopolitan Rome. As Antoine Chavasse has demonstrated, this practice contributed to a sense of unity among the faithful, especially during Lent when such unity was important to the preparation for baptism and for upholding the shared Lenten fast [illustration 116].

We have already noted how Roman books were imported into the realm by Charlemagne in order to promote the use of the Roman liturgy throughout the kingdom. The sacramentary, such as that sent by Pope Hadrian [quotation 201], contained an outline of the stational system as it existed in Rome in the eighth century. Because the Christians in the North did not live in cities like Rome or Constantinople, with sprawling networks of urban churches, they adapted the idea of the stational liturgy to their own circumstances. Sometimes this meant a very modest pattern of processions between two or three churches. Frequently, a single church or monastery was treated as though it was the city of Rome. Numerous altars were erected as symbolic parallels to the Roman stations, first within Carolingian churches and later in Romanesque churches.

Choir Area

Evidence indicates that by the early fifth century, the laity in some places were restricted from designated areas close to the altar. We have already recognized certain theological and cultural factors that contributed to the movement of the altar from the nave area into the apse and the consequent separation of table from the gathered community. Even previous to this move, however, there was a growing instinct to create a sacred precinct in the middle of the nave, prompting a number of architectural solutions. In the West, a low barrier was often constructed to contain the crowds [illustration 70]. This barrier created a pathway within the larger processional space, ordinarily open only to the clergy and the choir that took part in the entrance procession at the beginning of worship. The choir, often consisting of men and boys, commonly led such processions and created a kind of honor guard once inside the barrier, through which the rest of the processing clergy would pass. In time this ritual action would receive more elaborate architectural support and attention.

One factor that contributed to the enlargement and separation of this "choir" space concerned changes in the celebration of the

118. Reconstruction of the interior of the third church at Cluny (begun in 1088) illustrating the enclosed choir set off from the nave by a solid wall, in front of which are altars for the services attended by the laity. (After Conant as cited in Norberg-Shulz, p. 171)

Liturgy of the Hours. Increasingly monks and secular clergy were the central and sometimes sole participants in the Liturgy of the Hours, since it was celebrated in a language most Christians north of the Alps did not understand (i.e., Latin) and, because of the prohibitive expense of books, ordinarily requiring the memorization of all 150 psalms by the participants. In many churches the sanctuary was expanded and the apse elongated to provide a space for this celebration. The result was a hybrid basilica with an extended sanctuary that contained a choir area for the monks or canons [illustration 117]. Screens or walls were sometimes built to separate the choir from the nave, demarcating the place of the monks or clergy from the place of the laity. These were often known as "rood" screens (from Old English *rod* = cross), as they were frequently surmounted by a large cross or crucifix. By the eleventh or twelfth century, some of these walls were solid, presenting the laity with a visual obstacle to the Eucharist and other services that transpired in the sanctuary. Because of this, a second altar was often built for the people outside the boundaries of the choir [illustration 118].

Ambulatory

Quotation 210: *To clerics and monks . . . it is not proper that women should approach the altar.* (Charlemagne, *General Admonition* [789], 17)

The importance of relics for the new churches generated large numbers of pilgrims. Droves of visitors to relic-bearing churches, combined with the increasingly restricted access to the main altar area, especially for women [quotation 210], led to an important development in pre-Romanesque and Romanesque churches: the ambulatory. The ambulatory was an architectural solution for the problems that arose when large numbers of people tried to move through churches, especially in quest of relic veneration. The church's most important relic was usually in or under the main altar, which, because of both canonical and architectural constraints, was inaccessible to ordinary laity. A further problem was the throng of pilgrims surging through narrow side aisles or trying to squeeze into cramped corners where side altars or reliquaries sometimes were placed. The solution was the development of a passageway along the outermost ring of the apse, which allowed pilgrims to circulate through this part of the church while the monks or clerics were chanting the Liturgy of the Hours [illustration 119]. This also gave people access to relics located in a chapel off the ambulatory or in the main sanctuary. If the relics were located in the main sanctuary, they could be viewed from the back through an opening in the wall of the apse. Because ambulatories could be cordoned off, they aided any communities wanting to exact a monetary toll from a visiting pilgrim who wished to pass into the ambulatory and see the relic. Such practices exist yet today. The ambulatory also provided room for more side chapels, which were common in the great pilgrimage churches of the Middle Ages and would become a standard feature of most great churches of the Romanesque and Gothic era. Ambulatories also provided resident monks and clerics processional routes for enacting their modified versions of stational liturgy. The first such ambulatory seems to have originated in the now-destroyed church of St. Martin in Tours.

Summary

Architecturally, this period saw the full flowering of trends begun in the previous period. The sanctuary area was definitively separated from the body of the church both by legal and architectural barriers. The transition was made from a wooden table around which the

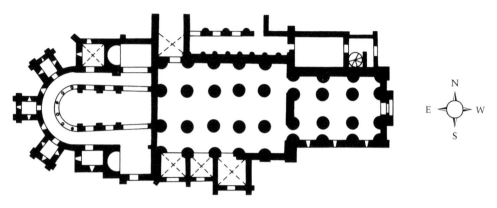

119. Church of Saint Philibert in Tournus (950–1120), showing an early form of an ambulatory around the apse, with main relics in the far eastern chapel. (After Poinard, *Tournus: Abbaye Saint-Philibert*)

assembly could gather to a large stone altar, often in the shape of a sarcophagus, pushed up against the back wall and embellished with an ornamental screen known as a reredos. A central choir space was carved out for monks or clerics, highlighting their increasingly privileged place as the ecclesiastical and liturgical elite. And the number of altars multiplied. Because many of these developments occurred in countries north of the Alps where the language of the liturgy was no longer the language of the people, they contributed to the separation of the community from the liturgical action.

MUSIC

The tendency toward architectural subdivision of the church building during this era serves as a visual analogy for the musical developments in the Christian West at this time. Architecturally, larger churches allocated special places for the priest (sanctuary), the monks or clerics (choir), and the laity (nave and transepts). The liturgical music of the era could similarly be said to be divided among the priest, the choir, and the laity. To the extent there was music, the choir would have been the dominant voice in the music of the Eucharist. The priest gradually retreated into private or silent prayer, while the assembly was increasingly excluded from the central musical action.

Different from the previous era was the emergence of eucharistic worship patterns that were essentially non-lyrical. This occurred because of various developments, some of which we have already noted, for example, the growing acceptability and then demand for the celebration of the Eucharist for the dead or as part of the commutation of a penance. Many, if not most, of these celebrations

Quotation 211:
Characteristics of Feudal Europe

- *Feudalism is a decentralized organization that arises when central authority cannot perform its functions and when it cannot prevent the rise of local powers.*

- *In a feudal society, civil and military powers at the local level are assumed by great landowners or other people of similar wealth and prestige.*

- *These local leaders and their retinues begin to form a warrior class distinct from the people of their territory.*

- *The distinction between private rights and public authority disappears, and local control tends to become a personal and even hereditary matter.*

- *The feudal leaders often take over responsibility for the economic security of their territories, and dictate how resources are to be used, while at the same time establishing monopolies over some activities. This strengthens their presence at the local level and also makes their possessions even more valuable.*

- *The feudal aristocracies are usually organized on the basis of private agreements, contracts between individuals.*

- *The private agreements that formed the network of mutual services were called contracts of homage and fealty, "homage" because one of the contractants agreed to become the servant [homme], or "man" of the other, and fealty, because he promised to be "feal, faithful" to him.* (Nelson, *Lectures in Medieval History*, chap. 18)

occurred without a choir and often occurred without the presence of an assembly as well. Such private Masses were devoid of music, and they were eventually silent. Thus it is during this era in the West that the previously noted "heightened auditory environment" of eucharistic worship waned, and the intimate connection between Eucharist and lyricism was broken. Henceforth it will be possible and even common to celebrate Eucharist as a recited rather than sung or chanted event.

Another contributing factor to the emergence of non-lyrical eucharistic worship was the growth of small rural "parish" churches. While originally Christianity was, to a large extent, an urban phenomenon, during the early medieval period most Christians lived in rural settings. It is commonly calculated that 90–95 percent of all northern Europeans during this era lived in small villages or on the land. The countryside was not the site of large cathedrals, though most great monastery churches were outside the cities. More common in the countryside were very small churches. Some of these had been founded by bishops and offered services under his mandate and authority. As Kevin Madigan notes, however, the most common type of church at the end of the first millennium was one founded and governed by a local lord. These "proprietary churches"—numbering in the tens of thousands—were especially common north of the Alps, and were a consequence of the Germanization and parallel feudalization of Europe [quotation 211]. These modest structures, often built of wood with a dirt floor, were divided into nave and sanctuary with no choir area. While there may have been some instances in such churches that vernacular singing punctuated the worship, here as well the auditory environment of the worship was more often muted if not silent.

Many great cathedrals in this era were important centers for the development and performance of liturgical music. Overall, however, it was the great monasteries of the early medieval period that served as centers of learning for the Christian West, and they were home to the musical-liturgical developments of this era as well.

The *Schola*

When Pepin III and Charlemagne after him mandated the use of the Roman liturgy throughout their kingdom, they also required that the official liturgical music of Rome be employed [quotation 212]. In order to accomplish this task, Roman musicians were imported into the Frankish kingdom to teach the chants. Sending singers was essential to accomplish this musical goal in this era when an accurate system of notation was yet to be developed. While not the work of Gregory the Great, it appears that choir schools (Latin = *schola cantorum*) did exist in Rome shortly after his death, and McKinnon believes it is safe to assume such an organization to be well established by about 675 (p. 87). The central role of the *schola cantorum* is quite evident in the first Roman Ordinal dating from around the year 700 [quotation 157]. Eventually choir schools were established north of the Alps in great centers such as Metz, St. Gall, and in the British Isles at York.

Trained singers were critical to the musical-liturgical leadership in the great episcopal centers and monasteries of the early Middle Ages. For Eucharist this meant that such musical specialists led the chants for the various proper and ordinary parts of the Mass, with the community initially supplying refrains or responses. The importation of Roman singers, Roman singing practices, and Latin chants

Quotation 212: *To every cleric: All are to sing Roman chant in its entirety, which is to be properly executed both for the office and for Mass. This is to be accomplished according to the wish of King Pippin, our father of happy memory, and because of the peaceable alliance between Gaul and the holy church of God, accomplished in complete agreement with the apostolic see.* (Charlemagne, *General Admonition* [789], 80)

120. Tunnel vaulting in the nave of the third church at Cluny, begun in 1088. (After Conant as cited in Norberg-Schultz, p. 171)

121a. Early form of polyphony (organum of the octave) in note-against-note style, ca. 850. (Davidson and Apel, p. 21)

121b. Example of free organum from the eleventh century. (Davidson and Apel, p. 22)

Quotation 213: *Two cities and two scholas can take credit for the creation of the Gregorian Mass Proper. There was Rome and its schola, which performed the first miracle, the fundamental one of creating the Mass Proper in its original guise, with its marvelous sets of texts for the temporal and sanctoral cycles, and its melodies that we can dimly discern in their Frankish manifestation. And there was Metz with its schola, which adjusted the Roman melodies into the form that we know and love.* (McKinnon, *The Advent Project,* pp. 402–3)

into the Frankish kingdom—where Latin was largely unknown by the laity—was the beginning of a process that would lead to the gradual exclusion of the congregation from joining in the singing of the ordinary and proper parts of the Mass.

Most scholars agree that it was in this period that what we call "Gregorian chant" developed. We have previously noted some of the debate about the exact origin and nature of this chant, and the differing views on the relationship between Gregorian chant and Old Roman chant. Recently James McKinnon has suggested that the *schola* chants developing in Rome from the end of the seventh century were exported outside of Rome where they were definitively written down by the Franks within a century of their transmission. These he calls "Gregorian," whereas the same original chants that remained within Rome were not written down until the eleventh century, and thus the origin of "Old Roman chant." Virtually all scholars agree that whatever chants were transported north of the Alps were modified in the process of their being codified and recorded. It was this intersection of Roman original with Frankish modification—maybe centered in a great liturgical well such as Metz—that produced what today we call Gregorian chant [quotation 213]. This linear form of music sounded very good in the long, Romanesque churches—especially those with tunnel vaulting [illustration 120].

Besides Gregorian chant, gifted musicians north of the Alps also developed polyphony, in which two or more lines of music sounded simultaneously. In its earliest form, known as organum, a second line of music was matched note against note to an original chant line. The earliest forms of organum utilized a single text simultaneously

S Anctus, * Sánctus, Sánctus Dóminus Dé-us Sá-

ba-oth. Pléni sunt caéli   et tér-ra gló-ri- a tú- a.   Ho-

sánna   in excél-sis. Benedíctus qui vé-nit   in nómine

Dómini.   Ho-sánna   in excél-sis.

122. *Sanctus* from Gregorian setting XV (*Dominator Deus*), tenth century. (From *Liber Usualis*, p. 58)

sung on parallel pitches (parallel organum); later forms included the simultaneous singing of the same text on different pitches (free organum) [illustration 121]. Further developments in polyphony, with multiple and complex lines of music and increasingly intricate rhythmic patterns, contributed to the obscuring of the liturgical texts. In contrast, Gregorian chant was word-centered music that supported and enhanced the text [illustration 122]. In this respect Gregorian chant was in continuity with the tradition of earlier church music, although it was performed in a language ordinary people no longer understood. Polyphony, on the other hand, contributed to the ever-widening gap between music and the liturgical texts it was originally intended to enhance.

In the monastic centers of the North, systems for notating music developed. Until this time, only the chant texts could be recorded, while the music had to be memorized [quotation 151]. By the mid-ninth century, a relatively effective system of signs or "neumes" was developed to aid the singer in recalling a previously learned chant [illustration 123]. By the mid-eleventh century the system was so accurate that music could be learned from the page alone [illustration 124].

The Laity

The early Middle Ages was a transitional era for the participation of the laity in the church's sung prayer. At the beginning of this era, at least in cathedrals and more prominent worship centers, people still joined in singing some parts of the ordinary of the Mass, though they shared little if any musical role in the proper of the Mass apart

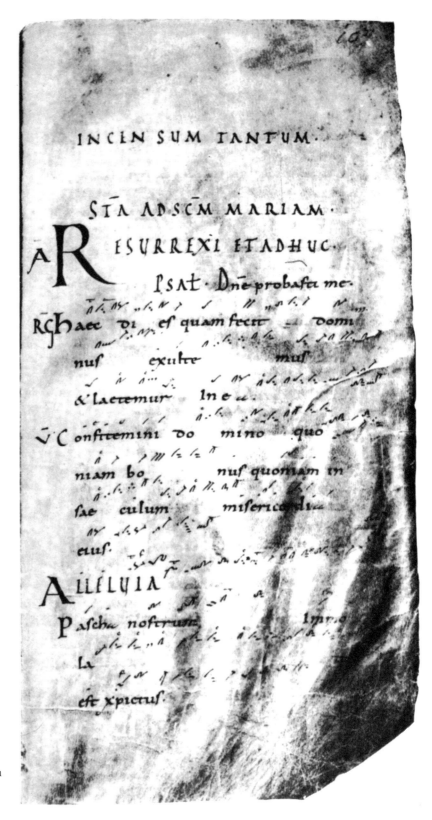

123. Example of an early stage of notation
from ca. 900, Manuscript Saint Gall 359.
(Apel, *Gregorian Chant*, plate 1)

124. Example of an eleventh-century notation, featuring notation in neumes as well as in letters. (Apel, *Gregorian Chant*, plate 4)

from joining in an occasional *Gloria Patri* (Latin, "Glory be to the Father) as part of the Introit (Latin = *introitus*, "entrance"). While the first Roman Ordinal (ca. 700), for example, presents only the *schola* singing the *Kyrie*, there is evidence from the Frankish kingdom well into the late ninth century that the people joined in this chant. More than any other part of the ordinary, however, it was the *Sanctus* that continued to be the song of the people. Various decrees, from Charlemagne [quotation 214] to those of important bishops, ensured that people would share in the *Sanctus*, in some places well into the twelfth century.

One of the factors that contributed to the survival of the *Sanctus* as a song of the assembly was the strong tendency to set the text to a single-line chant melody, even when polyphony was developing. Even though the people did not understand the language, may not have understood the text, and were never "taught" the music, the continuous repetition of a Gregorian setting of the *Sanctus* [illustration 122] by the *schola* could have been enough to sustain the assembly's involvement in this part of the ordinary. Eventually, however, the proliferation of polyphonic settings of the ordinary, plus the growing tendency to recite the canon silently, would virtually silence the assembly during the singing of the *Sanctus*.

Quotation 214: *The priest with the holy angels and the people of God are to sing "Holy, Holy, Holy" with a common voice.* (Charlemagne, *General Admonition* [789], 70)

While the congregation's voice was increasingly no longer essential to the eucharistic liturgy, this does not mean that the community stopped raising its musical voice during this worship. Of particular importance in this period was the development of vernacular religious songs, which were sometimes allowed or even invited into the Mass. Already in the writings of Bede (d. 735), who penned a celebrated history of the English church, there is a report that such religious song existed in England in the early eighth century [quotation 215].

We have already noted the stational practice in Rome and the various ways it was imitated and truncated in churches north of the Alps. Processions were an important part of Roman stational liturgies, and during these processions people joined in singing, often litanies or other responsorial chants. Parallel processions in the Frankish realms were moments when vernacular religious songs were employed. The great pilgrimage movement of the era to shrines like Santiago de Compostela also spawned a huge repertoire of vernacular pilgrim songs. Such processional songs occasionally found their way into eucharistic worship as well.

Another place within the Mass that seemed to allow vernacular song with some regularity was the time after the homily. When it took place, the homily was virtually always a vernacular event, even if the rest of the worship was not. Consequently, the homily often precipitated responses from the assembly, as in fifth-century Hippo where members of Augustine's congregation alternately cheered, sighed, laughed, or audibly beat their breasts when the great bishop preached. Probably less because of ancient precedents and more because of natural response, there is evidence from at least the tenth century in the Germanic territories that a brief acclamation of one or two lines known as a *Ruf* (German, "call") was sometimes sung after a sermon. Sometimes the people would also employ various forms of the refrain *Kyrie eleison* after the sermon. This ubiquitous refrain—which later medieval evidence demonstrates was even sometimes sung by the people during the creed—appeared after the sermon on at least some occasions as a relic from the old prayer of the faithful, which earlier had disappeared from the Roman liturgy.

The Priest

As the people's voice was increasingly silenced at Eucharist, so did the priest develop a silent mode of prayer. At Masses with a congregation, the priest often chanted some of the liturgical texts, reminiscent of a time when no public speech could be rendered without music. Two developments, however, contributed to the diminution of the musical role of the presider and to the musical dominance of the choir in the Eucharist. The first of these was the growing tendency for the priest to pray silently at Mass. During this era, for example, a large number of personal prayers for the presider were introduced into the Mass. One of the most prominent types of such prayers are what Jungmann calls the *apologiae* (Latin, "apologies"), which he describes as personal avowals of guilt and unworthiness, usually joined to prayers begging for God's mercy—prayers that Jungmann considered quite alien to the ancient Roman tradition (*Mass of the Roman Rite*, I:78). The introduction of these deprecatory prayers is understandable given the anti-Pelagian and anti-Arian teaching that was so powerful at the dawn of the Middle Ages. As previously noted, by the beginning of the early Middle Ages ordinary Christians considered themselves more sinful than graced, more unlike than like God, and unworthy for something as sacred as communion. The clergy, as well, were clearly mindful of their unworthiness before God, especially in so awesome an act as Eucharist.

One of the most dramatic examples of the silencing of the eucharistic presider is the complete silence of the priest during the canon of the Mass. Evidence from Gaul around 775 suggests that the presider changed his tone of voice when he began the canon so that only those standing around him could hear [quotation 216]. Toward the end of the ninth century, similar sources indicate that the canon had become completely silent [quotation 217].

A second development that marked the diminution of the sung role of the presider was the private Mass, which we previously noted developed during this period. In a private Mass, the priest assumed virtually all of the ministries—except when he had an assisting acolyte—including the silent reading of chant texts that normally would have been sung by the choir. Evidence of priests saying Mass without a congregation may come from as early as the seventh century. Originally, certain elements such as the chant texts simply were dropped. Evidence exists that Masses for the dead in the ninth century were without chant texts from their beginning; they apparently originated as silent Masses without music. Evidence that priests began to recite chant texts during private Masses comes from the ninth century [quotation 218]. It is from this time, therefore, that one can first distinguish between what will be called the sung Mass (*miss cantata*) from what will be known as the read Mass (*miss lecta*).

Summary

Although musical specialists appear in the time of Constantine, they came into increasing prominence during this period of Germanization, and the congregational voice was proportionally diminished at Eucharist. It is true that the congregation did sing and that they did sing at Eucharist. Such singing, however, was no longer in the official

Quotation 216: *And the pontiff begins the canon in a different voice so that it may be heard only by those standing around the altar. (Roman Ordo* XV [ca. 775], 39, in Andrieu, *Les Ordines Romani)*

Quotation 217: *And when the Sanctus is finished, the pontiff alone rises and begins the canon silent. (Roman Ordo* V [ca. 850], 58, in Andrieu, *Les Ordines Romani)*

Quotation 218: *Repeatedly we make this recommendation to all, so that every priest who desires can offer a reasonable and acceptable sacrifice to God. . . . When one celebrates Mass, first begin with a psalm and then the Gloria Patri or antiphon followed by the Kyrie eleison. Similarly at communion, employ an antiphon and psalm, always adding the Gloria Patri, which is praise of the Holy Trinity. (Roman Ordo* XV, 155, in Andrieu, *Les Ordines Romani)*

125. Carolingian writing centers in Gaul.

language of the liturgy, nor was it generally considered essential, much less integral, to the worship. One exception seems to have been the *Sanctus*, and there appears to be a particular propensity among some Germanic peoples to sing during the liturgy. The congregational music that did develop was more often wedded to pilgrimage, or devotions, or even in some places the Liturgy of the Hours rather than to the Eucharist. As the musical role of the congregation diminished, so did the presider begin to disregard the musical nature of the liturgical texts he was required to recite. Not only did presiders read what in a previous era would have been sung, but they also changed from reading the texts audibly to reading them silently.

BOOKS

It is not surprising that in the current study of liturgical history there is more interest in architecture and music than in the history and development of liturgical books. Architecture and music are powerful and enduring art forms that easily capture the religious imagination. In this computerized age of mass-produced paperbacks and downloadable E-books, the power of the handcrafted liturgical manuscript may be difficult to grasp. Ironically, however, manuscripts of the early Middle Ages played a decisive role in both the communication of the Roman Rite and its transformation into the Franco-Roman Rite.

We have already noted that importing of books from Rome was a key strategy in the plan of Pepin and Charlemagne for introducing the Roman liturgy into their kingdom. In an ironic twist, however, the Frankish kingdom became a great center for the production of liturgical manuscripts [illustration 125], which were transformed in the process and eventually reintroduced to Rome, contributing mightily to the official adoption of the Franco-Roman Rite at the heart of Western Christianity [quotation 201]. Benedictine monasteries were central to this development.

As Richard Clement has noted, even though the Rule of St. Benedict does not mention book production, it does require monks to read every day. Since private ownership of books was forbidden, a communal library was essential. Scriptoria eventually became an integral part of every major monastery in order to meet this need [illustration 126]. A parallel influence according to Clement was the founding of a monastery by Cassiodorus (d. ca. 580) who, in the midst of societal decline, understood that one task of a monastery was to serve as a repository of classical culture. To that end he provided various guidelines for book production and raised the monastic scribe to a person of considerable status. Though his own monastery

126. The scriptorium was designed to allow the maximum amount of sunlight throughout the day. Camaldolese hermitage, Fonte Avellana, built ca. 1000.

did not outlive him, Cassiodorus's work did inspire Gregory the Great. "The example provided by Cassiodorus as well as the direct involvement of Gregory redirected the Benedictine movement so that the production and preservation of books became an integral part of western monasticism" (Clement, p.16). It was in such monasteries that the vast majority of liturgical books in this era were crafted, and in the process the liturgy of the era was notably transformed.

Two somewhat contradictory tendencies marked the development of liturgical books during this period. The first, continuing the trend of the previous period, was the creation of new books for the liturgy. A second, quite different, tendency was the conflation of a number of liturgical books into a single volume. The result of this second evolution was the appearance of a new genre of self-contained liturgical books that facilitated more individualized liturgical prayer, such as the private celebration of the Mass and the individual recitation of the Liturgy of the Hours.

Almost all of the previously mentioned books—the antiphonary, cantatory, Bible, gospel book, epistle book, lectionary, calendar, martyrology, sacramentary, and ordo—continued in various forms. Only the *libelli missarum* disappeared. Of the existing books, the lectionary and the sacramentary underwent the most development in this period. Even though liturgical books were being employed as a way to unify a kingdom, there was yet enormous diversity in the way these evolving books were shaped and named. Thus, like so many other aspects of medieval worship, there is no strict categorization here to outline, but rather major trends within the liturgical books of this era.

The Antiphonary for Mass and the Gradual

As noted in the previous chapter, the various chant texts for the Mass were contained in a number of different books in Rome. As the Roman liturgy was imported into other parts of the West, these books like the liturgy itself both spread and changed. In the Frankish kingdom, there is evidence for the production of some books containing only sections of the Mass chant texts, such as the cantatory, which ordinarily contained the texts sung between the readings, though the Franks called this book the gradual (Latin = *gradale* or *graduale*). More often, however, the various chant texts for Masses were being gathered into a single book called the "antiphonary for Mass" (*antiphonarius missae*) [quotation 164]. Another type of antiphonary also existed at this time; it contained the chants employed during the Liturgy of the Hours. In time, the term antiphonary was abandoned as a designation for any book containing the Mass chants, and instead the name "gradual" was adopted as the proper term for this book. The term antiphonary eventually was restricted to refer to the book containing the chants for the Liturgy of the Hours. As the centuries passed, these books began to include not only the texts to be chanted but also the primitive musical markings, which helped the singer recall the previously learned melody for a particular text. Eventually, these books were fully notated.

Lectionary

In the last chapter we noted that, after the time of Constantine, the Bible began to be replaced as a Christian liturgical book. In its place a community might read from a Book of the Gospels, used alongside a "capitular," listing the specifics of each reading for each liturgical feast. In conjunction with such a book, a community would also have to have a book containing complete texts of epistles, for example, those of St. Paul, which would have its own capitular. These books were forerunners of a true evangeliary and epistolary, which did not contain all of the texts of the four gospels or all of the writings of St. Paul, but only those segments that were to be read during Eucharist, and these arranged according to the liturgical calendar. As Gy has noted, the development of evangelaries and epistolaries are symbolic of important ecclesiological developments. A specific type of book (e.g., epistolary) was identified with a particular person, liturgical role, and ecclesiastical status in the church (e.g., subdeacon). These books both expressed evolving distinctions in orders and symbolically contributed to cementing such distinctions. Thus, for example, while subdeacons already appear in the third century [quotation 102], and a fourth century document such as the *Apostolic Constitutions* speaks of their ordination, their exact role and placement as a step to priestly ordination and the lowest of the "major orders" in the West was not theologically clarified and accepted until the thirteenth century. Their distinctive role in the medieval Roman Mass and their identification with a particular liturgical book during this period certainly contributed to that eventual consensus.

Besides individual epistolaries, evangelaries, and books of the gospels that continued to be very popular during this period, lectionaries were clearly under development in this period. We have already noted that documentary evidence about lectionaries existed from the end of the fifth century [quotation 167] and partial manuscripts survive from the sixth century. As Martimort has noted, however, the first complete lectionaries that survive are from the end of the eighth and the ninth centuries. These books containing all of the readings for Mass arranged according to the liturgical year continued to multiply, but they will not displace epistolaries, evangelaries, and even books of gospels until the next era. Before that occurred, however, full lectionaries were combined with sacramentaries. This eventually led to the development of the full missal, which appeared by the tenth century.

Full Missal

One of the most significant new books of this period was the full missal. This book ordinarily contained materials from five other books: chant texts from the antiphonary for Mass, readings from the epistolary and evangeliary, the priest's prayers from the sacramentary, and rubrical instructions from the ordo. Numerous factors contributed to the emergence of the missal. One of these was the previously noted rise of the private Mass. Multiple ministers meant multiple books, but in a private Mass the priest assumed virtually all of the roles himself. A single book was useful for this purpose. Aside from issues of practicality, another contributing factor was a changed attitude toward the chants of the Mass. In the Christian West, the official Mass chants were increasingly the sung prerogative of scholas. Not only the laity but even the priest began to lose his role as a central music maker at Eucharist. In many situations, like those of the proprietary churches of the era, there were no trained singers or schola and the ritual chants were well beyond the ability of the congregation. It did not seem appropriate to drop these chants altogether. Furthermore, as Eric Palazzo observes, there was a developing piety among priests in this period that began to define Eucharist more in terms of personal devotion than ecclesial celebration. In such an atmosphere, reciting musical texts could render the Eucharist a more complete devotional activity. Eventually, instructions would direct that chant texts—first in the absence of a choir [quotation 218] and then even in their presence [quotation 260]—were to be recited by the priest.

Pontifical

Another new type of book that appeared during this period was the bishop's book or "pontifical" (Latin = *pontifex*, "bishop"). Like the full missal, the pontifical combined materials from a variety of books into a single volume. Initially this usually meant the rubrics from the Roman Ordinals with the corresponding prayers from a sacramentary. The pontificals, like the sacramentaries, began as small *libelli* (Latin, "little books"), which sometimes contained the text of a single liturgy at which the bishop would have presided, such as an ordination or the consecration of a church. Alongside these ninth century *libelli* there is also evidence that the scroll (Latin, *rotulus*) made a brief comeback as a preferred format in some places for pontificals—as well as magnificently decorated formats for the *Exultet* (Latin, "exult") sung at the Easter Vigil [illustration 127]. Like the sacramentaries, these *libelli* were often gathered together, creating a rudimentary form of the pontifical. As Rasmussen has demonstrated, there was a certain randomness about these primitive ninth- and tenth-century sacramentaries, and they lacked any fixed structure or content. That was to change with the composition of the Romano-Germanic Pontifical, composed between 950 and 962 in Mainz. This large book, containing 258 sections, is a well organized, true pontifical that has been lauded as one of the main liturgical monuments of the Ottonian Empire. Like so many other Germanic liturgical books, it eventually migrated back to Rome, where it became foundational for the development of the Roman Pontifical.

127. Tenth-century *Exultet* scroll, Benevento, Italy.

The reasons for the appearance of this new book are manifold. There is certainly an element of practicality here, as demonstrated by the proliferation of diverse *libelli* containing rubrics and texts for a particular episcopal ritual. It was undoubtedly easier to preside using a single book, than to juggle sacramentaries, ordinals, and other volumes at the same time during a service. Yet, as previously noted, the emergence of such a book symbolizes profound ecclesiological changes, particularly in the redefinition of priesthood and the episcopacy during this period. In the previous era we noted that priests were becoming ordinary presiders at Eucharist but that the bishop was yet understood to be the primary liturgist of a church, not only celebrating Eucharist but also the ordinary presider for initiation, reconciliation, and the other rites of the church. With the development of so many proprietary churches in this era, however, the priest became the ordinary presider in the eyes of most Christians, especially north of the Alps. Bishops, on the other hand, acquired new social and political influence during the Carolingian and Ottonian empires. They were important advisors to kings and emperors, not only on theological matters but also on educational, financial, and political issues. As Palazzo notes, this was increasingly true under Otto I who established a *Reichkirchensystem* (German, "imperial ecclesiastical system") that linked the bishop directly to the emperor. Some bishops held civil as well as ecclesiastical appointments in the empire, and under Otto I, the archbishop of Mainz (the place of composition for the Romano-Germanic Pontifical) was also arch-chancellor for the empire; he also happened to be the emperor's son.

The cumulative result of these changes would be the redefinition of the bishop, less as a pastoral office directly connected to the ordinary worship life of Christians, and more as an administrative and juridical figure. Theologically, this would eventually result in the

128. First page of a ninth-century sacramentary, Saint Gall 348. (After Righetti, 1:215)

removal of the episcopacy as the culmination of the ordination process. Rather, priesthood would be the apex of the various rites of ordination; bishops, on the other hand, would be "consecrated" not ordained—a rite conferring new dignity and jurisdiction but no longer a major order in the church. Pontificals, similar to other liturgical books, were symbols of and vehicles for this evolution.

Sacramentaries

This was a period of unusual growth for the sacramentary, and more manuscripts of sacramentaries exist from this than from any other period. Eventually superseded in the late Middle Ages by the full missal, sacramentaries were the predominant liturgical book of the early Middle Ages [illustration 128]. The Frankish church definitely shaped the content and form of the sacramentary for Western Christianity. We have already alluded to this in observing the central role that the sacramentary of Pope Hadrian played in the development of the Franco-Roman liturgy. This *Hadrianum* was of the Gregorian type, or that type used for papal Masses in Rome. A second type of sacramentary in use at Rome in the previous era was the Gelasian, intended for worship presided over by presbyters in the *tituli*. Outside of Rome there were other types of sacramentaries not directly drawn from either of these sources, like old Gallican or Frankish sacramentaries. When the *Hadrianum* was received by the Franks, though a splendid looking volume that was actually put on display, it was deemed quite incomplete, missing texts for a large number of Masses, including those for the Sundays after Epiphany, funeral rites, penitential rites, and a variety of votive Masses. Thus, Benedict of Aniane was commissioned to write an extended supplement of the *Hadrianum*, called the *Hucusque* (the first Latin word of the supplement, "Up to this point"). In doing so, he drew from mostly these non-Roman sources [quotation 219]. Over the next few centuries this "supplemented Hadrianum" was rearranged, acquired more materials (e.g., from eighth-century Frankish sacramentaries of the Gelasian style), and evolved into what is sometimes called the mixed-Gregorian type of sacramentary [illustration 129]. It was this hybrid genre of Frankish-Roman materials that was reintroduced to Rome and played a pivotal role in the development of the Roman Missal.

Summary

Books are more than convenient means for communicating liturgical texts or rubrical directions. They are, among other things, a dynamic embodiment of the church's ecclesiology. We have seen, for example,

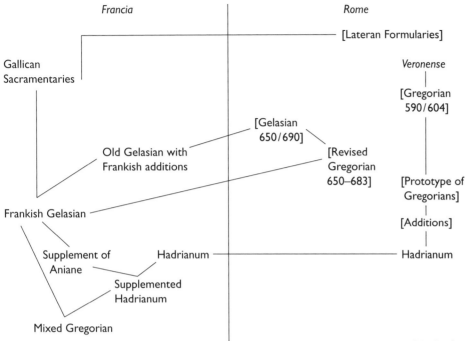

Francia   *Rome*

[Lateran Formularies]

Gallican   *Veronense*
Sacramentaries

[Gregorian
590/604]

[Gelasian
650/690]

Old Gelasian with   [Revised
Frankish additions   Gregorian
                                 650–683]   [Prototype of
                                                 Gregorians]

Frankish Gelasian   [Additions]

Supplement of   Hadrianum ——————————— Hadrianum
Aniane

        Supplemented
        Hadrianum

Mixed Gregorian

129. Outline of sacramentary developments.
(After Vogel, p. 401)

that materials for individual ministers, such as the liturgical chants
for the singers, were eventually consolidated into a single volume
for a single liturgical genre, for example, the *graduale* for the sung
celebration of the Eucharist. Eventually every minister in what would
be called "major orders" (subdeacon, deacon, and priest) had their
own liturgical book (epistolary, evangeliary, and full missal). The
bishop as well, who had originally been the intended presider for
different forms of the sacramentary, acquired a new book (the pontifical) indicative of his changing status. Taken together, these changes
in books illustrate sweeping ministerial developments in this era: the
consolidation of central musical responsibilities by specialists, the
redefinition of ministries so that they are aligned with the ultimate
goal of priestly ordination, the centrality of the priest in Christian
worship to the point that even the congregation could be eliminated,
and the distancing of the bishop from the center of pastoral liturgy.

     Some liturgical books of the early Middle Ages, as those of the
previous era, were illuminated, sometimes lavishly bound and crafted
as beautiful works of art. Because of their beauty, occasionally a
biblical or liturgical manuscript was given as a gift, never to be employed in worship itself, but now a liturgical or biblical artifact,
valuable because of how it appeared rather than how it enabled a

130. Ivory book cover of the Lorsch gospels, eighth century.

community to pray [illustration 130]. Even in the artistry of books intended for liturgical use, however, some medieval liturgical books seem to indicate a distancing from the baptized, whose ordinary existence was far removed from such richness and beauty.

VESSELS

Bread and Its Vessels

Quotation 220: *The bread which is consecrated into the body of Christ ought to be most pure without leaven or any other additive.* (Alcuin, *Letter 90 to the brothers in Lyons* [798])

From the beginning of Christianity, the bread used at Eucharist was made from similar ingredients and often looked like that used for ordinarily meals. We have already noted, however, that while crafted from common ingredients, by the fourth century bread intended for eucharistic worship was often stamped, marked, or shaped in a particular way, setting it apart from ordinary table fare. One tradition was to prepare eucharistic bread in the shape of flat disks. Bread stamps from the period [illustration 93] demonstrate that these disks were larger and thicker than the hosts (from Latin, *hostia*, "victim") of a later era. After the ninth century, however, there is a significant shift in the recipe for eucharistic bread, with unleavened bread becoming customary and eventually mandatory in the Christian West. Alcuin of York (d. 804), a key advisor on educational and church issues to Charlemagne and one of the most prominent figures of the Carolingian renaissance, provided one of the first testimonies for this change [quotation 220]. This new restriction against the use of leaven and other additives eventually produced eucharistic bread that was round, flat, and white.

The reasons for this change were many and complex. Contributing factors included a sustained emphasis on the unworthiness of the laity, something already noted at the end of the last chapter. Unworthy people did not go to communion regularly, nor by consequence did they bring gifts and bread and wine to the church as an offering. Thus, the number of communicants declined significantly, and offertory processions were eliminated in many places. With the growth in private Masses during this era such a procession would have served no purpose. Where the offertory procession did survive, the people's gifts were not used in the Mass. Increasingly, the elements offered in the Eucharist were prepared by monks or clerics, and the baking of hosts became a highly ritualized procedure in monasteries and other religious houses [quotation 221]. Furthermore, as the otherworldliness of the Eucharist was emphasized, using bread that was completely different from ordinary table fare became appropriate. The image of unleavened, specially prepared bread employed in Jewish temple sacrifices provided a biblical precedent for employing pure, specially prepared bread in the Eucharist. Another factor in the use of unleavened bread was the widespread understanding of the Eucharist as the reenactment of the life and death of Jesus. Russell believes this is one of the influences of Germanization, which produced a more dramatic and representational interpretation of the liturgy with emphasis on the historical drama of Christ's passion and death (p. 6). This perspective gave support to the use of unleavened bread, for this is what Jesus is remembered as having used at the Last Supper. Though evidence can be found for eucharistic breads that are ring-shaped [illustration 131] or other forms, at the turn of the millennium the ordinary eucharistic fare was the "host."

Increases in the number of private Masses and decreases in the number of communicants along with the change to unleavened bread all contributed to a reduction in the size of the host. The practice of placing the bread on people's tongues instead of in their hands, evident since the ninth century [quotation 222], also was a factor in the decreasing size of the host. By the eleventh century, small hosts were ordinarily prepared for communicants.

Patens   Changes in eucharistic bread brought about changes in the vessels that held it. Baskets disappeared as eucharistic vessels during

131. A ninth-century ivory tablet, part of a book cover portraying early medieval episcopal worship. A chalice with handles stands upon the altar and three ring-shaped hosts lie upon the paten.

Quotation 221: *It is [the sacrist's] task to prepare the hosts, and he should take every care to ensure that they are perfectly pure and seemly. In the first place, if it be possible, the wheat is to be picked out grain by grain with great care, and then put into a clean sack made of good cloth and prepared and reserved for the purpose; a servant of good character shall carry it to the mill, and there shall see that other corn is ground first, so that that from which the hosts are to be made may be ground without any admixture of dirt. When the flour is brought back the sacrist shall draw a curtain round the place and the vessel in which the flour is to be bolted, and he shall carry out his work in an alb and with an amice over his head. On the day the hosts are to be made, the sacristan and those who help him shall wash their hands and faces before they begin; they shall wear albs and amices, save for the one who is to hold the irons and ministers with them. One shall sprinkle the flour with water as it lies on an absolutely clean table, and shall knead it firmly and press it thin, while the brother who holds the irons in which the wafers are baked shall have his hands covered with gloves. Meanwhile, while the hosts are being made and baked, these brethren shall recite the "familiar" psalms that go with the hours, and the canonical hours themselves, or, if they prefer, psalms of equal length taken in order from the psalter. Absolute silence shall be maintained. (The Monastic Constitutions of Lanfranc [ca. 1077], no. 87, in Knowles, p. 125)*

Quotation 222: *None are to place the Eucharist in the hands of lay men or women, but only in their mouth.* (Synod of Rouen [878], canon 2, in Mansi, *Sacrorum Conciliorum*)

Quotation 223: *We prohibit making a chalice or paten for the sacrifice from the horn of an animal.* (Synod of Celchyth/ Chelsea [787], canon 10, in Mansi, *Sacrorum Conciliorum*)

this period. Patens, formerly large enough to hold a large piece of bread—if not all the bread for communicants—became smaller. Small patens already were in use in the post-Constantinian period. In the early Middle Ages, however, they became the rule regardless of the size or nature of the worshiping community. Because it was increasingly common to reserve whatever bread might be distributed in a pyx, the paten was no longer a vessel for the people's communion but rather only had to hold the priest's host. Jungmann notes that during this period it becomes customary to put the host on the paten at the offertory and that the practice grew of bringing the paten and chalice together to the altar at this moment in the Mass. This combination of vessels contributed to the concern and then requirement that the paten should lie smoothly on top of the chalice. The result, already present by the tenth century, was the evolution of the small paten in the shape of a concave disk [illustration 132].

During this period, scattered directives about the materials for the paten and other eucharistic vessels appeared, especially in England. The first requirements were prohibitive—forbidding the use of certain materials such as wood or animal horn [quotation 223]. In general, however, few directives about the material for the paten appear before the end of the Middle ages. Much more legislation developed around the material for the chalice. In general, the paten was forged from the same elements as the chalice; gold and silver became common materials for both. These special vessels, distinguishable by their precious materials and reduced size, were further set apart by special rituals and prayers of consecration [quotation 224]. This Gallican concern for consecrating vessels—something not seen in Rome during this era—lends support to Russell's theory for what he calls the more "magical" outlook of the Germanic peoples contributing to increased focus on the objects employed in worship.

Pyxes   As noted in chapter 3, the pyx—a vessel that held the eucharistic bread outside of Mass—assumed a number of forms. A new development in this era that contributed to the evolution of the pyx was its transformation from a vessel used outside of the eucharistic celebration to one that would eventually become a standard eucharistic vessel within the Mass. We have already observed how patens diminished in size during this period and eventually became the exclusive receptacle for the priest's host. The small hosts for the laity were placed in a pyx. Its original purposes were carrying the consecrated to the sick, giving oneself communion, or carrying the consecrated bread as a talisman [quotation 179]. There is evidence that such pyxes would sit on the altar during the Mass, suggesting that there was at least some continuation of the practice of bringing communion for the sick directly from the eucharistic table rather than from a tabernacle, which became ordinary procedure [quotation 225]. This practice foreshadowed a time when the pyx would commonly sit on the altar during Eucharist, no longer holding an "offering" for the sick, but containing small hosts for the communion of the faithful at Mass. Like patens, it was increasingly customary during this period to consecrate pyxes before they were used in the liturgy [quotation 226].

Wine and Its Vessels

There do not appear to be as many directives about the ingredients used for wine as there are for bread in the first millennium of Christianity. According to Patrick McSherry, one of the reasons for this is the cultural presumption that wine by definition equals "grape wine" (p. 10). The Fourth Council of Orleans is one of the few early sources providing a directive on the necessity of using grape wine for the Eucharist [quotation 227]. While wine, by definition, is fermented, there is also evidence that unfermented juice from the grape or *mustum* (Latin abbreviation for *vinum mustum*, "new wine") was used for Eucharist. The *Decretals of Gratian* (ca. 1140) quote Pope Julius I (d. 352) as having allowed the use of unfermented grapes for Mass [quotation 228]. While this saying appears to be a forgery— maybe by Burchard of Worms (d. 1025)—its apparent papal lineage lent it credibility, and the use of *mustum* was thus allowed by the leading canonists and theologians of the Middle Ages, and is yet allowed today with certain restrictions.

Chalices   There is evidence that, especially early in this period, large chalices comparable in size to those of the previous period were still used. Some chalices were designed with handles [illustration 131], reminiscent of drinking goblets. A few early Irish chalices in this style that have survived are particularly beautiful works of art [illustration 133]. Chalices with handles are increasingly rare and disappear in the West after the twelfth century. As in the previous period, chalices of different sizes could have been used at the same Mass, especially when the congregation was large and the consecrated wine was shared with the faithful by smaller "communion" chalices. Increasingly, chalices of this period were smaller than those of the previous era, largely because of a decline in the communion of the people, particularly their drinking from the cup, and the growing prevalence of private Mass. Even when people did receive communion, it was with progressive rarity that they actually drank from the chalice, often for fear that the precious Blood would be spilled. As we will discuss

132. Example of an eleventh-century chalice with a paten small enough to fit on top of the cup and large enough to hold the priest's host.

133. The eighth-century Ardagh Chalice, 7.01 inches in height and 7.68 inches in diameter.

Quotation 224: *Lord, deign to consecrate and sanctify this chalice through this anointing and our blessing, in Christ Jesus our Lord, who lives and reigns [with you forever and ever].* (Missal of the Franks [*Missale Francorum*, eighth century], 63)

134. Communion tube.

below, one stage in the separation of the people from the cup was requiring them to communicate the precious Blood through a tube.

One design development, apparent in most of the chalices fabricated during this period, was the inclusion of a node on the stem separating the base from the cup. There are some examples of chalices from the previous era with this design characteristic [illustration 100]; though it was by no means a standard feature on all chalices, it increasingly became one. One of the factors that contributed to the standardization of this element was the growing practice of priests holding together the thumb and forefinger after they had touched the consecrated host. Though challenged by some [quotation 229], this practice became the general rule by the thirteenth century. A node on the chalice stem made it easier to pick up the chalice without spilling the sacred contents (e.g., for the priest's communion) while one's fingers were so joined together.

Legislation concerning the material for fabricating chalices first appears during this time. Initially, certain materials were disallowed, as had been the case with the paten [quotation 223]. Eventually, directives required that the chalice be made from gold or silver. The laws were not consistent on this point, and various materials such as bronze or copper were also permitted, according to different synods or individuals. Exceptions were also made for poor churches that, for example, were allowed to use tin. Eventually, the preference that chalices should be made only of gold, silver, or at least tin was incorporated into the law of the church [quotation 230]. As chalices came to be forged almost exclusively from previous metals and were removed from the hands of the laity, their sacrality was further emphasized by the rites of consecration that, similar to those for other eucharistic vessels, appeared at this time.

Tubes One of the more unusual eucharistic utensils of this period was the eucharistic tube or reed (Latin = *calamus, fistula, pugillaris*), employed as a kind of straw when receiving communion from the cup [illustration 134]. The earliest evidence for this utensil comes from eighth-century Rome, where the tube was employed for the communion of the people during the bishop's Mass [quotation 231]. From at least the thirteenth century until the reforms of Vatican II, the tube was used on special occasions by the pope and his deacon and, less often, by bishops during a pontifical liturgy. The earliest sources, however, do not indicate that the people or other clergy used the tube for communion. Some scholars suggest that because certain communion tubes were fashioned from gold, one could conclude that these were employed by the clergy. It is also reasonable to conclude, however, that silver and gold were used not because of the dignity of the communicant but because of the precious nature of the consecrated wine. In general, the tube was used for the communion of the laity during Mass, though it also seems to have been used to give communion to the sick outside of Mass. This distinctive eucharistic vessel served in the transition from the time when people drank directly from the chalice to a period when ordinary people did not receive the consecrated wine. Lay communion from the chalice disappeared in most places by the late thirteenth century.

Summary

The eucharistic vessels of this period underwent a reduction in their capacity for holding the eucharistic species, if not in their overall size. At the same time, insistence increased on the use not only of precious materials but specifically of gold and silver in the fabrication of these vessels. These phenomena symbolized certain developments in eucharistic theology that we will explore below. In particular, some during this period increasingly focused on the localization of Christ's presence in the bread and wine. This emphasis on Christ's presence under the eucharistic species virtually ignored other modes of Christ's presence, especially his presence in the assembly. In the Germanized environment north of the Alps, the vessels that held the sacred species to a certain extent came to be considered more precious than the community itself. Vessels were consecrated at the same time that people began to be restricted in the way they could receive communion. Transformed bread in the form of a host was no longer put in their hands but on their tongues. Drinking through a tube replaced drinking from the cup, and eventually the cup was completely withdrawn from the laity. In a metaphoric way, beautiful chalices and patens came to replace the baptized as the primary vessels of the presence of Christ.

EUCHARISTIC THEOLOGY

In discussing the eucharistic developments at the end of the last two chapters, we have attempted to indicate where there have been strands of both continuity and discontinuity with the eucharistic theologies of previous ages. One could most certainly do the same thing when considering the eucharistic theologies that emerge in these early Middle Ages. On the other hand, the Christian church in the West at the end of this period can seem very distant from the church of the fifth or sixth century. Much of this can be explained

Quotation 227: *No one should presume, in the offering of the sacred chalice, to offer anything except that which is trusted to be from the fruit of the vine mixed with water, because it is judged to be sacrilege to offer anything other than that which the Savior instituted in accordance with his most sacred commands.* (Fourth Council of Orleans [541], canon 4, in Mansi, *Sacrorum Conciliorum*)

Quotation 228: *But if it be necessary, a bunch of grapes may be squeezed into the chalice and water added, because the cup of the Lord, according to the precepts of the canons, must be offered with wine mixed with water.* (Decretals of Gratian, part 3 ["Concerning Consecration"], distinction 2, canon 7, in McSherry, *Wine as Sacramental Matter*, p. 68]

Quotation 229: *Thus fingers are not always to be joined, even if some do so out of excessive caution. . . . This having been said, however, we may not touch anything with our fingers except the body of the Lord.* (Bernold of Constance [d. 1100], *Micrologus*, canon 16, in Migne, *Patrologia Latina*)

Quotation 230: *If the chalice with the paten is not from gold, it should be entirely of silver. If, however, some place is very poor, the chalice should at least be made of tin.* (Decretals of Gratian, part 3 ["Concerning Consecration"], distinction 1, canon 45, in Migne, 187:1720)

Quotation 231: *Then the archdeacon accepts the chalice from the head bishop and pours the contents back into the above mentioned larger chalice. The archdeacon then hands the smaller chalice to the regional subdeacon, who gives him a tube [pugillarem] with which he communicates the people.* (Roman Ordo I, no. 111)

from the perspectives of politics and geography, particularly in regard to the rise of Islam. As a consequence of the enormous success of Islam throughout the Middle East, North Africa, and the Iberian peninsula, the Western churches became much more separated from their Eastern counterparts during the early Middle Ages. This, coupled with the political rise of the Germanic tribes and the subsequent Germanization of the church and its worship, set the Roman Eucharist and its theologies on a quite distinctive trajectory in thought and practice.

What Is Real?

It is common to find theological references to the "Augustinian synthesis." While the phrase can mean many things, in terms of sacramental or eucharistic theology it ordinarily refers to the celebrated way in which Augustine fused biblical teaching and the Christian faith with late Platonic philosophy. Thus, just as Plato could speak about the visible pointing to essentials that could not be seen, Augustine could speak about sacraments as "signs" pointing to spiritual essentials [quotation 232]. Thus, when speaking about the Eucharist, Augustine taught that at the Last Supper, Christ gave the disciples the "figure (Latin, *figura*) of his body and blood" (*On Psalm* 3) and further, when explaining the Eucharist, insisted that "what you see is transitory, but the invisible reality therein signified does not pass away, but remains" (*Sermon* 227). For Augustine, there was no inseparable chasm between the visible and the spiritual; rather, there was continuity between the two. The visible "*figura*" was both helpful and essential for pointing to the eternal truths that could not be grasped by the senses alone.

Authors such as Jaroslav Pelikan remark about the confused state of this Augustinian synthesis during the early Middle Ages. Such confusion is obvious in the writings of various authors of this period who increasingly demonstrate an inability for such elastic or symbolic thinking, and instead resort to more literal understandings of sacraments and Eucharist. One celebrated example comes from Florus (d. ca. 860), a deacon in Lyons. Amalarius of Metz had once briefly governed the diocese of Lyons. During that time Florus learned of Amalarius's teaching that the three different parts of the host stood for the three different bodies of Christ: the resurrected Christ, the Church, and the faithful departed [quotation 233]. To symbolize this, Amalarius taught that the host must be divided into three parts, with one part to be put in the cup, one on the paten, and one on the altar. Florus, however, accused Amalarius of subdividing the single Body of Christ, and found sufficient support for his more

Quotation 232: *These things . . . are called sacraments [in Latin, the word sacramentum means "sign"] for the reason that in them one thing is seen, but another is understood. That which is seen has physical appearance, that which is understood has spiritual fruit.* (Augustine, Sermon 272 [ca. 405–411], in Sheerin, The Eucharist)

Quotation 233: *The body of Christ is triform . . . first, the holy and immaculate [body] assumed from the Virgin Mary; second, that which walks on the earth; third, that which lies in the sepulcher.* (Amalarius, The Book of Offices, 3.35.1-2, in Pelikan, The Christian Tradition)

literal interpretation of Amalarius's writings to have him censured at the Council of Quiercy in 838.

A more pivotal witness to the confused state of the Augustinian synthesis during this period is Paschasius Radbertus (d. ca. 860), a monk and eventually abbot of the monastery of Corbie. In order to help the other monks understand better the mystery of the Eucharist, Paschasius wrote the first extensive work in the West on eucharistic theology, *On the Body and Blood of the Lord* (originally composed 831–833, revised 844). As Gary Macy points out, Paschasius was fundamentally concerned about questions of salvation and how Eucharist contributed to our salvation by uniting us with Christ. Paschasius believed that salvation takes place by our being united to Christ's "real" body. In order to explain how Eucharist contributes to our being united to Christ's real body, Paschasius reflected upon the relationship between the eucharistic Body of Christ and the historical body of Christ. He concluded that the historical and eucharistic Body of Christ are not only related or similar but identical, and it was communion with this body of Christ born of Mary that enabled our salvation. In what Macy calls his crudest formulation of this belief, Paschasius writes in a letter to a certain Fredugard, "(Christ), however, lives on account of the Father because he was born the only-begotten one of the Father, and we live on account of Him because we eat him" (Macy, *Theologies of the Eucharist*, p. 28).

Paschasius was sensitive to some of the problems of this more literal approach to eucharistic presence and thus finds it necessary to speak of Christ's presence as a mystical event that can only happen through God's miraculous power [quotation 234]. He was also aware that salvation did not come magically through eating Christ's body, but required the discipline of Christian living. Despite such awareness, however, Paschasius—like every theologian—was limited by the resources of his culture and his age. Living in the interim between the decline of the Augustinian synthesis and the rise of a new synthesis to be offered by theologians like Thomas Aquinas (d. 1274), he lacked the tools to nuance his explanation of Christ's presence in the Eucharist. Macy summarizes:

> Paschasius wished to assert the presence of Christ, as God and as man, in the Eucharist, for it was only through our contact with the nature of the God-man that our own nature could be redeemed. Paschasius' theology was a simple and unified attempt to explain the role of the Eucharist in the salvation of the Christian. Its simplicity which might in itself be seen as a virtue, may also be it's major vice, for although it could be understood as implying a spiritual contact of our natures with that of the true God-man . . . it could also be understood as the crassest kind of capharnaism [quotation 235].

Quotation 234: *Because it is not right to devour Christ with the teeth, [God] willed in the mystery that this bread and wine be created truly his flesh and blood through consecration by the power of the Holy Spirit . . . so that it might be mystically sacrificed for the life of the world; so that as from the Virgin through the Spirit true flesh is created without union of sex, so through the same, out of the substance of bread and wine, the same body and blood of Christ may be mystically consecrated.* (Paschasius Radbertus, *The Lord's Body and Blood* [844], in McCracken, *Early Medieval Theology*, 4.1)

Quotation 235: *Capharnaism is a name given to the belief that the Body of Christ in the Eucharist is His physical Body miraculously concealed from our senses in order that we might not be shocked by seeing that we were eating human flesh. The term is a reference to the Jews of Capernaum in the gospels who asked, "How can this Man give us His flesh to eat?" (John 6:52).* (Macy, *Theologies of the Eucharist*, p. 28)

Paschasius was not the only voice attempting to discern what was "real" about Christ's eucharistic presence at this time. Another monk of his own monastery was actually drawn into the discussion at the invitation of the emperor. When Charles II became emperor, Paschasius sent him a revised version of *On the Body and Blood of the Lord*. Charles, in turn, wrote to Ratramnus (d. 868), also a monk of Corbie, and asked two questions: 1) Did the faithful receive the body and blood of Christ in mystery or in truth? and 2) Did they receive the same body and blood as that born of Mary? Ratramnus, who was a little closer to the thought of Augustine, distinguished between two different kinds of reality: reality in form or appearance (*in figura*) and the underlying reality discerned by faith (*in veritate*). This distinction allowed Ratramnus to admit the difference between the physical or sensed reality (like the eucharistic bread) and spiritual realities (like the Body of Christ), which are not perceivable to the senses but accessed only by faith. For him, like Augustine, spiritual realities were more "real" or more important than physical realities. Thus, he could conclude that the eucharistic presence of Christ is real, but Christ is received in mystery not as a physical reality. Consequently, in communion we do not receive the body of Christ born of Mary, but rather we receive the spiritual Body of Christ.

It is notable that these two monks holding very different perspectives on eucharistic presence apparently lived in peace with each other within the same monastery. Furthermore, neither of them was condemned in his lifetime, despite the fact that their theological views were almost polar opposites for their age. It is, however, the view of Paschasius—more compatible with the Germanic imagination—that came to dominate the religious imagination of most Christians and many theologians in the coming centuries. Ratramnus himself seems to have been largely forgotten, and his writings were eventually attributed to John Scotus Erigena (d. ca. 877) and under that name were condemned by the synod of Vercelli in 1050.

The climax of the controversies about the "real" in eucharistic presence during this period converged around the gifted but somewhat cantankerous theologian Berengar of Tours (d. 1080). By the end of the eleventh century, most theologians in the West—such as the celebrated doctor of the church Peter Damian (d. 1072)—held that, as Paschasius had taught, the historical and the eucharistic body of Jesus were identical [quotation 236]. Berengar vigorously refuted this position; many of his arguments are summarized in his major work on the topic, *On the Holy Supper*.

On the one hand this would seem to align Berengar with Ratramnus and indicate that the Augustinian synthesis was yet alive and operative in the eleventh century. As Macy notes, however,

Quotation 236: *What the catholic faith holds, what the holy church faithfully teaches . . . [is that] the very body of Christ that the blessed Virgin bore . . . this very body, I say without any doubt, and no other, we now receive from the holy altar.* (Peter Damian [d. 1072], *Sermon 45*, in Pelikan, *The Christian Tradition*, p. 193)

Berengar is actually far removed from Augustine and the late Platonic view that things of this world, grasped by the senses, pointed to otherworldly things that were only grasped by the mind or by faith. For Berengar, the physical and spiritual realms were quite distinctive, and there was an unbridgeable gap between them. This basic philosophical stance could not allow Berengar to believe that there was anything of the historical Christ or the "body born of Mary" present in the Eucharist.

One of the eucharistic issues that revealed Berengar's thinking concerned the kind of "change" that took place in the bread and wine through the consecration. His basic belief was that bread and wine cannot stop being bread and wine, because that would be against nature [quotation 237]. In a celebrated example, Berengar holds up the image of Saul of Tarsus who, in Berengar's language, was "changed" into Paul the apostle, but in that change the apostle continued at the physical level to be who he previously had been, while at the same time he became something new spiritually. The analogous belief that the bread continued to be bread as well as the mystery of Christ's presence after the consecration was labeled "impanation" (from the Latin *panis*, "bread").

Quotation 237: *Through the consecration at the altar bread and wine become the Sacrament of faith, not by ceasing to be what they were but by remaining what they were and being changed into something else.* (Berengar [d. 1080], Opusculum, in Pelikan, *The Christian Tradition*, p. 198)

Besides his arguments based on philosophy, Berengar also put forth a relatively crude but pointed Christological argument which proved, from his perspective, that consecrated Eucharist could not be identical to the historical body of Christ. Simply stated, Berengar reasoned that the historical body of Christ, born of Mary, left this world at the Ascension. The divine rift between heaven and earth did not allow Christ to be physically but only spiritually present in the Eucharist. To think otherwise would be to believe that the ascended body of Christ was capable of being cut up, and innumerable bits of the divine flesh were dispatched to earth where they were devoured [quotation 238]. Furthermore, "if the body of the Lord appeared every day in every liturgy all over the world, then surely every day the body of the Lord would grow bigger and bigger, and finally there would be a mountain of Jesus' body" (Macy, *Banquet's Wisdom*, p. 76). This was, of course, absurd and, in Berengar's mind, cemented his argument that Christ was received spiritually not physically in the Eucharist.

Quotation 238: *A portion of the flesh of Christ cannot be present on the altar . . . unless the body of Christ in heaven is cut up and a particle that has been cut off from it is sent down to the Altar.* (Berengar, On the Holy Supper 37, in Pelikan, *The Christian Tradition*, p. 194)

In the process of these explanations Berengar employed the useful distinction between the *sacrumentum* or outward sign and the *res* or underlying reality. Thus he could describe a sacrament as a visible form of an invisible grace, a formulation that would become a standard definition of a sacrament in later medieval theology (Macy, *Theologies of the Eucharist*, p. 40). Such distinctions between the visible and invisible, the physical and the spiritual, however, were

Quotation 239: *I confess . . . that the bread and wine which are placed on the altar are not merely a sacrament [non solum sacramentum] after consecration but also the true body and blood of our Lord Jesus Christ, and that these are truly, physically and not merely sacramentally [non solum sacramentum sed in veritate] touched and broken by the hands of the priests and crushed by the teeth of the faithful. (Confession of Berengar, 1059, in Patrologia Latina 150:411)*

Quotation 240: *[I affirm that] the bread and wine which are placed on the altar . . . are changed substantially into the true, proper and living body and blood of Jesus Christ, our Lord, and that after the consecration it is the true body of Christ which was born of the Virgin . . . and the true blood of Christ which was poured out from his side, not only through the sign and power of the sacrament but in their real nature and in true substance. (Confession of Berengar, 1079, in Mansi, 20:524)*

not well accepted by his contemporaries. Most considered Berengar's work an attack on the thought of Paschasius and a frontal assault on the very foundations of eucharistic theology. Berengar was alternately chastised and condemned. Summoned to a Roman Synod in 1059, he was required to sign a confession that Macy calls "one of the most unfortunate and theologically inept statements every put forward by the church on the subject of Eucharist" (*Banquet's Wisdom*, p. 77). In the statement, which bore the official stamp of orthodoxy from Rome, one reads not only the ideas of Paschasius, now summarized in the church's most literal pronouncement on the nature of Christ's eucharistic presence, but also language that suggests that "sacrament" is almost the opposite of real [quotation 239].

The irascible Berengar was not deterred by his censure and returned to Tours where he rejected the confession of 1059, attacked its theological errors, and reiterated his previous beliefs. The firestorm was rekindled and within twenty years Berengar was back in Rome, swearing a new oath about eucharistic faith [quotation 240]. While similar in many respects to the oath of 1059, this more nuanced statement introduced the language of substance, borrowed from the thought of Aristotle (d. 322 B.C.E.) whose writings were being rediscovered in the Christian west. This language foreshadowed the rise of a new synthesis in the following era. With increasingly nuanced language tools, theologians would continue to probe the nature of the "real presence" of Christ in the Eucharist and struggle for acceptable language that would both satisfy the human need for understanding and simultaneously respect the mysterious nature of this God reality.

Sacred Things

Christianity is by definition an incarnational religion, given that a fundamental belief for all Christians is that the Word became flesh (John 1:14). One consequence of the incarnation is a belief that, just as God chose to mediate divine presence through Jesus Christ once in history, so can other people and even the gifts of creation be reflections of God and mediators of the divine presence, though none as perfectly or absolutely as Jesus. This Christian belief in the mediating potential of people and even of things for shaping a relationship with God is sometimes known as the "sacramental principle." While it took some time for this understanding to evolve, it is clear from the beginning that Christians valued things like bread and wine, oil and water as mediators of God's presence and useful agents for bringing us into closer relationship with God. This attitude makes sense among a people whose religiosity is grounded in a basic instinct of gratitude for all that God has done for them in creation and human history (see pp. 31–32 above). In some respects, this entire book is built upon the presumption of such a sacramental principle and has attempted to demonstrate how things such as vessels, books, architecture, and musical arts have had an effect on the way various Christian communities have expressed and created relationships with the God of Jesus Christ.

As we have seen, Christians of previous eras showed great reverence to things like the consecrated bread, the vessels that held the consecrated elements, and other liturgical objects such as the Book of the Gospels. We have also noted that long before the rise of the Franks there was evidence that eucharistized bread was being used as a kind of sacred talisman, and there was a decline in the reception of communion by some believers. There also emerged new methods for explaining the eucharistic mystery, which challenged an Augustinian understanding of symbols. Nathan Mitchell speaks of this as a move from symbol to allegory [quotation 241].

Thus one can find strands of evidence that suggest that, before the rise of the Germanic tribes, the Eucharist was treated more like a sacred object than a sacred encounter with the God of Jesus Christ, and that the eucharistic liturgy was more a sacred drama to be watched in awe from a distance than the communal rehearsal of the baptismal call to become what we eat. These tendencies in eucharistic piety and practice, however, were neither pastorally widespread nor theologically in the mainstream. The multiple forces of the early Middle Ages, especially in northern Europe, would change that.

The Germanic imagination not only magnified previous trends in eucharistic piety and thought, it did so in the context of a different worldview. Thus, the tendency to emphasize the importance of eucharistic elements more than the eucharistic relationships they were to foster produced a quite different effect in a Germanic world that, according to Russell, had an instinct for the magical over the ethical, and easily invested sacred power in objects. Similarly, understanding of the meaning of key biblical phrases like "This is my body" resulted in radically different understandings of presence in a world that no longer embraced the Augustinian synthesis and had difficulty believing that symbols—or even "sacraments"—were real.

In the context of this new mindset, vessels were not only forged of precious metals, they underwent a special rite of blessing or consecration. Doing so affirmed a worldview that presumed that the things of this world were not worthy of liturgical usage unless they were ritually transformed from profane to sacred objects. In a parallel move, ordinary people were increasingly disallowed from even touching these sacred objects. In order to be able to touch sacred objects—much less change an object from profane to sacred, or from mere bread to the Body of Christ—people themselves had to be blessed,

Quotation 241: *Allegories tend to reduce the inherent ambiguity of persons, things and events by assigning one meaning to each action or object. . . . The movement from symbol to allegory is thus a movement from ambiguity to clarity, from multiple meaning to single meaning, from revelation to explanation. The ambiguous strategy of symbols provokes action; the reductive strategy of allegory provokes passivity. Whereas symbols require one to search and struggle for meaning, allegories explain meaning.* (Mitchell, *Cult and Controversy,* pp. 52–53)

consecrated, and "changed." Earlier this transformation was accomplished through the sacraments of initiation, especially baptism and Eucharist. For medieval Christians, such transformation increasingly occurred through the rites of ordination.

While the rituals of Rome certainly had liturgies of ordination, these were relatively modest rites that ordinarily included the laying on of hands and a central prayer of blessing. As Sharon McMillan explains, the sparsity of this ritual made sense when it was located in the rich ecclesial context of the Roman church, which would have included an ample process of nomination and election by the community. In the Carolingian Empire, however, the ecclesial context was much different, particularly since the election process was first abbreviated and then virtually abandoned, with the result that ordination was effectively reduced to the "blessing stage" (McMillan, pp. 164–65). In the process that blessing stage was radically transformed by the addition of multiple rites that invested the priest with new powers, including the ability to move things from the realm of the profane to that of the sacred, and effectively moved him from one realm to the other as well.

One of the more telling ritual additions in this regard was the inclusion of the anointing of the hands in the ordination rite for priests. We have noted throughout this chapter the penchant in this era for consecrating altars, vessels, and even churches with newly composed prayers and inventive ritual actions. It stands to reason, therefore, if a priest is going to touch these altars and hold these vessels and, most important, change the bread and wine into the Body and Blood of Christ, he would have to undergo similar ritual transformation. Since the hands are key sacramental instruments for such touching, holding, and changing, it was the hands of the priest that received special liturgical attention in the Germanized rites of ordination. It was, again, the eighth-century Missal of the Franks that contains the first extant texts for this ritual [quotation 242].

Maybe even more striking was the introduction of the ritual known as the *traditio instrumentorum* (Latin, "handing over of the instruments"), in which the bishop handed to the ordination candidate a paten with an unconsecrated host and a chalice containing unconsecrated wine. As McMillan notes, this imitated the previously noted practice contained in the fifth century *Ancient Statutes of the Church*, in which the bishop handed over various instruments to symbolize the ministry of various "minor orders," such as the lector, doorkeeper, and acolyte [quotation 186]. For the first time in the Romano-Germanic Pontifical (composed between 950 and 962), however, we see liturgical vessels being handed over in the ordination rite for priests. Furthermore, the text that accompanied this ritual made it clear, in McMillan's words, that "this act constitutes the very

Quotation 242: *May these hands be anointed with sanctified oil and the chrism of sanctification: as Samuel anointed David king and prophet, so may they be anointed and perfected in the name of God the Father and the Son and the Holy Spirit, making the image of the holy cross of the Savior our Lord Jesus Christ, who redeemed us from death and leads us to the kingdom of heaven.* (Missal of the Franks [8 c.], no. 34, in McMillan, "How the Presbyter Becomes a Priest")

essence of the presbyteral ordination" for "the bishop proclaims this declarative formula [quotation 243] at the same time as the candidates touch the "instruments" (McMillan, p. 169). This ritual was so important that in the coming centuries theologians no less than Thomas Aquinas would consider the *traditio instrumentorum* to constitute the essential rite for priestly ordination.

The cumulative effect of these Germanizing tendencies, which placed great import on sacred things in the context of a new world-view that was distrustful of the symbolic, was a growing "reification" (from the Latin *res*, "thing") of the liturgy. While symbolic actions employing things that expressed and created relationships had always been important in the Christian cult, now such things seemingly took on a life of their own, often outside of the sacramental actions that originally defined them, and sometimes irrespective of any communal or divine relationships that were their proper context. Said in another way, just like the transformed ordination rites of the priest, Christian Eucharist increasingly became "instrumentalized," or treated like a tool for achieving spiritual ends. Increasingly more a noun than a verb, more a thing to be reverenced than an action in which one was to be engaged, Eucharist and its theologies were less a privileged activity that founded, shaped, and missioned the baptized, and more a sacred treasure to be safeguarded and reverenced.

Sacramental Theology

An interesting and common phenomenon in history is the occurrence of change without any necessary or adequate labeling of that change until years or maybe even centuries later. We noted such an occurrence earlier in this chapter when we observed that while there was general agreement that "Romanesque" architecture, properly speaking, was an eleventh- and twelfth-century development, the term itself was not coined until 1818 by the French archaeologist Charles-Alexis-Adrien de Gerville (d. 1853). This often happens in the arts, and so J. S. Bach (d. 1750) had no inkling that his death would eventually be hailed as the close of the "baroque" musical era in the West. The same phenomenon often occurs in theology and philosophy. Thus, for example, Gregory the Great (d. 604) was totally unaware that his death would be considered by many to mark the end of the so-called patristic (from the Latin, *pater* or "father") era in Christian theology.

It is clear that the monks Paschasius and Ratramnus, as well as the teacher Berengar, knew that they were engaged in very important debates about the church's eucharistic theology. They also were very conscientious about their connection with past theologies: Paschasius, for example, drew from key writings of Hilary of Poitiers (d. 367),

Quotation 243: *Receive the power to offer sacrifice to God and to celebrate Mass for the living as well as for the dead, in the name of the Lord.* (Romano-Germanic Pontifical [960–962], in McMillan, "How the Presbyter Becomes a Priest")

and Berengar drew on the teachings of Ratramnus—although, as we have seen, by Berengar's time the works were wrongly attributed to John Scotus Erigena. What Paschasius, Ratramnus, Berengar, and many of their contemporaries were not particularly aware of, however, was that they were changing the path of eucharistic theology in a new and different direction.

Many contemporary writers recognize, for example, that Paschasius wrote the first systematic theological work on Eucharist that we know. A multitude of early teachers and saints had written about the Eucharist, but their teachings—like that of Augustine, whom we have often cited—were often scattered across various sermons, commentaries, and other theological tracts that dealt with other theological and pastoral matters besides the Eucharist. Nathan Mitchell further points out that Paschasius is the first Christian writer known to us who speaks extensively about the Eucharist in isolation from the other sacraments of initiation (i.e., baptism and confirmation), and he does so in an abstract way that seems separated from the experiences of any particular community of faith.

At the end of chapter 3 we drew attention to the tradition of "mystagogical instruction" from great bishops who drew forth celebrated theological reflection from initiates whose journey to full communion with the church culminated in the Eucharist. As noted, such reflections and teachings about the Eucharist were pastorally driven by the liturgical needs or challenges of a local church rather than by some speculative reality. This is why so much mystagogical material came to us from working bishops concerned with pressing pastoral realities.

Unlike the mystagogical reflections of Ambrose, Cyril, Augustine, and others, however, the theology of Paschasius and others of this era was separated from the whole initiatory process. Furthermore, it was separated from any community's real experiences of those processes—something completely foreign to authentic mystagogical reflection. As Mitchell summarizes,

> For the earlier fathers, doctrine was derived from doxology, from the liturgical actions of prayer and thanksgiving in the Eucharist: *lex orandi, lex credendi* [Latin, "the law of praying {establishes} the law of believing"]. For Paschasius, however, it was possible to raise questions about eucharistic doctrine that did not flow immediately from the experience and ritual action of a community at prayer. (Mitchell, *Cult and Controversy*, p. 74)

In contemporary theology, writers will sometimes distinguish between a "theology *of* or *about* the liturgy" and a "theology *from* the liturgy." While multiple other distinctions can be made about the relationship between theology and liturgy, this simple framework can help illuminate Mitchell's contrast between the earlier fathers and the writings of Paschasius. While Augustine and Hilary and so many Christian theologians who antedated the Germanization process did make more speculative theological statements *about* the liturgy that could be considered theologies *of* the liturgy, it is fair to say that their theological reflections were ordinarily and consistently *from* the liturgy. This means that actual liturgical practices and people's experiences of those practices—including the experiences of the theologians themselves—were the foundation for such theologizing. This was not generally true of the work of Paschasius and those who followed him. While Paschasius was clearly concerned about the spiritual lives of the monks he instructed—a characteristic that must have had something to do with his being elected abbot of his monastery—his style of theologizing did not rely upon their experiences. Rather, his theological method was more abstract, relying on certain understandings of salvation and incarnation. Furthermore, we know virtually nothing about how the liturgy in Paschasius' abbey was enacted from his writings. His theology was less drawn *from* liturgical events and people's experiences of those events, and more a theology *about* or *of* the liturgy.

Eventually theology and the teaching of theology in the West will undergo what Edward Farley considers significant fragmentation. This is such a widespread reality today that many who study theology simply take it for granted and do not always notice the subdivisions of or even the separations within the theological enterprise. The study and teaching of Scripture is different in method and content from church history, as is moral theology from Christology. In that same vein, consider how often the theology of sacraments is taught by one person in a school, while sacramental practice is taught by another. Sometimes the former is positioned in a department of "systematic theology" while the latter is lodged in a "ministry" or "practical" division.

While Paschasius and his colleagues are not responsible for such developments, the seeds of these current separations can be found in their work. These early medieval theologians launch a trajectory that will eventually allow people to theologize about sacraments without grounding such theologizing in the liturgical event itself. Using other language, one can say that some early medieval theologians paved the way for the development of a theologizing about the liturgy or sacraments that will eventually be known as "sacramental theology." This is quite different from the theologizing of an earlier age (e.g., mystagogy), grounded in liturgical events and the experiences of those events by the faithful, which in the late twentieth century was deemed to be a theology *from* the liturgical event or "liturgical theology."

Summary

In many ways, this was not a period of great synthesis in eucharistic theologies. Rather, it was more a time of questioning and theological exploration. The impetus that made this questioning and exploration necessary was a series of seismic shifts in the political, cultural, and religious landscape of Europe. Like imaginary tectonic plates, the worldview that flowed through Christianity south of the Alps and across the great centers of North Africa created increasing stress as it confronted the religious imagination and cultural frames of the Germanic peoples. In the ideological earthquakes and aftershocks that followed, many of the theological frameworks of the patristic church were abandoned. While great theologians like Augustine and Ambrose and Hilary would continue to be quoted, the internal logic of their thinking was often incomprehensible to the thinkers of this era who were no longer in dialogue with the bodies of knowledge accumulated before the fall of Rome and who suffered more than they knew from a general decline in learning after the Germanic invasions. Ironically, however, though credible and sustainable eucharistic syntheses among theologians would not arise until the next era, the religious imagination of many ordinary Christians was on its way to a certain synthesis. The Germanic imagination is, in many respects, still with us, and many Roman Catholics today share more of an instinct for a magico-religious interpretation of sacraments than an ethical, doctrinal, or even eschatological instinct. Thus, while theologically not all that determinative, this era has left an undeniable devotional and spiritual stamp on Christian practice.

BROTHER AELRED

Brother Aelred does not remember his age. Neither does anyone else in the monastery. The record of his entry into the abbey was lost in the great fire of 836. Now blind and lame, Aelred does remember that he was already a professed monk when the cornerstone for the new church was laid in 838. That was almost eighty years ago. Some of the young monks joke that "old Brother Aelred actually knew Saint Benedict."

Aelred does not have much contact with the young monks. He spends most of his days propped up near the big window in the infirmary, dozing in the sun. The infirmary on the second floor of the abbey overlooks the main cloister. Sounds from the abbey workshops, refectory, and chapter room drift through the window into the infirmary. These sounds are Aelred's faithful companions.

Although he is unable to see the new dormitory wing or watch the processions through the cloister, the sounds of the monks at work or at prayer reassure him that his beloved abbey continues to thrive. The bells in the towers of the abbey church are special friends, calling the monks to prayer, to meals, and to bed. Whether it is the bells, shouts in the cloister, or chants from the church, almost everything that Aelred knows about the monastery these days he learns through hearing. This is appropriate for the monastery's former choirmaster.

It is late in the afternoon on the patronal feast of the monastery. Aelred dozes off while listening to the monks chant the hour of None. He suddenly awakens to a strong arm beneath him and knows that Brother Accadam—or Brother Ox, as Aelred calls him—has arrived to carry him to bed. At least that is what Aelred presumes. But instead of carrying him down the south corridor toward Aelred's cell, Brother Ox takes the main corridor into the central dormitory and then descends the stairway into the church. Brother Aelred is going to the afternoon's solemn Mass for the patronal feast.

The chants that rise from the abbey choir bring tears to the old monk's eyes. Unable to walk for almost a decade, Aelred seldom joins the monks in the choir anymore. Only on rare occasions does the prior give Brother Accadam permission to bring the old monk into the church. Maybe the prior thinks that this will be Aelred's last patronal feast with them. Aelred does not care about the reason as the Ox gently lowers him into an upper choir stall. Aelred is back in his beloved church.

Aelred knows all the chants by heart. The introit begins, and after the antiphon the choir erupts with Psalm 99, "Iubilate Deo omnis terra, servite Domino in laetitia." Although eighty-plus voices join together on the psalm, Aelred easily picks out the uncertain voices of the novices sitting across from him on the left. They struggle through the seldom-employed solemn tone for this text. One young voice misreads the cantor's cue and instead of Psalm 99 sings the opening phrase from Psalm 65, "Iubilate Deo omnis terra psalmum dicite nomini eius." Aelred remembers his own years as postulant and novice, struggling to memorize all of the psalms before his profession of vows.

Over the years, he learned not only the psalms and their simple chants, but also hundreds of other tunes and texts. He learned them from Brother Romanus, who had trained as a cantor in the Monastery of the Holy Apostles in the Eternal City. Aelred had been such a good student that Brother Romanus had asked him to tutor the oblates in the simple chants. And in the year that the new choir was dedicated, when Brother Romanus went to God, Aelred succeeded him as choirmaster in the abbey.

"Desiderium animae eius"—the opening phrase of the offertory chant draws Aelred out of his reverie. Father Abbot now must be at the altar, holding aloft the great silver paten and chalice that miraculously survived the fire. Aelred smiles to himself as the antiphon rises from the voices of these sons of Benedict. What more perfect time and place to make the final offering? "Posuisite in capite eius coronam de lapide pretioso," chant the monks. "You placed on his head a crown of precious stones." The offertory verse becomes the old monk's final epithet. Before the last notes fade from the vault, Aelred accepts his own crown of glory.

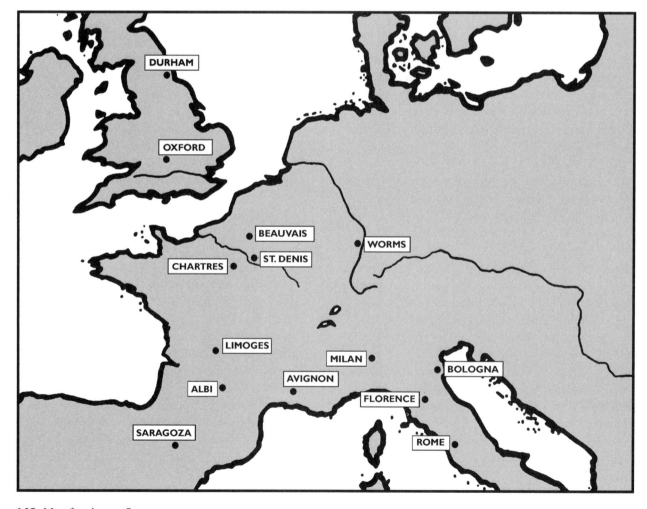

135. Map for chapter 5.

CHAPTER FIVE

Synthesis and Antithesis as Prelude to Reform: 1073–1517

The era under consideration in this chapter is a wellspring of rich and diverse narratives, many of which continue to captivate the contemporary imagination. This was a time of crusades and new world explorations, of towering monarchies, devastating plagues, trade routes to the Far East, and a scandalous schism between the churches of the East and West. Monuments in stone and glass, music and marble from this period populate our museums, and libraries are yet filled with classics of literature, philosophy, and political thought from this time. These so-called High Middle Ages are thought by some to provide basic directions for the arts and education in the West that stretch into our own day. Others find here not only the emergence of new languages and the birth or redefinition of countries and nations but also the dawn of what we now know as Europe. We cannot, of course, retell or hope to outline even the broadest strokes of such developments. Rather, we need to consider a few main cultural and political currents from this era that will allow us to contextualize and appreciate the eucharistic developments of the time.

One critical development for liturgical history was the reassertion of papal influence and control over the church. While Roman ideals were honored and emulated in the previous period, after the fall of the empire Rome itself was greatly reduced in population, political power, and theological influence. To survive, various popes forged alliances with stronger allies to the north, and in the process ceded authority for matters as basic as the naming of bishops or abbots, and the right to claim the primary allegiance of these prelates. Sometimes feudal lords or monarchs simply appointed themselves to ecclesial positions, such as the Emperor Charles II (d. 877) who took over as abbot of the famed abbey of St.-Denis, followed by his successors and other minor royalty for almost a century. The tide began to shift, however, with the ascendancy of a series of strong popes in

136. Twelfth-century depiction of conflict between Gregory VII and Henry IV.

Quotation 244:

The Dictates of the Pope

1. *That the Roman church was founded by God alone.*
2. *That the Roman pontiff alone can with right be called universal.*
3. *That he alone can depose or reinstate bishops.*
4. *That, in a council his legate, even if a lower grade, is above all bishops, and can pass sentence of deposition against them.*
5. *That the pope may depose the absent.*
6. *That, among other things, we ought not to remain in the same house with those excommunicated by him.*
7. *That for him alone is it lawful, according to the needs of the time, to make new laws, to assemble together new congregations, to make an abbey of a canonry; and, on the other hand, to divide a rich bishopric and unite the poor ones.*
8. *That he alone may use the imperial insignia.*

the late eleventh century, particularly Gregory VII (pope from 1073–1085). Symbolic of his reforming spirit was his excommunication of the recalcitrant German Emperor, Henry IV (d. 1108) [illustration 136]. This was quite a reversal, given that it was ordinary in the eleventh century for emperors to depose popes. While Gregory lost the short-term battle to Henry and was himself driven from Rome, his vision for reform eventually prevailed, and at the Concordat of Worms (1122) the so called "investiture controversy" was resolved.

This new papal vigor would manifest itself in an expansive belief that popes were not just "vicars of Peter," but now "vicars of Christ." The so-called Dictates of the Pope ascribed to Gregory VII present the pope not only as a person invested in power in the spiritual realm, and even in a position of almost hereditary sanctity (no. 23), but also invested with power in the political realm, where princes kissed his feet (no. 9) and he could depose any emperor (no. 12) [quotation 244]. While such statements may sound far fetched to the contemporary reader, they made sense in a world in which Christianity and all of Europe were virtually synonymous. R. W. Southern notes that this identification of the church with the whole of organized society is the fundamental feature that distinguishes the Middle Ages from earlier and later periods of history (Southern, p. 16). Not only *in* the world, the church was clearly *of* the world, appearing as a state alongside other states, with its own law courts, tax system, and bureaucracy. Analogously, it was increasingly necessary to reckon with the pope, like other monarchs of the age, as the temporal leader of this vast though often fragmented empire.

Christianity had become Christendom, and the sacramental implications were enormous. As Southern observes, baptism became as involuntary as birth for large segments of this population, and the obligations assumed in baptism were there forever, along with their ensuing obligations and penalties, in both the worldly and spiritual realms (Southern, p. 18). As for liturgical and eucharistic practice, there was a notable exercise of Roman direction, critique, and control over liturgical matters not seen before. This is not to suggest that there was some overarching papal plan to employ liturgy as a vehicle for unifying or controlling the diverse strands of European Christianity—parallel to what we saw with Pepin and Charlemagne. Rather, the concern was more about the stability and redefinition of the papacy and the church. Liturgy, as the most important ritual enactment of the church, was by consequence drawn into this service. It was the pope and his expanding curia who increasingly approved feasts, decided which eucharistic teaching was orthodox, assumed control of canonizations, and dispensed indulgences.

Because of the growing influence of Roman ways, even local liturgical decisions had far-reaching impact. Under Innocent III (d. 1216), for example, the workload of the clerics doing papal business was so taxing that their obligation for reciting the Liturgy of the Hours was becoming unusually burdensome. As a result, a new ordo for the breviary (from Latin, *breviarium*, "abridgment") of the papal household was developed. When Francis of Assisi (d. 1226) developed a rule for his followers, he instructed that they follow the prayer of the Roman church [quotation 245]. Numbering in the thousands by the time of his death, Francis's followers spread this particular practice of the papal household across Europe and beyond.

Even more influential was the acceptance and eventual dissemination of what in the last chapter we identified as the "Franco-Roman" liturgy. After centuries of Germanization, the eucharistic liturgy of Rome had been transformed, and that transformed liturgy was embedded in the prayer texts and rubrics of the liturgical books of the day. Such books were almost exclusively produced in the northern countries where the Germanizing influences were strongest. In the early Middle Ages, Rome had a limited capacity for producing liturgical books, and stories report that the bishop of Rome sometimes

9. *That of the pope alone all princes shall kiss the feet.*

10. *That his name alone shall be spoken in the churches.*

11. *That this is the only name in the world.*

12. *That it may be permitted to him to depose emperors.*

13. *That he may be permitted to transfer bishops if need be.*

14. *That he has power to ordain a clerk of any church he may wish.*

15. *That he who is ordained by him may preside over another church, but may not hold a subordinate position; and that such a one may not receive a higher grade from any bishop.*

16. *That no synod shall be called a general one without his order.*

17. *That no chapter and no book shall be considered canonical without his authority.*

18. *That a sentence passed by him may be retracted by no one; and that he himself, alone of all, may retract it.*

19. *That he himself may be judged by no one.*

20. *That no one shall dare to condemn one who appeals to the apostolic chair.*

21. *That to the latter should be referred the more important cases of every church.*

22. *That the Roman church has never erred; nor will it err to all eternity, the Scripture bearing witness.*

23. *That the Roman pontiff, if he have been canonically ordained, is undoubtedly made a saint by the merits of St. Peter; St. Ennodius, bishop of Pavia, bearing witness, and many holy fathers agreeing with him. As is contained in the decrees of St. Symmachus the pope.*

24. *That, by his command and consent, it may be lawful for subordinates to bring accusations.*

25. *That he may depose and reinstate bishops without assembling a synod.*

26. *That he who is not at peace with the Roman church shall not be considered catholic.*

27. *That he may absolve subjects from their fealty to wicked men.*

(Henderson, *Select Historical Documents of the Middle Ages*, pp. 366–67)

137. Seal of the University of Paris.

offered gifts or privileges to Frankish monasteries in return for these precious items [quotation 246]. Such books and their accompanying practices made their way back to Rome where this hybrid liturgy was embraced, particularly by a series of German popes who were formed in this mixed tradition. The sources of these Germanic influences were soon forgotten, and this liturgical amalgam was eventually known simply as the Roman Rite.

Also important for the development of eucharistic theology in the period was the rise of the great universities. Many factors contributed to this new phenomenon, including the success of outstanding cathedral and monastic schools like those of Tours and St.-Denis, the migration of many peasants off the land into burgeoning towns and villages that could support these institutions, and the explosion of new learning stimulated by things such as the recovery of Aristotle's writings, doctrinal controversies, and the growth of canonical literature. Paris [illustration 137], Bologna, and Oxford were three of the great schools that rose to prominence in the thirteenth century. While in receipt of privileges and immunities from monarchs and popes alike, the universities were often considered a "third power," strategically positioned between church and state. Secular and ecclesiastical leaders were both keen to support these institutions and, in turn, sought the support of their scholarly opinions, especially in the faculties of theology and law. Because one key method in the teaching of theology and philosophy in the universities was disputation, these institutions also became places of controversy and dissent, where powerful challenges would arise to confront the church and state, and even the very theological syntheses that were formed in these universities.

The growth of the universities and the increased attention to speculative learning in such institutions contributed to the growing divide between the belief and understanding of common people and those of theological specialists. As we saw, Paschasius was concerned that his monks had an adequate grasp of eucharistic theology. Increasingly, however, the explanations about Eucharist and eucharistic presence required a level of theological sophistication even beyond that of ordinary clergy. Consequently, while the religious imaginations and devotional practices of ordinary believers and many clergy continued to evolve, they did so often in contradiction to the speculative views of great theologians like Aquinas or Bonaventure (d. 1274).

Besides this growing dissonance between speculative sacramental theology and the devotional practices of ordinary people, there were other points of contention and reversals during this dynamic era. For example, there was growing unrest and ecclesial critique among an increasing population of freed peasants struggling to survive in the new urban environments. While many ordinary people scraped along at a subsistence level, celebrated monasteries and churches that had acquired substantial wealth and privilege were viewed with suspicion. The relatively meager formation for secular clergy often left them ill equipped to represent the teachings of the church or to live a respectable life in ministry. In this void, charismatic lay preachers sometimes arose to expose contradictions in the public life and teaching of the church and its ministers. Some, like Francis of Assisi, were cautiously

138. "The Three Living and the Three Dead," medieval manuscript depiction of the plague.

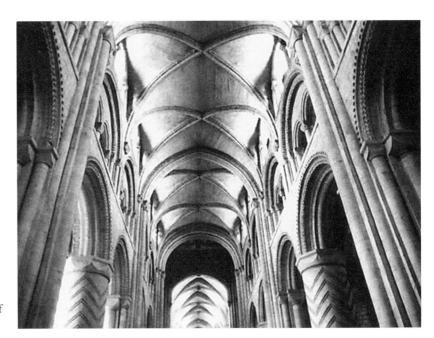

139. Durham Cathedral, example of ribbed vaults.

welcomed by the church and eventually spurred effective reform movements within the church. With others like Peter Valdes (d. ca. 1217) and the Poor Men of Lyons (or Waldensians), however, the alienation became too great, official condemnation followed, and often crusades were launched against such heretics.

The papacy, which some believe reached its apogee in the thirteenth century, subsequently experienced serious decline and disarray. For most of the fourteenth century popes lived outside of Rome in Avignon (1309–1377), often pawns of an increasingly powerful French monarchy. When the papal court finally returned to Rome, antipopes abounded during the period of the so-called great schism (1378–1417). This internal ecclesial strife mirrored growing disarray across the continent: the weather worsened to the point that Brian Fagan has called this the "Little Ice Age"; famine struck, wars abounded, and the bubonic plague [illustration 138] swept across Europe. Estimates project that as much as one-third of Europe's population was devastated by these cumulative disasters.

The fourteenth and fifteenth centuries certainly witnessed a renaissance in the arts and literature. Humanistic studies of Latin and Greek classics opened a new era of learning in the West, and an age of discovery was blossoming. For the church and its liturgy, however, the era ended on a less-promising trajectory than when it began. The new theological synthesis was under assault, as were many liturgical and devotional practices of the church. Reform and counter-reform were soon to follow.

ARCHITECTURE

Early in this era what would later be known as the Gothic style of architecture was born in the North. Almost three centuries later, the Renaissance style emerged in Italy. The evolution of these new styles signified more than advanced engineering prowess, new skills in constructing buttresses, or imaginative ways of rethinking the arch. More than a compilation and refinement of old architectural elements into pleasing forms, these distinctive architectural developments reflected new ways of viewing the cosmos, the world, and the faithful who inhabited them. They also embodied particular views of what it meant to be church, in which every ministry and person had an assigned place and role in a well-defined hierarchical order.

The Birth of Gothic

Like other designations, what we call Gothic was not originally known by that name but was called *opus modernum* (Latin, "modern style"). The architectural use of the term Gothic may have originated with Florentine architect Leon Battista Alberti (d. 1472). The word is derived from the Latin term for the Goths, the Germanic tribe that sacked Rome in 410 [illustration 104] and carried the derogatory implication of "rough" or "crude." Gothic architecture borrowed and refined key elements already present across the landscape of late Romanesque churches. For example, we previously noted that Romanesque architects had successfully constructed stone and masonry vaults, usually semicircular or "barrel vaults." Because of their weight, these roofs exerted tremendous lateral stress, and the walls had to bear all of the weight. Consequently, such load-bearing walls were often very thick and had few windows. By the end of the eleventh century at places like Durham Cathedral in England, however, architects were constructing ribbed rather than barrel vaults [illustration 139], which directed the weight vertically to piers. The webbing between the ribs consisted of lightweight masonry, which lessened the stress on the support system below and allowed the walls to be pierced with windows and galleries. The piers, in turn, could be strengthened by masonry buttresses—sometimes called "flying buttresses" because they appeared to "fly" from the pier being reinforced, usually over the roof of a side aisle, and connecting to the stronger superstructure that made up the exterior walls and supports of the building.

While Durham Cathedral had ribbed vaulting, flying buttresses, and even the pointed rather than rounded arches so characteristic of Gothic architecture, it was not a Gothic building. Otto von Simson argues that though such buildings had the construction technology

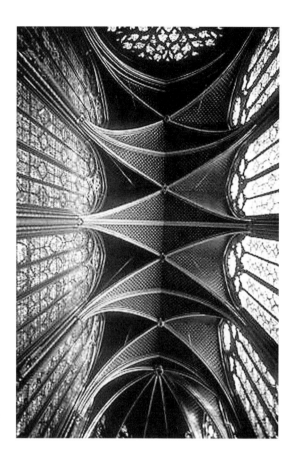

140. Ste. Chappelle in Paris, vaulting of
the upper chapel.

Quotation 247:

Whoever though art,
  if though seekest to extol the glory of
    these doors,
Marvel not at the gold and the expense
  but at the craftsmanship of the work.
Bright is the noble work;
  but, being nobly bright, the work
Should brighten the minds
  so that they may travel through the true
    lights,
To the True Light
  where Christ is the true door.
In what manner it be inherent in this world
  the golden door defines;
The dull mind rises to truth
  through that which is material
and, in seeing this light,
  is resurrected from its former submersion.

(Abbot Suger [d. 1151], poem on the
doors of St.-Denis, in Panofsky, *Gothic
Architecture and Scholasticism*, pp. 47–49)

similar to that found in later Gothic structures, they were missing central elements. One was a new way of using light. Gothic "luminosity" is not to be confused with "brightness," for these are not the same thing. This is evident in many Gothic churches, such as Chartres, whose rich stained-glass windows can make the nave of the church seem quite dark even in the middle of the day. Von Simson instead notes that the special kind of luminosity that characterizes Gothic is the relationship of light to the material substance of the walls. He explains, "In a Romanesque church, light is something distinct from and contrasting with the heavy, somber, tactile substance of the walls. The Gothic wall seems to be porous: light filters through it, permeating it, merging with it, transfiguring it" (von Simson, p. 3). The refined skeleton of the Gothic building, with the downward thrust of the roof diverted to pillars and buttresses, allowing huge open spaces filled with windows and galleries [illustration 140], was the engineering feat that allowed this new aesthetic to emerge. In doing so such buildings also made a distinctive theological statement. In the medieval mind, light was a privileged and mysterious mediator of God. The Gothic cathedral, with large and breathtaking stained-glass windows, offered a new kind of invitation to a powerful encounter with the divine [quotation 247].

Besides luminosity, another characteristic of Gothic was its embodiment of order [illustration 141]. These centuries were times of great achievement, especially in systematizing and organizing ideas in the West. Ageless examples of this are the theological compendiums or *Summas* (Latin, "summary"), such as those of Thomas Aquinas and Bonaventure. As gifted minds were attempting a vast synthesis of the divine order on paper, architects were undertaking a parallel synthesis in stone. Thus, one way to consider the Gothic cathedral is as an architectural synthesis of the divinely ordered universe. Internally, for example, the building was well ordered, with each individual part integrated into the whole [quotation 248]. Within the medieval universe, every person had a specific place and function ordained by God. The Gothic cathedral embodied this hierarchical vision. It acknowledged and accented the centrality of the priest and the mysteries he enacted within the sacred precincts of the sanctuary. If the Gothic cathedral was the epitome of order, it also personified a notable degree of liturgical exclusion. As Ernst Cassirer has noted, during the Middle Ages a person's importance was demonstrated according to how close one was to the first cause [quotation 249]. In the eucharistic liturgy, this meant physical proximity to the altar where God became present. The distancing of the laity, and even the various orders of clergy from the altar during the eucharistic celebration, was a clear message about degrees of holiness or unworthiness in the medieval church.

Given that Gothic churches were erected in the context of European Christendom, in which church and society were thought to be one, their personification of order and parallel messages of worthiness

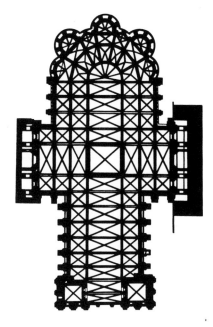

141. Ground plan of Chartres Cathedral, begun in 1145 and rebuilt after the fire of 1194. (After Norberg-Schulz, p. 195)

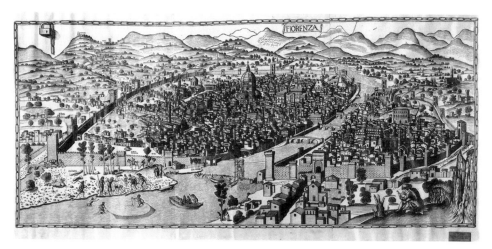

142. Fifteenth-century map of Florence with cathedral complex in the center.

Quotation 248: *Like the High Scholastic summa, the High Gothic cathedral aimed, first of all, at "totality" and therefore tended to approximate by synthesis as well as elimination one perfect and final solution; we may therefore speak of the High Gothic plan or the High Gothic system with much more confidence than would be possible in any other period. In its imagery, the High Gothic cathedral sought to embody the whole of Christian knowledge . . . with everything in its place and that which no longer found its place, suppressed. In structural design, it similarly sought to synthesize all major motifs handed down by separate channels and finally achieve an unparalleled balance between the basilical and the central plan type. (Panofsky, Gothic Architecture and Scholasticism, pp. 44–45)*

Quotation 249: *In the religious system of the Middle Ages, every phase of reality is assigned its unique place; and with its place goes a complete determination of its value, which is based on the greater or lesser distance which separates it from the first cause. (Cassirer, The Philosophy of the Enlightenment, p. 39)*

were not confined to the church's interiors. As Christian Norberg-Schulz recognizes, these buildings are symbolic of a re-envisioning of the medieval town. In his language, Romanesque churches often appeared more as "strongholds" against the outside world. Gothic churches were different, and through their open structures radiated a divine presence to the surrounding environment that was shaped around the cathedral [illustration 142]. Thus, Norberg-Schulz concludes that "the Gothic age extended the concept of *Civitas Dei* [Latin, "City of God"] to the urban environment as a whole, with the town conceived as a meaningful organism," (p. 185) certainly with the church at its center.

Gothic as the embodiment of order eventually evolved into Gothic as the embodiment of the extreme and the frantic. The flamboyant Gothic style of the late thirteenth and fourteenth centuries came to obscure the synthesis and order of early and middle Gothic. This evolution in stone and glass mirrored the increasingly confused and contested order of late medieval church and society. Liturgically, as well, there was increased confusion, some extreme practices and a general focus on what could be considered secondary rather than primary liturgical actions and symbols. Popular devotion focused on seeing the host rather than receiving it; concern for reducing the time one would have to spend in purgatory led to problematic, even scandalous, practices around Mass stipends and indulgences. Eventually, like the great vault of Beauvais Cathedral, eucharistic practices that had been shaken free from their biblical and patristic foundations, began to collapse under their own weight.

The Italian Renaissance Style

As the forward movement of Gothic architecture began to stall and then dissipate, a powerful new social and artistic movement was flowering south of the Alps. Although the word "renaissance" (from Latin *renasci*, "to be born again") has been used to describe many eras and movements, English usage of this term today ordinarily refers to the Italian Renaissance of the fourteenth to sixteenth centuries. Many factors contributed to the birth of this era. One distinctive foundation for this movement was the return to the literature and philosophy of the ancient Greeks and Romans (thus the language of "rebirth"). Medieval figures like Thomas Aquinas and other Scholastics had previously drawn upon the writings of Aristotle and Plato in shaping their theologies. Yet, the return to the classics in the Italian Renaissance was a much more sweeping endeavor with a very broad societal impact.

In the Christian context of the High Middle Ages, these classics were decidedly "pagan," and their worldview or ethics often contradicted the Bible and church teachings. Thus, such writings spurred a new appreciation for the pleasures of this world rather than supporting any aesthetic that delayed worldly pleasures for the reward of a future life. Another characteristic of Greco-Roman classics was an emphasis on the value, dignity, and unity of human nature. While early Christianity certainly taught the value of the individual, this teaching waned in the course of time. With increased emphasis on the sinfulness of the baptized, the growing division between clergy and the laity—symptomatic of the growing division between heaven and earth—and the collective impact of feudalism, the individual human being was not highly valued in the medieval scheme of things [quotation 250]. In an amazing inversion of this trend, the Renaissance, in imitation of the ancient classics, not only valued the individual but sometimes imaged the human being at the center of the universe [illustration 143]. This broad intellectual movement, foundational to the Italian Renaissance, is thus aptly named "humanism."

Renaissance architecture also returned to the classics of the Greco-Roman world for inspiration. The architectural vocabulary of ancient Rome, still visible in this era (though often in ruins) with their columns, rounded arches, and domes, replaced the Gothic

Quotation 250: *Medieval civilization suppressed the ego. In the feudal regime the isolated individual had little standing. He acquired status and protection mainly as a member of a definite group, whether lordly or servile. The manorial system revolved around the community rather than the individual. When the cities threw off the yoke of feudalism, they promised collective and corporate liberty rather than individual freedom. In commercial relations group life was paramount, both in the town guilds and the peasant villages on manorial estates. Everything was regulated by law and custom. The individual who attempted to challenge authority and tradition, in matters of thought or action, was either discouraged or crushed. (Kreis, "Renaissance Humanism")*

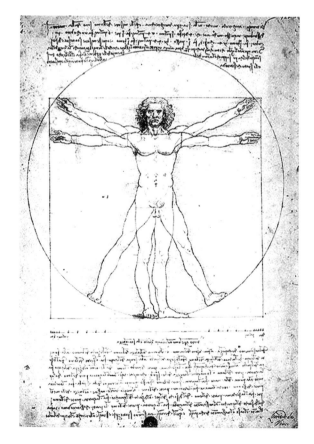

143. Sketch by Leonardo da Vinci illustrating the principles of proportion.

144. Florence Cathedral.

vision. An important written source for this "rebirth" was *De Architectura* (Latin, *About Architecture*) by the ancient Roman Architect Vitruvius (d. after 27 C.E.). While employing the advances made by Gothic builders, Renaissance architects found new ways to vault and buttress that incorporated classical rather than medieval elements. Their works were marked by a new sense of harmony founded on the Vitruvian belief that the human body [illustration 143] provided the ideal proportion for architecture and art [quotation 251]. There was also a preference by some Renaissance architects for central-plan churches rather than the longitudinal basilica so characteristic of the Gothic period.

While certainly not the first building of the Italian Renaissance, one of the most enduring symbols of this architectural revolution is the domed cathedral of S. Maria del Fiore (Italian, "St. Mary of the Flowers") in Florence [illustration 144]. Begun in 1296 as a Gothic structure, in 1366 the city leaders decided that the Gothic style should no longer be followed and that a new type of building in the Roman style should be built. The *Duomo* (Italian, "dome" or "cathedral") still remained unfinished at the beginning of the fifteenth century, largely because no one could propose a credible plan for creating a dome capable of spanning an open space over 140 feet across. It was sculptor turned architect Filippo Brunelleschi (d. 1466) who engineered the feat, with a bold design that employed both an inner and outer dome, resulting in what is still the largest masonry dome in the world.

The completed cathedral of S. Maria del Fiore epitomized many aspects of Renaissance architecture. For example, it was a civic rather than an ecclesiastical venture, and the town leaders not only hired the original architect in 1296 but decided to change the style of the building in 1366, and mounted a competition in 1418 to find an architect to complete the dome. Unlike virtually all of the Gothic cathedrals, we actually know the names of the three major architects (Arnolfo di Cambio, d. before 1310; Francesco Talenti, d. about 1369; and Filippo Brunelleschi) who created the structure, and the genius of an individual like Brunelleschi was well celebrated even in his own lifetime. The building, but especially the dome with its octagonal design, embodied the principles of symmetry espoused by the ancient Roman architect Vitruvius. Finally, we noted that Gothic buildings radiated a kind of divine presence (from the inside out) to the surrounding environment. Conversely, the *Duomo* can be considered a building that is turned inside out, with exterior ribs on the dome calling attention to Brunelleschi's octagonal ingenuity; a soaring, independent bell tower (over 275 feet tall) designed by Giotto (d. 1337); and a vivid exterior of white, green, and pink marble bands in contrast to a quite simple, almost barren interior. This is not a building that radiates from the inside out, but one which rather proclaims by its exterior the political prowess, financial power, and genius of the people of Florence. Certainly this was a humanistic vision of how God was to be glorified.

Division of Space

There were significant differences between Gothic and Renaissance architecture, including the way the interiors of churches were shaped. At the same time, there were many parallels in ecclesiastical architecture in the West during this period, including similarities in the ways interior spaces were divided.

Main Altars   One key convergence point in these buildings was the main altar, whether it was positioned at the back of a long Gothic choir or centered under a Renaissance dome. Often raised on many steps, sometimes marked with elaborate reredos, it dominated the most sacred precinct and was a focal point for worshipers, even though it was often a great distance from the faithful. This was the place where Christ was made present and where he was raised up under the appearance of bread at the elevation of the Mass.

In Roman Ordinal IX (ca. 880–900) there is evidence that at the end of the canon, the bishop raised the consecrated elements from the altar. According to Nathan Mitchell, by the end of the twelfth century in the West there developed a new practice of lifting up the host when the priest recited the part of the institution narrative that began, "On the night before he suffered, he took bread . . ." This

145. Elevation of the host.

innovation would be well explained by the Germanizing tendency toward a dramatic and representational interpretation of the liturgy that we noted in the previous chapter. This practice coincided with a theological debate about when exactly the consecration took place. Peter Cantor represented what Mitchell calls the "single consecration" school, which held that the one encompassing act of consecration included both bread and wine, and that neither could be consecrated alone [quotation 252]. It seems that in response to this position, which was eventually rejected by the church, and to avoid any question about when the consecration did take place, a Parisian synod around 1208 ordered that before the consecration the bread was to be held chest high, and only after the repetition of Christ's words over the bread was it to be elevated [illustration 145] so that it could be seen by all (Mitchell, p. 156). While it would take centuries for the elevation of the chalice to become customary, this elevation of the bread became so significant in the late Middle Ages that everything possible was done to ensure that the host might be seen. Sometimes a dark curtain was drawn behind the altar as a contrast to the white wafer. At other times a special consecration candle was held aloft by a server to illuminate the bread. Often bells were rung to signal this pivotal moment. One of the more unusual gestures of reverence was the construction of a mechanical device above the

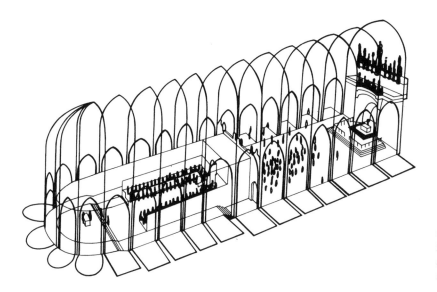

146. Schematic drawing of the cathedral at Albi, indicating the positions of clerics in the choir, the high altar, the rood screen, and the people outside the rood screen. (After Quinn, p. 40)

high altar in early sixteenth-century England. At the time of the consecration, this device caused angels to descend to the altar, where they remained until the conclusion of the Our Father (Thurston, pp. 380–81). While somewhat bizarre, this practice underscores that the elevation had became the ritual center of the liturgy, celebrated at the architectural center of the church.

Choir Area   Already in the previous period the area where monks or clerics prayed the Liturgy of the Hours had begun to develop into a permanent and restricted zone that separated the assembly from the main sanctuary. Rood screens continued to evolve, sometimes appearing as elaborate and impenetrable barriers that virtually excluded the faithful from the central liturgical action [illustration 146]. The increased interest in seeing the consecrated host often made it necessary to design these screens with doors that could be opened during the canon of the Mass so that people could view the elevation. Pulpits were sometimes raised on top of these barriers so that people could hear whatever preaching occurred during the liturgy, something that happened with increasing frequency under the influence of preaching orders like the Dominicans and Franciscans. Within the confines of the choir were often found magnificent choir stalls where the monks or clerics celebrated the Liturgy of the Hours or attended Mass [illustration 147].

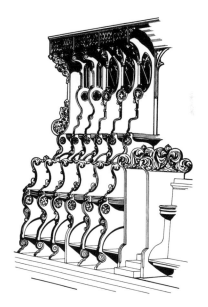

147. Choir stalls from Maulbronn, fifteenth-century carving. (After Atz, p. 154)

Side Altars   The popularity of the private Mass as well as increased veneration of relics led to a multiplication of side altars within the churches of this era. In older churches, not always designed to accommodate simultaneous private Masses, additional side altars were added wherever a convenient open space could be found. By the late Middle Ages, however, the need for multiple side altars was incorporated into the very design of the building. Often small chapels for these altars radiated from the apse or nave. In the hands of a genius like Brunelleschi [illustration 148], the result was an amazing combination of a wondrous open nave flanked by numerous circumscribed spaces. The embedded theology in such a building is one that recognized a faith community with an official public liturgy, while at the same time admitting that the spiritual needs of the community (lay and ordained) were not always or even essentially met by the official public worship.

Pews   Since the beginning of Christian worship, allowances were made for the seating of certain people during the Eucharist. In the homes that served as the first gathering spaces, a bench was sometimes placed along the wall in the dining room where Christians gathered. As the community abandoned the Greco-Roman tradition of lounging while dining and chose to stand during Eucharist—a symbol of resurrection—benches or stools were seldom available for the whole community, and when people sat, they sat on the floor. Seats were provided for the bishop and, less frequently, for other ministers or elders. In the post-Constantinian period, seating was also provided for the emperor and other dignitaries. In monasteries or cathedrals benches were provided for the monks or clerics who occupied the choir area before the altar. From the Carolingian period, some evidence exists that scattered benches, mats, or stools were available to the laity, often provided through their own initiative. During the fourteenth and fifteenth centuries the availability of benches and stools became more widespread. Churches filled with

148. Church of S. Spirito in Florence by Brunelleschi, begun in 1436 and completed in 1482, illustrating how a multitude of side altars with individual chapels are integrated into the design of a church. Brunelleschi intended to express the inclusion of so many side chapels externally by articulating the exterior wall of each chapel with a semicircle. These were later concealed with a straight wall around the periphery of the building. (After Kostof, p. 383)

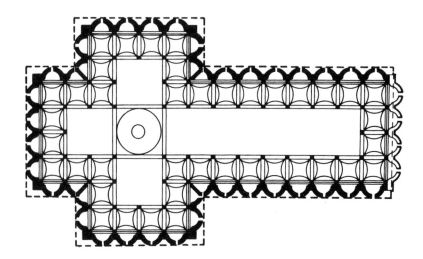

pews became common after the sixteenth century. Though a common feature in Western churches today, their appearance symbolized a significant shift in the attitude of the assembly and contributed to their increasingly static stance within worship [quotation 253].

Summary

The High Middle Ages was one of the most inventive periods in the history of church architecture. Two unusual syntheses in the Gothic and Italian Renaissance left a permanent stamp on Western visions of how worship spaces were to be designed. Along with magnificent artistic and engineering achievements, these developments signaled significant shifts within the eucharistic assembly. For example, the historical and geographic proximity between the introduction of the elevation and the birth of Gothic architecture was more than a coincidence. Rather, they were analogous elements that affirmed both the predominance of the visual aspects of liturgy and the tendency to reduce the role of the assembly to that of eucharistic spectator. Both Gothic and Renaissance buildings were designed less for the hearing and responding of the assembly and more for their viewing. In the process, ordinarily believers were kept at a distance from the sacred action of the priest, who occupied the architectural and liturgical center of these buildings. With the addition of pews, the community assumed a new degree of stasis in the eucharistic liturgy.

MUSIC

The musical landscape of late medieval Eucharist was a diverse and paradoxical state of affairs. On the one hand, *scholas* and choirs had assumed a new prominence in the eucharistic liturgy, especially in the cathedrals and other large urban churches. As far as musical composition for these elite musicians, this was an unusually fertile period of development for church music. On the other hand, the growing phenomenon of private Mass indicates that very frequently Eucharist was celebrated without music. As for the faithful, their musical role in the public celebration of the Eucharist clearly declined, but their voices could not be completely silenced. In order to chart this complex situation we will consider two basic musical trends of the time: the addition of more than one line of music during a piece, and the textual changes that accompanied this musical development. In light of those two changes, largely effecting the music of *scholas* and choirs, we will then consider how and when the voice of the congregation was heard.

Quotation 253: *Beginning in the fourteenth century, a revolution occurred in many parish churches. The congregation literally sat down on the job as pews were introduced. The congregation, once mobile and able to go where preaching was best heard or the Mass best seen, became static. . . . A seated congregation may have been the most significant change in Christian worship since Constantine.* (James White, A Brief History of Christian Worship, pp. 101–2)

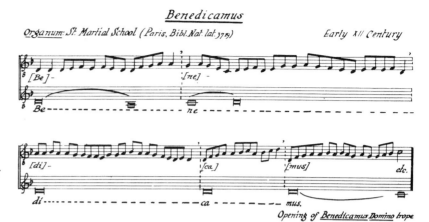

149. Two-part organum with slow-moving Gregorian melody in the lower voice and florid ornamentation in the upper voice. Early twelfth century. (Gleason, p. 30)

Multiplication of Musical Lines

Polyphony appeared in the ninth century and grew to prominence during the late Middle Ages. Assuredly, chant works continued to be performed in the liturgy, and new works of chant were also composed. There is even a celebrated woman mystic from this period, Hildegard of Bingen (d. 1179), whose liturgical chants written for the nuns of her convent have come down to us. Yet, as convents and monasteries gave way to cathedrals as the centers of Christian worship in the West, so did chant yield its prominence to polyphony.

Simple two-part works of organum, already extant in the previous era, were succeeded by three- and four-part compositions. Besides the addition of more musical lines to these compositions, sometimes the writing was in a more florid style. In some works based on Gregorian melodies, the chant was performed very slowly in the lower voice while ornate passages were sung in the upper voice(s) [illustration 149]. In chapter 4 we noted that, no matter what its origin, Gregorian chant was word-centered music that was designed to support and enhance the liturgical text. Successive developments in polyphony often contributed to the obscuring of the liturgical text as well as overshadowing the original melody, which was reduced to an underlying drone, sometimes performed on the primitive organs of the period.

These melodic developments were matched by rhythmic advances, such as the introduction of a repeated rhythmic pattern. This repeated pattern was one of the techniques thirteenth-century composers used for organizing their compositions [illustration 150]. The resulting music—marked with a new rhythmic coherence and verticality created by many lines piled one upon the other—was much like the Gothic cathedral of the day, with its soaring vaults and repetitive patterns of piers and buttresses. Both had a similar effect on

Mode	Meter	Musical equivalent
1	Trochaic: long short	
2	Iambic: short long	
3	Dactylic: long short short	
4	Anapaestic: short short long	
5	Spondaic: long long	
6	Tribrachic: short short short	

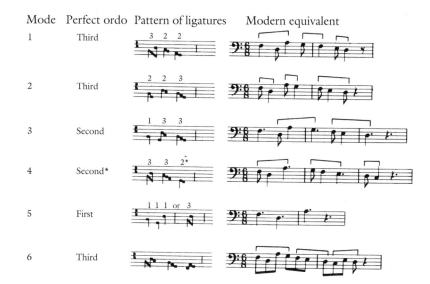

Mode	Perfect ordo	Pattern of ligatures	Modern equivalent
1	Third		
2	Third		
3	Second		
4	Second*		
5	First		
6	Third		

150. The six rhythmic patterns known as "rhythmic modes" employed in organizing the rhythm of some later medieval music. (Hoppin, pp. 222, 224)

the assembly as well: they exceeded the comprehension of ordinary people while invoking a sense of awe and wonder.

Early polyphonic composition for the Eucharist was confined to the changeable or proper parts of the Mass. In the fourteenth century some composers shifted their attention to polyphonic settings for the ordinary of the Mass. One reason for this shift was the awareness that settings of the ordinary could be more useful than propers, which generally were sung only once a year. It is also possible that the texts of the ordinary, which had been in use for many centuries, were considered a more venerable part of the ritual. Thus for a long time musicians were less inclined to depart from traditional Gregorian settings of the ordinary. During the late Middle Ages, however, Western music underwent significant artistic developments independent of the liturgy. In this context, because of the newfound independence of the musical arts from the church's liturgy, and because of the desire to push into new compositional territories, composers felt bold enough to apply polyphonic techniques to the ordinary of the Mass. The first complete setting of the ordinary of the Mass by a single

151. Example of a trope text sung in the upper voice (*Stirps Jesse*) against an original Gregorian *Benedicamus Domino*. Early twelfth century. (Gleason, p. 33)

composer was *La Messe de Notre Dame* by Guillaume de Machaut (d. 1377). While chant melodies and most works of early polyphony were composed anonymously, Machaut and his musical contemporaries became some of the first composers to achieve fame for their individual achievements. Parallel to the previously noted rise of individual architects, this development further signaled that music was assuming a life apart from worship. Artistic independence, be it in music or in architecture, contributed to the artists' growing tendency to use the liturgy as a setting for their artistic achievements, regardless of whether these contributed to the prayerful engagement of the assembly. This is not to suggest that such artists were not concerned about glorifying God with their arts, for many were. God's glorification, however, was not necessarily wed to people's sanctification.

Textual Changes

The addition of numerous lines of music to a single melody can be a work of great beauty. The simultaneous sounding of independent lines of music in polyphony, however, makes it difficult—especially for the musically untrained—to identify or reproduce any of the melodies in such a piece. While this was no doubt inspiring music, the obscurity of the various melody lines made it inaccessible to most people. One would not leave church humming a polyphonic work.

This melodic obscurity found a parallel in the growing obscurity of the texts in the liturgical music of the day. The propers and ordinary of the Mass developed out of a common textual stock: psalms, litanies, and traditional hymns or prayers. Even if the people did not speak Latin, years of listening to the sung *Sanctus* or other chants allowed ordinary people to become familiar with these texts. The simultaneous singing of one text in two or three different rhythms or the singing of two or three different texts at the same time did not enable such familiarization.

152. Motet based on gradual for Easter, *Haec Dies* (This is the day), with a Latin text *Virgo virginum* (Virgin of virgins) in the second voice and either a Latin text *O mitissima* (O Sweetest Virgin Mary) or an old French text *Quant voi* (When I see returning the summer season) in the upper voice. (Davidson and Apel, p. 33)

Various developments in polyphony contributed to a progressive obscuring of liturgical chants. In organum, a trope or second text sometimes was sung against the original texts [illustration 151]. At times only a fragment of the original text was employed in the lower voice. This type of composition was called a *clausula* (from Latin, *claudere*, "to falter"). A Latin text eventually was added to the upper voice(s) of the *clausula*, thus creating the motet (from French, *mot*, "word"). In some motets, a second text in Latin or French occasionally was added [illustration 152]. The resulting polytextuality wed to musical polyphony greatly obscured the texts. While this is a decidedly extreme example, there was a growing concern at the end of this era about the inability to hear or understand the liturgical texts. This was true not only for ordinary people but even for highly educated humanists. Thus the great linguist Erasmus (d. 1536) could complain about the obscurity of the liturgical texts [quotation 254].

Vernacular Song

Although it is not possible to keep people from singing, it is possible to restrict when and where their singing is allowed. At no time in the history of Christian worship has the song of the assembly been completely suppressed. During the late Middle Ages, however, their singing was increasingly marginalized in the eucharistic liturgy. Previously, the assembly joined in singing various parts of the ordinary and even the proper of the Mass. The last part of the ordinary that seems to have belonged to the people was the *Sanctus*. Literary evidence suggests that in some places this ancient text was considered a chant of the people as late as the twelfth century. Musical evidence also attests to a lingering conviction that the *Sanctus* belonged to the people. When composers began to apply polyphonic techniques to the ordinary of the Mass, they did not write complete settings that would have included a *Kyrie*, *Gloria*, *Sanctus*, *Benedictus*, and *Agnus Dei*. Rather, they set individual pieces. The *Sanctus* was one of the last parts of the ordinary to receive polyphonic treatment. For example, the "Mass of Tournai" is the earliest known example in which all five movements of the ordinary were collected under a single title. The ordinary is actually a compilation of materials composed between the late thirteenth and mid-fourteenth centuries. Each Mass part is set polyphonically, except the *Sanctus*. This piece, which dates from the earlier period, is set monophonically except for the polyphonic setting of the words *in excelsis* that occur at the end of each *Osanna* section. This does not necessarily mean that the congregation was able to sing this simpler setting of the *Sanctus*. It does, however, at least attest to the living memory that congregations once sang this part.

As polyphonic composition overtook the *Sanctus*, the assembly's voice was excluded from what could be considered their last integral liturgical chant. From this point on, while the voice of the assembly still sounds within the eucharistic liturgy, their musical role could be considered both peripheral and expendable, more occurring "in" the liturgy than actually a voice "of" the liturgy. A symbol of this change was the growing tradition for the assembly to sing in their own language, rather than singing the official parts of the Mass in Latin. It was especially among the Germanic speaking people that vernacular singing was liturgically prominent [quotation 255]. There were three places in the Mass where vernacular song seems to have occurred with some regularity.

Processions   In the previous chapter we noted how the faithful vocally participated in the processions that accompanied the stational liturgy practice in Rome and other cities. There are innumerable sources from the Middle Ages that relate how popular religious songs were employed in processions outside of Eucharist. English carols were sometimes used as processional songs. Italian *laude* (from Latin, *lauda*, "praise") played an important role in popular religious processions. German *Geisslerlieder* (German, *Geissel*, "whip" + *Lied*, "song" or "flagellant song") accompanied the processions of the flagellants. Also, the great pilgrimage movements of these centuries spawned a large repertoire of pilgrim songs. While there is not a great deal of explicit evidence documenting the use of such processional songs in the Eucharist, there is sufficient evidence of their religious usage in other liturgies to suggest that they also may have been sung, for example, during the entrance rites of the Mass on special days. This is probably one of the reasons why diverse diocesan and provincial synods in the late Middle Ages ordered that the Latin chants of the Mass must neither be truncated nor abandoned in favor of vernacular chants.

Sequences   The sequence, which still exists in the Catholic Mass on special occasions like Easter, was a particular type of hymn chanted after the Alleluia, which developed in the ninth century. These were ordinarily in Latin and sung by musical specialists, though vernacular paraphrases developed in some places alongside the official texts, allowing for the assembly to join in. Sometimes the parallel vernacular text was interpolated into the sequence, with the congregation singing a strophe after each Latin verse [quotation 256]. In other situations the vernacular text was performed after the sequence.

Quotation 255: *All the earth exalts in praise of Christ with vernacular songs, but especially the Germanic people, whose language is especially suited for communal singing.* (Gerhoh of Reichersburg (1148), in Ruff, "A Milennium," p. 11)

Quotation 256: *Around other feasts such as the Resurrection, Ascension and Corpus Christi, several songs are joined with sequences: for example, in the sequence "Victimae pascali laudes"* the vernacular "Crist ist erstanden" *occurs regularly every two verses or so. . . . Also, around the sequence for the Ascension,* "Summi triumphum etc." *there is sung the vernacular prosa* "Crist fuer gen himel." ("Crailsheimer Schulordnung" [1480], in Crecelius, *Alemannia*)

Many well-known texts arose from the popular appropriation of sequences by the people.

Sermon   A third "soft spot" in medieval Eucharist that allowed for the insertion of popular vernacular song occurred after the sermon, which itself was virtually always a vernacular event, even when the rest of worship was not. As previously noted, there is evidence from at least the tenth century that Germanic speaking people inserted a brief acclamation of one or two lines, called a *Ruf,* after the sermon. In later centuries a *Leise* (from Greek *eleison*, "have mercy") could be sung here as well. These were Germanic folk hymns that developed from the refrain *Kyrie eleison*, a shortened form of which (*Kyrieleis*) concluded each stanza. Italian *laude* (from Latin *lauda*, "praise") with their congregation refrains were closely connected to the preaching of Franciscans and other penitent groups; Francis himself had composed vernacular praises. Most evidence is that *laude* were sung in special services of the laypeople who formed confraternities known as the *laudesi*, which cultivated the singing of these praises [illustration 153]. Because of the intimate connection between *laude* and mendicant preaching, it is possible that on occasions when such mendicants preached within the context of Eucharist—especially to the *laudesi*—*laude* could have been sung as well.

Eventually a kind of vernacular office attached to the sermon evolved. It incorporated aspects of the old prayer of the faithful, song, and announcement. Known as the prône (from Latin *praeconium*, "announcement"), nascent forms of this service appear already in the late ninth century, though a fully developed service is not apparent until the fourteenth century. While not an official part of Mass, this service became quite common and was probably one of the most consistent places in the eucharistic liturgy where the faithful would have sung.

Summary

As noted at the outset of the section, the musical landscape of this era was both rich and paradoxical. The creative and compositional richness we have sketched, but the paradox has only been hinted at. One framework for grasping something of the musical contradictions of this period is the previously noted distinction between music "in" the liturgy and music "of" the liturgy. There are many types of music that can occur in the liturgy but are not necessarily integral to or essentially connected to the church's official worship. Thus liturgical music can be defined as that music which unites with the liturgical action, serves to reveal the full significance of the rite, and, in turn,

153. Fourteenth-century lauda manuscript.

derives its full meaning from the liturgical event and not simply from its liturgical setting.

Previous to the High Middle Ages there are few examples of music occurring in the eucharistic liturgy that did not meet such a definition of liturgical music. During this period, however, we can begin to identify developments that led to musical composition that was religious or sacred but not necessarily liturgical. Gifted musical geniuses, for example, sometimes seemed more interested in pushing compositional boundaries than enhancing the eucharistic action. For the first time in Christendom, such musicians had nonreligious venues for writing and performing their works, and sometimes there was little differentiation between what they wrote for court or church. As previously noted, this is not to suggest that their motives were not religious, but rather than intimately wed to the ritual actions, their musical artistry often took on a life of its own. This is understandable in an era when the priest was at some distance, often with his back to the people, praying inaudibly, and even (as we will see below) reciting to himself at his own pace the very texts that the musicians were singing. These developments did not pass without

Quotation 257: *Certain disciples of a new school . . . are turning their attention to new kinds of music . . . for they trivialize the melody with a second or third line and sometimes they go so far as to burden it with additional secular texts. . . . By the sheer number of additional notes the plain-chant melodies—with their modest ascending and descending patterns by which the various modes are distinguished—are obscured.* (John XXII [d. 1334], Teaching of the Holy Fathers [1324–1325])

critique. John XXII (d. 1334) issued one of the first authentic papal documents specifically dealing with music, which challenged the introduction of many contemporary compositional practices into the liturgical music of the day [quotation 257]. This did little, however, to change the practice.

Similarly, laypeople were developing devotional activities outside of what we might consider the church's official liturgy. Their religious songs might accompany a procession blessing a crop, punctuate a town fair, or even be sung during the liturgy. While often inspired by liturgical texts like the *Kyrie*, these religious songs began to assume an identity apart from the liturgy. Thus, while there were occasions when such religious songs did punctuate the liturgical action, they were neither circumscribed nor defined by such action. Liturgical music was less and less the purview of the baptized, and in this void devotional and religious songs abounded.

BOOKS

Similar to cathedrals, musical settings of the ordinary, and liturgical vessels, every liturgical book is a rich and complex symbol. Each symbolizes, for example, something about what it means to be church. As already seen in the previous era, the trend of combining materials from two or more liturgical books into a single volume continued during the High Middle Ages. While new books did develop, the overall trend for books in this era was consolidation. The lectionary, for example, was a combination of the epistolary and evangeliary, thus containing all of the readings necessary for the celebration of Mass. The pontifical gathered together all of the texts that a bishop would need for Eucharist and other special ceremonies. If the previous era could be considered the age of the sacramentary, then this era of consolidation was most of all the era of the full missal, the most important liturgical compilation of the age. Ecclesiologically, this central Mass book symbolized the primacy of the priest, whom theologians like Aquinas defined essentially in terms of his eucharistic role during the consecration [quotation 258]. In the thirteenth century, it was the priesthood and not the episcopacy that was considered the summit of the ordination process, and bishops were no longer thought to be ordained, but only consecrated.

Quotation 258: *A priest has two acts: one is the principal, namely to consecrate the body of Christ; the other is secondary, namely to prepare God's people for the reception of this sacrament.* (Thomas Aquinas, *Summa Theologica*, Suppl., quest. 40, art. 4, respond.)

Books of the era also point to wider trends in the cultures of the time. One of these was the growth in literacy among the laity. Some of this growth was the result of the expansion of the merchant class, for whom reading was an increasingly valuable skill. Furthermore, there were many other professions of the time, from English sheriffs

154. A woodcut from the romance *De Claris Mulieribus* (Latin, "Concerning famous women") by Giovanni Boccaccio (d. 1375).

to royal clerks, that required skill in reading. The spread of universities, with their degrees in arts, law, and medicine as well as theology, testify to spreading literacy in the late Middle Ages as well. Apart from politics, church, or commerce it also seems that reading provided a form of entertainment in social circles. Thus, in the fourteenth century there appeared the "romance," a genre of literature for the upper class that related entertaining tales with clear moral overtones [illustration 154]. Books of a more explicit religious nature were also produced for the laity.

Two other trends shaped both the appearance and the content of liturgical books of this era. One was the amazing artistic developments in manuscript illustration during the late Middle Ages. Often anonymous artisans crafted books of visual magnificence. Some genres, like books of Hours, had virtually no text in them, so that they were more looked at than read. At the height of this manuscript art, a very different development occurred in the art of printing. Many in the West celebrate Johann Gutenberg (d. 1468) as the inventor of printing as we know it, although the Chinese had already printed books in the sixth century with a woodblock method, and Koreans had a moveable type printing press by 1241. The convergence of multiple developments in the quality of ink, paper, and technology, combined with Gutenberg's skill and vision, enabled him to produce books of unusual distinction, still celebrated for their unparalleled quality.

The move from manuscript to printed liturgical book was to have a significant effect on worship practices. Because manuscripts were individually produced, they captured the liturgy of a very particular time, place, and worship practice. While a thirteenth-century missal or ordinary contained standard material found in similar books of the era, it would also include distinctive texts, rubrics, and illustrations. Thus, for example, the thirteenth-century Ordinary of St.-Denis included additional prayers for the blessings of grapes to be inserted in the canon of the Mass on the feast of the Transfiguration (August 6). Some liturgical books included vernacular texts along with the Latin, such as a fourteenth-century epistolary from Spain, which, according to Martimort, contained a Latin text of the prophet Isaiah for Christmas with a parallel text in Catalan. Printing, on the other hand, had the potential to introduce a uniformity in texts never before experienced within Christian worship. Such textual uniformity was not achieved until the next era, but the explosion of printing presses throughout Europe in the fifteenth century prepared the way for this development. Elizabeth Eisenstein estimates, for example, that by the year 1500 there were 220 printing presses in operation throughout western Europe and at least eight million books in print (pp. 13–17).

We will now examine particular genres of these books in view of this shifting symbolization in the liturgical books of the late Middle Ages. First we will consider two key books for clerics and then examine the rise of prayer books for the laity.

Full Missal

The full missal was not new to this era and had already appeared in some places by the ninth century. This volume was a combination of five other books (Mass antiphonary, epistolary, evangeliary, sacramentary, and ordo) and greatly facilitated the celebration of Mass by a single priest without other ministers. Though rare before the turn of the millennium, the full missal became one of the most frequently produced manuscripts of the late Middle Ages. As the full missal became more popular, the sacramentary diminished in popularity [quotation 259].

As noted in the previous chapter, the full missal developed for a number of reasons. Chief among these were the requirements of the private Mass and the tendency to reduce sung texts to read texts. Regarding the latter, we have seen that already by the eighth century there was evidence in some places that priests were reading song texts, such as the entrance psalm or the communion psalm, in the absence of a choir [quotation 218] or even repeating song texts privately while a schola or cantor chanted them. This practice spread, and by the mid-thirteenth century legislation appeared directing that all

Quotation 259: *In the first half of the twelfth century, the sacramentaries were a small minority, in the thirteenth they were exceptional and in the fourteenth they were archaic leftovers.* (Vogel, *Medieval Liturgy*, p. 105)

In Die Sancto Pasche. Ad Matutinas primitus sonet classicum.
Postea sonent campane duppliciter et non dicatur *Ad Dominum*.
Sollempnitas ista sollempnitatum dicitur. Matutine hoc modo
celebrentur. Primitus abbas incipiat *Domine labia mea* at postea
dicatur *Deus in adiutorium et Gloria Patri*. Post Gloriam statim
cantetur Invit. *Alleluya Surrexit Dominus vere* inter duo altaria
a IIII in cappis. Ps. *Venite exultemus*. Remaneant cantores in
choro et non cantetur Hy. set mox incipiat ebdomadarius Ant.
super Ps. *Ego sum qui sum*. Ps. *Beatus vir*. Ant. *Postulavi Patrem*.
Ps. *Quare*. Ant. *Ego dormivi*. Ps. *Domine quid multiplicati*.
Ant. omnes dicantur sine neumate et per totam ebdomadam.
V. *Surrexit Christus*. Prima Lc. a diacono alba dalmatica induto
qui veniens stet abbatem et abbas benedicat incensum . . .

On the Holy Day of Easter. At Matins first ring the bell. After that
sound the tower bells in doublets. *To the Lord* is not said. This
solemnity is called the feast of feasts. Matins is celebrated in this
way: First the abbot begins *Lord, open my lips* and afterwards is
said *O God, come to my assistance* and *Glory be to the Father*.
Immediately after the doxology the invitatorium *Alleluia, the Lord
is truly* risen is sung by four cantors in copes standing between the
two altars with the Psalm *Come, let us sing joyfully*. The cantors
remain in the choir. The hymn is not sung. The leader next begins
the antiphon before the psalm *I am who am*. Psalm *Blessed is the
man*. Antiphon *I asked the Father*. Psalm *Why*. Antiphon *I slept*.
Psalm *Lord, how many*. All the antiphons are said without
modulation through the whole week. Versicle *Christ rose*.
The first reading is read by a deacon robed in a white dalmatic.
He stands before the abbot who blesses the incense . . .

155. Directions for the celebration of Easter from the early thirteenth-century ordinary of the
Abbey of St.-Denis near Paris. A Latin transcription and English translation follow in which the
rubrics are in plain type and the prayer texts are in italics. (Foley, *First Ordinary of the Royal
Abbey of St.-Denis in France*, p. 386)

Quotation 260: *[After the priest has kissed the altar] the deacon places the missal on the right side of the altar and the subdeacon the gospel book on the left side. . . . Then all the ministers, assembling at the missal and standing to the right of the priest [in order of their rank] say the Introit and the Kyrie eleison. [Then all are seated while the choir finishes singing]. . . . At the end of the Kyrie eleison the priest rises from his seat and, standing in the middle of the altar . . . begins the Gloria in excelsis—if it is to be said that day—with the other ministers arranged behind him according to rank, as previously noted. When the priest says "Deo" he joins his hands. Then, beginning with the priest and the others following, they move to the right side of the altar where the other ministers stand to the right of the priest according to their rank, as previously noted. When they have finished saying the Gloria, the priest and deacon remain there while the choir completes the singing of it. (Ordinarium juxta ritum sacri Ordinis Fratru Fraedicatorum* [The Dominican Ordinary of 1267], nos. 47 and 49)

chant texts must be read by the presider [quotation 260]. This practice not only symbolized the centrality of the priest to the eucharistic action but effectively announced that even though choirs or people could sing texts at Mass, their singing was neither essential nor effective for fulfilling the requirements for Eucharist. All texts and actions critical for the valid celebration of Mass belonged to the priest.

Finally, one should not forget that this was an era of mobility and pilgrimage. The phenomenon of so many laypeople and clerics on the move would also have contributed to the growing need for portable books. Issues of mobility were especially important for members of some of the new religious orders—like Franciscans and Dominicans. These were not monks but mendicants (from Latin *mendicare*, "to beg"), who were forbidden to own land and were to make their living by begging. Mendicants did not take a vow of stability to a single monastery like Benedictines, but were itinerants whose ministry and livelihood required them to travel from place to place. Portable books were very important for supporting this new form of religious life.

Ordinary

In the centuries following the conversion of Constantine, collections of rubrics developed to help ministers execute the increasingly complex Roman liturgy. The earliest collections of these ordos—the previously quoted Roman Ordinals—dated from seventh-century Rome. During the period of Germanization, these collections were widely used. By the late Middle Ages, new influences led to the gradual expansion of these ordos. One such influence was the desire to include instructions for all the days of the church year and not just those for the special rituals outlined in the ordos. Another factor was the need to use Roman rubrics in places other than Rome. This necessitated further adaptations of the collections. In the process, the rubrics or directions were combined with the opening few words or the *incipit* (Latin, "it begins") of the relevant liturgical texts [illustration 155]. The result was a new genre of liturgical book called an "ordinary" (Latin, *liber ordinarius*). Like a Roman Ordinal, the ordinary was never used during worship but rather was consulted beforehand in the preparation process. The ordinary was, therefore, an auxiliary liturgical book that supplied texts and directions for celebrating the offices, the Eucharist, and a variety of other rites and devotions. The book was arranged according to the liturgical calendar and usually was composed for a specific church or religious community, thus manifesting one of the characteristics of liturgical manuscripts noted above. The local character of these books was one of their chief assets because, in the midst of the diverse liturgical practices that marked the Middle Ages, they clarified how specific rites were enacted in particular monasteries or cathedrals. Ordinaries appeared for the first time in the twelfth century, but they soon became obsolete. Two main factors contributed to their obsolescence. The first was the growing presumption that every liturgical book should include all of the necessary texts along with the rubrics. Thus one of the unique features of the ordinary—the inclusion of rubrics—was eventually incorporated into all liturgical books. A second fact was the gradual standardization of liturgical books in the West. This development, greatly enhanced by the evolution of the printing industry, eventually eliminated the need and even allowance for descriptions of local rites and customs so characteristic of the ordinary.

People's Prayer Books

In the previous era we saw that special liturgical books were developed for the various ministers, but none developed for the use of the laity. Songbooks went to the singers, epistolaries to the subdeacons, evangeliaries to the deacons, and so forth. Not only were liturgical books assigned to these various clerics, there is also increasing evidence prohibiting the laity from even touching them. Thus, for example, there is evidence that north of the Alps the laity may actually have participated in kissing the Book of the Gospels during the Eucharist [quotation 261]. Jungmann reports, however, that by 1221 Pope Honorious III decreed that the right to venerate the gospel book was henceforth restricted to *personis inunctis* (Latin, "anointed people"), so that only priests and bishops were allowed this privilege (*The Mass of the Roman Rite*, I:449–450), rather than deacons, subdeacons, and the raft of other minor clerics regularly included in the ritual until this time. Disallowed from even handling the official books of the liturgy, the laity began to develop its own books. This process is not unrelated to the musical trends of the Middle Ages: the people were increasingly eliminated from the official song of the liturgy and consequently developed their own religious songs, mostly for use outside the confines of official worship.

Although liturgical books generally were the property of worshiping communities, evidence suggests that after the conversion of Constantine, some individuals had books for their personal prayers. The great Christian prayer book was the Psalter, and some individuals—especially the wealthy or the powerful—had personal copies [illustration 130], thought it was not always clear that these books

Quotation 261: *And when the deacon descends from the ambo, the subdeacon [who is standing next in order of rank] receives the gospel book which [holding before his chest outside of the vestment] he extends to be kissed: first to the bishop or priest, then to all in order of position who were standing near, and then all of the clergy and the people.*
(Roman Ordinal V [ca. 900], n. 38)

156. Saint Anne teaching the Blessed Virgin to read, from a book of hours (1524). (Rosenwald manuscript 10, Library of Congress)

Quotation 262:

Loued [praised] be thou, kyng [king];
and blessed be thou, kyng;
of alle thy gyftes [gifts] gode [good],
and thanked by thou, kyng;
Ihseu, al my ioying [joying]
that for me split thy blode [blood]
and dyed upon the rode [rood]
thou gyue [give] me grace to sing
the song of thy louing [praising]

(early 14 c. English translation of an elevation prayer, in *The Lay Folks Mass Book*, p. 40)

were actually used for prayer. Previous to the Carolingian period, the laity had little need for books to aid in following the eucharistic liturgy, because the liturgy was ordinarily in a language and style native to them and thus more easily understood. The importation of the Roman Rite into non-Latin speaking communities and the progressive distancing and ultimate marginalization of the laity from the central eucharistic activity, however, provided a climate appropriate for the development of prayer books for lay use during and outside the Eucharist.

Many times these books did not offer a translation or even the original Latin text of the prayers that the priest prayed at the altar. Rather, these books often contained various psalms, litanies, and offices of the dead or of the Blessed Virgin. These were eventually called "books of hours," and in England they were known as "the prymers," as they were sometimes employed as the "primary" text for teaching someone to read, be that in Latin or in English. Symbolic of this purpose was the frequent inclusion of an illustration of St. Anne teaching the Blessed Virgin how to read [illustration 156]. Eventually Eucharist-related prayers and meditations were added to some books of hours [illustration 157]. Prayers similar to those said by the priest were occasionally included in these books as well, sometimes for almost the entire Mass. In other instances, meditations or allegorical interpretations of the Mass were offered, and the layperson was instructed to pray so many Our Fathers and Hail Marys for each part of the Mass. Finally, there appeared at this time books and sections of books more specifically focused on instructing the laity about how to attend or "hear" Mass. The *Lay Folks Mass Book*, for example,

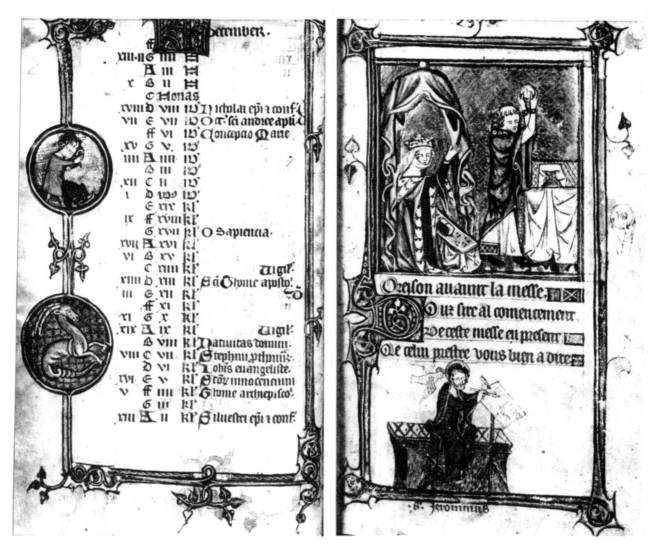

157. Two pages from the *Taymouth Hours*, an early fourteenth-century book of hours written for a noblewoman of the time, probably Joan, daughter of Edward II of England. The reproduced pages show the last page of a liturgical calendar, which began the book, and a prayer said before Mass (*Oreison avaunt la messe*) along with an illustration, possibly of the noblewoman herself attending Mass. Though the prayer is said before the Mass, the illustration is of the most characteristic and important ritual moment of the Mass, the elevation. (Harthan, p. 46)

appeared in the late twelfth century in France and over the years was translated into other languages, acquiring additional prayers and other materials in the process. It contained some of the earliest prayers for greeting the host during the elevation [quotation 262]. In this and other books of the period, however, the canon of the Mass and the changeable propers were seldom if ever printed, either in Latin or in translation.

Summary

The subdivision of the late medieval church building into various segments for priest, choir, and laity found an analogue in the liturgical books of the day. Each group had its own place in the building, and the priest's place at the main altar in the sanctuary was clearly the most important. Similarly, distinctive books developed for each group. The book for the priest was of preeminence here, incorporating within its covers the essential material from virtually every other liturgical book for the celebration of Mass. Implicit acknowledgment of the revered nature of this book was the growing practice, already evident by the thirteen century, of resting the missal on a cushion or wooden stand that could be draped with richly embroidered cloth. As Cyrille Vogel has noted, the full missal was not just a new book, it also was a symbol of a new understanding of the Mass [quotation 263]. By the end of the Middle Ages, the ordinary baptized were quite marginalized from the central activity of the Eucharist and, to some extent, could even be considered irrelevant to the eucharistic action.

The creation of prayer books for laypeople could be understood as a partial response to this situation. The emergence of such books was aided by a religious movement among some people in the latter part of this era toward more interiority and meditation. As noted in the introduction to the chapter, in many places there were enormous discrepancies between the opulence of the church and the poverty of ordinary people. Strands of resistance to religious emphases on externals were evident in many groups who, instead, stressed the interior life and meditation, particularly on the passion of Christ. Francis of Assisi and his followers were early examples of this trend. More extreme groups like the Cathars (Greek, *katharos*, "pure") rejected the material and things of the flesh as evil, including the doctrine of the incarnation and all the sacraments. They were condemned and persecuted. A more mainstream yearning for things interior was symbolized in the influential movement of the fourteenth and fifteenth centuries known as the *Devotio Moderna* (Latin, "modern devotion") and the most famous spiritual manual of that movement, the *Imitation of Christ* (ca. 1418) [illustration 158], probably authored by Thomas à Kempis (d. 1471).

While individual books for prayer and meditation were helpful aids for personal reflection, they also contributed to the liturgical isolation of individuals, not only from the action of the priest but also from each other. Watching, listening, and eventually reading were the dominant forms of participation available to the faithful during the Eucharist. Because of the widespread practice of silent Mass, the inability of most laity to understand Latin, and the complexity of whatever music might have been performed, listening was

Quotation 263: *The plenary missal is . . . the result of a new way of regarding the Mass. The eucharistic celebration ceases to be an actio liturgica [Latin, "liturgical action"] in which the celebrant, ministers, singers and people collaborate and have distinctive and cooperative roles to play. As a result the priest-celebrant, as the sole actor in this liturgical process, will be provided henceforth with a new kind of book.* (Vogel, Medieval Liturgy, p. 105)

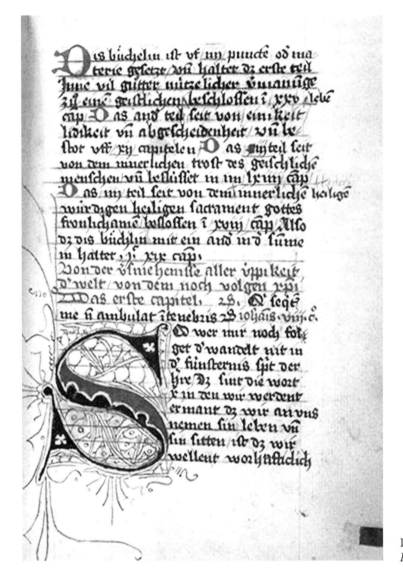

158. A fifteenth-century manuscript page of the *Imitation of Christ*.

a decreasingly important mode of participation. Instead, the assembly was left to watch the liturgy, pray, or read silently during it. These activities were certainly satisfying for many laypeople, but they nonetheless contributed to the people's liturgical isolation and the fragmentation of the liturgical assembly.

VESSELS

During the late Middle Ages, two somewhat contradictory trends influenced the development of eucharistic vessels. The first was a continued increase in the number of vessels for the bread. Most important was the emergence of vessels for the display of the host.

As the types of vessels for holding the consecrated bread increased, the number of vessels or utensils for the consecrated wine decreased. During this period the cup was entirely removed from the people. Communion for the laity was given only under the form of bread. Theologically, this practice was supported by the new theory of "concomitance" (Latin *per concomitantiam*, "by association"), defended by theologians such as Thomas Aquinas, which held that when the bread was consecrated into Christ's Body, the Blood of Christ was also present.

These trends underscored the increased rarity of communion by the laity. The reasons for this situation were multiple and complex. On the one hand, this was the cumulative result of centuries of theology and practice that emphasized the unworthiness of the baptized, their second-class ecclesial status, and their need for penance. On the other hand, ordinary people found ritual satisfaction in a wide variety of other devotions and popular practices in which they were more active participants. Thus, despite the restrictions on receiving communion, most baptized did not feel eucharistically deprived and some could go years or even longer without ever receiving communion. Theologically this practice was justified by a developing theory that proposed that the priest received communion for the people [quotation 264]. In response to the diminished reception of the Eucharist by the faithful, the church decreed—under threat of being denied a Christian burial—that all the baptized must go to communion at least once a year during the Easter season; given the presumption of their sinfulness and need for penance, the decree first required their annual confession [quotation 265]. The decree seems to have been effective, and as Vauchez notes, it was a rare layperson who did not make confession at least once a year; on the other hand, as he notes, frequent communion remained the preserve of an extremely limited spiritual elite (p. 105). It is also important to acknowledge that when people did go to communion, it was seldom actually at Mass during the communion rite, but ordinarily either before or after the eucharistic celebration, usually at a side altar.

One exception concerning frequency was the desire on the part of some mystics, particularly women mystics, for more regular communion. As Caroline Walker Bynum has argued, many teachers, preachers, and confessors emphasized the magnificence of this sacrament and the consequent danger in reception, sowing the seeds of eucharistic terror in the hearts of many faithful. This, along with a well-rooted sense of unworthiness, effectively kept many people away from communion. On the other hand, Bynum believes that some of the devout found that through this pious fear, their eucharistic hunger actually intensified. That does not necessarily mean that such

Quotation 264: *Otto of Bamberg [d. 1139] said that the converted Pomerangians should communicate through their priests if they could not receive themselves. Berthold of Regensburg [d. 1272] explained that the communicating priest "nourishes us all," for he is the mouth and we are the body. William Durandus the Elder [d. 1296] suggested that the faithful receive three times a year "because of sinfulness" but "priests [receive] daily for us all." Ludolf of Saxony [d. 1377] argued that the Eucharist is called our daily bread because ministers receive it daily for the whole community."* (Bynum, *Holy Feast and Fast,* p. 57)

Quotation 265: *Let everyone of the faithful of both sexes, after he has arrived at the years of discretion, alone faithfully confess all his sins at least once a year to his own priest, and let him strive to fulfill with all his power the penance enjoined upon him, receiving reverently the sacrament of the Eucharist at least in Paschal time, unless by chance on the advice of his own priest for some reasonable cause it shall be decided that he must abstain from the precept temporarily; otherwise, both while living let him be barred from entrance to the church, and when dying, let him be deprived of Christian burial.* (Fourth Lateran Council [1215], ch. 21, in Denzinger, *The Sources of Catholic Dogma*)

devout communicated more often. To illustrate that point, Bynum relates the story of Margaret of Cortona (d. 1297), "who pleaded frantically with her confessor for frequent communion, but when given the privilege . . . abstained out of fear at her unworthiness" (p. 58). For some mystics, this tension was resolved through visions; for others, the acceptable substitute was gazing at the host during its elevation at Mass, or in a monstrance during times of benediction or adoration. This "ocular communion" became an important spiritual exercise for ordinarily faithful during this period, achieving the status of a "second sacrament" alongside receiving (Bynum, p. 55).

Bread and Its Vessels

By the eleventh century, the use of unleavened bread first noted in the ninth century became universal in the West. The practice of baking hosts of two separate sizes—a larger one for the priest and smaller ones for lay communicants—also became general practice. As early as the fourteenth century, the baking of hosts had, in some places, become a business that required ecclesiastical approval. New in this era will be the development of vessels, such as Easter sepulchers and monstrances, designed for holding the consecrated bread without any anticipation of it being consumed by the faithful. In a special way, these signal the culmination of centuries of development, noted above, which left the faithful more as watchers or adorers of the Eucharist than actively participating recipients of communion.

Ciboria   In this era, vessels for carrying the Eucharist outside of the church were increasingly distinguished from those employed for reserving the Eucharist within the church. The pyx was the vessel used for holding the Eucharist outside of church, especially for taking communion to the sick. We previously noted that at the end of the first millennium it was becoming customary in some places to place the pyx for communion for the sick or dying on the altar during the Eucharist [quotation 225]. Presumably this held unconsecrated hosts, which were consecrated during the ensuing Eucharist. Eventually it became customary to use the pyx for the communion of whatever faithful were to receive, ordinarily before or after Mass. This occurred, in part, because of the reduced size of the paten, which was large enough only for the one large host to be consumed by the priests. The smaller hosts baked for lay communicants had to be held by another vessel. The pyx, already in use for communion of the sick and dying, was adopted for this purpose. In the process, the shape of the pyx evolved. The Mass pyx was shaped like those previously employed outside of the Eucharist—often round, with a conical lid, sometimes surmounted by a cross—but now, similar to the chalice,

Quotation 266: *On that day we solemnize the burial of the Body of our Saviour . . . on that part of the altar where there is space for it there shall be a representation as it were of a sepulchre, hung about with a curtain, in which the holy Cross, when it has been venerated, shall be placed. . . . When they have laid the cross therein, in imitation as it were of the burial of the Body of our Lord Jesus Christ, they shall sing . . . and during the night let brethren be chosen by twos and threes . . . who shall keep faithful watch, chanting psalms. . . . On the holy day of Easter . . . before the bells are rung for Matins, the sacrists shall take the Cross and set it in its proper place. . . . While the third lesson is being read, four of the brethren shall vest, one of whom, wearing an alb as though, for some different purpose, shall enter and go stealthily to the place of the "sepulchre" and sit there quietly, holding a palm in his hand. . . . The other three brethren, vested in copes and holding thuribles in their hands shall . . . go to the place of the "sepulchre" . . . as though searching for something . . . in imitation of the angel seated on the tomb and the women coming with perfumes to anoint the body of Jesus. When . . . he that is seated shall see these three draw nigh . . . he shall begin to sing softly and sweetly "Quem quaeritis" [Latin, "Whom do you seek"]. . . . The three shall answer together "Ihesum Nazarenum" ["Jesus of Nazareth"]). Then he that is seated shall say, "Non est hic. Surrexit sicut praedixerat. Ite, nuntiate quia surrexit a mortuis" ["He is not here. He is risen as he had foretold. Go, announce it, because he has risen from the dead"]. At this command the three shall return to the choir saying "Alleluia. Resurrexit Dominus" ["Alleluia, the Lord has risen"]. When this has been sung, he that is seated, as though calling them back, shall say the antiphon "Venite et videte locum" ["Come and see the place"], and then, rising and lifting up the veil, he shall show them the place void of the Cross and with only the linen in which the Cross had been wrapped.*
(Regularis Concordia, nos. 46–51)

159. Mid-fifteenth-century ciborium from southern Germany, consisting of a typical pyx-shaped container on a stem.

they became attached to a stem [illustration 159]. The Mass pyx came to be called a ciborium (Greek = *kiborion*, a vessel for seeds shaped like a cup).

Easter Sepulchers   One of the more unique "eucharistic vessels" particular to this era was the Easter Sepulcher. It developed out of a dramatic practice, already recorded in the English document *Regularis Concordia* (Latin, "Monastic Agreement"), written for English monks and nuns between 970 and 973. The document contains rubrics and texts for what many consider to be the birth of liturgical drama. On Holy Saturday they "buried" the cross, before Easter Matins the sacristan removed the cross, and during Easter Matins they briefly reenacted the Easter morning encounter between the women and the angel recorded in the gospels (e.g., Matt 28:1-7) [quotation 266]. This practice spread throughout England and on to the continent and continued in England until the sixteenth-century Reformation. Originally only a cross was "buried" in this ritual, but eventually people also began burying a consecrated host as well. The first sepulchers were portable wooden structures [illustration 160]; though there is widespread literature about the evidence of stone sculptured sepulchers as well, Christopher Herbert has recently shown that they are exceedingly rare and virtually nonexistent in this era. Occasionally the wealthy and prominent designed their tombs with a raised flat top so that the portable sepulchers could rest on

160. Wooden Easter sepulcher. (*Birmingham and Midland Institute Transactions*, Archaeological Section, p. 80)

them on Holy Saturday, sometimes in the hope that while the consecrated host was resting on their tomb, they would not suffer in purgatory. The development of such sepulchers and their surrounding rituals were one of the more powerful examples of the medieval instinct for a dramatic, almost literal representation of Christian beliefs in the liturgy. They also were tangible testimonies to the deep concern among Christians about purgatory and the strong expectation of most believers that this stage of suffering and purgation was a presumed part of their transition into eternal life.

Monstrances   No vessel is more symbolic of eucharistic theology in the late Middle Ages than the monstrance. It developed in response to a complex of liturgical and devotional trends, some of which we have already noted: for example, the removal of the cup from the faithful, the increased focus on the consecrated bread, the sense of unworthiness for communion on the part of the laity, the tendency toward more dramatic and visual liturgical display, the emergence of the elevation, and the literalism that—as evidenced by the Easter sepulcher tradition—tended to treat the consecrated host like a relic of Christ, the divine martyr. These same forces contributed to the emergence of the feast of *Corpus Christi* (Latin, "The Body of Christ") in the mid-thirteenth century, with its celebrated processions and other rituals honoring Christ's presence in the consecrated bread. It is notable that a feast for the "Precious Blood," on the other hand, did not appear until the nineteenth century. Eventually specific vessels were fashioned for a more permanent display of the host. The first clear literary evidence of such vessels comes from the life of Dorothy of Montau (d. 1394), who was later beatified and declared patroness of Prussia. Her biographer noted Dorothy's intense devotion to the Blessed Sacrament and described how, when she was living the life of an anchoress in a cell inside the church of Marienwerder, the Eucharist was daily displayed for her in a primitive monstrance [quotation 267].

Some monstrances survive from the fourteenth and early fifteenth centuries [illustration 161]. Certain of these were modeled after reliquaries of the time, which held relics in a glass or crystal cylinder. This evolution was not only the result of a practical adaptation of one vessel for another use but implicit acknowledgment that the Eucharist was venerated as the ultimate Christian relic, and Christ was the supreme martyr. Eventually the monstrance developed into a distinctive vessel consisting of a stem with a node and a flat window for holding a large, consecrated host. Monstrances were sometimes designed to resonate with the surrounding architecture. The prevailing custom of fashioning sacred vessels out of gold or silver continued with the monstrance. As these were vessels for display, containing

Quotation 267: *Her confessor decided to succor her with the delectable feast of the body of our Lord for which she yearned so fiercely during the mass. . . . It happened daily for about twenty weeks before her death that her confessor . . . with the permission of the bishop of the diocese and the prior, locked the host into an appropriate reliquary where chalices and other mass utensils were kept under lock and key. This reliquary was attached to a pew facing Dorothea's cell. That this locking up of the host in the pew and this nightly communion were pleasing to God the most beloved made obvious to Dorothea in word and deed.*
(von Marienwerder, The Life of Dorothea von Montau, p. 169)

161. Monstrance, ca. 1400.
(Brukenthal Museum)

162. Example of a wall tabernacle, thirteenth century, from San Clemente in Rome. (After Righetti, 1:436)

the most precious sacrament of the church, they were often adorned with precious gems and intricate metal work.

By the end of the Middle Ages, devotion to the exposed Blessed Sacrament was widespread. The practice was both a source of deep spiritual nourishment and mystical experience as well as the occasion for dubious, even magical belief. Thus, there was both great support for the practice and serious concern about it. Pope Leo X (d. 1521), for example, gave permission for the exposition of the Blessed Sacrament during Mass, a practice that was meant to add more solemnity to the eucharistic celebration. On the other hand, Nicolas of Cusa (d. 1464), one of the most learned church leaders of the late Middle Ages, recognized certain dangers in this practice, which often led to very popular but theologically untenable beliefs [quotation 268]. Despite such objections, however, this practice and its accompanying vessels developed further in the coming centuries.

Tabernacles   In many places, the Eucharist continued to be reserved as it had been in the previous era, for example, in a pyx suspended over the altar, in a special box or tower, or in a sacristy cupboard or closet. Eventually more secure places for public reservation developed. Concern for the security of the sacrament prompted some councils of the period to prescribe that the Eucharist should be kept in a locked and safe environment [quotation 269]. Permanent wall tabernacles appeared in Italy by the twelfth century [illustration 162]. More common in northern Europe was the "sacrament house." These places of reservation could be towering structures, sometimes resembling cathedral spires, usually located within or near the sanctuary [illustration 163]. Sometimes these larger tabernacles were designed so that they could accommodate exposition of the sacrament, either by allowing a monstrance to be positioned behind a grille within the tabernacle or sometimes by having a receptacle for holding the consecrated host built right into the front of the tabernacle. Occasionally one can find examples of tabernacles or sacrament houses built directly on the high altar [illustration 164]. While initially the exception, this practice was to become the rule in Catholic churches during the next period.

Wine and Its Vessels

We previously noted that it was the custom from earliest times to use grape wine in the celebration of Christian Eucharist. There were few prescriptions about the wine intended for sacramental use, one exception being the Fourth Council of Orleans in 541 [quotation 227]. During the late Middle Ages, however, theologians like Aquinas argued that only grape wine was the proper matter for Eucharist [quotation 270]. The eighth session of the Council of Florence (22 November 1439) confirmed that only grape wine was acceptable matter for Eucharist, a position that in the early twentieth century became part of Roman Catholic canon law and continues in force today. The production of wine for sacramental use was largely monastic work through the Middle Ages.

Chalices   While new vessels for the bread were developing, the number of vessels for the wine decreased. The chalice was clearly a secondary vessel when it came to lay devotion, which was so influential in contributing to some of the developments of the vessels for bread noted above. The cup was not an object of great devotion by the laity because it had been withdrawn from the people in most places by the twelfth century. Although it contained the Blood of Christ, this species could not be seen during the liturgy nor easily reserved after it. Thus the eucharistic wine was not an object of intense veneration as the host was. Symptomatic of this was the belated introduction of the elevation of the chalice during Mass. Though some evidence suggests an elevation of the chalice as early as the thirteenth century, this was a rare occurrence, spreading more widely in the fourteenth century. As Jungmann notes, however, the practice was not much in evidence in Rome, and the printed Roman Missals of the early sixteenth century (1500, 1507, and 1526) do not mention the elevation of the chalice. It was only with the *Missal of Pius V* (1570) that Rome indicated that this second elevation would be equal to that of the consecrated host (*The Mass of the Roman Rite*, II:207–208).

Two-handled chalices fell into disuse during the late Middle Ages, and communion from the cup by the laity came to an end. The cup part of chalices from this period were often cone shaped and attached to a hexagonal or octagonal stem. The node was often enameled, carved with images, or even shaped into an elaborate architectural design, reflecting in miniature the style of the surrounding building. Bells were added to some chalices, possibly to draw attention to them when raised during the elevation [illustration 165]. The enlarged base of the chalice frequently was divided into six or eight compartments and sometimes adorned with enameled medallions. Various synods regulated the materials acceptable in the fabrication of chalices. Wood, glass, and copper were usually forbidden. Tin was permitted, often as a concession to poor churches, while gold and silver were preferred [quotation 230].

Cruets   In chapter 3 we related the evidence, possibly from as early as the fourth century, for special vessels that carried the water and wine before they were poured into the chalice at the Eucharist. These

Quotation 270: *This sacrament can only be performed with wine from the grape. First of all on account of Christ's institution, since He instituted this sacrament in wine from the grape, as is evident from His own words, in instituting this sacrament [Matt 26:29]: "I will not drink from henceforth of this fruit of the vine." Secondly, because . . . that is adopted as the matter of the sacraments which is properly and universally considered as such. Now that is properly called wine, which is drawn from the grape, whereas other liquors are called wine from resemblance to the wine of the grape. Thirdly, because the wine from the grape is more in keeping with the effect of this sacrament, which is spiritual; because it is written [Ps 103:15]: "That wine may cheer the heart of man."* (Thomas Aquinas, *Summa Theologica*, part 3, quest. 74, art. 5, respond.)

163. A late medieval sacrament house from Austria. (After Righetti, 1:439)

164. A tabernacle (1471) by Mino da Fiesole on the high altar of the Cathedral in Volterra, with a round receptacle for holding the consecrated host built into the face of the tabernacle.

Quotation 271: *In some churches, the subdeacon carries the chalice in his left hand, the paten in his right and places them upon the corporal. One cantor carries the host in a cloth and wine in a cruet; another cantor offers the water to be mixed with the wine.* (William Durandus [d. 1296], *Guillelmi Duranti Rationale [The Rationale of the Divine Offices]*, 4:25)

Quotation 272: *Hold up, Sir John, hold up. Heave it a little higher.* (Fortescue, *The Mass*, pp. 341–42)

vessels largely belonged to the baptized, who used them for bringing their gifts of bread and wine to the liturgy. For a variety of reasons that practice died out over the centuries. One factor contributing to this change was the shifting rules on the shape and quality of the eucharistic bread, which disallowed ordinary people from bringing this as a liturgical offering. Then there was the slow withdrawal of the cup from the baptized. Since they no longer were offered the consecrated wine at Mass, there was little motivation for bringing this as a eucharistic gift. From a more mundane perspective, in the northern countries wine was not as widespread a drink as it was around the Mediterranean. Instead, beer was more popular, first produced by some Benedictine monasteries in the eighth and ninth centuries and then commercially brewed in some of the new urban centers by the year 1000. For many people, wine was simply not a drink they ordinarily imbibed and thus not a gift ordinarily accessible to them for Eucharist.

Though there is some evidence that the offertory procession of gifts survived on special occasions into the twelfth century—and some places even longer—it was missing from the medieval Roman Rite as practiced by the Roman Curia. By at least the thirteenth century, it is the subdeacon who brought the chalice and the paten with the host to the altar at the beginning of the offertory. As Jungmann reports, there was some disagreement even in the fifteenth century about when the wine and the water should be poured into the chalice. Some priests poured these elements before Mass began (*The Mass of the Roman Rite*, II:60). In his famous liturgical work *Rationale Divinorum Officiorum* (Latin, "The Rationale of the Divine Offices") from the late thirteenth century, Bishop William Durandus (d. 1296) described the practice that, with some variation, became commonplace: a subdeacon brings an empty paten and chalice to the altar, followed by two singers carrying the host, a cruet of wine, and a cruet of water [quotation 271].

With the transposition of this pouring and commingling of wine and water to the altar, the cruets become ordinary vessels for every celebration of the Eucharist. While they were secondary vessels, used in preparation of the gifts and never in contact with the consecrated species, they were liturgical vessels nonetheless. These were ordinarily small flasks that held only a few ounces of liquid, since they only supplied wine for the priest's communion and water, a few drops of which was added to the chalice before its consecration; a little water was also needed for the washing of the priest's fingers during the offertory rite, as well as for cleansing the priest's chalice after communion. Often these vessels were crafted of glass or crystal, so that the wine and water could easily be distinguished. With the increased use of white rather than red wine, however, it became customary to mark the cruets with an "A" (*aqua* = Latin, "water") and "V" (*vinum* = Latin, "wine"). Sometimes the cruets, like the primary eucharistic vessels, were crafted of precious metals [illustration 166] and sometimes even encrusted with jewels.

Summary

The development of eucharistic vessels in this period illustrates some significant trends in eucharistic theology we will address below. One overall tendency was the increased evidence on seeing rather than hearing as the fundamental way to belief. Seeing was believing, and belief for many Christians was inspired and sustained by seeing the host, which became the ritual high point of the eucharistic liturgy. It also was the occasion for many dubious beliefs [quotation 268]. Seeing the host was of such importance that priests were sometimes paid a special stipend for prolonging the elevation or inserting other elevations, for example, after the "Lamb of God." One story is told of a congregation in England crying out to the presider to lift the host higher if it could not readily be seen [quotation 272]. The vessels of this period reflect this preoccupation with the bread. Receiving the wine became unthinkable. Given the unworthiness of ordinary laypeople, receiving the bread became a dangerous undertaking and so infrequent that the church had to mandate yearly reception. Seeing the bread was the ordinary substitute for receiving it.

165. Chalice showing Gothic architectural influence with bells.

EUCHARISTIC THEOLOGY

While it may begin to sound like a well-worn formula, the developments in eucharistic theology in this period, parallel to those we have considered in late medieval arts and artifacts, are diverse. Yet there were a number of central tendencies or what sociologists call "flows" in the theological developments of the time. Some of these ritual and theological flows actually contradicted each other. This was an increasing tendency in the late Middle Ages that eventually erupted in the sixteenth-century Reformation and Counter-Reformation. We will consider three major issues that occupied center stage in the eucharistic developments in this era: 1) the academic debates over the "what" and "how" of Christ's presence in the Eucharist, 2) the popular understanding of the nature of the eucharistic Body of Christ, and 3) consideration of the "effect" of Christ's presence for believers.

166. Cruets.

Today the Roman Catholic Church holds to certain truths or dogmatic formulations that emerged during this period. At the time, however, these ideas were not as uniform or as universal as we might imagine. It might be helpful to remember that one of the key forms of instruction at the universities in this period and one of the basic methods of Scholastic theology was disputation. Thus it was common to find learned and respected teachers and church leaders holding different positions on a subject.

Eucharistic Presence: The Academic Debate

In the previous chapter we charted something of the innovations in eucharistic thinking in the ninth-century with the work of Paschasius Radbertus. This theological pioneer was the first to attempt to explain, in a systematic way, how Christ was present in the Eucharist. Because of various cultural factors, as well as the underdeveloped state of theological language and systems at the end of the millennium, his formulations were somewhat crude and prone to what was ultimately judged to be an erroneous position, asserting that Christ's presence in the Eucharist was identical to his historical presence, and was thus literal, corporal, and physical.

Like all important thinkers, Paschasius's work generated a great deal of response, not only in his own time but for centuries to come. This was due, at least in part, to the broad acceptance of his eucharistic instincts about the physical nature of presence by both influential teachers and ordinary people. Early on, however, there were also many who objected to his formulations. The evolution of an appropriate response to Paschasius's very appealing but highly problematic ideas relied upon developments in language and philosophy. We already saw that in the second oath of Berengar in 1079 [quotation 240] there appeared the language of "substance" (from Latin, *sub* + *stare* = "to stand under"), borrowed from the thought of Aristotle (d. 322 B.C.E.), whose writings were reemerging at this time in the Christian West. Besides this language of substance, or the *essence of a thing*, theologians in the late eleventh century began borrowing another idea from Aristotle, that of "accidents," or the *characteristics of a thing* that do not alter its essence or substance but are merely accidental to it. Thus one substance is a rose, and its accidents may be that it is red, or thorny, or long stemmed; another substance is bread, and its accidents may be that it is wheat, round, unleavened, and white. The substance of a thing can never be touched or perceived with the senses, but only with the mind. Accidents, on the other hand, are perceived through the senses.

These two concepts or frameworks allowed medieval theologians like Thomas Aquinas to offer a very nuanced explanation of how the bread was changed into the Body of Christ, even though after the consecration the host still looked like bread. Aquinas explained that before the consecration the substance of the host was bread and the accidents were of a particular kind of bread; but after the consecra-

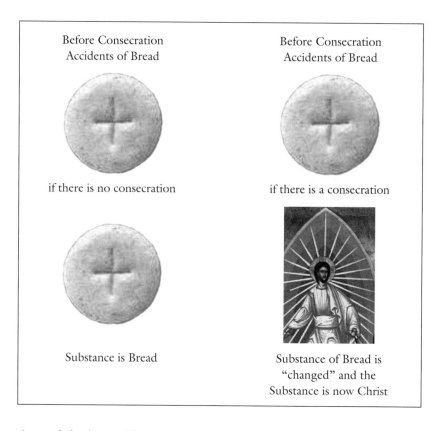

Before Consecration
Accidents of Bread

Before Consecration
Accidents of Bread

if there is no consecration

if there is a consecration

Substance is Bread

Substance of Bread is
"changed" and the
Substance is now Christ

167. A visual metaphor of Aquinas's understanding of transubstantiation.

tion, while the accidents remained the same, the substance had been changed into the Body of Christ [illustration 167]. The technical term for this "trans-formation" of the substance was transubstantiation, a term that already appeared in the twelfth century.

Aquinas was a man of great faith, and he was not so bold as to suggest that this framework could completely "explain" the mystery of Christ's eucharistic presence. Early on in his *Summa* he recognized the problem of speaking about divine mysteries in human language. Aquinas realized that language about God or about mysteries like the Eucharist was not exact but what he considered "analogical." An analogy can be defined as a "similarity in difference." Thus, while Aquinas taught that Christ's presence under the form of bread was "like" or "similar" to a change in the substance of bread, he fundamentally recognized that this was a miracle beyond human understanding. Aquinas's attempt to explain Christ's presence was brilliant, but he was aware of its flaws. One of them was that Aquinas actually contradicted Aristotle, who taught that you could never have the accidents of one thing with the substance of another. Aquinas used the language of Aristotle, but he did not offer an "Aristotelian" explanation. Rather, he offered an explanation from the viewpoint of faith, which Aristotle did not have. Anselm of Canterbury (d. 1109) once defined theology as "Faith seeking understanding." Like Anselm, Thomas Aquinas was a man of faith who sought understanding. He also recognized, however, that understanding did not replace faith, but required it. Transubstantiation was a faith explanation, not a logical proof of Christ's eucharistic presence.

Gary Macy has clearly shown that, while many today hold that the term transubstantiation has a fixed meaning, this was not true in the High Middle Ages, where there were multiple understandings of the term, even after it was officially used for the first time in the decrees of the Fourth Lateran Council in 1215. Various positions differed in regard to not only "what" substance was present after the consecration but also "how" any change in the substance took place [quotation 273]. Thomas Aquinas's position would eventually become the standard teaching of the Roman Catholic Church and appeared in the documents of the Council of Trent (1545–1563). That council, however, did not decree that Catholics must believe in this formulation but, rather, called this explanation most appropriate (Latin, *aptissime*) and highly recommended it to believers. Early on, however, Aquinas's position was challenged. The brilliant Franciscan philosopher John Duns Scotus (d. 1308), for example, teaching at the University of Oxford, argued that Thomas's explanation caused more problems than it solved. The English theologian John Wyclif (d. 1384) also rejected Aquinas's explanation because it was nonbiblical. Eventually, the concept of transubstantiation became a central point of dispute among many sixteenth-century reformers.

Popular Belief about the Eucharistic Body of Christ

University theologians like Aquinas and Dun Scotus had abandoned the somewhat crude formulations of Paschasius and employed sophisticated philosophical frameworks and arguments in attempting to explain the eucharistic mystery. While the theological elite were engaged in sometimes very rarefied debates, ordinary people as well as many religious and clergy held to a different kind of eucharistic faith that was much more in keeping with the teachings of Paschasius. Most people in the late Middle Ages—like most people today—did not understand the distinctions between substance and accidents, nor did they understand that in Aristotle's framework substance was not perceivable with the senses but was what philosophers called a "metaphysical" (from Greek *meta* + *physika* = "beyond nature") rather than a "physical" reality. For them, Christ's presence in the Eucharist was indeed a miracle; this miracle was not only a sacramental or a mystical miracle but one in flesh and blood.

Symbolic of this belief, as Bynum documents, was the growing emphasis on "flesh and blood" rather than the "bread of heaven" or the even more metaphoric "Body of Christ" in the sermons, hymns, and stories of the thirteenth and fourteenth centuries. Maybe most emblematic of this tendency was the explosion of eucharistic miracle stories. Some of these relate the appearance of the infant

Quotation 273: *". . . there was no common understanding of the category of substance, much less agreement on either the use of the term transubstantiation or on what the term might have meant when used. In fact, theologians at the time of the Fourth Lateran Council [1215] fell roughly into three camps in regard to the eucharistic change. 1) Some believed that bread and wine remained present along with the Body and Blood of the Lord; 2) others felt that the substance of the bread and the wine were annihilated, the substance of the Body and Blood alone remaining. Finally, 3) a third group argued that the substance of bread and wine was changed into the substance of the Body and Blood at the words of consecration. Modern terminology would categorize the first theory as "consubstantiation," the second as "annihilation" or "succession" theory, and the third as "transubstantiation."* (Macy, *Treasures from the Storeroom*, pp. 82–83)

168. Detail of Raphael's Miracle of Bolseno (1512–13) in the Vatican Museums.

Jesus in place of the host. Others were shockingly graphic, sometimes describing the appearance of raw flesh. Common were stories of bleeding hosts. One of the most celebrated was the "Miracle of Bolseno," immortalized in a fresco by Raphael [illustration 168]. The thirteenth-century story concerns a young priest from Bohemia who was plagued by doubts about whether Christ was actually present in the consecrated host. While on a pilgrimage, the priest stopped in Bolseno north of Rome where he celebrated Mass. When he spoke the words of consecration blood began to drop from the host, trickle over his hand, and onto the corporal. The shocked priest stopped the Mass and was taken to the neighboring city of Orvieto where Pope Urban IV (d. 1264) was living. After hearing the story, and a brief investigation, the pope ordered that the host and bloodstained corporal be brought to Orvieto where he enshrined them. The corporal bearing the bloodstain is yet venerated in that cathedral.

We have already rehearsed some of the factors that explain, to some extent, why such stories were so popular and powerful in the medieval mind. They certainly resonated with a Germanized imagination that was prone toward the physical and had a penchant for what Russell called a "magico-religious" interpretation of sacraments. Furthermore, these miracles would be more easily accepted in a religious climate, like the late Middle Ages, where seeing was becoming more important than hearing in the confirmation of one's faith. There also may be some deeper theological and psychological reasons for the centrality of such stories in the faith of medieval Christians.

It was during this period that the laity stopped receiving communion from the cup. We have already noted how this practice was supported theologically by the theory of "concomitance," which held that when the bread was consecrated into Christ's Body, the Blood of Christ was also present. In some ways, these stories of bleeding hosts are graphic folk images demonstrating the acceptance of this theology. The laity did not receive the Blood of Christ, and even though the elevation of the chalice was eventually introduced, they never actually saw the consecrated wine but only the cup containing it. It was only such miracle stories that confirmed in a visual, graphic way this new teaching of the church and reassured the faithful that the redeeming Blood of Christ, often reported seeping from a consecrated host, was still at the center of this sacrament.

Eamon Duffy offers another interpretation of these stories and their importance for medieval believers. More than simply announcing salvation in the Blood of Christ, Duffy argues that images of Christ's Blood, like that of Cain spilling the blood of Abel in the book of Genesis, "cried out for vengeance" (Duffy, p. 104). Evidence for this interpretation comes in the many eucharistic stories of this era that serve as a type of morality tale about the Eucharist, illustrating that when someone attempts to use the consecrated host inappropriately, raw flesh or a bleeding host appear as vivid images of divine wrath and punishment for such defilement [quotation 274].

One of the darker sides of this devotion and its powerful stories of guilt and vengeance was the connection between stories of eucharistic desecration and the persecution of heretics, and especially persecution of the Jews. In her *Gentile Tales: The Narrative Assault on Late Medieval Jews*, Miri Rubin offers a disturbing look at this genre of eucharistic stories. In its most generalized form, the host-desecration narrative is the tale of a Jew who acquires a consecrated host and then subjects it to various forms of abuse [illustration 169]. The host miraculously bleeds, the terrified Jew attempts to rid himself of the host, but wherever it is hidden the host reveals itself to Christians who then enact varied forms of vengeance on the Jew and others in the Jewish community. Miracles of bleeding hosts thus become extraordinary tales of judgment, orthodoxy, and right belief. They were graphic warnings to believers as well as nonbelievers that proper eucharistic faith and reverence were necessary if one was to avoid God's vengeance.

The Effects of Christ's Presence

Christians have always believed that celebrating Eucharist gave glory to God but also offered benefits both to the church and to individual Christians. Long before an independent sacrament of penance existed, for example, Eucharist was considered the first sacrament of reconciliation and an important action for healing the Body of Christ. It was considered by the ancients an "antidote" to sin and a source

Quotation 274: *Miracles of bleeding hosts, which proliferate from the twelfth century on, sometimes have sinister overtones. The host becomes flesh to announce its violation; the blood is an accusation. When the nun Wilburgis [d. 1289] took the host to her enclosure to help her avoid sexual temptation, it revealed itself, in a quite common miracle, as a beautiful baby who spoke the words of the Song of Songs. But when another nun hid a host that she dared not swallow because she was in mortal sin, it turned into flesh. . . . Similarly, Peter Damian tells of a host that protested its abuse when used superstitiously: a woman who tried to conjure with it found that half of it had turned into flesh. Caesarius of Heisterbach reports that when another women tried to use the consecrated wafer as a love charm and then guiltily hid it in a church wall, it turned to flesh and bled.*
(Bynum, *Holy Feast and Fast,* pp. 63–64)

1. A Christian steals a host from a monstrance on the altar.
2. A Christian sells the host to a Jew.
3. Jews carry the host into a synagogue.
4. Blood flows from the host when it is desecrated.
5. Hosts are sent to other Jews in Prague and Salzburg.
6. When the Jews try to burn the host, angels and doves fly out of the oven and a child appears in place of the host.
7. Jews are arrested.
8. Some Jews are beheaded.
9. Some Jews are tortured.
10. Jews are burned.
11. The Christian is also punished.
12. The synagogue is converted into a church.

169. Broadsheet from Passau (ca. 1490) relating a desecration story in twelve panels. (Rubin, *Gentile Tales*, p. 82)

Quotation 275:

Thy fote that day shall not the fayll;
Thyn eyen from ther syght shall not blynd;
Thi light spekyng, eyther in fabill or tale,
That veniall synnes do up wynd,
Shall be forgeven, & pardon fynd..
Thy grevouse othes that be forgett,
In heryng of messe are don a-way;
An angel also thi steppis doth mete,
& presentith the in hevyn that same day . . .
Thyn age at messe shall not encrease;
Nor sodeyn deth that day shall not the spill;
And without hostill [housel] yf thou hap to
dissease,
It shall stond therfore; & beleve thou this skyll,
Than to here messe thou maste have will,
Thes prophitable benefitts to the be lent,
Wher God, in fowrm of bred, his body doth
present.

(Poem from Balliol College manuscript 354 [ca. 1530], in Duffy, *The Stripping of the Altars*, p. 100)

of divine charity. Eucharist was traditionally understood as the invitation to unity with other Christians and the sacrament by which believers are conformed to the image of Christ, even "divinized."

In the late Middle Ages there was increased emphasis, especially in the preaching of the day, on the effects of "hearing" Mass—whether or not one received communion. These "fruits" of the Mass were often gathered into lists of six or ten or twelve virtually guaranteed effects of attending the eucharistic liturgy. While theologians and church leaders criticized such preaching, it was very popular and continued unabated. While such lists often included common beliefs—such as the belief that hearing Mass was a way to be more united with Christ or to be strengthened against temptation—other promised fruits of the Mass appeared to be more magical. Thus it was common belief that when you went to Mass you did not age, you would not suffer sudden death on that day, your house or barn would not be struck by lightning, and you would be cured of disease [quotation 275].

Given the centrality of the elevation, which as already noted was a time of special prayers and acts of reverence, it is not surprising that many magical beliefs were associated with seeing the host. Thus, as Eamon Duffy summarizes, "mothers in labour could secure safe delivery, travellers safe arrival, eaters and drinkers good digestion, by gazing on the Host at Mass" (p. 100). While such beliefs may seem foolish to us, they made sense to people who lived under the threat of eternal damnation, were often reduced to spectators at the church's liturgy, and were surrounded by a eucharistic practice that stressed intercession rather than praise or thanksgiving. Here the Germanic imagination, with all of its magico-religious tendencies, met the needs of ordinary Christians for whom life was a real struggle. Many preachers were no different than their parishioners, and with poor education and sometimes little direction from church authorities, they were happy to repeat such beliefs that were also solace for themselves.

Besides the common belief about various benefits available to those who attended Mass or viewed the consecrated host at the elevation, there also developed at this time theologies and practices that underscored how the benefits of the eucharistic liturgy could be applied to those not present for worship, including the dead. As Gil Ostdiek has documented, one of the important changes in understanding that allowed for this practice concerned the role of Christ in the Eucharist. Earlier Christ had been considered the central actor in the eucharistic action and the one who led the assembly in offering this prayer. Over the centuries, however, Christ eventually became the object of prayer and worship, and he was replaced by the priest who assumed the role of the central actor in the Mass. Because of this shift, there emerged various opinions regarding the priest's ability to direct the benefits of the Mass to certain groups or individuals.

Duns Scotus was the first to elaborate a systematic theology of these "fruits of the Mass." According to his widely accepted teaching, the saving grace or "fruits" of Christ's death were a threefold source of blessing: 1) first and foremost for the priest who celebrated the Mass, 2) then for the whole church, and finally 3) for those for whom the Mass was offered. While Scotus based his teaching on a reasonable theology of intercessory prayer, he was in fact offering his best theological rationale for a well-known practice of the time: Mass stipends. We have already seen how Mass stipends appeared in the Carolingian period, usually related to the commutation of a penance [quotation 209]. Increasingly, however, stipends became associated with Masses for the dead. This was perfectly understandable, given the medieval imagination about purgatory. It also, however, led to practices and beliefs prone to exaggeration and even abuse.

In the popular imagination more was better, and there was widespread concern for quantity more than quality in prayer for the dead. It was common practice to arrange for multiple Mass offerings for a beloved relative. Moreover, concern for one's fate after judgment prompted many who had the means to provide money for the celebration of Masses for themselves after their own death. Last wills and testaments of this period are filled with such examples. Because stipends were becoming an important part of the local church economy, they also were the occasion for sometimes scandalous activity. Despite teachings and legislation to the contrary, priests sometimes took multiple stipends for a single Mass. Other times they took a stipend for celebrating a "dry Mass" (Latin, *Missa* sicca), usually celebrated without a chasuble, in which the priest simply read the Mass texts (except the offertory, consecration, and communion) without any bread or wine. Although priests were ordinarily allowed to celebrate only one Mass a day, there were no such restrictions on "dry Masses," which could be offered repeatedly, each time for a new stipend. Eamon Duffy reports that, at least in late medieval England, reading the gospel was accepted as a substitute for celebrating Mass, and "reading a Gospel was exploited by clergy anxious to maximize their incomes" (p. 215). Church authorities repeatedly condemned such practices, and virtually none of them survived past the sixteenth century. Such abuses, however, fueled various individuals and movements who increasingly criticized the liturgical and devotional practices of the church, anticipating the reform movements of the sixteenth century.

Summary

This was an era of major theological advances, with the appearance of great schools of theology, celebrated philosopher-theologians, and enduring *Summas*. It was also a time when there was a significant distance, even separation, between the teaching of the great school figures or Scholastics and that of ordinarily clergy or laity. Maybe most notable in this era were the theological reversals that took place in the eucharistic theologies of this era when compared with those of an earlier time in the church. We have seen, for example, that it was no longer Christ but the priest who was seen as the main actor in the worship. The priest also substituted for the assembly, no longer requiring their response, and even received communion for them according to some. Worship was less an act of thanksgiving and more about offering and intercession, with great attention on the effects of Christ's sacrifice. In some respects, the eucharistic liturgy of this period was more focused on the dead than on the living. A final reversal touches the basic understanding of what was the true Body of Christ.

In his classic study on the Eucharist and the church in the Middle Ages, Henri de Lubac studied the Latin phrase *corpus mysticum* or "mystical Body" (of Christ). While in our own day we usually think of the mystical Body as a reference to the church, de Lubac shows that from its origin in the fifth century and through the Carolingian period, the phrase *corpus mysticum* usually referred to the consecrated host. The church was the "Body of Christ" or the *corpus verum* (Latin, "true body"). Given all of the eucharistic controversies of the medieval period, however, it seemed necessary to affirm with new vigor that Christ was truly present in the Eucharist, even if that presence was not the same as his historical body. Sometimes this was done by affirming that the consecrated bread was the "sacramental body" of Christ. Eventually, however, it became common to refer to the consecrated host as the "true body" (*corpus verum*) and, in a telling reversal, the church became the "mystical body" (*corpus mysticum*). In de Lubac's analysis, this change symbolized and con-tributed to a widening gap between the sacramental body and the ecclesial body, between the Eucharist and the church. Thus, rather than a source of spirituality and mission for the church, the Eucharist became almost a commodity in some people's view, a noun rather than a verb, and a power outside their lives rather than nourishment for Christian living.

CLOTHILDE

Although it was winter and she could feel the dampness of the stone pavement through her many layers of clothing, Clothilde never considered standing. She remembered being taught as a child that the raising of the host was the most sacred of all events; even the trees swayed in adoration at the elevation of the wafer. And, as her mother often reminded her, if nature in all its majesty was so responsive, then Clothilde, as one of the least of God's creatures, should kneel as well.

After the priest lowered the host to the altar and genuflected slowly, Clothilde struggled to her feet. This past winter her arthritis had worsened. She found it difficult to kneel and even more difficult to get up. Now that her children were grown with families of their own, Clothilde no longer had their help when she visited the cathedral. But this never stopped her from making her daily pilgrimage to the great church at Chartres.

Clothilde walked away from the side altar of St. Martin, slowly working the blood back into her aching legs. She gazed into the vault as the sunshine exploded against the clerestory windows on the south wall of the nave. Although she had been there a thousand times before, Clothilde never ceased to marvel at the miraculous windows and their many moods in the shifting sunlight. Only God could have imagined so many shades of blue! As she watched the colors play against the stone, she thought of her husband who had worked on the cathedral for so many years. It was while he was working on the roof in the south transept that the accident that killed him occurred. The funeral in the unfinished cathedral seemed a fitting memorial to a man who had labored in this building his entire lifetime. Although it was almost thirty years since his death, Clothilde always felt a special closeness to him when she was in "their" cathedral. As she lowered her eyes from the ceiling, Clothilde noted an unusual amount of movement within the great church that morning. There was always a flurry of activity in the cathedral, but this Sunday seemed to be an especially busy one. Dozens of small groups clustered around the innumerable altars in the church, attending Mass. All the while,

scores of visitors from near and far roamed the cathedral, gaping at the stained glass or buying candles from one of the many stalls along the south aisles of the church. Some days, there seemed to be as many vendors as visitors, selling everything from herbal medicines to relics of the Three Kings. Clothilde herself had once owned a piece of cloth that had touched a relic of the true cross. She gave her little treasure to a friend whose child was sick with fever. After the child recovered, Clothilde left the relic with the family who now had a special devotion to the cross.

Like all of the townspeople of Chartres, Clothilde was proud of the cathedral. But more than the towers, the stained glass, or the soaring vault, she prized nothing more than the veil of the Blessed Virgin. It was this mantle of the Mother of God that spurred the townspeople to build such a monumental edifice, and it was this precious relic that served as the focus for endless pilgrimages. Even now a large group of pilgrims was making their way around the ambulatory on their knees to the altar where the tunic was displayed.

Clothilde herself was thinking of making a visit to the Lady Chapel to view the relic when a bell rang, announcing the beginning of the bishop's Mass. Although she seldom attended the whole Mass, Clothilde did enjoy the opening flourishes of this ritual. From the side sacristy she could see the long procession beginning. First out the door was a large young man carrying the bishop's cross emblazoned with his coat of arms. A stream of singers and minor clergy followed. Clothilde never could remember who among these was a priest, who was going to be a priest, or who wasn't going to be a priest. She decided years ago that the simplest solution to this dilemma was to call all of them "Father." That way she never would be embarrassed and they never would be offended. After the ordained and unordained "fathers" came the canons of the cathedral, wrapped in layers of purple and white. Their robes were certainly more beautiful than anything Clothilde had ever owned. Some of their garments were lined with fur—a luxurious antidote to the winter chill. At the end of the procession was the mitered archbishop. As he passed, the crowds knelt and received a blessing from the gloved hand adorned with a huge amethyst ring.

The music that accompanied the procession was glorious. The organ played a slow, simple tune that the choir embellished with melody upon melody. As the Introit ushered the archbishop into the sanctuary, the gates of the great screen closed behind him. She still could hear the music on the other side of the screen, but she no longer was able to watch the ritual. It was just as well, Clothilde thought to herself, for it was time to make her own pilgrimage to the Virgin's veil. Turning away from the barred sanctuary, Clothilde hurried to the Lady Chapel where she would join her friends in prayer. Even as she entered the ambulatory she could hear the invitation from a distance, "Ave Maria, gratia plena . . ."

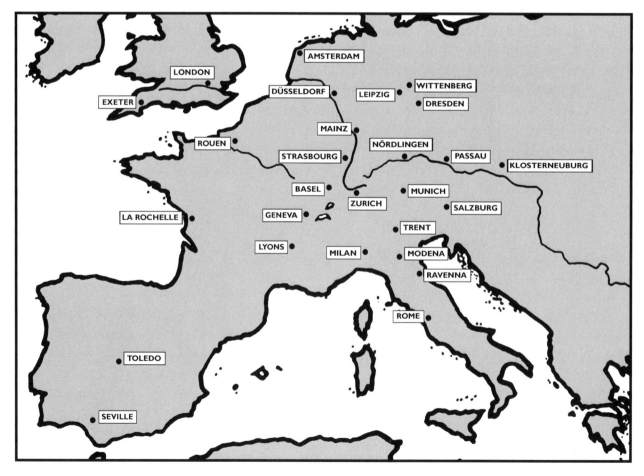

170. Map for chapter 6.

CHAPTER SIX

Reform and Counter-Reform:

1517–1903

By this stage in our study it is clear that while there are central and core beliefs about the Eucharist throughout the centuries, change is also a constant. Thus, while noting continuities, we have given significant attention to the changes, particularly in the arts and environment, for Eucharist. There have also been considerable changes in the way Eucharist has been both accessed and understood by the faithful, theologians, and church leaders through the centuries. In this chapter we will continue to see such constancy and change, but in some ways the speed of change will increase. This is especially apparent politically, socially, and culturally. Liturgically there was also momentous and rapid change, particularly in the sixteenth century. Because of the stabilizing and counter-reforming nature of the Council of Trent (1545–1563) and its aftermath, however, the pace of change in Roman Catholic eucharistic practice slowed after the sixteenth century, and in some places even appears to have stalled. As James White has demonstrated in *Roman Catholic Worship*, however, even in the period following the Tridentine reforms, ferment abounded in Roman Catholic eucharistic practice and thought.

Politically the landscape underwent a radical reshaping during this era. In the early sixteenth century monarchs ruled what we know today as England, Spain, Portugal, France, and Germany. The pope was also an important temporal ruler, and in the eighteenth century controlled most of central Italy. These and other monarchs of the period were concerned with both protecting and expanding their domains. Thus the 1500s, sometimes called the "age of exploration," was a time when most great European powers devoted significant energy to continued colonization of Africa and the exploration of the "new worlds" of North and South America. Major European powers accumulated vast holdings around the globe, and several touted the mythology that the sun never set on their empires. The splendor of the European monarchies, however, was not to continue, and by the end of this era no major ruling monarchy remained in Europe. To the extent that there were monarchs, they were recon-

Quotation 276: *The ordering of worship as sacrifice and the ordering of worship as sacrament of gift and grace relate to two different perceptions of the social order. . . . A medieval society which lived by a division of the populace into social ranks, and which perceived the total order of things as one which united the faithful of heaven, purgatory and earth, could find its spiritual unity, and even its temporal unity, in the act of sacrifice. On the other hand, the ordering of worship as sacrament reflects a perception of society which starts with the fundamental fellowship of all in the grace of Christ, and in this unity of sacrament sees the model of a social order to be constructed. It is less prone to sanction the hierarchical rankings of social or ecclesial order, and more attuned to the ordering of society as the work of all the people. That the grace of Christ prevails over this ordering is expressed in the gratuity of sacrament . . . in which all participate in the equality of the common calling . . . around the images of the holy fellowship and the common table of the Lord's Supper. (Power, The Sacrifice We Offer, p. 145)*

figured as "constitutional monarchies," with the real political power residing in an elected government as in contemporary England and Spain. The pope continued to be a temporal as well as an ecclesiastical ruler, but with the loss of the papal states in the nineteenth century, the Vatican was reduced to the smallest independent nation-state in the world, and the pope's temporal influence was proportionately reduced.

Tension between such powerful nations shaped both the political and religious landscape of the period. England's Henry VIII (d. 1547), for example, was honored by Pope Leo X (d. 1521) with the title "defender of the faith" because of Henry's objection to the reforming ideas of Martin Luther (d. 1546). Within a few years, however, Henry was excommunicated by Rome for what was considered an invalid second marriage. Obsessed with producing a male heir, he had sought an annulment from Rome, and when it was not forthcoming, Henry set in motion a series of legal procedures that resulted in his being declared the Supreme Head of the Church of England. For Henry this was essentially a political move rather than a theological or liturgical reform. Unlike many reformers on the continent, Henry was theologically conservative and remained committed to Roman Catholic doctrine. Thus in 1539 he passed a series of laws affirming beliefs like transubstantiation as well as the practice of private Mass and confession. After his death, however, the Church of England enacted more dramatic liturgical and theological reforms.

Political forces on the continent also helped shape religious and liturgical reforms. For example, from the fourteenth century on there existed a confederation of small states or "cantons" in what today we know as Switzerland. In growing numbers these cantons united against the Holy Roman Emperor, achieving independence from him at the end of the fifteenth century. In the process, local leaders sought independence from the church, and attempted to diminish the church's influence on its political, educational, and economic life. Switzerland's early experiments in political and social democracy offered a climate where some of the most radical theological and liturgical reforms of the sixteenth century took root. The theological instincts of such reformers to remove priestly intermediaries between God and the baptized, and to seek eucharistic images more tuned to fellowship than sacrifice are explained, in part, by this powerful social context [quotation 276].

These political and social forces help to explain why Martin Luther's reforms ignited across Europe so quickly. Before him, John Wycliffe (d. 1384) had already translated the Bible into the vernacular in 1382 and was speaking out against transubstantiation. Similarly, the Bohemian reformer Jan Hus (d. 1415) preached against indul-

171. Tetzel indulgence. Translation: "In the authority of all the saints, and in compassion towards you, I absolve you from all sins and misdeeds, and remit all punishment for ten days."

gences and demanded that the cup be returned to the people. These reforming calls, however, did not enkindle a significant wave of reform in the church and its worship, but smoldered beneath the surface. By the early sixteenth century, however, the climate had changed. The papacy was in serious decline, plague and terrible weather had battered Europe, peasant revolts and civil unrest challenged kings and emperors, new ideas questioning the old ways abounded in the universities, and corruption in the church was rampant [quotation 277].

In this context Luther's challenges to the pastoral practices and teachings of the church found deep resonance. A Catholic priest and Augustinian monk, Luther was professor of Sacred Scripture at Wittenberg University in Germany who was undergoing a personal religious struggle in the second decade of the sixteenth century. Jaroslav Pelikan believes that the immediate context for this struggle was the failure of the sacrament of penance and Luther's lack of certainty about whether his or anyone's contrition was adequate (*The Christian Tradition*, 4:129). Luther resolved this dilemma through teaching and studying Scripture, particularly passages like Romans 4 that stressed justification by faith, not by works. This personal resolution prepared him to denounce the selling of indulgences [illustration 171]. As a priest in Wittenberg he noticed that few people were coming to confession. Instead they were buying indulgences, substitutes for doing penance that seemed to offer the promise of forgiveness and salvation, whether people reformed their lives or not. In 1517 Luther composed a series of ninety-five theses [quotation 278], meant to serve as a basis of a discussion about indulgences. He nailed these to the church door of the castle in Wittenberg and sent them in a letter to his superior, a few bishops, and friends. By the end of the year they had been published in multiple places and soon ignited the unrest that was smoldering across Europe.

Quotation 277: *Depravity has become so taken for granted that those soiled by it no longer notice the stench of sin.* (Hadrian VI [d. 1523], as cited in Jedin and Dolan, *History of the Church*, V:7)

Quotation 278: *Thesis 21: Thus those indulgence preachers are in error who say that a man is absolved from every penalty and saved by papal indulgences.* (Martin Luther, Ninety-Five Theses (1517), in *Luther's Works*)

172. Papal bull, *Exsurge Domine* ("Arise, O Lord"), condemning the errors of Martin Luther (June, 1520).

Quotation 279: *It is also considered an abuse that a priest would accept gifts from several people for the celebration of Mass and then seek to satisfy these requests with only a single Mass. This admitted abuse leaves a lasting impression, because the title of Mass is actually applied to simple monetary gains. Herein are innumerable scandals, and no little harm thus befalls Christ the Lord and the Church. . . . The abuse also is noted that while the conventual Mass is being celebrated, cadavers are carried into church, which completely disrupts the sacred rites. . . . Still more serious is the oft-noted scandalous act of very many priests who balance the chalice on their head with both hands after the consecration, so that sometimes . . . there is the greatest danger of spilling the chalices.* ("Abuses, relating to the Sacrifice of the Mass," reported by a specially appointed commission of the Council of Trent [8 August 1562], in Mansi, *Sacrorum Conciliorum*)

Unfortunately, the sale of indulgences that upset Luther was authorized by Pope Leo X. In 1520 Luther was condemned by Leo [illustration 172]. Though Luther was called before Emperor Charles V (1558), he was supported by a number of German princes who hoped to use this religious unrest to weaken the political influence of the emperor and the pope. Sheltered by Prince Elector Friedrich of Saxony (d. 1525), Luther hid in Wartburg where he produced a German translation of the Bible in eleven weeks. Meanwhile, the reform raced across Europe. Luther's ideas were condemned by some, embraced by others, and also critiqued for not going far enough. More radical reformers like Ulrich Zwingli (d. 1531) in Zurich thought that Luther allowed too many ideas and practices not found in the Bible and called for a reform strictly prescribed by the New Testament. Martin Bucer (d. 1551) laid the groundwork for the reform in Strassburg and tried to take a middle position between Luther and Zwingli. It was especially over issues of Eucharist and the nature of real presence that these reformers differed. In October of 1529 Luther, Zwingli, Bucer, and others met at the castle in Marburg in the hopes of coming to agreement. While the participants did sign articles demonstrating a shared belief in things like infant baptism and the rejection of the sacrifice of the Mass, they could not agree on the nature of real presence. As James White summarizes, this wide gulf between the views of Luther and Zwingli on the Eucharist became permanent and led to divisions within the reforming traditions that still remain. (White, *Protestant Worship: Traditions in Transition*, 59)

By the 1530s virtually all of Scandinavia and the British Isles as well as significant portions of Germany, Austria, and even some of France had broken ties with Rome. Calls arose already in the 1520s for a church council to address the situation. The wars between Charles V and the French king made it difficult to convene such a council. Also, some popes were afraid that a council might limit their authority or challenge some of their views, a fear quite real since the Council of Constance (1414–1418) had deposed three popes to end the "Great Schism," designed the election of an alternative pope, and declared such councils as the ultimate authority of the church. After many false starts, a council in Trent finally convened in 1545 and met sporadically for almost twenty years (1545–47, 1551–52, 1562–63). The council addressed many of the abuses that had sparked the reform [quotation 279]. As a consequence, the training of the clergy was greatly improved, regular preaching was encouraged at Sunday worship, and the people received better preparation for receiving the sacraments. On the other hand, the council seemed unwilling and was probably unable to reconcile with the reformers.

The teachings of Luther, Zwingli, and others were soundly condemned. The Roman Catholic Church held fast to most of the teachings challenged by the reformers, resulting in something of a theological entrenchment that lasted for centuries. This Catholic Counter-Reformation was both reforming and divisive for Western Christianity, and even for the Roman Catholic Church itself.

The teachings of the Council of Trent were not everywhere accepted or implemented by Roman Catholics. This was especially true in France, where a movement for freedom from the authority of the papacy had deep roots. Because of this widespread "Gallicanism," Roman Catholic worship in France did not conform to Rome's directives well into the nineteenth century. For political and cultural reasons the Holy Roman Emperor Joseph II (d. 1790) moved to restrict the pope's control, which included directives to make the liturgy simpler and more intelligible in the empire: a move known as "Josephinism." The Emperor's brother Leopold (d. 1790) was Grand Duke of Tuscany, where he supported similar reforms. The Synod of Pistoia (1786), held under his auspices, embraced the principles of Gallicanism and Josephinism but went even further directing that there should be only one altar in each church, one Mass on each Sunday, and outright condemning the use of Latin in the liturgy. Even in the United States, the first Roman Catholic bishop in the new country, John Carroll (d. 1816), was moved by principles of intelligibility and self-determination and so argued for participation of the laity in running the church, for the people's right to choose their own bishops, and even for celebrating liturgy in the vernacular.

Because of the enormous diversity among the various "Protestants" (from Latin, *protestans* = "testifying or protesting")—a diversity respected at the meeting at Marburg—the reform apart from the Roman Catholic Church continued to evolve [illustration 173]. For example, "Anabaptist" (from Greek *ana* + *baptismos*, "again baptism") reformers, more radical than Zwingli, rejected infant baptism as nonbiblical and separated into their own communities of faith. In centuries to come Quakers would reject all external sacraments, while John and Charles Wesley would spark a reform within

	Left-Wing	*Central*	*Right-Wing*	
16th c.	Anabaptist	Reformed	Anglican	Lutheran
17th c.	Quaker	Puritan		
18th c.		Methodist		
19th c.	Frontier			
20th c.	Pentecostal			

173. James White's outline of the traditions of Protestant worship.

174. William Blake's (d. 1827) illustration of *Newton* as a divine geometer.

the Church of England that would come to be known as Methodism, and the United States would witness the flowering of distinctive free church styles of worship.

As the face of Western Christianity was fundamentally reconfigured during this period, amazing developments in the sciences and philosophy also occurred. Already in the sixteenth century Nicolaus Copernicus (d. 1543) reimagined the universe with the sun rather than the earth at its center, a position strengthened by the work of Galileo Galilei (1642). Isaac Newton (1727) subsequently reinvented our understanding of optics, mathematics, and the laws of gravity. Parallel changes in philosophy, the birth of the social sciences, and advances in communications and industry swept through this era at an astounding rate, heralding the onset of what we call the "modern" era. Many of these developments revealed a belief in people's capacity to understand the workings of the universe and maybe even to harness creative powers previously thought only possessed by God [illustration 174]. An era of reason and empiricism, or the Age of Enlightenment, thus arose offering both new tools and powerful challenges to the theology and worship of the churches. Enlightenment principles were foundational for changes in Protestant worship during the latter part of this era and were similarly a force behind Gallicanism, Josephinism, the Council of Pistoia, and even the vision of John Carroll. The full impact of the Enlightenment on the liturgy would not become apparent, however, until the twentieth century.

ARCHITECTURE

The ecclesiastical upheaval of the sixteenth century and its radical reshaping of Western Christianity had a significant impact on church architecture. In Roman Catholicism, for example, the post-Tridentine church emerged from the challenges of the reform with a new optimism and sense of vitality. The energetic architectural style that symbolized this exuberance—or what sometimes is perceived as triumphalism—came to be known as the baroque. Although other architectural styles such as rococo and neoclassicism ensued, they never displaced baroque as the architectural symbol of the post-Tridentine Roman Catholic Church.

It is true that some Protestant communities, such as Lutherans and Anglicans, employed the baroque style as well in their church buildings. Many Protestant churches, however, were more concerned with enabling the community to hear and respond to the word than creating the visually impressive buildings characteristic of the baroque. Challenges to eucharistic practice and theology contributed in some strands of Protestantism to a diminished role for the Eucharist. Zwingli, for example, suggested that the Lord's Supper should be celebrated only four times a year. As a consequence, altars assumed much less significance in some Protestant communities, whereas the pulpit acquired a renewed importance.

Saint Peter's in Rome

More than any other building project of the sixteenth century, the reconstruction of St. Peter's in Rome chronicled the transition from renaissance to baroque architecture. The fourth-century basilica built by Constantine had been in disrepair for sometime when Julius II (d. 1513) laid the cornerstone for the new church in 1506. Ironically, the sale of indulgences that so stirred Martin Luther was the financial support of this reconstruction. The sixteenth-century church was first conceived in grand renaissance style. Donato Bramante (d. 1514) designed a central-plan space consisting of a series of small Greek crosses (four arms of equal length) surrounding one large Greek Cross. This plan was to express symbolically the church's position at the center of the Western church, Christianity, and the world. After Bramante's death, work slowed until Michelangelo (d. 1564) took over as architect in 1546. By simplifying Bramante's design and

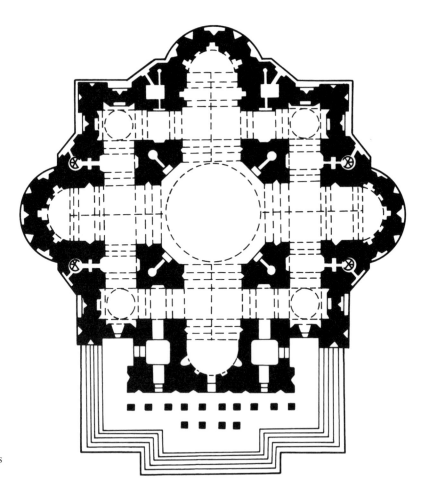

175. Michelangelo's plan for Saint Peter's in Rome. (After Gardner, p. 552)

enclosing the space in a transverse square, Michelangelo converted St. Peter's from a renaissance building composed of related but somewhat independent parts to a massive work of dynamic unity, announcing the onset of the baroque [illustration 175].

After Michelangelo's death, the plan of St. Peter's was altered by the addition of a nave, transforming it from a Greek cross to a Latin Cross (three equal and one elongated arm) [illustration 176]. This addition better accommodated the Roman liturgy and the processions so integral to that liturgy. Unfortunately, the addition obscured Michelangelo's great dome, which today can be appreciated only from the back of the building. The final stage in St. Peter's transition from a renaissance to a baroque building was the addition of a piazza designed by Gian Lorenzo Bernini (d. 1680). This enormous space (almost 790 feet across at its widest point) is surrounded by a two-armed, elliptical colonnade consisting of 284 travertine columns surmounted by 162 twelve-foot-high statues of saints. Dedicated in 1666, Bernini's piazza is one of the most dramatic public spaces ever created. True to the artist's intentions [quotation 280], the piazza beckons all into the embrace of the mother church of Rome.

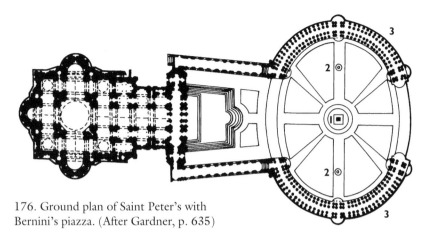

1. Obelisk
2. Fountain
3. Colonnade

176. Ground plan of Saint Peter's with Bernini's piazza. (After Gardner, p. 635)

Il Gesù and the Baroque

Among the first of the true baroque churches stands Il Gesù (Italian, "the [Church of] Jesus"), the mother church of the Jesuits. Il Gesù symbolized the vitality and ingenuity of this new community and its founder, Ignatius of Loyola (d. 1556). The Jesuits were a novel form of religious life in the sixteenth century: highly centralized, well organized, mobile and free from the demands of a common liturgical life, especially the Divine Office, which Ignatius did not require his followers to chant together. Their new church embodied the fresh spirit of this community, a much more open and dynamic space compared to the subdivided space of many Gothic churches. Designed and built in Rome between 1568 and 1584, Il Gesù became one of the most copied designs in ecclesiastical history [illustration 177]. Its popularity was the result of a number of important innovations including the elimination of side aisles, the shortening of the apse, and the removal of the choir from its place between the altar and the congregation—an architectural affirmation of the elimination of the Divine Office as a community exercise among the Jesuits. The

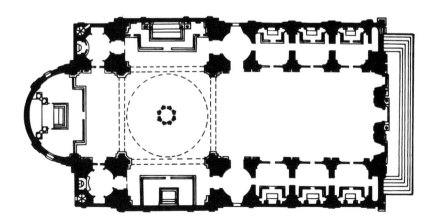

177. Ground plan of Il Gesù. (After Norberg-Schulz, p. 277)

result was a large open space with its central area emphasized by a dome. Like the hall churches of thirteenth-century Germany, so popular with medieval preaching orders, these churches gave new attention to the pulpit and the act of preaching. With no choir of monks to obstruct the view, no rood screens, and no elongated apse to distance the people from the sacred action, Il Gesù drew the laity into closer proximity to the liturgical action.

The people's direct participation in the Eucharist, even at a church like Il Gesù, however, remained limited. James White (*Roman Catholic Worship*, 2–3) explains this phenomenon by comparing this new design for churches to that for a theater. The raised sanctuary, shortening of the apse, and elimination of visible barriers, including the lack of interior columns, turned the high altar into a virtual stage. Like an audience, the assembly could watch the drama of the Mass unfold before them with few visible obstructions, and the improved acoustics enhanced by the shortened apse and stone vault rendered the preaching more audible as well. The actors in the liturgy, however, did not include the assembly, but only the ministers in the sanctuary, particularly the priest. Thus, while the assembly was physically closer to the eucharistic action in such a building, they remained liturgically distant.

Common Liturgical Arrangements in Roman Catholic Churches

As we will continue to see, the Council of Trent and the work done in its aftermath contributed to a new uniformity within Roman Catholic worship. There was, for example, clearer uniformity in eucharistic doctrine and, because of the revisions of the liturgical books, much more uniformity in the celebration of the Mass. While there were no real architectural directives within the decrees of the Council of Trent, the tendency toward uniformity in doctrine and rubrics generated by that council spurred a similar instinct for conformity in the liturgical arrangements within Roman Catholic churches. This was first apparent in places like northern Italy, then across Europe, and ultimately across the globe as European missionaries exported the Roman Rite and architectural presumptions about the celebration of that rite around the world. Many components of a typical arrangement of a Roman Catholic church were never initially mandated by law, but became so customary that they were widely presumed, and some eventually did become legally binding.

For example, there is a widespread tendency for tabernacles in this era to make the final transition from a liturgical vessel to an architectural fixture. As we shall see, custom dictated and eventually

Quotation 281: *Beyond the celebration of the Eucharist, the Church has had a most ancient tradition of reserving the eucharistic bread. The purpose of this reservation is to bring communion to the sick and to be the object of private devotion. Most appropriately, this reservation should be designated in a space designed for individual devotion. A room or chapel specifically designed and separate from the major space is important so that no confusion can take place between the celebration of the Eucharist and reservation. Active and static aspects of the same reality cannot claim the same human attention at the same time.* (Bishops' Committee on the Liturgy, *Environment and Art in Catholic Worship*, 78)

178. High altar of the Mexico City Cathedral.

law required that the tabernacle was to be fixed to the altar table. In many places the tabernacle and adjoining reredos became a focal superstructure that could accommodate exposition of the Blessed Sacrament, with tabernacle and exposition platform flanked by a cadre of niches filled with adoring angels and saints or candles and flowers [illustration 178]. Such a heightened theatrical backdrop sometimes dwarfed the eucharistic action at the table and contributed to the blurring and confusion between what a later Roman Catholic document would characterize as the "active" space for eucharistic celebration and the more "static" place of reservation [quotation 281].

Another addition, common to many Roman Catholic and other churches through the twentieth century, was a low communion rail.

Quotation 282: *There is nothing whatever in the rubrics about an altar rail; it is nowhere prescribed. It is purely utilitarian, to protect the chancel from irreverence [especially in a crowded church]; but it has become a necessity for the giving of the Holy communion in large churches. (O'Connell, Church Building and Furnishing, p. 13)*

According to Jungmann, these seem to have developed from the practice of spreading a cloth for communicants kneeling at the altar; eventually these cloths were placed over tables or benches, which evolved into the communion rail (*Mass of the Roman Rite*, II:375). The first legislation regarding this manner of receiving communion comes from Milan at the end of the sixteenth century. While ubiquitous in Roman Catholic churches (and some other Christian churches as well) after the Council of Trent, communion rails are never mentioned in the law or even in the rubrics of the Tridentine Rite [quotation 282].

Influential in the standardization of some liturgical arrangements was Charles Borromeo (d. 1584), archbishop of Milan, who published the very detailed *Instructions on the Architecture and Furnishings of Churches* (1577). He stated a clear preference for cruciform church design, affirmed the importance of the tabernacle on the altar, gave clear instruction about the need and design for the innovation we have come to know as a "confessional," and even prescribed the shape, size, and materials for the fonts that provided holy water for the faithful who were to bless themselves with it upon entering a church. While most of these ideas did not carry the weight of law, Borromeo's influence was significant. As Vatican Secretary of State he had helped reopen the Council of Trent and participated in its final session (1562–63). He was also in charge of producing the *Roman Catechism* (1566) after the close of the council; he worked on the revisions of the Breviary (1568) and Roman Missal (1570); and even held the position of "Prefect of the Tridentine Council" (1564–65). Thus, the liturgical vision of an Italian cardinal who presided in sumptuous Milan Cathedral had ramifications for the most ordinary Roman Catholic parishes around the world.

Reformation Churches

While Roman Catholic church buildings were increasingly similar in their internal arrangements, the growing diversity within Protestantism spawned a new pluriformity in the liturgical arrangements of these houses of worship. Initially reforming communities took over existing churches and adapted them to their own needs. In some places this meant removing statuary and iconography (as in Zurich in 1524), and in other places it meant creating new images that were considered more theologically correct [illustration 179]. As for the interior design of such churches, in England, the rood screens that divided the church into a nave and a choir area [illustration 180] were often maintained, the nave being used by the assembly for Matins and Evensong, and the choir area employed for communion

179. Lucas Cranach the Elder's (d. 1553) altarpiece for the City Church in Wittenberg.
Top panels, left to right: Baptism, Lord's Supper, confession. Lower panel: The Crucifixion.

180. Late fifteenth-century rood screen from York Cathedral in England.

services. This division symbolized what would become the increasingly secondary role of the Eucharist in Anglican worship, eclipsed by morning and evening prayer. The choir area was smaller than the nave, and, as the site of the Lord's Supper, presumed the presence of fewer worshipers, while Sunday matins in the nave became the main worship service of the week. It is true that the 1549 *Book of Common Prayer* presumed daily communion—even going so far as to provide an exhortation to be given by the priest "if upon the Sunday or holydaye the people be negligent to come to the communion." Just three years later, however, the 1552 *Book of Common Prayer* included the injunction that "every Parishioner shall communicate, at the least thre tymes in the yere: of which, Easter is to be one." This minimum requirement eventually became the norm for most of this era.

181. Sacrament house, built between 1460–80, in Ulm Cathedral.

On the continent, the renovation of worship spaces usually included the elimination of rood screens as well as the removal of elaborate reredos and tabernacles. In many renovations the pulpit was commonly moved toward the center. Given the growing diversity of traditions and decentralized nature of the Protestant Reformation, however, it is difficult to generalize about the liturgical rearrangements in existing buildings and exceptions can always be found. Thus, the eighty-five foot tall, fifteenth-century sacrament house survived in the Cathedral at Ulm [illustration 181], though no longer used for reservation of the Eucharist, and the Lutheran Cathedral in Stockholm actually received a new ebony and silver altar and reredos in 1640.

182. Saint George's United Methodist
Church in Philadelphia, built in 1769.

Dissatisfaction with some of these renovations as well as the need
for additional churches led to the creation of new buildings for Protestant worship. One element common to virtually all of these new
churches was the centrality of the pulpit [illustration 182], which
underscored the new reverence for God's word in the Scriptures and
the importance of preaching in Protestant worship. This emphasis
on the Word overshadowed the celebration of the Lord's Supper,
which Zwingli, for example, thought should be celebrated only four
times a year in Zurich. While most of these churches did have altars,
they were often simple, portable tables that were stored or set to the
side on those Sundays when communion was not celebrated. Leipzig
at the time of J. S. Bach (d. 1750), on the other hand, provided a
very different and somewhat exceptional practice, since the main
Sunday worship service in this very Lutheran town "always included
celebration of the Holy Communion" (Stiller, p. 49). In such a setting a permanent altar was more appropriate.

As Spiro Kostof has noted, one commonality in emerging Protestant architecture was "a shift from a processional to an auditorium
space, from a longitudinal to a centralizing plan." Kostof further
points out that this centralization is not only horizontal but vertical
as well, generating "the gallery, sometimes successive rows as in an
opera house, drawing in the whole congregation around the focal
spot" (p. 539). One stunning example of such horizontal and vertical

183. Dresden Frauenkirche, restored and rededicated in 2005 following its destruction during World War II.

centralization is the recently reconstructed *Frauenkirche* in Dresden, with its multiple galleries all focused on the sanctuary with its baroque altar, Silbermann organ, and centrally positioned pulpit [illustration 183]. Most centrally planned Protestant churches were more austere, however, and the Roman Catholic emphasis on the visual elements of worship was rejected by major segments of the Reformation. It was the renewed emphasis on the Word and preaching that compelled Reformation architects such as England's Christopher Wren (d. 1723) to construct buildings more suitable for hearing than for seeing [quotation 283]. The shift from processional to auditorium space— from a place that emphasized movement to one that focused on hearing—contributed to the increased popularity of seating, first in Protestant and then Roman Catholic churches, especially in northern Europe and North America. Like theaters of the day, churches were filled with pews, which symbolized something of the immobility and even passivity of worshipers. In some cases, the introduction of pews coincided with a renewed separation of women and men during

Quotation 283: *The Romanists indeed, may build larger churches, it is enough if they hear the murmur of the Mass and see the elevation of the host, but ours are to be fitted for auditories.* (Christopher Wren [d. 1723] as cited in Addleshaw and Etchells, *The Architectural Setting of Anglican Worship*)

worship [quotation 284], something that Charles Borromeo had even suggested for Roman Catholics in 1577, though this one of his ideas seemed to have gone unheeded.

Summary

The Reformation and Counter-Reformation produced diverse, even contradictory theologies about Christian belief and sacramental practices, especially regarding Eucharist, baptism, reconciliation, and ordination. That a similar diversity developed in the worship spaces for an increasingly fragmented Western Christianity is strong testimony to the theological significance of the architectural arts. Thus ordinary believers intuited that it was incongruous to worship in the same, traditional space when fundamental teachings about the nature of real presence or the role of the Word had significantly changed. In the midst of this diversity there were clear currents at work in the church buildings of this period. Protestants, and to a lesser degree Roman Catholics, placed renewed emphasis on preaching, which resulted in churches designed with shorter apses and other concessions to acoustical concerns. Some Protestant and even Jewish communities embraced the baroque style, but it was particularly the Roman Catholics who reveled in the visual display and maybe even triumphalism of this style. The more "left-wing" reformers [illustration 173] ordinarily rejected this highly embellished style and instead favored simple, even austere interiors shaped in a central plan.

As the theological creativity of the Reformation and the Counter-Reformation waned, church authorities from various Christian perspectives often occupied themselves more with apologetics than constructive or speculative theology. Thus, as the lines between various denominations and churches solidified, the leadership often became more concerned with defending previously defined positions than in reflecting on doctrinal differences as a source of new insight or even reconciliation. In some ways, the architectural developments in succeeding centuries symbolized something of this entrenchment or even stagnation. There is, for example, a devolution of the baroque, epitomized by the furiously designed St. John Nepomuk in Munich (1733–1746) [illustration 184]. This building, as many of those in the rococo style, is more about the decorative, inventive surfaces and visual pleasure than architectural substance. Maybe even more telling were the many architectural "revivals," such as neoclassicism (ca. 1750–1850), the Romanesque revival (ca. 1840–1900), and the Gothic revival (nineteenth and early twentieth centuries). These revivals occurred during the Enlightenment when Western scholars were increasingly interested in a more "objective" study of history.

184. Detail of the sanctuary and side wall of Saint John Nepomuk in Munich.

In this era of so much rapid change and the questioning of basic Christian beliefs, James White opines that these stylistic revivals, maybe like the study of history itself, indicated a deep longing for a secure past, even a past that never existed. Nostalgia for a previous era was a spiritual reality that found expression in revival architecture.

MUSIC

While some architectural innovation such as the baroque might have radiated from Rome, innovations in liturgical music—especially in congregational song—belonged to the reformers. The reasons for this included the musical skill of early reformers such as Martin Luther, the Reformation's focus on God's Word coupled with music's ability to serve the Word, and the strong tradition of vernacular song in the German-speaking areas where the Reformation began. While reformers emphasized congregational song, officials in the Roman Catholic Church sought a more restrained style of Latin polyphony. The influence of Reformation hymnody, and the influences which spawned it, however, could not be avoided completely. As Protestant composers continued to explore hymnody and its many derivatives, some Roman Catholic communities did the same. Overall, however, Roman Catholic liturgical music was not focused on the congregation and—like the surrounding architecture—drifted toward the theatrical. In both traditions, the influence of opera and developments in orchestral music were unmistakable.

Reformation Song

Martin Luther was not only a gifted reformer but a talented musician. Convinced of the primacy of the Word of God, he was also convinced that music was one of the most important ways to communicate that Word [quotation 285]. Dedicated to the theological principle of the "priesthood of all believers," Luther shifted emphasis from the music of clerical *scholas* and what we would consider professional musicians to that of the congregation. With simple musical and textual building blocks—many of them borrowed from previously composed chants and even secular songs—Luther constructed scripturally based music that was both singable and enduring. His melodies usually were written in stepwise motion, within the range of a ninth, in syllabic settings, often employing a self-rehearsing musical form [illustration 185]. More effectively than others, Luther was able to transform non-liturgical, religious song into liturgical music. By doing so, he further integrated the community and vernacular hymnody into the worship.

Although Luther's influence was widespread, his views were not shared by every reformer. Zwingli, for example, considered music to be an essentially secular element that had no place in worship. The most musically gifted of the leaders of the Protestant Reformation, Zwingli nevertheless eliminated all music from the churches in Zurich during his lifetime. John Calvin (d. 1564) held the middle ground between Luther and Zwingli. On the one hand he banned polyphony from worship because it obscured the Word; he also thought that instrumental music distracted one from God. On the other hand, he encouraged singing from scriptural texts and sought out some of the best musicians (for example, Louis Bourgeois, d. 1561) and poets (especially Clément Marot, d. 1544) of his day. His enduring contribution to congregational song was the introduc-

185. "A Mighty Fortress" by Martin Luther. (Leupold, *Luther's Works*, vol. 53, p. 284)

186. Psalm 136 from the 1562 *Geneva Psalter*. (Grout, *A History of Western Music*, p. 317)

tion of vernacular metrical psalmody into the reformed liturgy. The resulting collection of rhymed verses set to simple melodies was the *Geneva Psalter* (1562) [illustration 186].

Roman Catholic Responses

Aware of the many musical and liturgical abuses that contributed to the onset of the Reformation, the Council of Trent emphasized intelligibility and restraint in church music [quotation 286]. In language reminiscent of John XXII [quotation 257], the twenty-second session of the council (17 September 1562) issued a supplemental decree that banished from the Roman Catholic Church all music that contained things "lascivious or impure." While Trent sought to restrain composers and performers from indulging in the theatrics of secular music, it never challenged the predominance of clerical choirs and cantors over the congregation in liturgical music. Insistence on the intelligibility of texts, for example, referred only to the intelligibility of Latin texts, which were often recognized because of their repetition but seldom understood by the laity and even some of the poorly trained clergy. Although a few Roman Catholic leaders favored a vernacular liturgy, Trent decreed that it was not "deemed advisable that [Mass] should be celebrated everywhere in the vernacular tongue" (17 September 1562, trans. Schroeder [p. 148]). The suggestion that polyphony should be banned from the Eucharist also did not prevail.

The reaffirmation of Latin and polyphony, plus the somewhat paradoxical emphasis on intelligibility, contributed to Trent's implicit affirmation of the work of Giovanni da Palestrina (d. 1594). More than virtually any other composer of the Counter-Reformation, Palestrina achieved a clarity and restraint that respected both the dictates of the council and the polyphonic tradition. Although Palestrina was a composer of polyphony, his works shared certain characteristics with the hymnody of Martin Luther. Like Luther, Palestrina often wrote parts in stepwise motion, frequently within the range of a ninth, relying on consonant harmonies, avoiding chromaticisms, and demonstrating great respect for the text. There is a well-circulated story that—possibly under the auspices of Charles Borromeo (one of the cardinals charged with the reform of church music)—Palestrina performed his *Missa Papae Marcelli* [illustration 187] for church leaders (maybe even the pope himself). This performance supposedly helped convince church leaders not to ban polyphony from the liturgy. While the story can be neither proven nor refuted, it is undeniable that Palestrina's compositions were celebrated even in his own time as paradigms of intelligible polyphony. Such an assessment appears in print as early as 1607 in the writings of the Italian composer Agostino Agazzari (d. 1640). On the other hand, these were evaluations of professionals steeped in the polyphonic tradition and fluent in liturgical Latin. History tells us little of what ordinary believers thought of Palestrina's music.

While not supported by the Council of Trent, vernacular song did continue to exist and develop within Roman Catholic worship. This development was spurred, in part, by the example of reformers like Martin Luther. It also seems rooted in the nationalism that marked this era, as well as in the Enlightenment, which stressed reason and intelligibility. Michael Vehe's *Ein neue Gesangbuchlein Geistlicher Lieder* (German, *A New Little Songbook of Spiritual Hymns*, 1537) is often identified as the first vernacular Roman Catholic hym-

187. *Kyrie* from Palestrina's *Missa Papae Marcelli*, composed ca. 1561. (Eulenburg edition)

nal. Though Vehe (d. 1559) publicly refuted many aspects of the Reformation and became the Roman Catholic bishop of Halberstadt, he apparently understood that the powerful tradition of vernacular hymnody in German-speaking areas could not be ignored in the Counter-Reformation. Anthony Ruff catalogs a raft of Roman Catholic hymnals and directives for singing in the vernacular in the century after Trent in German-speaking areas [quotation 287]. By the eighteenth century, hymns were permitted in some (often German-speaking) places as substitutes for the proper and ordinary of the Mass. This *Singmesse* (German, "sing Mass") gave the people a new sense of participation.

In the New World, too, vernacular hymnody was taking root among Roman Catholics, but for reasons different than those that spurred such singing on the continent. Vernacular singing was a practice that helped missionaries both attract converts and impart religious teaching. The missionaries who brought Catholicism to New Spain brought the Latin liturgy and its rich tradition of polyphony, especially that of sixteenth-century Spain. They also composed or encouraged the composition of hymns and ritual music in local languages. Today there are extant examples of hymns written

Quotation 287: *"A provincial synod in Salzburg approved the 'ancient custom' of singing congregational hymns for various seasons of the church year. Michael Peterle published a German-language hymnal in Prague in 1581 which gave the people a hymn to be sung after the first reading for each feast and season . . . [and] vernacular metrical versions of the Kyrie, Gloria, Credo and Lord's Prayer. . . . The Jesuits at Innsbruck issued a Catholisch Gesangbuechlein ["Little Catholic Hymnal"] in 1588 . . . Nicolaus Beuttner's . . . Catholisch Gesang-Buch ["Catholic Hymnal"] [was] published in 1602 . . . [and] reprinted at least ten times through 1718. . . . In 1625 David Gregor Corner . . . issued a German hymnal; the 1631 reissue in Vienna contained almost five hundred hymns. . . . [A] hymnal published in Prague in 1655 advocated singing German hymns at the Latin High Mass, a common practice in German-speaking lands."* (Ruff, p. 13)

188a. *Kyrie* from *Missa Salisburgensis*, often attributed to Orazio Benevoli (d. 1672), but possibly the work of Heinrich Biber (d. 1704) and written for the eleven-hundredth anniversary of the founding of the Diocese of Salzburg. Top half of page one. (*Denkmaler der Tonkunst in Osterreich*, 20:1)

in numerous indigenous languages that existed throughout New Spain, such as Nahuatl and Mochica. Similarly, when missionaries followed the conquistadors into what we know as Peru, they encountered rich cultures with highly developed ritual and musical arts. Some missionaries were known to have encouraged the singing of Quechua (the language of the Incan Empire) at different parts of the Mass and relied upon local music for shaping liturgical song. This dual missionary practice of importing the Latin liturgy while simultaneously drawing upon indigenous musical gifts is a sixteenth- and seventeenth-century phenomenon that extended from Mexico to the Philippines. Roman Catholic hymnody in the English-speaking U.S. is a later but well-documented phenomenon. By 1787, for

188b. Bottom half of *Kyrie, Missa Salisburgensis.*

example, Roman Catholics in the U.S. had their first collection of English vernacular hymns in John Aitken's *A Compilation of the Litanies and Vesper Hymns and Anthems as They are Sung in the Catholic Church* (Philadelphia, 1787). Although vernacular hymnody was recommended by the First National Synod in Baltimore in 1791 [quotation 288], it was never a dominant trend in Roman Catholic Eucharist in the English-speaking U.S. during this era. While there were exceptions, it is fair to suggest that the active participation of the congregation was not highly valued in Roman Catholic Eucharist after Trent. Consequently, congregational song—to the extent that it existed—was more music *in* worship than music *of* worship. The assembly was clearly musically dispensable.

Quotation 288: *[On Sundays and feast days] Mass is to be solemnly celebrated with song. . . . It is hoped that during the various services some hymns or prayers in the vernacular would be sung.* ("Statuta Synodi Baltimorensis Anno 1791 Celebratae" [First National Synod in Baltimore 1791], 17)

Quotation 289: *The victorious temper of the post-Tridentine age, which once more felt the courage to absorb the entire wealth of the contemporary culture into the Catholic cosmos . . . found its triumphal voice in this music. . . . It sometimes happened that this church music, which had fallen more and more into the hands of laymen, forgot that it was meant to serve the liturgical action. As a result of this, the music often fitted very poorly into the liturgical setting. And since this latter was but little understood, and because esthetic consideration began to hold sway, the liturgy was not only submerged under this ever-growing art but actually suppressed, so that even at this time there were festival occasions which might best be described as "church concerts with liturgical accompaniment."* (Jungmann, The Mass of the Roman Rite, 1:148–49)

Quotation 290: *I have found to my astonishment that the Catholics, who had music in their churches for several centuries, and sing a musical Mass every Sunday if possible, in their principal churches, do not to this day possess one which can be considered even tolerably good, or in fact, which is not actually distasteful and operatic. This is the case from Pergolese and Durante, who introduced the most laughable little trills into their Gloria, down to the opera finales of the present day. Were I a Catholic, I would set to work at a Mass this very evening; and whatever it might turn out, it would at all events be the only Mass written with a constant remembrance of its sacred purpose.* (Felix Mendelssohn [d. 1847], Letter to Pastor Bauer, Dusseldorf [12 January 1835], in Wienandt, Opinions on Church Music, p. 122)

Elaboration, Reform, and Pietism

Although it took longer to develop, the characteristics that marked baroque architecture during the sixteenth and seventeen centuries eventually came to characterize baroque music during the seventeenth and eighteenth centuries. Opera was becoming a dominant musical form in Europe, and its emphasis on heroic performance that showcased gifted soloists supported by large choruses and lavish orchestras clearly influenced church music [quotation 289]. While all Christian traditions did not embrace operatic forms in public prayer, worship music in virtually every denomination did undergo a process of elaboration during this era. Contrary to the will of Calvin, who sanctioned only single-line melodies, Calvinists turned to multiple-part settings for the Psalter. Composers of the English reform wrote polyphonic anthems and settings of the Service, which included music for Morning Prayer, Evening Prayer, and Holy Communion. Lutherans composed Masses, chorale motets, chorale concerti, and chorale or church cantatas. In the Roman Catholic Church, the compositional restraint of Palestrina was largely abandoned. One of the most unusual examples may have been the *Missa Salisbergensis* (Latin, "Salzburg Mass") for sixteen voices, orchestra, and organ [illustration 188]. While extreme, this was not an isolated composition, and instrumental music such as the *sonata da chiesa* (Italian, "sonata for church") by Arcangelo Corelli (d. 1713) or the operatic *Stabat Mater* by Giovannin Pergolesi (d. 1736) typified composition of the era that simply overwhelmed the liturgy [quotation 290].

While opera influenced the composition of larger musical pieces for worship, a new spirit of pietism influenced the smaller congregational works of the era. Inspired by English Puritanism and the Swiss reform, pietism emerged in seventeenth-century Lutheranism. Reacting to what some considered an overemphasis on dogma and confessional statements that were often a source of conflict, some spiritual leaders called for a renewed emphasis on a heartfelt Christian faith and ethical living. This more personal, even subjective approach to Christianity, stressing the personal piety and morality of believers, exerted a significant influence on the congregational song of most Christian denominations. One result of this movement was a rich and beautiful body of hymnody [illustration 189]. Such hymns were often simply written in the first person singular and wedded to attractive and accessible melodies. In the hands of less talented composers and poets, however, this tendency could devolve into sentimental, formulaic, and unimaginative music. Hymns were also composed in order to teach doctrine. This was particularly true of the hymns of John (d. 1791) and especially Charles (d. 1788) Wesley—over 5500 of them—whose texts served to impart the basic

1 Je - sus, price - less Treas - ure, Source of pur - est pleas - ure,
2 In   thine arm   I   rest me; Foes who would mo - lest me
3 Hence, all thoughts of sad - ness! For the Lord of glad - ness,

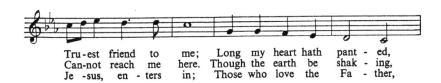

Tru - est friend to   me; Long my heart hath pant - ed,
Can - not reach me   here. Though the earth be shak - ing,
Je - sus, en - ters in; Those who love the Fa - ther,

Till   it   well - nigh faint - ed, Thirst - ing af - ter thee.
Ev - 'ry heart be quak - ing, God dis - pels our fear;
Tho' the storms may gath - er, Still have peace with - in;

Thine I   am,   O   spot - less Lamb, I   will suf - fer
Sin and hell   in   con - flict fell With their heav - iest
Yea, what - 'e'er we   here must bear, Still in   thee lies

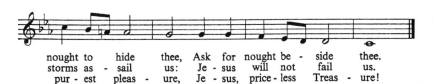

nought to   hide   thee, Ask for nought be - side thee.
storms as - sail   us: Je - sus will not fail us.
pur - est pleas - ure, Je - sus, price - less Treas - ure!

189. Example of a pietist hymn with tune by Johann Cruger (d. 1662) and text by Johann Franck (d. 1677). "Jesus, priceless treasure," translation by Catherine Winkworth (d. 1878). (*The Catholic Hymnal and Service Book*, Benziger, 125)

doctrines of John Wesley's Methodist movement. In the introduction to *A Collection of Hymns for the Use of the People Called Methodist* (1780), John Wesley points out that this large collection contains "all the important truths of our most holy religion."

Important moderating voices did exist in the midst of the theatrical and sentimental tendencies of the seventeenth and eighteenth centuries. Because the organ and other instruments were forbidden in the papal chapel, the *a cappella* (Italian, "[as] in the chapel") style of Palestrina found a permanent home and sponsor in Rome. In Germany, the Lutheran master Johann Sebastian Bach (d. 1750) was a thoroughly liturgical baroque composer who could deftly illuminate a text while achieving new heights of musical expression. By the end of the eighteenth century, however, vocal and choral liturgical music was in a general state of decline as the churches were displaced as patrons of the arts by secular princes. Although some great religious works were written for the liturgy (such as the Masses of Mozart, d. 1791), most, like Beethoven's (d. 1827) *Missa Solemnis* (Latin, "Solemn Mass") or Brahms's (d. 1897) *Ein deutsches Requiem* (German, "a German Requiem"), were written for non-liturgical performances in churches or concert halls. The prevalence of the low Mass in Roman Catholicism meant a great decline in the number of Mass compositions. Instead, incidental motets and organ interludes occupied church composers.

The emergence of sacred music composed for the concert hall was met by a new reform in Roman Catholic church music. This restoration movement sought a return to Gregorian chant and polyphony in the style of Palestrina. One of the most celebrated proponents of this reform was the Society of St. Cecilia, whose work was sanctioned by Pope Pius IX in 1870. Effective in rejecting the elaborations characteristic of the baroque and romantic periods, this reform also opposed the singing of vernacular translations or paraphrases of the ordinary of the Mass (known as the *Deutches Hochamt*, German, "German High Mass") that were popular in German-speaking countries at the time. The nineteenth century was also a time of much scholarly work on chant, especially at the French monastery of Solesmes, which provided much of the scholarship for a new Vatican edition of chant that appeared in the early twentieth century.

Summary

Although the various reforms that emerged during the sixteenth century were not musical at their root, the music of the period well reflected the positions of the Reformation and the Counter-Reformation. In the ensuing centuries, music continued to symbolize and serve the basic trajectories of Protestant and Roman Catholic theology and worship. One main trajectory of Protestantism was a turning away from emphasis on the visual that was increasingly characteristic of Roman Catholic worship, and turning instead to the auditory. Luther's belief in the centrality of God's Word and music's ability to serve the Word was foundational for this development. The Roman Catholic Church corrected many musical and liturgical abuses but ultimately maintained an implicit affirmation of the primacy of the visual in worship. Celebrated for its architectural developments

190. Letter of Saint Jerome on the opening page of the first volume of the Gutenberg Bible.

during this period, the Roman Catholic Church made few musical concessions to the assembly in its Counter-Reformation. Consequently, they were often silent, and to the extent that they did sing, it was seldom central to the liturgical action.

BOOKS

In the previous chapter we noted the birth of the printing industry in the West and noted that some estimated that by the year 1500 there were 220 printing presses in operation throughout western

Europe and at least eight million books in print. Over half of these books were religious in nature. Popular works included books by theologians like Thomas Aquinas, the *Imitation of Christ* [illustration 158] by Thomas à Kempis, and especially the Bible. The early alliance between this new technology and religion, and particularly between printing and the Bible, was symbolized by Gutenberg's first printed book: the forty-two-line Bible (1453–55) [illustration 190]. This printing of Jerome's fifth-century translation of the Bible into Latin, known as the Vulgate (from Latin *vulgata*, "common" or "well known"), was followed by over one hundred other printings of this biblical translation by 1500.

In addition to producing biblical or classical texts, this revolutionary invention was also employed to disseminate new ideas through books, pamphlets, and even single pages. We have already seen the power of this single-sheet publication in the anti-Semitic broadsheet disseminating the anti-Semitic story of host theft by a Jew in Passau [illustration 169] and in the sale of indulgences [illustration 171] that sparked Luther's challenge to the church. Given the debate about indulgences, it is ironic that the earliest datable example of printing from moveable type in the West is a letter of indulgence issued by Pope Nicholas V in 1451 and printed by Gutenberg in 1454.

Quotation 291: *With Gutenberg, Europe enters the technological phase of progress, when change itself becomes the archetypal norm of social life.* (McLuhan, *The Gutenberg Galaxy,* p. 155)

Printing enabled the rapid exchange of ideas and served as a catalyst for change [quotation 291]. Paradoxically, it also served to stem the tide of change in some quarters by creating new standards of uniformity. Previous to the printing press, manuscripts had to be copied by hand. Sometimes errors were made, changes introduced, or glosses added to traditional texts. No matter how conscientious the scribe, no two medieval manuscripts were exactly alike [illustration 155]. Even changes in the Roman Canon—despite the fact that the word "canon" means unchanging"—were commonplace, as in the previously noted example of the thirteenth-century ordinary of St.-Denis that included additional prayers for the blessings of grapes to be inserted in the canon of the Mass on the feast of the Transfiguration (p. 212). The printing press, however, made it possible to produce identical copies of the same book. For those who tried to impose such books, and for those who accepted them, a new age of liturgical uniformity had begun.

Protestant Books

In the early stage of the Reformation, printed liturgical books seldom were meant to be comprehensive. Often a combination of instruction, rite, and commentary, these books frequently had more affinity with the early church orders of Mass than with the liturgical books of the Middle Ages.

Early Efforts   In 1520 Martin Luther issued a vehement challenge to the Roman Catholic sacramental system in his pamphlet *The Babylonian Captivity of the Church* [illustration 191]. Although this document severely criticized the Roman liturgy, Luther did not publish a revision of the Mass. On Christmas of 1521 another reform theologian by the name of Andreas Karlstadt (d. 1541) did celebrate a modified Eucharist in which the institution narrative was read in German, the elevation was eliminated, and communicants took the bread and wine into their own hands. At that time Luther was sequestered in the castle in Wartburg and from a distance very much opposed this reform, although it was officially accepted by the city council of Wittenberg in early 1522. The first published reform Mass was probably the 1522 *Evangelical Mass* of the Carmelite brothers in Nördling. In 1523 another Mass was authored by the Anabaptist Thomas Müntzer, who also published a German setting of the Divine Office. In December of 1523 Luther finally published *The Rite for Mass and Communion for the Church of Wittenberg*. This Latin revision satisfied few reformers—including its author [quotation 292] —and vernacular liturgies continued to appear. Zwingli's pamphlet *An Attack upon the Canon of the Mass* (1523) included a proposal for the reform of the eucharistic liturgy. His *Action or Use of the Lord's Supper* (1525) offered an even more radical revision. In 1523 Leo Jud (d. 1542) produced a vernacular rite for Zurich, and in January 1524 Matthis Zell (d. 1548) and Theobald Schwartz (d. 1561) did the same for Strasbourg. About the same time William Farel (d. 1565) prepared the first reformed liturgy in French and John Oecolampadius (d. 1531) published *Form and Manner of the Lord's Supper in Basil*. This avalanche of vernacular liturgies pressured Luther to produce the *German Mass and Order of Worship*, which he celebrated in October of 1525 and published in early 1526.

The Maturing of Reformed Rites   The decades following these first reformed rituals witnessed the slow emergence of more comprehensive publications. In addition to the numerous hymnals that appeared during this period, followers of Luther—such as the popular Wittenberg pastor Johann Bugenhagen (d. 1558)—produced *Kirkenordnungen* (German, "church orders") for most major cities and principalities in Germany, Denmark, and Sweden, where Luther's reforms had been adopted. These contained instructions for reformed church life and worship, including instruction on the shape of the ritual, the content of the preaching, and even church arrangements and appropriate vesture. Similar church orders for the followers of Calvin were drawn up in the Netherlands and in Swiss cities such as Bern, while such documents for the followers of Zwingli appeared in Zurich.

191. Woodcut portrait of Martin Luther on the title page of his pamphlet, *The Babylonian Captivity of the Church*, printed in Strasbourg by Johann Pruess in 1520.

Quotation 292: *I would gladly have a German Mass today. I am also occupied with it. But I would very much like it to have a true German character. For to translate the Latin text and retain the Latin tone or notes has my sanction, though it doesn't sound polished or well done. Both the text and notes, accent, melody, and manner of rendering ought to grow out of the true mother tongue and its inflection, otherwise all of it becomes an imitation in the manner of the apes.* (Martin Luther, *Against the Heavenly Prophets* [1524], in *Luther's Works*, vol. 40, p. 141)

192. Title page of the first edition of the *Book of Common Prayer* or the *First Prayer Book of King Edward VI*, published in London in 1549.

Martin Bucer (d. 1551), who exerted significant influence on Calvin's thought, revised the Strasbourg liturgy in his *Psalter, with Complete Church Practice* (1539). John Calvin published a now-lost rite for Strasbourg in 1540, although both a 1542 and a 1545 edition of his *The Form of Church Prayers and Hymns* still exist. In England, the death of Henry VIII in 1547 paved the way for new liturgical publications that were largely the work of the Archbishop of Canterbury, Thomas Cranmer (d. 1556). The first *Booke of the Common Prayer and Administracion of the Sacraments* [illustration 192] appeared in 1549 during the reign of King Edward VI (d. 1553). Discontent with this work, sometimes known as the *First Prayer Book of King Edward*, led to a second edition of the *Boke of Common Prayer* in 1552. These were foundational works in English liturgy and continue to be a font for Anglican and Episcopalian worship today. Under the influence of Calvin and Cranmer, the Scottish reformer John Knox (d. 1572) published *The Form and Prayers and Ministration of the Sacrament* (1556) for English Protestant congregations in Geneva. This work was adopted by the Scottish Church in 1562. Puritans adapted Knox's work in their *Book of the Forme of Common Prayers* (1586).

The Seventeenth and Eighteenth Centuries   Although the general directions for reformed liturgy emerged during the sixteenth century, significant liturgical publications continued to appear during the seventeenth and eighteenth centuries. For example, in the midst of its struggles with its monarch Charles I (d. 1649), the English Parliament abolished the *Book of Common Prayer* and in 1645 accepted in its place a new *Directory for the Public Worship of God*, also known as the *Westminster Directory for Worship* (1644). This *Directory* was only employed for fifteen years in England, and with the ascent of Charles II (d. 1685) and the restoration of the English monarchy in 1660, the *Book of Common Prayer* was restored and a new edition issued in 1662. Though officially rejected in England, the *Directory* found sustained use in the Church of Scotland and, in the words of James White, was destined to become normative for all Presbyterians. The first service intended for use solely in North America also appeared during this time. It was John Wesley's *The Sunday Service of the Methodists in North America* (1784).

Roman Books

The call to rework Rome's liturgical books was sounded long before the Reformation. As early as the fifteenth century, the previously mentioned Nicholas of Cusa [quotation 268], who became bishop

193. Canon from the 1474 *Missale Romanum*.

of Brixen, ordered that all missals in his diocese should be brought into conformity with one approved model. During the early sixteenth century similar demands for reforms emanated from various quarters. Soon there were calls not only for the realignment of books within a single diocese but for uniform books throughout the Latin Church. Actually, for some centuries there were some trends in this direction for books like the Roman Missal. The missal of the papal court had become quite popular in the Middle Ages, particularly the revision by Haymo of Faversham, the general of the Franciscan Order (1240–44). His revision was eventually adopted by the papal court itself and formed the basis of the first printed missal in 1474 [illustration 193]. Some estimate that there were over 325 printings of this

Missale Romanum (Latin, "Roman Missal") between 1474 and 1570, when it was replaced by the 1570 missal.

The fourteenth session of the Council of Trent anticipated the work on liturgical books in its decree on Scripture (8 April 1546). In this decree, the council fathers ordered that books of Scripture and commentaries could not be printed without ecclesiastical approval [quotation 293]. On 20 July 1562, Pius IV (d. 1565) appointed a commission to compile a list of abuses in the Mass. The first list, circulated on 8 August 1562, was long and implied enormous work for a council that was drawing to a close [quotation 279]. While condemning some of the most blatant abuses in the twenty-second session (17 September 1562), the council left the reform of the liturgy and its books to the pope [quotation 294].

Initially, only the missal and breviary were to be reformed. Their appearance in 1568 and 1570 led to the adoption of the Roman breviary, missal, and rubrics by the whole Latin church. Considered more a purification of the existing rites than original works, this Roman Missal and breviary were imposed on all dioceses and religious communities whose own liturgical traditions were less than two hundred years old. The hoped-for uniformity eventually achieved with these books was hailed in the bull of Pius V, printed in every Roman Missal from 1570 until 1965 [quotation 295]. Such uniformity could not have been achieved without Gutenberg's contribution. The success of the new breviary and missal encouraged further reform. The Roman martyrology was promulgated in 1584, the pontifical in 1595, and the Roman ritual in 1614. Though minor revisions of these rites occurred in succeeding centuries, the liturgical books published in the fifty years after Trent remained in force until the second half of the twentieth century.

Summary

Similar to the different ways that Roman Catholics and Protestants developed music and architecture during the sixteenth century, the different ways that various segments of the Reformation and Counter-Reformation used the printing press are notable. For Protestant reformers, the printing press was largely an instrument of change. Innumerable orders of worship rolled off primitive presses into the hands of ministers and laity alike. These vernacular rites, economically and linguistically accessible to many believers, did much to support the belief in the priesthood of the laity, a primary tenet of the reform. While most Protestants, however, used the printing press as an agent of change, the Roman Catholic Church used the printing press to achieve uniformity and obedience—a goal shared by Thomas

Cranmer who, contrary to other Protestant reformers, promoted an ideal of uniformity in English worship. Texts and rubrics approved by Rome were reproduced for the entire church. These Latin texts, however, were produced only for the clergy. In the seventeenth century there was a movement in France concerned with making the liturgy more understandable to ordinary people. To that end Josef de Voisin published a French translation of the missal of the Council of Trent in 1660. This work prompted a swift papal condemnation [quotation 296], which not only suppressed that translation movement but provided the foundation for a general prohibition of translating Roman liturgical books, a prohibition that lasted into the nineteenth century. Contrary to this prohibition, many unofficial prayer books for the laity did appear, such as the first U.S. vernacular missal, *The Roman Missal, Translated into the English Language for the Use of the Laity* (1822), by Bishop John England of Charleston. Such translations, however, were usually not matched by moves to draw the people into active participation in the liturgy. Rather, they tended to encourage private prayer in the midst of what was supposed to be a public prayer, ironically led by a priest praying privately at the altar. Such use of vernacular prayer books in public worship lends credence to Marshall McLuhan's insight that print is the technology of individualism (p. 206).

VESSELS

As already noted, the size and style of eucharistic vessels often is related to the size and architectural style of the worship spaces in which they are used. Domestic spaces were complemented by domestic vessels, imperial buildings required impressive cups and plates forged of previous materials, and ornate Gothic churches were the setting for chalices and monstrances adorned with bells and tiny Gothic arches. After the sixteenth century, a visible relationship between the surrounding architecture and eucharistic vessels was still apparent in some segments of Roman Catholic worship. Within the Protestant churches, divergent trends such as the emphasis on communion for everyone from the cup and the decline in the frequency of Eucharist led to disparate and sometimes contradictory developments in eucharistic vessels.

Roman Catholic Vessels

Following the Council of Trent, no new genres of vessels developed within the Roman Catholic Church. The major structural change,

Quotation 296: *It has come to our attention, and we perceive it with great sorrow, that in the kingdom of France certain sons of perdition, curious about novelties, which is dangerous to souls, and disdainful of the regulations and practice of the Church, have had the audacity to translate into French the Roman Missal, which until now has been written in Latin, following the usage approved for so long in the Church; once it was translated they had it put into print, thereby making it available to every person of whatever rank or sex. Thus they attempted by a timorous effort to cast down and trample the comprehensive majesty the Latin language has given to the sacrosanct rites and to expose the dignity of the divine mysteries to the vulgar crowd. . . . We abhor and detest this novelty which deforms the perpetual beauty of the Church and which easily engenders disobedience, temerity, audacity, sedition, schism, and many other evils. Therefore . . . we damn, reprove, and interdict perpetually the Missal already translated into French by anyone or which in the future might be translated and published by someone. (Pope Alexander VII [12 January 1661], in Swidler, Aufklärung Catholicism, p. 75)*

Quotation 297: *We decree that the Eucharist, viaticum, or the body of Christ as well as chrism, holy oil and the oil of the sick—in order that they may be cared for with appropriate devotion in a distinct and secure place—may be stored in churches or in sacristies in places designated and prepared for this. (Synod of Ravenna [1311], in Mansi, Sacrorum Conciliorum)*

Quotation 298: *The bishop should take the utmost care so that in cathedrals, collegiate churches, parishes and any other churches where the sacred Eucharist is customarily reserved, it should be located on the main altar, except in case of necessity or for what seems to be another valid reason. (Council of Milan [1565], in Mansi, Sacrorum Conciliorum)*

194. Tabernacle built into the high altar in Modena, Italy. (After Anson, p. 88)

195. Baroque chalice from the seventeenth century.

noted previously, was the wedding of the tabernacle to the high altar. In effect, this development was a final stage in the tabernacle's transition from a "vessel" to an architectural feature. Stylistically, the baroque and rococo styles were especially influential in the design of chalices and monstrances.

Tabernacles   Before the sixteenth century, the Eucharist was usually reserved in a pyx suspended over the altar, in a sacristy cupboard, in a wall niche in the church, or in a sacrament house. Although there are instances of the Eucharist being reserved on the altar as early as the ninth century, this was a relatively rare occurrence before the fifteenth century, and clearly only one option for reservation [quotation 297]. During the sixteenth century, reservation in a tabernacle affixed to the main altar became a preferred option in Italy [illustration 194], as reported in various diocesan and provincial synods [quotation 298]. It is this new and somewhat regional preference that Charles Borromeo canonizes in his *Instructions on the Architecture and Furnishings of Churches* (1577). The 1584 ritual for the diocese of Rome contained the first explicit Roman directive for placing the tabernacle on the altar. A similar directive was included in the Roman Ritual of 1614 [quotation 299]. As Pierre Jounel notes, however, unlike the other ritual books produced after the Council of Trent, the Roman Ritual was only proposed for—not imposed upon—the universal church (Martimort, pp. 18–19). The propositional character of this ritual implicitly recognized the wide diversity of practices in things like the placement of tabernacles as well as the innovative nature of such new proposals. While the Roman Ritual was widely accepted, wall tabernacles in France and sacrament houses in Germany continued to be commonplace. Only in 1863 did the Sacred Congregation of Rites forbid churches to reintroduce the practice of reserving the Eucharist in sacrament houses, suspended pyxes, or other ancient methods of reservation. This did not mean that churches that could demonstrate an uninterrupted custom of one of these alternate forms of reservation had to abandon them. Rather, it simply prohibited old or new churches that did not practice such forms of reservation from adopting them. Such a directive was not surprising and simply underscored the custom of the era not only to place tabernacles on the altar but also to build them into the church's high altar. Ultimately, the tabernacle was transformed from an independent eucharistic vessel to a facet of a church's architecture.

Chalices and Monstrances   Most of the artistic developments in Roman Catholic vessels during the post-Tridentine era concerned vessels that had little to do with the sacramental communion of the faithful. The removal of the cup from the laity in the previous era contributed to the standardization of the chalice's shape and size. Chalices only needed to hold a small quantity of wine and a few drops of water for the priest's communion. While there continued to be artistic elaborations of chalices, these had virtually no ritual function. Because of their size relative to the priest's paten and the artistic possibilities with a vessel that stood upright rather than lay directly on the altar, chalices were usually the most beautiful eucharistic vessel employed during the Mass. Frequently, chalices as well as monstrances in this era reflected the baroque and rococo architecture of the period. The conical shape, so popular in the Gothic era, often was abandoned for a rounded bell- or tulip-shaped cup. Angular stems with single nodes and geometric bases were replaced by rounded stems with softly defined nodes that often melded into two or three smaller nodes and terminated in a mound-like base [illustration 195].

196. Baroque monstrance from Klosterneuberg (1712–14), Germany.

197. The ornate high altar of the Toledo Cathedral (ca. 1500) includes a statue of Saint Mary in the center section of the lowest level; an enormous monstrance is above the statue.

Monstrances often reflected the architecture of post-Tridentine churches as well. Rather than the static and geometric monstrances of the Gothic or Renaissance periods, baroque monstrances often were exuberant vessels sometimes adorned with bejeweled rays of precious metals emanating from the host at the center [illustration 196]. Sometimes the lavishness and even oversized dimensions of a monstrance were necessary in order for it to stand out in a church building whose lavish interiors could easily dwarf a more modest vessel. An extreme example is the enormous monstrance constructed in the late Gothic style for Toledo Cathedral [illustration 197]. Like the tabernacles of the sixteenth century, such monstrances were no longer simply eucharistic vessels, but a permanent design feature of what could be considered eucharistic architecture. Besides these monumental architectural features, it is also possible to find—often in Spain—monumental processional monstrances, particularly important for the feast of Corpus Christi [illustration 198].

Protestant Vessels

As we have seen, various Protestant groups held divergent views on the role and frequency of eucharistic celebrations. Luther, for example,

198. A Spanish processional monstrance.

considered weekly Eucharist normative. Zwingli preferred a weekly preaching service, with Eucharist celebrated only four times a year. Emphasis on the Word of God in virtually every segment of Protestantism, coupled with the influences of pietism and rationalism during the eighteenth century, contributed to a general decline in the frequency of Eucharist, even in the most sacramental traditions. Thus, in a sacramental revival such as Methodism [quotation 300], the ideal of weekly Eucharist in practice eventually became three communion services a year.

These divergent theological views and pastoral practices produced a similar divergence in eucharistic vessels. In some places beautiful new eucharistic vessels were created, while in other places such vessels were virtually eliminated. When new vessels were required after a purge of the old chalices and patens, domestic pieces often were used, similar to what first happened with worship vessels at the birth of Christianity. In time, new types of vessels developed. We will consider these developments under the rubrics of adaptation, elimination, substitution, and invention.

Adaptation   Luther and Cranmer were two of the reformers who held the Eucharist in high esteem. Not surprisingly, their traditions and those influenced by them produced communion vessels that were fine works of art. In Germany, for example, this meant crafting vessels similar to those once used in Roman Catholic worship, but with a distinctive Protestant aesthetic. There were beautiful *Abendmahlskelche* (German, literally "Lord's Supper cups" or chalices) crafted for use during the Eucharist [illustration 199] as well as *Hostiendosen* (German, literally "Host boxes" or pyxes) [illustration 200]. As previously noted [illustration 179], there was a necessary change in the pictorial arts in reformed churches, which often, for example, eliminated images of saints and relied upon more biblically founded images. So, too, in these newly crafted eucharistic vessels, there is a new Protestant aesthetic, evident in the scripturally based iconography, such as vines and grapes reminiscent of John 15, or an image of the Lamb from Revelation 5. Sometimes a Scripture passage is engraved directly on the vessel accompanying such imagery, such as a seventeenth-century communion cup from northern Germany with the inscription *Ego sum Pastor bonus* (Latin, "I am the good Shepherd," John 10:11) over an image of Christ as the Good Shepherd.

Elimination and Substitution   Many Reformation churches during the sixteenth century underwent purges, including the destruction of images, the elimination of architectural barriers, the removal of tabernacles, and the dismantling of pipe organs. The need for some reformers to establish a definitive break with the traditional Roman

199. A silver chalice created for an Evangelical community at Oberwinter, Germany (1659); approximately seven inches high.

200. Pyx or host container from a Reformation church in Essen, in the Rhineland of Germany, made in 1685.

201. Large silver salver similar to one transformed into a "credence paten" given to the church of St. Martin's, Salisbury in 1662.

Catholic Mass contributed to the elimination of many eucharistic vessels. In England, for example, during the reign of Edward VI (d. 1553) it was mandated that all but one cup and plate were to be removed from every church. Yet, as Eamon Duffy has documented, local adherence to such demands was sometimes slow and often reluctant [quotation 301]. Monstrances and pyxes, as well as cups and plates, were destroyed, sold, or given away [quotation 302].

On the continent, a simplified Eucharist celebrated only three or four times a year often resulted in a drastic reduction in the number of sacred vessels retained by a particular congregation. When the need arose for new vessels, it was customary in many places on the continent, in England, and in the New World to borrow secular vessels. Tankards, porringers, wine glasses, and mugs became communion cups for many congregations. A similar array of trays and plates held the eucharistic bread. Sometimes these vessels were exceedingly plain, like the wooden plates that Zwingli preferred. Other times vessels that originally graced the tables of the wealthy were donated to churches for use [illustration 201].

Invention The restoration of the cup to the laity by the reformers eventually produced two new vessels for wine. Special vessels for carrying wine before its consecration had appeared by the fourth century. Such vessels were emptied into chalices, which then held the wine for the duration of the service. Evidence indicates that during the Reformation containers other than the chalice held the wine before and after its consecration. Flagons or tankards were used to convey the wine to the table, where some was poured into a cup. Because the cups of the period were seldom large enough to hold sufficient wine for all the faithful, a large amount of wine remained in these flagons, which were used to refill the cups during communion. Some of the flagons or tankards, produced for domestic use, were donated to churches. Others of this type of vessel were crafted intentionally for worship purposes [illustration 202].

Another vessel that resulted from returning the "cup" to the community was the communion tray. This U.S. contribution to eucharistic vessels consisted of a tray that held several small cups for wine [illustration 203]. Such trays appear to have been a nineteenth-century invention. Concern for hygiene apparently contributed to this development in the same century that Louis Pasteur (d. 1895) and others established a basic understanding of the nature and spread of bacteria. The use of individual cups—which Daniel Sack links to a physician in Rochester, New York, about 1896 (p. 37)—placed popularized scientific theory and pastoral convenience above the ancient symbol of one cup for the one community of faith.

A second U.S. contribution to be noted concerns, not the shape of the communion vessel, but its content. According to Sack, a

Methodist preacher turned dentist by the name of Thomas Welch was bothered by the use of alcohol for communion. His search for a nonalcoholic replacement resulted in "grape juice." While it was his son who founded the company that produced Welch's Grape Juice, it was the vision of Charles Welch [quotation 303] that eventually led to the widespread practice among some Protestants in the U.S. of substituting grape juice for wine during the Lord's Supper. As most reformers had reverted to ordinary, leavened bread in the sixteenth century, this nineteenth-century development led to the irony summed up by James White as "real wine for Roman Catholics, real bread for Protestants."

Summary

Although some changes in vessels occurred during this period, the time after the Reformation was not primarily an era when communion was emphasized. Consequently, communion vessels were not a significant liturgical concern. Roman Catholics were accustomed to watching the consecrated host and the chalice during the elevation at Mass, or watching the consecrated host during periods of adoration as it was exposed in a monstrance. The reception of communion for the faithful remained an infrequent event. Only the priest received the wine, and it was his chalice that received some elaboration in this period. More significantly, the tabernacle seemed to take a final step in its evolution, as it changed from a portable vessel into an architectural element. In the process, it was moved to the center of the worship space, a place restricted to the priest and designated ministers.

Generalizations about Protestant vessels are more difficult. In some places, tabernacles were retained and used, in other places they were retained but remained unused, and in still other places they were dismantled or destroyed. Some Protestant communities continued to make and use beautiful crafted vessels, while others reverted to the ancient Christian tradition of using cups and plates found in the homes of believers. It was the reintroduction of lay communion from the cup that led to the appearance of new vessels for some Protestant communities during this period.

202. Eighteenth-century Lutheran flagon.

EUCHARISTIC THEOLOGY

Disagreements about eucharistic theology and practice are neither new nor particular to this period of Christianity. From the birth of Christianity there have been questions about what Eucharist is, what it does, what ritual elements should be included, who is invited, and who should lead. Differing opinions on these issues have sometimes

203. A contemporary communion tray.

led to heated debate, condemnations, and even divisions between Christians. Never before, however, had these disagreements led to such a fracturing of Christianity. It is true that the division between Western Christianity and Eastern Orthodoxy in 1054 was a scandalous fracturing of the Body of Christ, but that division was not at its core a disagreement about liturgy or Eucharist. Issues of real presence, the number of sacraments, the role of ordination, the effect of sacramental confession, and the liturgical role of the Word of God, however, were central to the splintering of Christianity in the sixteenth century. Furthermore, it was not simply the theory about these issues that concerned the reformers but the pastoral practices and their effects on the lives and faith of ordinary believers. Unlike a Paschasius or Berengar or Thomas Aquinas, many of the eucharistic thinkers of the sixteenth century were thus concerned about changing rituals and not simply theologizing in the abstract. Consequently, the Reformation spawned a breadth of eucharistic diversity in theology and practice never before seen. It also provoked strong and restrictive responses that contributed to the polarization of Christians in the West during this era.

Real Presence

In *The Babylonian Captivity of the Church*, Martin Luther sounded many themes that would resonate throughout the Reformation. One of these was a "captivity" in which he believed Christians were metaphorically "carried away" from the teaching of the Scriptures by the "monstrous word and . . . monstrous idea" of transubstantiation. Luther refuted this idea on biblical grounds, noting that this was not the teaching of the church for twelve hundred years and that it even contradicted the teaching of Aristotle [see above p. 229]. Luther did not condemn people for believing in transubstantiation but argued that Christians should be allowed to hold other formulations of real presence. He clearly believed that Christ's real flesh and blood were present in real bread and wine—both "substances" together. This view is sometimes known as "consubstantiation," although Luther never used the term and explained the coexistence of Christ and the elements in a more pastoral vein [quotation 304].

As we noted in the previous chapter [quotation 273], there was a wide range of belief during the late Middle Ages about the exact meaning of the term "transubstantiation," and many held for the position that Luther eventually embraced. As Macy notes, however, theologies that held for the coexistence of elements of bread and wine along with the presence of Christ came under increasing criticism. Already at the end of the thirteenth century, Thomas Aquinas

Quotation 304: *If we heed the simple sense of language we can say of a glowing piece of iron, "It is fire," or, "The iron lying there is pure fire" . . . [this] is nothing more than saying that the iron and fire are in each other, so that where the iron is there the fire is also. And no one is so stupid that he here needs some great and clever sophistry to tell him that wood is not stone, fire is not iron, water is not earth. Since now iron is fire and fire is iron, according to the simple sense of language, and the two are in each other and as one, though each retains its own nature . . . "This is my body" . . . would mean the same as saying bread and body are as one or in each other as fire and iron.* (Martin Luther, *Against the Heavenly Prophets*, in *Luther's Works*, vol. 40, p. 196)

204. Zwingli by Hans Asper (d. 1571).

held that this teaching was erroneous and not an orthodox interpretation of the teaching on transubstantiation of the Fourth Lateran Council. The position was eventually rejected as an orthodox teaching by the fifteenth century, although it continued to be taught by some critics of Aquinas's transubstantiation theology, such as John Wycliffe.

Virtually all of the significant reform theologians of the sixteenth century agreed with Luther in rejecting the notion of transubstantiation, which was often incorrectly attributed to Aquinas. While there was unanimity around rejecting what had become the official teaching of the Roman Catholic Church on this topic, there was no such agreement on the appropriate theology of presence to accept, as the meeting at Marburg so pointedly underscored. The reformer who disagreed most with Luther and had the most divergent view of eucharistic presence was Zwingli [illustration 204].

While there are many factors that contributed to Zwingli's particular views on eucharistic presence, two seem especially important. First was his belief that nothing physical could affect the soul. The scriptural foundation for this belief was "It is the spirit that gives life; the flesh is useless" (John 6:63), a text that Zwingli inserted as the gospel in his reformed eucharistic liturgy of 1525. This idea pervaded much of Zwingli's reforming efforts and in part explains, for example, why he rejected music, which he felt was a worldly distraction and had no place in worship. Faith and belief for Zwingli were tuned to spiritual, not created or visible things. Thus there was a kind of dualism in his teaching that created a very clear division, even opposition, between the spiritual and the material. Sacraments were exercises of the spiritual and not material world. A second important issue shaping Zwingli's sacramental theology was the concept of oath, which we have already noted as one of the earliest meanings of "sacrament" [quotation 109]. For Zwingli, engaging in a sacrament was essentially announcing publicly one's commitment to God. It was not, as Luther and others held, only and essentially a sign of God's covenant with us. Rather, Zwingli placed new stress on the sacraments as ritual occasions for people to profess their faith, rather than as moments for receiving special graces.

In light of these foundational ideas, Zwingli held that Christ's presence in the Eucharist was spiritual or metaphorical rather than substantial. He interpreted the Last Supper words of Jesus, "this is my Body," to mean "this signifies my Body." He did not believe that the consecrated bread was the Body of Christ, but more a kind of visual aid to help the baptized announce belief in Christ, a belief that must be manifest in a truly Christian life [quotation 305]. As James White notes, the emphasis for Zwingli was not really on the "this is" part of Christ's Last Supper text, but much more on his command to "do this." In contrast to Luther, who was quite traditional in his focus on the eucharistic elements, Zwingli turned his eucharistic focus to the community, "stating in a new way the reality of Christ's presence as a transubstantiation of the congregation rather than of the elements" (White, *Protestant Worship*, p. 59).

There were many other important reforming voices offering new formulations for understanding the nature of Christ's eucharistic presence. John Calvin, who held something of a middle ground between Luther and Zwingli, believed that communicants really shared in the Body and Blood of Christ, but that presence was not on the altar but in heaven. Calvin's developed theology of the Holy Spirit allowed him to argue that the Holy Spirit was the only true *vinculum communicationis* (Latin, "bond of communication") between Christ and the baptized. The Holy Spirit, according to Calvin, does not bring about Christ's presence in the Eucharist on the altar, but unites us through the visible sign of the sacrament to his body that is in heaven [quotation 306]. The varying views of Calvin, Zwingli, and Luther illustrate something of the diversity of theological perspectives among the Protestant reformers and caution against any broad generalizations about what Protestants believe about real presence.

Quotation 305: *What does eating then mean? Just this that you proclaim before your brethren that you are a member of Christ, one of those who trust in Christ; and further, it pledges you to a Christian life, so that if you do not renounce your sinful ways, you are cut off from the other members."* (Ulrich Zwingli, in Brilioth, *Eucharistic Faith and Practice*, p. 158)

Quotation 306: *For as we do not doubt that Christ's body is limited by the general characteristics common to all human bodies, and is contained in heaven . . . until Christ return in judgment, so we deem it utterly unlawful to draw it back under these corruptive elements or to imagine it to be present everywhere. And there is no need of this for us to enjoy a participation in it, since the Lord bestows this benefit upon us through his Spirit so that we may be made one in body, spirit, and soul with him. The "bond of this connection" is therefore the Spirit of Christ, with whom we are joined in unity, and is like a channel through which all that Christ himself is and has is conveyed to us.* (John Calvin, *Institutes of the Christian Religion,* 4.17.12, in Battles, II:1373)

205. Council of Trent in session.

The definitive Roman Catholic response to these varying views and challenges came in October 1551, during the thirteenth session of the Council of Trent [illustration 205]. In its decree on the Eucharist, the council fathers announced that Christ is "truly, really and substantially contained" in the Eucharist under the appearances of bread and wine. Employing the language and perspectives of Thomas Aquinas, that same decree further stated that the consecration brought about a change through which the whole substance of the bread was changed into the Body of Christ, and the whole substance of the wine was changed into the Blood of Christ. It also, somewhat cautiously, used the language of transubstantiation. Given all of the debate on this topic since the thirteenth century, not only among the Protestant reformers but even among so many Roman Catholic theologians, the council decreed that this change was "properly and appropriately called" (Latin, *convenienter et proprie . . . est appellata*) transubstantiation. More pointedly, the council fathers appended a series of canons to the end of the decree on the Eucharist that forcefully condemned, among other things, those who did not hold for the substantial change, those who taught that Christ was only present as in a sign, and those who held that the substance of the bread continued after the consecration [quotation 307].

Quotation 307: *Canon 1: If anyone denies that in the sacrament of the most Holy Eucharist are contained truly, really and substantially the body and blood together with the soul and divinity of our Lord Jesus Christ, and consequently the whole Christ, but says that he is in it only as in a sign, or figure or force, let him be anathema. Canon 2: If anyone says that in the sacred and holy sacrament of the Eucharist the substance of the bread and wine remains conjointly with the body and blood of our Lord Jesus Christ, and denies that wonderful and singular change of the whole substance of the bread into the body and the whole substance of the wine into the blood, the appearances only of bread and wine remaining, which change the Catholic Church most aptly calls transubstantiation, let him be anathema.* (Decree on the Eucharist [1551], Council of Trent, in *Canons and Decrees of the Council of Trent*, p. 149)

Sacrifice and Priesthood

Another highly contested theological issue in the sixteenth century was the relationship between Eucharist and sacrifice. Martin Luther, in his *Babylonian Captivity*, challenged the Roman Catholic Church's official stance on sacrifice, considering it the "most wicked" of the three captivities (the other two being the removal of the communion cup from the people and the teaching of transubstantiation). His fundamental concern, as already apparent in his challenge to the use of indulgences, was that certain religious practices were being treated as somehow giving human beings leverage over God. Many religious practices, in Luther's view, were being treated like commerce [quotation 308]. Thus it was not simply a theological idea that Luther opposed, but a central pastoral practice gone awry. Instead of thinking of the Eucharist as a sacrifice, Luther emphasized that the Lord's Supper was Christ's testament and promise of the forgiveness of sin. Rather than something we offer God, he argued that the Eucharist was something that God offered us, a divine gift instead of a human work.

Just as there was a broad consensus among Protestant reformers in rejecting the concept of transubstantiation, there was virtually unanimous acceptance among this same group of Luther's critique of the Eucharist as sacrifice. In the public debates on religion in 1523, for example, Zwingli proclaimed that the Mass was not a sacrifice, but was a commemoration of the one sacrifice of the cross and a seal of redemption through Christ. Calvin also sought to protect what he considered the biblical heritage of the once-and-for-all sacrifice of Christ on the cross and thus considered it "devilish" to think of the eucharistic celebration as a sacrifice.

In part these reformers, like Luther, were responding to the sometimes scandalous practices associated with stipends and the "buying" of Masses for every need, but especially for the dead. Corruption was rampant in this system, which gave many the impression that graces and even salvation could be bought and sold. In the words of James White, it was difficult for ordinary laypeople of the period to consider the offering of a Mass "other than as a bribe to God" (*Protestant Worship*, p. 39). Related to this, and troubling to many people on both sides of the reform, was the frequent lack of connection between the offering of the Mass and the call to Christian discipleship. The threat of final judgment did not seem to spur many believers to radical Christian living, especially if they could acquire the right indulgences, set aside sufficient resources for, or rely upon relatives to have Masses celebrated for them after their death. The system of stipends and the offering of Masses, founded on questionable approaches to the doctrine of eucharistic sacrifice,

Quotation 308: *The holy sacrament has been turned into mere merchandise, a market, and a profit-making business. Hence participations, brotherhoods, intercessions, merits, anniversaries, memorial days and the like wares are bought and sold, traded and bartered, in the church.* (Martin Luther, *The Babylonian Captivity of the Church*, in *Luther's Works* 36:35-36)

supported an image of salvation more akin to magic than one of sustained personal conversion and commitment. This is not to suggest that there were few committed Roman Catholics among the faithful; they were probably as numerous in this period as in any age. Unfortunately, the sacramental system of the time did not always enhance their journey into discipleship.

Related to this critique of sacrifice was a rethinking of the priesthood so central to this offering action. Luther again took the lead here, hoping to remove what he perceived as intermediaries between God and the baptized. In his *Babylonian Captivity* he argued that all Christians are "equally priests" and all have the "same power in respect to the word and sacrament." These ideas were not completely original and, for example, could be found in the previous century in the teachings of the followers of John Wycliffe known as the Lollards. In his open letter to German nobility, Luther offered a scriptural exposition demonstrating that through baptism all are consecrated to the priesthood [quotation 309]. While his language can sometimes sound harsh, Luther's more moderate (what some reformers even considered a "conservative") approach to reform was apparent in the way he believed the practice of ordination should continue, though he did not consider ordination a sacrament but a "churchly rite." In Luther's thought, this was an appropriate way communities designated their pastoral leader and committed him to the work of administering the means of grace.

There was widespread agreement outside of Rome on this concept of the "priesthood of all believers," and it became a central tenet among most Protestant reformers. Most Protestant communities also maintained a clergy and taught that ordination was ordinarily required in order to preside at the two sacraments of baptism and Eucharist. Such ordination, however, was a matter of good order and appropriate authorization and did not, from the perspective of most Protestants, change the ordained in any theological sense. Because of this understanding, many of the medieval trappings of priesthood did not survive in the Protestant Reformation. Luther considered the Mass vestments, like many other externals, *adiaphora* (Greek, "indifferent things") or nonessentials and he did not forbid their use, which continued for some time among Lutherans. Others, like Andreas Karlstadt, opposed this practice, and in his radical celebration of the Christmas service in 1521 (see above, p. 271), this university professor—who conferred the doctorate on Luther at the University of Wittenberg—wore his black academic gown. This practice became commonplace, and even Luther was depicted wearing such a vestment [illustration 179]. This "Geneva gown" became commonplace among sixteenth-century reformers, who also rejected

Quotation 309: *We are all consecrated priests through baptism, as St. Peter says in 1 Peter 2 "You are a royal priesthood and a priestly realm . . ." When a bishop consecrates it is nothing else than that in the place and stead of the whole community, all of whom have like power, he takes a person and charges him to exercise this power on behalf of the others.* (Martin Luther, *To the Christian Nobility of the German Nation* [1520], in *Luther's Works* 44:128)

Quotation 310: *Since either through the depravity of the times or through the indifference and corruption of men many things seem already to have crept in that are foreign to the dignity of so great a sacrifice, in order that the honor and worship due to it may for the glory of God and the edification of the faithful be restored, the holy council decrees that the local ordinaries shall be zealously concerned and be bound to prohibit and abolish all those things which either covetousness, which is a serving of idols, or irreverence, which can scarcely be separated from ungodliness, or superstition, a false imitation of true piety, have introduced . . . as regards avarice, [they shall] absolutely forbid conditions of compensations of whatever kind, bargains, and whatever is given for the celebration of new Masses; also those importunate and unbecoming demands, rather than requests, for alms and other things of this kind which border on simoniacal taint or certainly savor of filthy lucre.* (Council of Trent, Decree concerning the things to be observed and avoided in the Celebration of Mass [1562], in *Canons and Decrees of the Council of Trent*, pp. 150–51)

Quotation 311: Canon 2: *If anyone says that by those words, "Do this for a commemoration of me," Christ did not institute the Apostles priests; or did not ordain that they and other priests should offer His own body and blood, let him be anathema.* Canon 3: *If anyone says that the sacrifice of the Mass is one only of praise and thanksgiving; or that it is a mere commemoration of the sacrifice consummated on the cross but not a propitiatory one; or that it profits him only who receives, and ought not to be offered for the living and the dead, for sins, punishments, satisfactions, and other necessities, let him be anathema.* (Council of Trent, Canons on the Sacrifice of the Mass [1562], in *Canons and Decrees of the Council of Trent*, p. 149)

the language of "priest" and referred to their clergy as pastors or presbyters. The issue of vestments was more controversial in sixteenth-century England, where eventually the directions found in the first Book of Common Prayer were imposed, requiring clergy to wear a cope for celebrations of the Eucharist and a surplice for all other presiding.

The Roman Catholic Church recognized that abusive eucharistic practices abounded, and the Council of Trent in 1562 promulgated a decree noting some of these abuses [quotation 310]. At the same time, the council did not shrink in any way from speaking of the "Sacrifice of the Mass" and issued a decree on the "Doctrine Concerning the Sacrifice of the Mass" in 1562. In actuality, the council used virtually no other image for the Eucharist except that of sacrifice. Furthermore, since the offering of the Mass was so closely tied to its understanding of priesthood—for Roman Catholics believed at the time that it was the priest who offered the sacrifice—the council condemned any who denied the role of the ordained priesthood, particularly in regard to the offering of the Mass [quotation 311].

As David Power has recognized, these two radically different systems of worship—one focused on Eucharist as testament or gift, the other emphasizing offering and sacrifice—need to be understood in terms of the differing images of society and divergent political forces at work among Protestant and Roman Catholic communities [quotation 276]. The more radical reforms, like those of Zwingli and Calvin, took place in communities that were exhibiting what we would call democratic tendencies. We have already noted how a small confederation of states in what is now Switzerland united against the Holy Roman Emperor and achieved independence at the end of the fifteenth century. This broader context allows one to understand how, for example, an elected town council in a Swiss city like Zurich could take over responsibility for religious decisions, including those about worship, and that such worship would itself appear more democratic. While not as advanced a form of democracy as Switzerland, even within the Holy Roman Empire of the fifteenth century there was a recognized need for reform, fueled in part by local rulers who were seeking more independence from the emperor and the pope. Thus in the mid-1400s there emerged loose confederations of German states, including Saxony, that collectively struggled for more local control. By 1489 the representative gathering of all states within the empire (the imperial diet or Reichstag) allowed for the first time the participation of representatives from imperial cities in the decision making. In 1495 the Diet of Worms even established a court to adjudicate disputes among princes. While the emperor and princes certainly held the balance of power, such developments would continue to challenge their power.

Within this changing social order one can understand why the democratization of worship, the removal of priestly intermediaries, an emphasis on the priesthood of all believers, the preference for a less hierarchical eucharistic theology based on koinonia rather than sacrifice, and a preference for the accessibility of vernacular languages in the Bible, hymnody, and liturgy would be embraced. In the Roman Catholic Church, on the other hand, no such democratic moves were officially supported, and an unquestioned monarchy continued. While the pope was eventually to cede his position as a temporal monarch with the loss of the papal states in the nineteenth century, his spiritual leadership was virtually unchallengeable and complete, culminating in the promulgation of the doctrine of papal infallibility at the First Vatican Council in 1870. Within this realm priestly sacrifice, traditional Latin texts, prohibitions against the vernacular, and a clear theological and political division between clergy and laity continued to make sense.

Inculturation

Although the term "inculturation" [quotation 312] does not appear until the twentieth century, the mutual influence between culture and worship has been occurring since the birth of Christianity. Often that process is a gradual one. The Protestant Reformation can, in one sense, well be understood as a radical move toward inculturation, whereby certain cultural or contextual sensibilities engaged the traditional theologies and worship practices of the church, and something new emerged. While it can appear that, in rejecting the positions of Luther and other Protestant reformers the Roman Catholic Church rejected any process of inculturation, a more nuanced perspective is useful.

Officially, the Roman Catholic Church in the sixteenth century recognized that there were several ancient rites that existed alongside the Roman Rite. Some of these emerged from religious communities, like the Cistercian or the Dominican Rites; others were related to specific geographic areas, like the Ambrosian Rite of Milan or the Mozarabic (also called "Visigothic" or "Old Spanish") Rite, which developed in Spain. In promulgating the Tridentine Roman Missal of 1570, Pius V acknowledged that any such rite over two hundred years old was allowed to continue. At the same time, this pope, who was very concerned about uniformity in worship [quotation 295], gave permission for those who celebrated according to other rites to use this new Roman Missal [quotation 313].

Aside from these officially sanctioned expressions of what could be considered liturgical adaptations, there were innumerable other practices and experiments in adapting the liturgy to various cultural

Quotation 312: *One may define liturgical inculturation as the process whereby pertinent elements of a local culture are integrated into the texts, rites, symbols, and institutions employed by a local church for its worship. Integration means that the cultural components influence the liturgical pattern of composing formularies, proclaiming them, performing ritual actions, and symbolizing the liturgical message in art forms.* (Chupungco, "Liturgy and Inculturation," in *Handbook for Liturgical Studies* II:339)

Quotation 313: *This new rite alone is to be used unless approval of the practice of saying Mass differently was given at the very time of the institution and confirmation of the church by the Apostolic See at least 200 years ago, or unless there has prevailed a custom of a similar kind which has been continuously followed for a period of not less than 200 years, in which most cases we in no way rescind their above-mentioned prerogative or custom. However, if this Missal, which we have seen fit to publish, be more agreeable to these latter, we grant them permission to celebrate Mass according to its rite, provided they have the consent of their bishop or prelate or of their whole chapter.* (Pius V, *Quo Primum* [14 July 1570])

contexts. Sometimes, as noted above, this meant the inclusion of vernacular hymnody within the official Latin Mass [quotation 287]. On the continent, a more radical form of liturgical adaptation occurred in France during the seventeenth and eighteenth centuries. Attempting to reassert their Gallican (from Latin *Gallicanus*, referring to the ancient church of "Gaul" or France) heritage, and insisting on more political independence from Rome, French civic and ecclesiastical leaders undertook various theological and legislative actions that affirmed the role of the French monarch over the pope, and supported distinctive forms of liturgical music and worship in French. This "neo-Gallican" movement produced a large body of chant, new missals, breviaries, and other liturgical books. Klauser estimates that by the French Revolution at the end of the eighteenth century, 80 out of 130 dioceses had abandoned the liturgy of Trent and were following a neo-Gallican form of liturgy.

This era was also a time of great exploration and missionary activity. Many of the liturgical adaptations that accompanied these missions were undocumented and have been lost. Of those that were documented, one of the most fascinating is that which occurred in China in the seventeenth century. Matteo Ricci (d. 1610) [illustration 206] was an Italian Jesuit missionary who arrived in China at the end of the sixteenth century. A gifted linguist, Ricci was a celebrated intellectual at the court of Peking where he became the court mathematician. Culturally astute, Ricci recognized that the teachings of the revered philosopher Confucius (d. 479 B.C.E.) were foundational for the life of the Chinese elite whom Ricci and the other Jesuits were intent on converting to Roman Catholicism. Belief in Confucianism included the practice of certain rituals, especially ceremonies for the honoring of ancestors. Ricci and his companions argued that these rituals were not superstitious, did not treat the ancestors like idols, and should be allowed for Chinese Catholics. After Ricci's death and following almost a century of controversy, Rome decreed that Chinese Catholics could not partake in these practices, which were condemned [quotation 314]. Pope Benedict XIV (d. 1758), who affirmed this decree of condemnation, further required that all missionaries to the region take an oath upholding the Roman Catholic Church's teaching on this matter and reject the rituals of Confucius—an oath that was in effect until withdrawn by the Propagation of the Faith in 1939.

Quotation 314: *2. The spring and autumn worship of Confucius, together with the worship of ancestors, is not allowed among Catholic converts. . . .*
3. Chinese officials and successful candidates in the metropolitan, provincial, or prefectural examinations, if they have been converted to Roman Catholicism, are not allowed to worship in Confucian temples on the first and fifteenth days of each month. . . . 4. No Chinese Catholics are allowed to worship ancestors in their familial temples. 5. Whether at home, in the cemetery, or during the time of a funeral, a Chinese Catholic is not allowed to perform the ritual of ancestor worship. . . . Such a ritual is heathen in nature regardless of the circumstances. (Pope Clement XI, *Ex Illa Dei* [1715], *China in Transition, 1517–1911*, p. 23)

Neo-Scholasticism and Manual Theology

Besides the biblical and pastoral challenges of sixteenth-century Protestant reformers, another formidable challenge to Roman

PMATTHEVS RICCIVS MACERATENSIS QVI PRIMVS E SOCIETAE
IESV EVANGELIVM IN SINAS INVEXIT OBIIT ANNO SALVTIS
1610 ÆTATIS 60.

206. Portrait of Matteo Ricci, S.J. (d. 1610).

Catholic theology in this era was the Enlightenment emphases on human reason (rationalism) and human experience. As Gerald McCool has suggested, the only adversary outside the church that Roman Catholic theologians took seriously was rationalism. In response there developed what, on the one hand, could be considered a more "scientific" approach to theology among some Roman Catholic theologians. As Francis Fiorenza describes it, this style of theology employs a deductive method and is highly reliant on a philosophical form of reasoning grounded in the work of ancient Greek philosophers, especially Aristotle.

While sometimes called "neo-Scholasticism" or "neo-Thomism," this form of theology was quite different from that of Thomas Aquinas and the other Scholastic theologians of the medieval period.

For thirteenth-century "school theologians" like Thomas, theology was an exploration, faith seeking understanding, and began with disputation. The theological enterprise in this period was consequently an expansive discipline, not driven by apologetics or a need to defend the official church, and closely related to the birth of universities, where new ideas were eagerly explored. Neo-Scholasticism, on the other hand, developed at a time when the Roman Catholic Church was in a more defensive position, was losing political influence in Europe, was challenged theologically by Protestantism, and facing intellectual adversity in the Enlightenment.

It was in this climate that neo-Scholasticism emerged. Symbolic of this "scientific" approach to theology was the theological "manual," a kind of encyclopedia of theological information, systematically arranged according to distinctive principles. As Fiorenza summarizes, one characteristic of these manuals is that they begin with church teaching rather than some disputed question, as was typical of Thomas and other Scholastics. For neo-Scholasticism, the teaching of the Roman Catholic Church was considered foundational and was the prism through which one considered other theological sources such as Scripture or the teaching of early Christian writers. This placing of Scripture in a second place is, in part, a response to Protestant reforms and their principle of *sola scriptura* (Latin, "by scripture alone"). Neo-Scholastic theologians argued that the Scriptures were often misinterpreted and required the official teaching of the church to safeguard against such errors. When Scripture or other texts from the tradition were employed, they were often "reduced to proof-texts for a particular proposition . . . cited independently of their context and were interpreted primarily as demonstrations of the truth of a particular doctrinal thesis" (Fiorenza, p. 32). As a result, this manual approach to theology in neo-Scholasticism was highly apologetic and authoritarian.

While centers of neo-Scholasticism were developing in Rome, France, Spain, and even the Philippines, the movement was particularly strong in Germany. The German Jesuit Joseph Kleutgen (d. 1883) was a key figure at this time and was central to the advancement of the whole neo-Scholastic movement. His seminal 1860 book *Philosophie der Vorzeit* (German, "Philosophy of a Past Era") was a combative work in which he argued that the fundamental principles of Thomism were the only principles capable of satisfying the needs of human reason. Kleutgen's influence extended to drafting the final version of the Dogmatic Constitution on the Catholic faith, *Dei Filius* (Latin, "Son of God"), promulgated at the First Vatican Council (1869–70), which articulated basic neo-Scholastic principles, particularly around the relationship of faith and reason. According to McCool, he is also to be credited as the principal author of the 1879 encyclical of Leo XIII (d. 1903), *Aeterni Patris* (Latin, "[The Only Begotten Son] of the Eternal Father"), which praised Thomas as the most noble philosopher-theologian [quotation 315] and ensured that a neo-Scholastic approach would be employed in the education of all future Roman Catholic priests and serve as the bedrock of Roman Catholic apologetics.

The effect of neo-Scholastic theology on eucharistic theology was broad and sustained. Like the approach to other sacraments, a "manual" approach to Eucharist gave virtually no attention to the liturgy itself but offered abstract reflection on what were considered foundational truths. Its "scientific" approach was direct, concise, and methodological. It was also reductionistic, and seldom gave the reader access to primary sources but, rather, offered summaries often lacking in nuance and sometimes even in accuracy. For example, discussions of a concept such as transubstantiation were considered outside of Aquinas's essential reliance on analogical language for speaking of divine realities (see above p. 229). The many different understandings of transubstantiation were neither understood nor recognized, and Trent's careful phrasing of transubstantiation that admitted that it was a most appropriate and yet nontraditional way of speaking about real presence was virtually ignored. Rather, transubstantiation was presented as a a timeless dogma [quotation 316], and to deny transubstantiation was essentially to deny belief in the real presence of Christ in the Eucharist. Such an approach was symptomatic of a eucharistic and sacramental theology less concerned with theological reflection than with surety and fidelity.

Quotation 315: *We exhort you, venerable brethren, in all earnestness to restore the golden wisdom of St. Thomas, and to spread it far and wide for the defense and beauty of the Catholic faith, for the good of society, and for the advantage of all the sciences. . . . Let carefully selected teachers endeavor to implant the doctrine of Thomas Aquinas in the minds of students, and set forth clearly his solidity and excellence over others. Let the universities already founded or to be founded by you illustrate and defend this doctrine, and use it for the refutation of prevailing errors.* (Leo XIII [d. 1903], *Aeterni Patris*, n. 31)

Quotation 316: *How is Jesus Christ Present? Not, as Osiander maintained, by impanation or a personal or hypostatic union into which the Godman enters with the bread; nor by consubstantiation, as maintained by Martin Luther, whereby Christ would co-exist with the bread and wine; but by transubstantiation whereby the substance of bread is changed into the substance of the body of Christ. This is of faith, otherwise the words "This is my body" would be meaningless.* (Berthier, *A Compendium of Theology*, II:76)

Summary

In some ways the theological developments of this era may well be understood through the polarities of inculturation and neo-Scholasticism, by the tensions between worship and theology that respects human experience and historical context, and those prone to uphold orthodox views validated by church structures, teaching, and leadership. In a new and contentious way in this era, local contexts challenged the "catholic" or universal. Broadly speaking, the Protestant reaction was diversity and a move toward the contextual pole, while Roman Catholicism moved toward uniformity and the neo-Scholastic pole. Like great tectonic plates, these two polarities continued to grind against each other. It is especially in the following era, however, that theological friction will give way to a new liturgical dynamism.

THOMAS

For as long as he could remember, Thomas had wondered what it was like behind the great choir screen. It seemed strange now to be sitting in those choir stalls that before he could only glimpse from a distance. How much things had changed in the cathedral since he was a child!

Thomas remembered the worship in the church when King Henry was still alive. Once the king himself had come to their cathedral for Mass. It was a glorious ceremony! There were banners and officials everywhere, more clergy and soldiers than Thomas had ever seen, and a corps of trumpeters in the gallery.

That day was also Thomas's first memory of the great stone screen. He was only four or five at the time, scarcely eight hands high, and his view of the pageant was blocked by the crowds. He caught only glimpses of the procession of clerics and royalty as it wound its way through the nave. Then it disappeared behind the choir screen. Thomas didn't think that was fair. He stood outside the screen with his uncle Geoffrey for a long time, trying to discover what was going on inside. Young Tom could hear the service, but he didn't understand it. Uncle Geoff told him that it was in Latin. For all young Tom knew, it could have been in Egyptian. It certainly wasn't the King's English. Tom felt cheated that he could not watch the king and the rest of the royal escort during the Mass.

Things certainly changed after the death of old Henry. Almost as soon as the boy Edward took the throne, the innovations began. Thomas doesn't remember much about the early variations in the service, except that the priests looked very confused. The only consolation, to Thomas's thinking, was that the service was in English, so that the priest and people could be confused together.

Just when things seemed to be settling down and the clergy and congregation were getting used to the new liturgy, Bloody Mary ascended the throne. Then, as Uncle Geoff used to say, "all hell broke loose." Within a few years, the Mass was back in Latin. This time Thomas knew it was Latin and he still didn't like it. But there were many, including his mother, who preferred the mysterious language. He never under- stood why. Happily for Thomas, that situation didn't last very long. Bloody Mary died just three years after restoring the Latin Mass. Then Elizabeth assumed the throne, and the following year the Mass was back to English. What years of turmoil those were!

Thomas liked many things about the new liturgy, besides the fact that he could understand it. After he attended the Mass for King Henry, he fought the choir screen in his mind. He wondered what it was like behind the stone wall, and he asked his mother why he couldn't stand inside the screen during the services. He promised that he would be quiet and no one would even know that he was there. His mother just gave him that look reserved for impossible re- quests and unanswerable questions. A few times after services, young Tom had taken matters into his own hands and stood at the edge of the doorway, looking into the great choir. He never got completely inside. Once he came close, but he was caught by the sacristan and pushed back outside the door.

Recalling that boyhood memory was a special pleasure as Thomas sat in his favorite seat in the choir stalls inside the great screen, behind the son of that retired sacristan. Being able to sit there during the communion service was maybe the best part of the new worship. Instead of standing out in the nave with the rest of the people during the Latin Mass, Thomas now sat in the choir stalls where they attended the new "Mass." Others called it Holy Communion, but it would always be the Mass to Thomas. Like the old Latin service, the new service had a lot of prayers and readings and a long sermon. He didn't mind so much though, because he could sit during the whole first part of the worship, studying all the carvings in the seats or pondering the fancy vault that towered above the choir. When he did have to stand or kneel, he was comforted in his old age by the presence of wooden risers, much preferred to the damp stone pavement of the nave. All in all, Thomas thought that the changes he had experienced over the years were welcome ones, though he still enjoyed regaling his own children with stories of the great cathedral from the time when he was a boy.

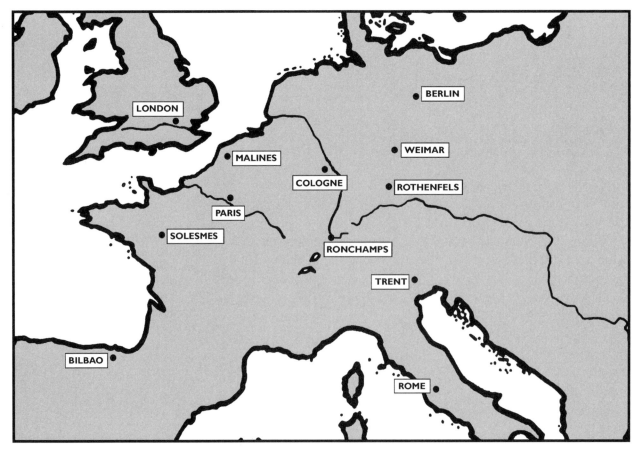

207. Map for chapter 7.

CHAPTER SEVEN

Renewal, Reaction, and an Unfolding Vision: 1903 to Tomorrow

It is too early for any definitive introduction to the current period of liturgical change and reform. Although much liturgically has happened since the dawn of the twentieth century that indicates significant variance from the previous period, there also exist strong counter-currents toward restorationism and the retrieval of medieval, Tridentine, and neo-Scholastic theologies and practice. These confluences have simultaneously generated exhilaration and angst among liturgical leaders, as well as comfort, confusion, and even rancor among the faithful.

Similar to previous eras, such developments are intimately wed to larger social, economic, and political trends. In the last chapter we noted that, while constancy and change have always marked the liturgical practices of the churches, the onset of "modernity" [quotation 317] contributed to the increased speed of change and reaction to change. With the dawn of the twentieth century, global change has occurred with a new breadth and velocity. For example, the number of nations that have won or reasserted independence since 1900 is staggering, challenging even the digital cartographer [illustration 208]. Population developments have been equally dramatic. In 1900 there were 1.6 billion people in the world; by 2000 that number had grown to over 6 billion, with the vast majority of the growth in developing countries in Asia, Africa, and South America [illustration 209]. Parallel to these political and demographic changes were rapid developments in communication technologies, world markets, and the geography of power at the end of the twentieth century. These fueled the international current known as "globalization," which Robert Schreiter defines as "the extension of the effects of modernity to the entire world and the compression of time and space, all occurring at the same time" (Schreiter, p. 8). The dominance of these worldwide trends, however, has not resulted in the homogenization of the global village or the suppression of the dis-

Quotation 317: *Modernity is sometimes identified as an historical period [often thought to have begun in the seventeenth century] contrasted with other eras such as the primitive, ancient, or medieval. Harvie Ferguson offers a more philosophical definition and suggests that the key to understanding modernity is "a genuine understanding of our experience." More recent forms of understanding in the West, particularly since the thought of René Descartes [d. 1650], are characterized by autonomy, creativity, and freedom. Generally, Ferguson claims that it is the category of experience, or more precisely "the sovereignty of experience," that marks modernity. (Ferguson, Modernity and Subjectivity, p. 199)*

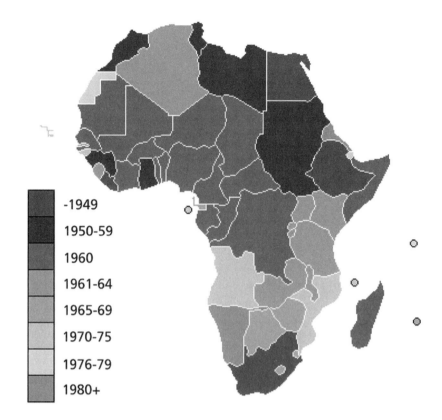

	-1949
	1950-59
	1960
	1961-64
	1965-69
	1970-75
	1976-79
	1980+

208. Map of African countries and their dates of independence in the twentieth century.

tinctively local. Often in reaction to these larger forces there arise new emphases on the particulars of a people, context, language, and environment. In the words of Roland Robertson, globalization has become "glocalization," a mixture of the global and the local.

Concurrent with such trends have been amazing developments and horrifying destruction. Since the nineteenth century there has been an evolution in philosophy and political theory that has emphasized the dignity of the individual. Freshly evolving social sciences such as psychology, sociology, anthropology, and ethnography similarly prize the human person and human experience. Such valuation has burgeoned into multiple liberation movements, which not only seek national or political freedom but also demand economic inclusion and equality across gender, ethnic, age, and class lines. Yet, the dignity of the human person has also been under new and debilitating assault. The twentieth century was the bloodiest in recorded history, with over 100 million war dead alone. Genocide reached unprecedented proportions, with over a million Armenians killed in 1915, at least six million Jews killed during the Holocaust of 1939–45, two million Cambodians killed under the Khmer Rouge (1975–78), and almost a million killed in the Rwandan Massacres

Population in the World's Major Regions, 1750-1995 (in Millions)

Year	Total	Europe & USSR	North America	Latin America[a]	Africa	Asia & Oceania
1750	694	144	1	10	100	439
(%)	100.0	20.7	0.1	1.4	14.4	63.3
1900	1,571	423	81	63	141	863
(%)	100.0	26.9	5.2	4.0	9.0	54.9
1950	2,520	549[b]	166	166	224	1,416[c]
(%)	100.0	21.8	6.6	6.6	8.9	56.2
1975	4,077	676	239	320	414	2,427
(%)	100.0	16.6	5.9	7.8	10.2	59.5
1995	5,716	727	293	482	728	3,487
(%)	100.0	12.7	5.1	8.4	12.7	61.0

[a] Includes Mexico, Central America and South America

[b] 1950 and later: excludes Asiatic republics of the former USSR

[c] 1950 and later: includes Asiatic republics of the former USSR

209. World population growth. (Carl Haub, "Global and U. S. National Population Trends," *Consequences* 1:2 [Summer 1995])

of 1994. Estimates of those killed in wars and atrocities during the twentieth century totaled almost 200 million lives. Given this social, political, and economic strife, it is not surprising that the world is currently experiencing unparalleled migration. In 2002 the United Nations reported that the number of immigrants in the world had doubled since 1975 and that over 175 million people were residing in a country other than that in which they had been born.

Christianity, like other world religions, responds to and is shaped by these global forces. For example, national independence movements have found an echo in the explosion of independent Christian churches across global Christianity. Now the largest group of Christian churches in places like southern Africa, these independent churches embody something of the twentieth-century's postcolonial spirit, rejecting the cultural dominance of their founding churches that were often

Euro-American. The growth of these independent churches—most with a strong evangelical orientation—are symptomatic of significant demographic shifts within worldwide Christianity. Over the last century, the Christian center of gravity has moved south. While over 80 percent of all Christians lived in Europe and North America in 1900, the Center for the Study of Global Christianity estimates that in 2005 that percentage had dropped to 40 percent and predicts that by 2050 it will fall below 30 percent. The fastest growing Christian country in the world has been Brazil, but by the middle of this century it could be surpassed by China.

Mainline Protestant churches have clearly declined in North America. In the U.S. alone, the United Methodist Church, Presbyterian Church, Evangelical Lutheran Church in America, Episcopal Church, United Church of Christ, and Christian Church (Disciples of Christ) have all experienced significant decline since 1965, while affiliation with evangelical churches—especially Pentecostal churches—has sharply risen. While Roman Catholicism has grown during this period it, like many other U.S. churches, is experiencing a major demographic shift as it becomes increasingly multicultural, especially with the growth of the Hispanic population. An unusually rich example of this growing multiculturality is the Archdiocese of Los Angeles. According to their official website, worship is regularly offered in at least twenty-nine languages in that diocese and some report that on any given Sunday, Mass is celebrated in as many as forty languages.

Along with these demographic and cultural changes, Christian theology and practice since the beginning of the twentieth century has been confronted by some of the same ethical and liberation issues that face secular society. While one could argue that Christian theology has always emphasized the dignity of the individual, there has been a strengthened Christian voice for the marginalized, oppressed, and the poor [quotation 318]. Concern for issues of oppression has not been limited to the economically disadvantaged, however, and church voices have also raised serious questions regarding marginalization based on gender, ethnicity, physical disabilities, and sexual orientation. This constellation of concerns has coalesced to the extent that Robert Schreiter considers theologies of liberation, feminism, and human rights to be three of the four major theological flows across the globe at the onset of the twenty-first century. Ironically, the twentieth century was a time when charges of oppression, marginalization, and even abuse were leveled at the church, which is under new scrutiny in an age of hyper-communication.

It is in this wider global and ecclesial context that we consider the worship dynamics of the current era, frequently considered an epoch

Quotation 318: *Such perspectives provide a basis today for what is called the "preferential option for the poor." Through the Gospels and in the New Testament as a whole the offer of salvation is extended to all peoples, Jesus takes the side of the most in need, physically and spiritually. The example of Jesus poses a number of challenges to the contemporary Church. It imposes a prophetic mandate to speak for those who have no one to speak for them, to be a defender of the defenseless, who in biblical terms are the poor. It also demands a compassionate vision that enables the Church to see things from the side of the poor and powerless and to assess lifestyle, policies, and social institutions in terms of their impact on the poor. It summons the Church also to be an instrument in assisting people to experience the liberating power of God in their own lives so that they may respond to the Gospel in freedom and in dignity. Finally, and most radically, it calls for an emptying of self, both individually and corporately, that allows the Church to experience the power of God in the midst of poverty and powerlessness.* (U.S. Catholic Bishops, *Economic Justice for All*, no. 52)

210. Prosper Guéranger, O.S.B. (1805–75).

of liturgical reform and renewal. Just as the modernity that flourished in the twentieth century had roots that reached back as far as the Renaissance, so was the liturgical ferment of the current era heralded long before the twentieth millennium. As suggested in the previous chapter, continuous liturgical reform marked the evolution of various Protestant churches in the preceding centuries. Some developments—such as Methodism in eighteenth-century America, the Lutheran confessionalism of Wilhelm Löhe (d. 1872) in nineteenth-century Bavaria, and the Oxford movement in nineteenth-century England—were strongly sacramental. We also noted some of the independent liturgical movements within Roman Catholicism in the eighteenth and nineteenth centuries such as Gallicanism, Josephinism, and the Synod of Pistoia.

One influential Roman Catholic liturgical force that arose in seventeenth- and eighteenth-century France was Jansenism. Centered in Paris, the Jansenists were named after the Flemish theologian Cornelius Otto Jansen (d. 1638), an Augustinian scholar who promoted the teachings of that African doctor rather than those of Scholasticism. Some Jansenist teachings appeared almost anti-liturgical —for example, their emphasis on confession and rigorous preparation for communion—which, in effect, discouraged many people from

Quotation 319: *The canon of the Mass [is recited] aloud in a voice intelligible to all the people; [as we are] certain that in [earlier] times what was said aloud and what was said in lowered tones was what was sung, and what was not sung was said intelligibly at the altar. . . . The clergy and the people receive communion at the Mass of their pastor and from his hand, and each responds according to the ancient custom, upon receiving the body of Jesus Christ, immediately after the pastor has pronounced the words: Corpus Domini nostri Jesu Christi. The people say Amen. (Church News [July 1690], trans. F. Ellen Weaver, in "Liturgy for the Laity")*

Quotation 320: *Efforts must be made to restore the use of Gregorian chant by the people, so that the faithful may again take a more active part in the ecclesiastical offices, as they were wont to do in ancient times. (Pius X, The Restoration of Church Music [1903], no. 3, in Seasoltz, The New Liturgy, pp. 5–6)*

Quotation 321: *. . . a remarkably widespread revival of scholarly interest in the sacred liturgy took place toward the end of the last century and has continued through the early years of this one. . . . The majestic ceremonies of the sacrifice of the altar became better known, understood and appreciated. With more widespread and more frequent reception of the sacraments, the worship of the Eucharist came to be regarded for what it really is: the fountainhead of genuine Christian devotion. . . . While we derive no little satisfaction from the wholesome results of the movement just described, duty obliges us to give serious attention to this "revival" as it is advocated in some quarters, and to take proper steps to preserve it at the outset from excess or outright perversion. (Pius XII, The Sacred Liturgy [1947], 4–7, in Seasoltz, The New Liturgy, pp. 108–9)*

frequent reception. On the other hand, they made significant strides in achieving lay participation within Roman Catholic worship, shaping what would be considered a French Catholic Rite, attentive to the language of ordinary people that would consciously engage them at the heart of the worship [quotation 319]. Although Jansenists eventually were condemned by Rome, their liturgical reforms continued to influence official worship and popular devotions in France. The French monk Prosper Guéranger [illustration 210]—who refounded the Benedictine order in France at the abbey of Solesmes—was a nineteenth-century reformer credited with helping to stem the influence of such "Gallicanisms" by reintroducing the Roman liturgy into France. Sometimes too focused on narrowly conceived historical accuracy, especially regarding medieval worship that he considered normative, he did not promote a participatory image of worship that was more characteristic of fourth- or fifth-century Christian liturgy. Nonetheless, he did manage to hold up traditional Roman liturgy as the model for public and private prayer. His liturgically centered reform generated great enthusiasm for the Roman liturgy, especially in certain monasteries of France and Germany.

The work of Guéranger and the monks of Solesmes was affirmed by Pius X (d. 1914), who approved their restoration of Gregorian chant for the whole church. Pius X's concern for sacred music was evident in his 1903 apostolic letter *Tra le Sollicitudini* (Italian, "Among the [pastoral] cares"). This letter also included a call for the active participation of the people [quotation 320]—one of the grand themes of twentieth-century liturgical reforms, resonant with the global currents of inclusion and liberation that widely marked the twentieth century. Although anticipated in the writings of Pius X, who also promoted more frequent communion, the modern liturgical movement found full expression through Benedictine Lambert Beauduin (d. 1960). His paper on active participation of the people for the Catholic Congress at Malines, Belgium, in 1909 is traditionally recognized as the birth of this movement.

After this, the twentieth century seems to have experienced a virtually uninterrupted avalanche of liturgical scholarship, pastoral experimentation, and dialogue directed toward the renewal of Christian liturgy, especially across Europe and North America. In the spirit of the Enlightenment, with its emphasis on human reason and its legacy of critical tools, scholars such as Louis Duchesne (d. 1922), Gregory Dix (d. 1952), and Josef Jungmann (d. 1975) produced great liturgical histories that offered an increasingly nuanced picture of the development of Christian worship. One important pastoral experiment was the *Missa recitata* [Latin, "dialogue Mass"], which encouraged the people's participation in reciting the prayers of the

Mass together and in responding to the priest. Requiring the permission of the local bishop, over 25 percent of the Roman Catholic parishes in Chicago had introduced the *Missa recitata* by 1939, and by the middle of the century it had become normative in as many as 75 percent of the parishes (Pecklers, *The Unread Vision*, pp. 55, 61). Even more influential were the various vernacular movements of the century. Pius X granted permission for certain areas of Yugoslavia to make permanent liturgical use of the classical Paleoslav language in 1906; Benedict XV (d. 1922) granted permission for limited use of Croatian, Slovenian, and Czech in church rites; and in 1929 Pius XI granted permission for a vernacular ritual in Bavaria (Pecklers, *Dynamic Equivalency*, pp. 32–33). A society promoting the vernacular was founded in England in 1942 and in 1946 a similar group appeared in the U.S. [illustration 211].

While the liturgical movement was not exclusively a Roman Catholic phenomenon, it first became systemic within Roman Catholicism. The 1947 encyclical of Pius XII (d. 1959), *Mediator Dei*—sometimes considered the Magna Carta of the liturgical movement—affirmed specifics like the value of the vernacular and, more generally, the liturgical movement for Roman Catholics [quotation 321]. A culminating moment in this movement was the first document issued by Vatican II (1962–65), the *Constitution on the Sacred Liturgy* (1963). While written for Roman Catholics, this document became pivotal in the reform of worship throughout the Christian churches. More than any other previous official document, this constitution richly articulated the authentic role of worship in the life and mission of the church [quotation 322].

Nathan Mitchell characterizes the first two decades after the *Constitution on the Sacred Liturgy* as a time open to change, collegial decision making, and diverse cultures. In some ways it could be considered a time when the Roman Catholic Church and its liturgy reckoned with the forces of modernity. Mitchell characterizes the period since 1984, however, as a period of increasing caution, restriction, and retrenchment (Mitchell, "Amen Corner," pp. 56–57). In 1984 the Vatican gave limited permission for Roman Catholics to reemploy the preconciliar Tridentine Mass, despite the fact that the Latin rite ordinaries of the world considered the Tridentine Mass to be a virtually nonexistent problem. If the first decades after Vatican II could be considered a time of *aggiornamento* (Italian, literally "update," indicating an openness to change and renewal) and reconciliation with the flows of modernity, Thomas O'Meara has suggested that since the 1980s the Roman Catholic Church seems to be returning to a nineteenth-century vision of the baroque. Symptomatic of this shift were various reversals by the Vatican, especially

The ENGLISH is coming!

211. Cartoon from the U.S. Vernacular Society's journal *Amen*.

Quotation 322: *The liturgy is the summit toward which the activity of the church is directed; it is also the source from which all its power flows. (Constitution on the Sacred Liturgy* [1963], 10)

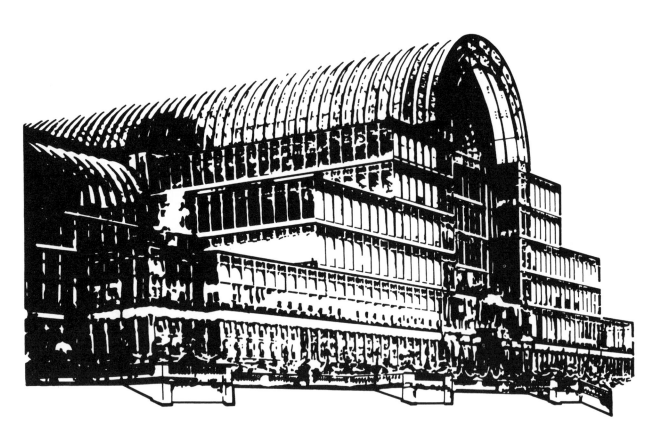

212. Joseph Paxton's Crystal Palace (London, 1851).

around issues of translation. One key symbol of the changes was a 2001 set of translation guidelines (Latin, *Liturgiam Authenticam*, "Authentic Liturgy") that not only replaced the previously published guidelines of 1969 and radically reversed the principles for translation but also reserved for Rome the right to "prepare translations in any language, and to approve them for liturgical use" (no. 104), despite the fact that the Council of Trent ceded authority to local bishops for approving translations.

There is little doubt that much of the worship of Christian churches, and most especially liturgy for Roman Catholics, has been permanently transformed in this period. This does not mean, however, that the transformation is settled or complete. Complementary, parallel, and competing forces in the world and in the church suggest that we will continue to live in a period of liturgical ferment. It is only hoped that the vision of active participation embedded in Vatican II, the voices for inclusion that echo around the globe, and the promise of charity that resides at the heart of Christian Eucharist will combine in rich and powerful ways to serve Christian worship in a new millennium.

213. Frank Lloyd Wright's Robie House (Chicago, 1909).

ARCHITECTURE

Baroque architecture, a product of Roman Catholicism, was the last Western architectural style with ecclesiastical roots. During the eighteenth century, architecture, like other arts and sciences in the West, became independent of the church. After the Enlightenment and the industrial revolution, the church and the nobility no longer dictated society's building needs. Instead, the industrial and commercial sectors became the driving forces in architecture. These developments must be considered before turning to ecclesiastical architecture in the twentieth century.

Secular Developments

Architecture is an expression of context and culture. The developments in secular architecture in the modern period were influenced by the philosophical and political movements that changed the face of Western civilization. The previously mentioned liberation flows and the concurrent rise of systems that upheld the value of the individual and the individual's inalienable right to basic freedoms were especially influential. In architecture, these ideals were expressed by open spaces that related to their environment—a spatial concept very different from that of the baroque era [quotation 323].

One early example of this new spatial openness was Joseph Paxton's (d. 1865) Crystal Palace [illustration 212], built for the

Quotation 323: *When discussing the architecture of the nineteenth century, we have repeatedly used the term "open space" to indicate the image of a limitless and continuous environment where people may act and freely move about—not for the sake of movement as such, but as an expression of a new freedom of choice, that is, the freedom to search and create one's own place. The new image, then, is the opposite to the Baroque. Whereas Baroque space represented an integrated system, the open space of the nineteenth century expressed a new ideal of human freedom.* (Norberg-Schulz, *Meaning in Western Architecture*, p. 351)

London Exhibition of 1851. Almost 1,900 feet long, this edifice was built completely of iron and glass framed in wood. Constructed in six months from thousands of prefabricated parts, the Crystal Palace announced a new architectural era through its materials, size, style, and even construction technique. This feat was possible because of technological advances from the industrial revolution. One such advance was the use of iron and, after the middle of the century, steel rather than masonry and wood in construction. Economical, fire-resistant, and strong, these materials allowed the construction of vast open spaces symbolizing a new freedom and openness. Eventually, buildings began expanding vertically rather than horizontally, and the skyscraper emerged, especially in Chicago and New York.

While some architects experimented on this grand scale, Frank Lloyd Wright (d. 1959) focused on the single-family dwelling [illustration 213]. Although concern for domestic architecture might appear to contradict the spirit of the Crystal Palace, both were statements about a new openness and freedom, one industrial and the other domestic. Wright considered his work an architecture of democracy. He abandoned the principle of a single room for a single use and, instead, arranged flexible spaces that flowed naturally from the outside, in which people could move freely [quotation 324].

Functionalism

At the turn of the century, a trend against ornamentation in building arose. Adolf Loos (d. 1933) offered a dramatic summation of this trend by suggesting that ornamentation was actually a crime [quotation 325]. The rejection of ornamentation contributed to a preference for buildings that did not hide their structure behind elaborate masonry, but rather revealed the essential elements of their construction and materials. This move against the artificiality of traditional ornamentation, combined with the emphasis on revealing the interior structure of the building exteriorly, is called "functionalism." A primary maxim of functionalism, articulated by the Chicago architect Louis Sullivan (d. 1924), was "form follows function." In Sullivan's view, the need for continuity between the interior and the exterior design did not eliminate the need for ornamentation. Sullivan, rather, shunned ornamentation that would obscure or hide the function of the building.

Functionalism became a dominant architectural principle during the twentieth century. In Germany this principle was foundational to the Bauhaus school of design established in Weimar in 1919. A former director of the Bauhaus, Mies van der Rohe (d. 1969) moved to Chicago's Illinois Institute of Technology in 1937, where he gave

214. Mies van der Rohe's Seagram Building (New York City, 1956–58).

215. Frank Gehry's Guggenheim Museum Bilbao (Bilbao, Spain; 1997).

new expression to functionalism [illustration 214]. The Swiss-born Charles-Edouard Jeanneret-Gris (d. 1966)—more commonly known as Le Corbusier—was a brilliant exponent of functionalism.

A broad acceptance of functionalism contributed to the development of an international style that spread throughout western Europe and the United States. This style avoided ornamentation. Its preferred construction material was reinforced concrete. Often employing white stuccoed walls, long horizontal bands of windows and flat roofs, buildings in the international style frequently projected a strong sense of volume, rather than simply a sense of mass. In recent decades, functionalism and the international style have given way to a more pluralistic approach to building. As Christian Norberg-Schulz explains, this postmodern pluralism does not begin with preconceived styles or basic principles. Rather, a pluralistic approach attempts first to understand the nature of each task and then to generate a series of compatible solutions. Thus, pluralism is more a method than a specific style and can allow for regional and stylistic variations.

Such pluralism has become more pronounced with important architectural developments outside of the Euro-American axis. Imaginative works continue to develop within this axis, for example, the titanium-clad Guggenheim museum in Bilbao, Spain, by Frank Gehry [illustration 215]. Increasingly, however, as world population shifts continue to gravitate south, some of the most imaginative architectural thinking is emerging in Asia, where urbanization is a new major force. Thus, it was Kuala Lumpur in Indonesia that laid claim to the

Quotation 324: *What then is the nature of this idea we call organic architecture? We are here calling this architecture "The Architecture of Democracy." Why? Because it is intrinsically based on nature-law: law for [people], not law over [people]. . . . It is simply the human spirit given appropriate architectural form. Simply, too, it is the material structure of every [person's] life on earth now seen by him as various forms of structure—in short, organic. Democracy possesses the material means today to be enlarged intelligently and turned about now to employ machine power on super materials for [human] superiority. Therefore, organic architecture is not satisfied to be employed merely to make money—not if that money is to be stacked against [humanity itself]. Our growing dissatisfaction with autocratic power or bureaucracy of any kind requires wisdom. Old wisdom and good sense are modern even now; it is their application that changes. Still more ancient is the wisdom, and it too is modern, that recognizes this new democratic concept of [humans] free in life wherein money and land-laws are established as subordinate to rights of the human being. That means first of all that all good architecture is good democracy. (Wright, The Living City, p. 28)*

216. Cesar Pelli's Petronas twin towers (Kuala Lumpur, Malaysia; 1998).

tallest building in the world [illustration 216], and it is outside of Beijing near the original Great Wall that leading Asian architects are reimagining the harmony between home and nature [illustration 217].

Ecclesiastical Architecture

Although the nineteenth century was a revolutionary time for Western architecture, this was not true for church architecture. The most notable developments in church architecture during this period were various revivals (see p. 258–59 above), most important the Gothic revival. Augustus Pugin (d. 1852) was this revival's most outspoken proponent [quotation 326]. Pugin's argument that Gothic was the

217. Kengo Kuma's Great Bamboo Wall House (near Beijing, 2002).

only appropriate ecclesiastical style was accepted not only by the Roman Catholic church but also by other religious traditions in his native England. This revival, however, had little impact outside of England, the United States, and, to a lesser degree, France.

Another nineteenth-century development in the U.S. was the emergence of "auditorium churches" for some Protestant communities. These buildings were often designed as radial-plan amphitheaters with large stages and comfortable seats fanning out from a sanctuary that was often dominated by an imposing organ and a theatrical pulpit. As Jeanne Halgren Kilde notes, these buildings could be part of sophisticated complexes that included parlors, lecture halls, and even sports facilities, integrating worship as one component of a comprehensive outreach to urban families. In some ways these buildings anticipated the megachurch structures of the late twentieth century and signaled the growing influence of entertainment models of worship. They also symbolized a shifting understanding in the U.S. of worshiper as consumer and worship as one of many services that a church provided the baptized. An implicit critique of such works might be found in an early church of Frank Lloyd Wright. His

Quotation 326: *The object of the present lecture is to set forth and explain the true principles of Pointed or Christian Architecture, by the knowledge of which you may be enabled to test architectural excellence. . . . Strange as it may appear at first, it is in pointed architecture alone that these great principles have been carried out; and I shall be able to illustrate them from the vast cathedral to the simplest erection. Moreover, the architects of the middle ages were the first who turned the natural properties of the various materials to their full account and made their mechanism a vehicle for their art.* (Augustus Pugin, *The True Principles of Pointed or Christian Architecture* [1841])

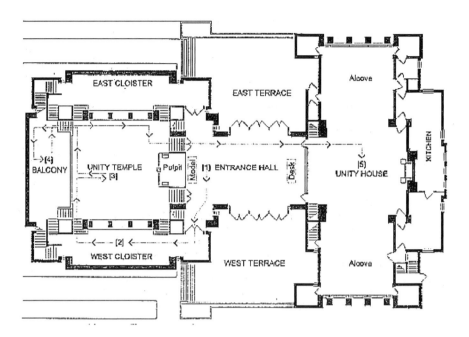

218. Floor plan of Frank Lloyd Wright's Unity Temple (Oak Park, Illinois; 1906).

1905 Unity Temple in Oak Park, Illinois, is an intimate central-plan space, often described as a gem of simplicity and beauty. The Temple is connected by a large entrance hall to the Unity House [illustration 218]. In the original brochure explaining the project, Pastor Rodney F. Johonnot notes how these complementary spaces meet (without confusing) the two basic requirements of a church building: the worship of God and the service of people.

Innovations, some of which were structural, occurred in early twentieth-century European church architecture. Saint Eugene (1854–55) in Paris, designed by Louis-Auguste Boileau (d. 1896), for example, was the first iron-framed church, and in 1928 Otto Bartning (d. 1959) created the steel and copper *Stahlkirche* (German, "Steel church") in Cologne that offered technological innovation within a traditional configuration. The development of reinforced concrete, patented by Joseph Monier (d. 1906) in 1867, allowed the creation of large open spaces that reflected a more democratic approach to worship. Northwest of Paris in Le Raincy, Auguste Perret (d. 1954) constructed the church of Notre Dame (1922–1923) completely out of reinforced concrete, a design that had much in common with the hall churches of the thirteenth century [illustration 219]. While offering a relatively conventional configuration of assembly and sanctuary, the church gives the impression of a single large room, even as it allows for traditional devotional activities. The result is a clearer image of the assembly as a corporate entity in the worship,

219. Auguste Perret's Notre Dame Church (Le Raincy, France; 1922–23).

whose clear sight lines to the sanctuary underscore the importance of the recent calls for their explicit and active participation. Even more influential was the 1928 remodeling of *Schloss Rothenfels* (German, "Castle Rothenfels), which served as the headquarters for the Catholic Youth Movement in Germany before the Second World War. While there was a small chapel in the castle, the influential piece was the multipurpose main hall. As Frédéric Debuyst describes it, this was a large rectangular space with pure white walls, deep windows, and a stone pavement. Devoid of decoration, the only furniture was a hundred little black cuboid stools whose placement could be easily rearranged according to need. When Eucharist was celebrated, a provisional altar was erected, which was surrounded by the faithful on three sides [illustration 220]. This radical placement of the assembly in proximity to the action of word and sacrament, as well as their unobstructed view of each other, signaled a new architectural integration of what it meant to be the "mystical body" of Christ. This visionary renovation was the collaborative result of liturgical leader Romano Guardini (d. 1968), professor of Catholic theology at the University of Berlin and chaplain to the Catholic Youth Movement, and the architect Rudolf Schwarz (d. 1961), who influenced generations of church architects with his overtly theological vision.

With the onset of World War II European leadership in liturgical architecture waned, with the exception of Switzerland [quotation 327]. After the war, bolstered by the growing strength of the liturgical renewal, innovative work resumed. Debuyst believes one mark

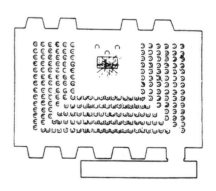

220. Floor plan of the main hall, configured as a chapel, at Schloss Rothenfels, Germany. (Debuyst, p. 36)

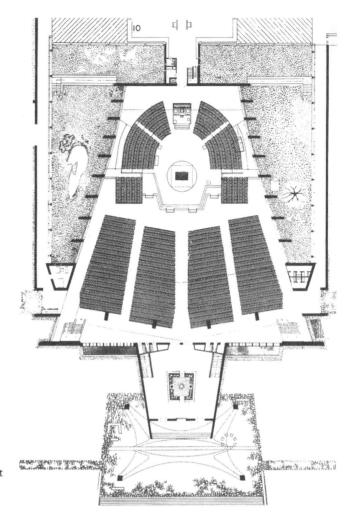

221. Floor plan of Marcel Breuer's Saint John's Abbey Church (Collegeville, Minnesota; 1958–61).

Quotation 328: *Among the symbols with which the liturgy deals, none is more important than this assembly of believers. (Environment and Art in Catholic Worship [1978], 28)*

of this period was the progressive abandonment of the rectangular plan. An important example in the U.S. of this trend is the Abbey Church at Saint John's Abbey in Collegeville, Minnesota. Long associated with the liturgical movement in the U.S., the monks of Saint John's selected the Hungarian-born, German-trained, Harvard professor Marcel Breuer (d. 1981) to create a fresh image of monastic worship in his reinforced concrete church that integrates a choir for three hundred monks and a worship space for seventeen hundred faithful fanning out around the sanctuary [illustration 221].

The most famous church of this era was Le Corbusier's Notre-Dame-du-Haut in Ronchamps (1950–55) [illustration 222]. Because it was designed as a pilgrimage church on a hill rather than a parish church, it has a strong devotional focus and is not as liturgically satisfying as a place like Schloss Rothenfels. For example, although

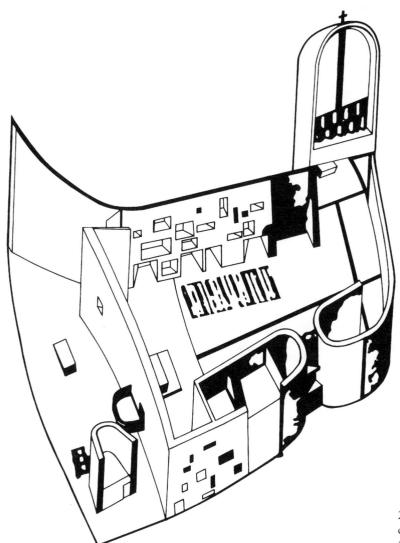

222. Floor plan of Le Corbusier's Notre Dame du Haut (Ronchamps, France; 1950–55). (Norberg-Schulz)

innumerable barriers traditionally placed between the assembly and the sanctuary were omitted, the space does not assert the primacy of the assembly [quotation 328] as did Schloss Rothenfels or even Raincy. Rather, the interior of Notre-Dame-du-Haut appears as a collection of devotional spaces under a single roof—a perspective that Le Corbusier's own words seem to confirm [quotation 329]. On the other hand, the processional path leading up the hill to the church and the exterior choir, which faces east—calling the eucharistic community to stand in the light of day—are compelling ritual elements. Overall, however, Notre-Dame-du-Haut exists more as a triumph of sacred architecture and one of the most lyrical buildings of the age rather than a model of interior liturgical space.

Quotation 329: *In building this chapel I wished to create a place of silence, prayer, of peace and spiritual joy. Our efforts were inspired by their sacred aim. . . . The Virgin is extolled by various symbols and some written words. The cross—the real cross of suffering—is erected in this ark; henceforth the Christian drama is in possession of the place. . . . What all of us have recorded here will, I hope, find an echo in you and in those who climb this hill.* (Le Corbusier's address to the bishop [June 25, 1955])

223. Sanctuary of Eero Saarinen's North Christian Church (Columbus, Indiana; 1964).

Ultimately, it was not the accumulation of technological advances or even the new vision of the sacred offered by Le Corbusier that changed the face of twentieth-century Christian architecture in the West. Rather, it was the success of the liturgical movement, which reasserted the corporate nature of worship and the centrality of the community's active participation. Although this perspective was held by many sixteenth-century reformers, who often opted for central-plan churches, many Protestant churches lost this vision. Under the influence of the nineteenth-century Cambridge Movement, many English-speaking churches returned to more traditional forms of the various architectural revivals (Gothic, classical, and Romanesque) that marked that century. James White has noted a similar return to traditional forms resulting from nineteenth-century revivalism, where emphasis on pulpit personalities and massed choirs developed the concert-stage arrangement—a move resonant with the emergence of auditorium churches.

A few visionaries, including Rudolf Schwarz and Otto Bartning, experimented with central-plan spaces as a way to affirm the unity and centrality of the assembly, but these were initially isolated experiments. Eventually the liturgical movement, reflecting broader cultural flows of freedom and equality, brought a greater emphasis to the communal aspect of worship. At first this emphasis took place mainly through scholarship, but it eventually had a broad impact on

Protestant and Roman Catholic worship forms and their space. In some sense, this meant a growing acceptance of the principle of "functionalism" in liturgy [quotation 330], more commonly expressed in terms of the "ritual requirements" of the space. Thus, a space must serve not only as a place for individual encounter with the Holy but also, and primarily, as a place for the enactment of public ritual. From this perspective, Christian liturgical space is rendered sacred first of all by the action of the community.

A turn to the principles of functionalism in shaping ritual spaces was reflective of architectural principles that dominated Europe and the United States earlier in the twentieth century: respect for individuals and their freedom; a preference for open, free-flowing, flexible spaces suited to their environment; the achievement of a sense of volume rather than of mass; a concern for the authenticity of materials; the exposure of the essential elements of the construction and the nature of the materials; and the rejection of ornamentation. Whereas Frank Lloyd Wright shaped his domestic spaces around a huge open hearth, an increasing number of liturgical churches shaped their space around the ambo and the altar [illustration 223].

A strong flow of functionalism still influences the shaping of new worship spaces as well as renovations of older churches in the West. In the closing years of the twentieth century, however, there was a growing reaction to this approach within Roman Catholicism and particularly to the 1978 document of the U.S. Bishops, *Environment and Art in Catholic Worship*, which espoused a more functional approach. Corroborating Mitchell's suggestion regarding a shift within the Roman Catholic Church after 1984 (see p. 303), there arose in the mid-1980s increasing concerns about what some perceived as a disproportionate emphasis on the role of the assembly, the poor aesthetic quality of some ritual spaces, a disconnection from the "Catholic vocabulary" of stained glass or statuary, and what some considered disrespect to the Blessed Sacrament, often reserved in spaces separate from the main worship space.

In response, some bishops and other pastoral leaders required that the flexibility that distinguished some church arrangements be delimited and that altars, ambos, and other liturgical furniture be fixed to the floor. Tabernacles were sometimes moved back into the main worship space and even fixed on a central altar of reserve, reminiscent of the sixteenth century. Most telling were the "corrective-renovations" of spaces previously constructed or renovated according to the vision of *Environment and Art in Catholic Worship*. While these comprise a very small percentage of the total number of church renovations over the past few decades, there have yet been numerous projects in which a traditionally arranged church, subsequently reconfigured as a central plan with the assembly gathered around the

Quotation 330: *A space acquires a sacredness from the sacred action of the faith community which uses it.* (U.S. Bishops' Committee on the Liturgy, *Environment and Art in Catholic Worship* [1978], 41)

224a. Renovation of the Madonna della Strada Chapel of Loyola University, Chicago (1983).

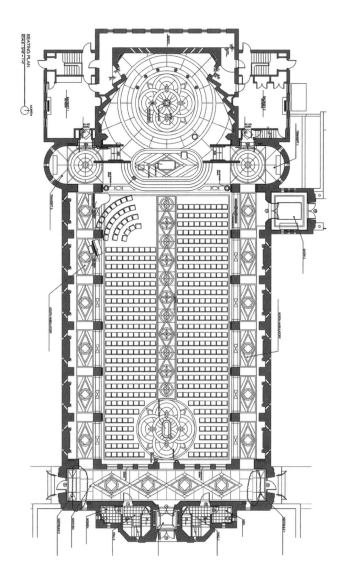

224b. Floor plan for the renovation of Madonna della Strada Chapel by Marvin Herman & Associates (2006).

sanctuary, has been refurbished and "restored" to the original con-figuration. One example of this is the Madonna della Strada chapel of Loyola University in Chicago, built in 1939, renovated in 1983, and renovated again in 2006 [illustration 224]. This architectural rethinking, even reversal, of some spaces finds an analogy in the new guidelines for liturgical art and architecture issued by the U.S. Catholic Bishops in 2000. Some find *Built of Living Stones* a welcome corrective to *Environment and Art in Catholic Worship*, offering a more balanced vision of architecture and liturgical reform. Others question some of its theological presuppositions and wonder aloud whether it will have the broad and positive influence of its predecessor, among both Roman Catholics and Protestants [quotation 331].

Apparently Debuyst's assessment in the early 1980s that "the architectural battles were over" was a bit premature (p. 46). There are many factors that have contributed to recent ferment in liturgical architecture, including different approaches to aesthetics. The stark, even severe architectural approach founded on Bauhaus principles does not inspire all worshipers. What a proponent of such an ap-proach might consider crisp and clean, many might consider bland and empty. Furthermore, much leadership in the liturgical renewal was connected to great monasteries, but the aesthetics of monks who might appreciate the purity of reinforced concrete might not be those of ordinary baptized whose own homes more often demonstrate a preference for the decorated or even vulgar. Important in this discus-sion is the role of popular devotion in liturgy and worship spaces. In the first decades following Vatican II, many liturgical efforts within Roman Catholicism were so focused on Eucharist and the sacraments that traditional devotional practices were often overlooked or even scorned. As a consequence, many new or renovated churches were, for example, devoid of the banks of votive candles, with their accom-panying statues and relics that were so important to the spirituality of masses of ordinary people. This tension is heightened in a place like the U.S. where the population of the baptized is shifting to peoples whose cultures have a long tradition of popular devotions. Aside from these aesthetic differences, theological rifts are also appar-ent in these tensions, in particular the appropriate balance—especially among Roman Catholics—in respecting both the ministerial priest-hood and the priesthood of the baptized.

Quotation 331: *[Built of Living Stones] is preoccupied with the location and symbolism of the presider's chair, the separation of the sanctuary from the assembly, and an excessive concern about the location of the tabernacle.* (Mauck, "Architectural Setting [Modern]," p. 25)

225. Richard Meier's *Dio Padre Misericordioso* (Jubilee Church) near Rome (2003).

Summary

Given the wider currents of pluriformity, regional diversity, and glo-calization in world architecture, it is unlikely that one can expect any synthesis in the foreseeable future. Multiple currents will continue to thrive and critique each other, as demonstrated by two churches from celebrated architects, both dedicated early in the new millennium.

Quotation 332: *Light is the protagonist of our understanding and reading of space. Light is the means by which we are able to experience what we call sacred. Light is at the origins of this building. . . . In the Jubilee Church, the three concrete shells define an enveloping atmosphere in which the light from the skylights above creates a luminous spatial experience, and the rays of sunlight serve as a mystical metaphor of the presence of God.* (Meier, in ArchNewsNow)

Dio Padre Misericordioso (Italian, "God the Merciful Father") [illustration 225] was designed by Richard Meier of New York, the youngest recipient of the 1984 Pritzker Prize for Architecture. Completed in 2003 in a working class suburb outside of Rome, the strikingly modern building with a modest worship space is designed in steel, concrete, and, most important, glass. Meier admits that light was the "protagonist" in the building [quotation 332]. Ironically, the modernistic shell houses a liturgical configuration that is almost preconciliar, and the stark interior does little to address the traditional devotions of the people. In contrast, 1995 Pritzker laureate Jose Rafael Moneo of Spain was chosen to design Our Lady of the Angels Cathedral in Los Angeles [illustration 226]. Located in a prized downtown location, this is a massive church that gathers the assembly and ministry around a central table, provides multiple devotional spaces, and places the baptismal font so that worshipers encounter it on entry. Of the thirty-six tapestries created by John Nava for the building, twenty-five along the north and south walls of the nave depict 135 saints and blessed from around the world.

These extraordinary, high-profile buildings are not typical churches. Yet, while designed by world-renowned architects for Roman Catholic worship, they do symbolize key issues and tensions across contemporary liturgical architecture. The polarities of monoculturalism and multiculturalism, sacred and liturgical, urban and suburban, priesthood and laity, modern and traditional, transcendent and immanent, local and global, are therein articulated but not resolved. It is unlikely that resolution will come soon, or easily.

226. Interior of Jose Rafael Moneo's Cathedral of Our Lady of the Angels (Los Angeles, 2002).

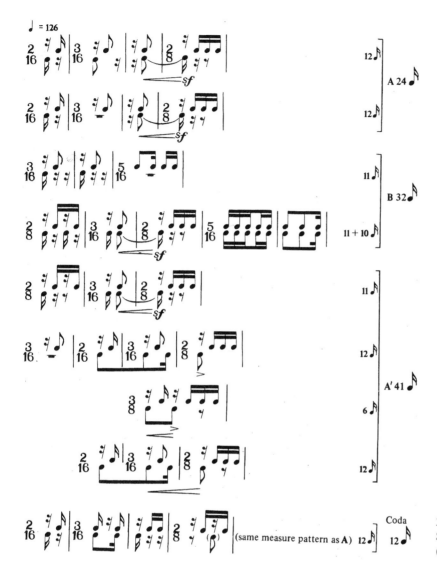

227. Examples of rhythms used by Igor Stravinsky in "The Rite of Spring." (Grout, pp. 844–45)

MUSIC

Just as ecclesiastical influence on Western architecture waned during the eighteenth and nineteenth centuries, so did Christianity lose its leadership in the musical arts in the West. The resulting division between worship music and non-liturgical sacred or religious music allowed the latter to flourish in the concert halls, outside a liturgical context. The division between the concert hall and the church was further marked by radically different musical styles. While composers of secular music explored new dimensions of rhythm, harmony, form, and instrumentation, church composers often took their inspiration from the past. Artistic advances did eventually influence church music, but the shape of worship music was less driven by the compositional vision of church musicians than by broader cultural forces outside of worship and the participatory vision of the liturgical movement from within.

Secular Developments

Outside the church, four important musical developments have affected contemporary liturgical music: 1) changes in Western compositional techniques, 2) the emergence of the musical science of ethnomusicology, 3) technological and commercial changes, and 4) the global flow of "world music."

Changing Sounds   Early in the twentieth century, dramatic musical changes erupted across the landscape of Western classical music. Harmonic, rhythmic, and melodic experiments abounded. Composers such as Arnold Schoenberg (d. 1951) explored atonal music in works such as his "Three Piano Pieces" (1909). Igor Stravinsky (d. 1971) shattered existing concepts of rhythm with "The Rite of Spring" (1913) [illustration 227]. Others, such as Béla Bartók (d. 1945) in "Music for Strings, Percussion and Celesta" (1936), experimented with new musical forms. Later in the century, visionaries such as Karlheinz Stockhausen (b. 1928) turned to the composition of electronic music. John Cage (d. 1992) redefined the avant-garde music scene in 1952 when his piece *4'33"* was performed, consisting of a pianist sitting down at a piano for four minutes and thirty-three seconds and doing nothing. Pierre Boulez (b. 1925) continued to push the envelope with electronic and computer music, and through his high-profile teaching and conducting became one of the leading voices for the new musics. Despite the critical acclaim of these and similar composers, their works are not yet central to the preferred repertoire of Western concert subscribers, and Mozart is still more likely to be heard than Bartók. On the other hand, late twentieth-century operatic works such as John Adam's *Nixon in China* (1987) and John Corigliano's *The Ghosts of Versailles* (1991) have been finding a place in the repertoire of major opera houses in the West.

Ethnomusicology   Another important influence in twentieth-century music was the emergence of the field known as ethnomusicology. During the nineteenth century, scholarly interest in the music of what Westerners considered "exotic" cultures generated a new musical subdiscipline known as comparative musicology. This combination of social sciences and traditional music studies acquired the name ethnomusicology in the 1950s. While originally focused on non-Western music, what distinguishes ethnomusicology as a discipline is its consideration of music as a dynamic aspect of culture. Combining the tools of anthropology, ethnography, musicology, and other

Quotation 333: *Focusing on the musical performance of kwaya [KiSwahili, "choir"] moves me beyond understanding and representing the phenomenon of kwaya solely as a musical genre; kwayas are distinct socio-cultural structures, or systems "compelled" into "engagement and union". . . . While I have found it important to understand and represent the musical sounds, structures and repertoires of traditional and indigenous kwaya music elsewhere, I also now find it important to address a different question: Why do members of Tanzanian kwayas gather on a regular basis to sing, pray, mourn, play sports, seek counsel and advice, learn about their spirituality, and look for potential spouses? The answers to these questions illustrate some of the many ways that a kwaya functions as a microcosm of an idealized social system. Perhaps most important is the function of a kwaya as a critical means for meeting the needs not only of a greater community but as a community in and of itself."* (Barz, *Performing Religion*, p. 81)

228. A song for the initiation of a girl in the Venda Society of South Africa.

fields concerned with culture and communication, ethnomusicologists study how music functions in various societies, how it serves as a means of social discourse, and especially how the performance of music provides an interpretive lens for understanding the dynamics of a culture or a particular group of people within a culture [quotation 333]. Because music is integral to the rituals of many peoples, ethnomusicologists often study the ritual music of traditional societies [illustration 228]. More recently, researchers have employed these techniques for studying musical phenomena within Western cultures, from the musical ambiance of shopping malls and airports, to the social significance of rap. In some ways, ethnomusicological studies are symbolic of the contemporary dynamics of glocalization. On the one hand, research in this field tends to focus on a very particular locale and context. On the other hand, ethnomusicologists recognize music making as a fundamental human phenomenon, with both local and global flows, as with "black music" and its sustained circulation around what Paul Gilroy has called "the black Atlantic" [quotation 334].

Technological and Commercial   Few arts have been affected by the technological changes of the last century as much as music. First was the invention of the phonograph in 1877 by Thomas Edison (d. 1931) and then a decade later Emil Berliner's (d. 1929) gramophone and record disks, whose popularity quickly surpassed that of Edison's cylinders for making and playing back recordings. Already in the late 1890s recorded music as a medium of entertainment had become firmly established in the U.S. This spurred the birth of a recording industry that first relied on classical music but then turned to jazz and popular forms. By 1919 a single recording (Paul Whiteman and his Orchestra's "Japanese Sandman") had sold a million copies. The widespread growth of the electrical industry in the early twentieth century was a boon to recording technologies and the commercialization of music. Magnetic tape, analog recording techniques, and tape recorders appeared in the mid-1930s, and by 1958 stereo recordings and playback equipment were available. Cassette recordings were introduced in the 1960s and by the 1980s their sales bypassed those of LP records. Dolby and digital recording changed the industry in the 1970s, and the compact disk became commercially available in 1983. More recently, the appearance of MP3 players along with the Internet have eliminated the need for records, cassettes, or disks, as consumers download music directly onto these personal storage and playback units.

Driving the growth in music consumption have been developments in mass communication. Commercial radio, largely a musical venture in the beginning, began broadcasting in 1922 in the U.S. Soon after, the first commercially successful movie with sound (*The Jazz Singer* of 1927) was released. Movies continue to be an important media for musical composition, performance, and marketing. Commercial TV became commonplace in the U.S. in the 1950s, and has been an influential venue for musical performance, from the early variety shows to contemporary music cable channels such as MTV. More recently, the Internet has become a global network for the exchange and promotion of music of every kind.

World Music   A more recent phenomenon from the later twentieth century has been the rise and recognition of "world music." This is not a new genre of music, but rather the appreciation and marketing of local music from around the globe—especially from outside of dominant Western cultures. Previously classified as indigenous, traditional, ethnic, or folk music, the term "world music" emerged in

Quotation 334: *Examining the place of music in the black Atlantic world means surveying the self-understanding articulated by the musicians who have made it, the symbolic use to which their music is put by other black artists and writers, and the social relations which have produced and reproduced the unique expressive culture in which music comprises a central and even foundational element.* (Gilroy, *The Black Atlantic,* pp. 74–75)

XI. In Dominicis infra annum.
(For Sundays throughout the Year.)
(Orbis factor)

229. Accompanied version of the *Kyrie* from Mass XI (1937). (*Kyriale* [Accompaniment by Achille P. Bragers], p. 58)

the early 1980s as part of a concerted effort to bring such music into the mainstream and give it the opportunity to be appreciated on its own merits. Western composers have been drawing on such music for centuries, for example, some of Antonin Dvorák's (d. 1904) music shows the influence of Czech folk dances. The growth of the field of ethnomusicology and the invention of recording devices contributed to the increased dissemination and influence of such indigenous music. A watershed event in Western popular music was the 1986 release of Paul Simon's album *Graceland*, which featured the South African vocal ensemble Ladysmith Black Mambazo. Their rise to prominence is symbolic of the growth of this global music current. In 1987 they were awarded a Grammy for "Best Traditional Folk Recording"; when they won their second Grammy in 2005, the title of the category had changed to "Best Traditional World Music Recording." The strength of this global musical flow has been aided by other late twentieth-century phenomena, such as the huge number of immigrants moving across national and international borders, the shifting of political and economic influence to the South and East, as well as the ubiquitous Internet and its ability to introduce local music into a global market: a true symbol of glocalization.

Church Music before Vatican II

During the first half of the twentieth century, two currents in church music were the revival of traditional music and experimentation with twentieth-century sounds.

Revivalism   Rather than advocating new sounds or musical forms, many churches during the nineteenth and early twentieth centuries advocated a return to traditional music. This musical revivalism was analogous to the various architectural revivals of the nineteenth century. The Roman Catholic Church, for example, sought to restore Gregorian chant in its worship [quotation 335]. Influenced by the work of Solesmes and other centers of chant study, Pius X (d. 1914) mandated chant for the universal church while simultaneously calling for the active participation of the assembly [quotation 320], which meant that congregations around the world were expected to sing music written for specialists. In most places, this was possible only by accompanying chant on the organ, which dramatically changed the nature of the music [illustration 229].

In the Church of England, adherents of the Oxford Movement sought to restore traditional carols, plainsong hymns, and German chorales to their worship. Of lasting significance were the translations of ancient texts by hymnologists such as John Mason Neal (d. 1866) [illustration 230] and Catherine Winkworth (d. 1878). Lutherans also experienced a musical revival during this period. After the death of Bach (d. 1750), the quality of Lutheran church music in Europe declined. The interest of King Friedrich Wilhelm IV (d. 1861) in traditional music, as well as the tendency of the age to value things from the past, contributed to a revival of older musical forms in nineteenth-century Lutheran Prussia. Interest in their musical heritage spread throughout Lutheranism.

These revivals were aided by advances in historical and musicological studies during the nineteenth century. Such advances, coupled with a renewed reverence for traditional music, helped generate a series of important denominational hymnals. Often produced by committees of experts, such hymnals raised the standards of church music by recovering quality composition from the past and encouraging contemporary composition of equal artistry.

New Sounds   Another development in church music before Vatican II was the work of outstanding Western composers in liturgical composition. Ralph Vaughan Williams (d. 1958) wrote a "Mass in G

Quotation 335: *Sacred music should consequently possess, in the highest degree, the qualities proper to the liturgy, and precisely sanctity and goodness of form from which spontaneously springs its other character, universality. . . . These qualities are possessed in the highest degree by the Gregorian chant which is, consequently, the chant proper to the Roman Church, the only chant it has inherited from the ancient fathers, which it has jealously guided for centuries in its liturgical codices, which it directly proposes to the faithful as its own, which it prescribes exclusively for some parts of the liturgy and which the most recent studies have so happily restored to their integrity and purity. Upon these grounds the Gregorian chant has always been regarded as the supreme model for sacred music so that the following rule may be safely laid down: The more closely a composition for church approaches in its movement, inspiration and savor the Gregorian form, the more sacred and liturgical it is. . . . The ancient traditional Gregorian chant must, therefore, be largely restored in the functions of public worship.* (Pius X, *The Restoration of Church Music* [1903], Introduction: 2–3, in Seasoltz, *The New Liturgy,* pp. 4–5)

Veni veni Emmanuel;	O come, O come, Immanuel (Isaiah 7:14)
captivum solve Israel,	and ransom captive Israel
qui gemit in exilio,	that mourns in lonely exile here
privatus Dei Filio.	until the Son of God appear.
Gaude, gaude, Emmanuel	Rejoice! Rejoice! Immanuel
nascetur pro te, Israel.	shall come to thee, O Israel.
Veni, o Jesse virgula;	O come, thou Rod of Jesse, free (Isaiah 11:1)
ex hostis tuos ungula	thine own from Satan's tyranny;
de specu tuos tartari	from depths of hell thy people save
educ et antro barathri.	and give them victory o'er the grave.
Gaude, gaude, Emmanuel	Rejoice! Rejoice! Immanuel
nascetur pro te, Israel.	shall come to thee, O Israel.
Veni, veni, o Oriens;	O come, thou Dayspring come and cheer (Luke 1:78)
solare nos adveniens;	our spirits by thine advent here;
noctis depelle nebulas	disperse the gloomy clouds of night
dirasque noctis tenebras.	and death's dark shadows put to flight
Gaude, gaude, Emmanuel	Rejoice! Rejoice! Immanuel
nascetur pro te, Israel.	shall come to thee, O Israel.
Veni, Clavis Davidica;	O come, thou Key of David, come, (Isaiah 22:22)
regna reclude caelica;	and open wide our heavenly home; (Revelation 3:7)
fac iter tutum superum,	make safe the way that leads on high,
at claude vias inferum.	and close the path to misery.
Gaude, gaude, Emmanuel	Rejoice! Rejoice! Immanuel
nascetur pro te, Israel.	shall come to thee, O Israel.
Veni, veni Adonaï	O come, O come, thou Lord of might (Exodus 20)
quo populo in Sinaï	who to thy tribes on Sinai's height
legem dedisti vertice	in ancient times didst give the law
in maiestate gloriae.	in cloud and majesty and awe.
Gaude, gaude, Emmanuel	Rejoice! Rejoice! Immanuel
nascetur pro te, Israel.	shall come to thee, O Israel.

230. John Mason Neal's translation of "Veni veni Emmanuel." (Routley, *A Panorama of Christian Hymnody*, p. 76)

Minor"; Igor Stravinsky contributed a "Mass for Mixed Voices and Wind Instruments"; Zoltán Kodály (d. 1967) and Benjamin Britten (d. 1976) each composed a *Missa Brevis*. On the one hand, such luminaries introduced many of the compositional advances of the century into church music. Somewhat like the church at Ronchamps, however, while providing a renewed artistic perspective, these works did not provide a renewed liturgical perspective that placed the assembly at the center of the prayer. On the other hand, noted composers such as Gustav Holst (d. 1934) and Ralph Vaughan Williams did compose hymns for the assembly, for example, the latter's *Sine Nomine*. Vaughan Williams was particularly influential in shaping church music by serving as music editor of the important *English Hymnal* (1906, revised in 1933).

Besides new sounds from the concert hall, there were also new sounds from the street that began to change the dynamics of twentieth-century worship music. Particularly important was the religious awakening that began in Los Angeles in 1906 and is known as the Azusa Street Revival, which took place under the leadership of an African-American Holiness preacher, William J. Seymour (d. 1922). Sometimes considered the birthplace of the modern Pentecostal movement, this religious, social, and cultural event unapologetically placed the richness of black religious heritage—with its body movement, clapping, song, dance, and storytelling—at the heart of this worship [quotation 336]. This movement also contributed to the introduction of wider instrumentation in Western Christian worship. Guitars and banjos were first employed, by the 1930s the piano was used, and by the 1950s the Hammond organ became the instrument of choice for many Pentecostal churches, supported by an array of percussion instruments enhanced by the introduction of electronic amplification systems. This was a sound that was to have a significant effect, not only on worship music in the West, but also on popular music currents indebted to this "gospel" sound.

The Liturgical Movement and Vatican II

Concurrent with these various musical flows was the growing influence of the liturgical movement. Because of its Roman Catholic origins, the effects of this movement first surfaced within that tradition. We have already noted the growing practice of the "dialogue Mass." In such Masses, the people recited some of those parts previously performed by the choir (such as the *Kyrie* and *Gloria*), first in Latin and eventually in the vernacular. As noted in the last chapter, some groups, such as Germans, Poles, and some Slavic communities, have had a long tradition of vernacular hymnody. Large immigrations of these people to the U.S. meant the introduction of these traditions here, which contributed to the currents of vernacular hymnody and other forms of congregational participation that anticipated aspects of the *Constitution on the Sacred Liturgy* (1963).

This pivotal document reiterated many insights from Pius X and others that music serves the liturgy and forms an integral part of the worship. One reason for music's integral role is its ability to serve liturgical texts. The constitution broke new ground, however, when it asserted that the "holiness" of the music is not determined by some intrinsic qualities or how similar it is to privileged forms of music like Gregorian chant, but by how closely the music is wed to the ritual [quotation 337]. This statement challenged the long-standing belief that worship music could be considered holy simply because it enhanced the worship through its beauty, as though it was art for art's sake. Music now must serve the liturgy, judged according to the council's first aim of reform, that is, the full, conscious, and

Quotation 336: *[William Seymour] affirmed his black heritage by introducing Negro spirituals and Negro music into his liturgy at a time when this music was considered inferior and unfit for Christian worship.* (Hollenweger, *Pentecostalism,* p. 20)

Quotation 337: *The musical tradition of the universal church is a treasure of inestimable value, greater even than that of any other art. The main reason for this pre-eminence is that, as a combination of sacred music and words, it forms a necessary or integral part of the solemn liturgy. Sacred scripture itself has praised sacred song. So have the Fathers of the church and the Roman pontiffs who in more recent times, led by St. Pius X, have explained more precisely the ministerial function of sacred music in the service of the Lord. Therefore sacred music will be the more holy, the more closely connected it is with the liturgical action, whether making prayer more pleasing, promoting unity of minds, or conferring greater solemnity on the sacred rites.* (Constitution on the Sacred Liturgy [1963], no. 112)

Peter Scholtes
Text and music © 1966, FEL Publications
Assigned to Lorenz Corp., 1991

231. "And They'll Know We Are Christians By Our Love" (1966).

active participation of the faithful (no. 14). Because of this emphasis on the ministerial function of music, a new set of standards for judging the effectiveness of worship music arose [quotation 338]. These new directions have not been without controversy and have sometimes contributed to the division between those who wish to emphasize the people's accessibility to the music and others stressing the need for compositional standards. This was particularly true right after Vatican II, with the publication of groundbreaking music resources such as the *Hymnal for Young Christians* (1966) [illustration 231]. As vernacular music for Roman Catholics matures and vast quantities of worship music in hymnals, missalettes, and octavos appear, the topic has become less controversial than other areas, such as liturgical architecture. Symbolic of this was the U.S. bishops reissuing the 1972 document *Music in Catholic Worship* in 1983 with virtually no changes. This was in stark contrast to the previously noted supplanting of the 1978 architectural guidelines by the U.S. bishops with *Built of Living Stones* in 2000.

Quotation 338: *To determine the value of a given musical element in a liturgical celebration, a threefold judgment must be made: musical, liturgical, and pastoral.* (U.S. Bishops' Committee on the Liturgy, *Music in Catholic Worship* [1972], no. 25)

P The Lord be with you.

C And al-so with you.

P Lift up your hearts.

C We lift them to the Lord.

P Let us give thanks to the Lord our God.

C It is right to give him thanks and praise.

29. The preface appropriate to the day or season is sung or said.

P It is indeed right and salutary . . . we praise your name and join their unending hymn:

C Holy, holy, ho-ly Lord, Lord God of

pow'r and might: Heav'n and earth are full of your

glo-ry. Ho-san-na in the high-est.

Bless-ed is he who comes in the name

of the Lord. Ho-san-na in the high-est.

232. Holy Communion, Setting Two. (*Lutheran Book of Worship* [1978], pp. 88–89)

While many Protestant churches never displaced the assembly's song in prayer, their worship still has undergone a significant change. As many Protestant churches have more intentionally recovered sacramental aspects of their traditions, especially the weekly celebration of the Eucharist [quotation 339], so have they more frequently placed music at the very heart of the Eucharist. Thus, numerous hymnal revisions for major Protestant denominations increasingly include acclamations, responsories, and various settings for the eucharistic liturgy [illustration 232], along with more traditional psalms and hymns. Although some traditions, such as the Scandinavian Lutherans, never lost this practice, they no longer are the exception. Even more common in these hymnals, as well as those of Roman Catholics, is music from nondominant and non-Western worship traditions, reflecting the wider currents of global music. Thus, it is not unusual to find adaptations of Swahili songs [illustration 233] or other indigenous chants side-by-side with the hymns of Charles Wesley and contemporary composers like Ruth Duck (b. 1947) and F. Pratt Green (d. 2000).

Quotation 339: *Christian faith is deepened by the celebration of the Lord's Supper. Hence the Eucharist should be celebrated frequently. . . . As the Eucharist celebrates the resurrection of Christ, it is appropriate that it should take place at least every Sunday. As it is the new sacramental meal of the people of God, every Christian should be encouraged to receive communion frequently. (World Council of Churches, Baptism, Eucharist, and Ministry [1982], nos. 31–32)*

South African
Text and music © 1984, Utryck, agent: Walton Music Corp.

233. Siyahamba, "We Are Marching in the Light of God," South African hymn, 1984.

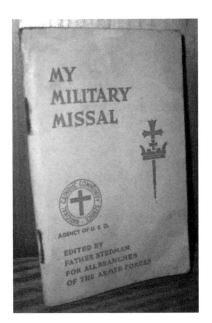

234. Stedman Military Missal.

Summary

As much or more than any other element in the liturgy, liturgical music has changed in response to concerns for congregational accessibility, cultural diversity, social redefinition, and shifting understandings of the ministerial function of music. Such changes, as in the other worship arts, reflect the challenge of balancing the new with the church's rich and varied musical traditions. As the sounds between some worship music and that of the secular music industry become blurred—symbolized by crossover artists who easily move between the sanctuary and Billboard.com's top 100—new concerns arise about liturgical music as entertainment. Sophisticated sound and lighting systems for musicians in some churches, the introduction of praise bands whose instrumentation and musical styles imitate those of the marketplace, and the commercialization of religious and even liturgical music with the boom of Christian radio and "easy listening" CDs demand more sophisticated theological reflection, especially on the part of pastoral leaders and pastoral musicians.

BOOKS

A steady stream of new liturgical books emanated from the Christian churches of the West during the twentieth century. The increase in the number of books from many denominations after Vatican II is especially noteworthy. To highlight this development, this section will consider books that appeared both before and after this pivotal council. Although a vast number of rituals and hymnals have been published throughout the world during this era, we will focus on books published in the U.S.

Liturgical Books before Vatican II

Few significant changes occurred in Roman Catholic official liturgical books between the Council of Trent and Vatican II. One exception was the reform of the breviary by Pius X in 1911. The heart of this reform was a reduction in the number of psalms—from twelve to nine—prayed at Matins, and the redistribution of the psalms throughout the offices. In theory, this was a startling innovation [quotation 340]. In practice, however, it went unnoticed by the faithful who had been excluded from this prayer for centuries. The restoration of the Easter Vigil (1951), which ended the practice of celebrating the Easter Vigil on Saturday morning, and the *Renewed Order of Holy Week* (1955) were more significant for ordinary believers.

There is no official Roman Catholic liturgical book for the laity's use at Eucharist. Instead, there existed innumerable prayer books filled with devotional exercises that occupied the faithful at Mass;

Quotation 340: *For the first time in the history of Christian morning praise in East or West, the psalms of lauds, Psalms 148–150, were not said daily, but one psalm of praise was assigned to each day of the week beginning with Saturday: Psalms 148, 116, 134, 145, 146, 147, 150. Furthermore, Psalms 50 and 62 were abandoned as fixed psalms at lauds, as were the traditional canticles except for Lent and vigils. For anyone with a sense of the history of the office, this was a shocking departure from almost universal Christian tradition.* (Taft, *The Liturgy of the Hours in East and West*, p. 312)

many said the rosary. A particular phenomenon in the twentieth century was the widespread use of unofficial daily missals. While they appeared in English in the nineteenth century, it was only at the turn of the century that permission was granted to translate the Mass into the vernacular, significantly contributing to this development. The most popular of these was the *Sunday Missal* published by Joseph Stedman (d. 1946), with thirty-two printings between 1932 and 1944 [illustration 234]. As Keith Pecklers documents in *The Unread Vision*, this missal received worldwide recognition—largely because of its use by solders during World War II—and was translated into Polish, Italian, French, Spanish, Chinese, Dutch, German, Japanese, Portuguese, and even one Native American language (p. 50).

In the early twentieth century, as James White documents throughout *Protestant Worship: Traditions in Transition*, Protestant

---

The Communion

¶ *After the Preface shall follow immediately:*

THEREFORE with Angels and Archangels, and with all the company of heaven, we laud and magnify thy glorious Name; evermore praising thee, and saying:

¶ *Then shall be sung or said the Sanctus.*

THE SANCTUS

HOLY, holy, holy, Lord God of Sabaoth; Heaven and earth are full of thy glory; Hosanna in the highest.
Blessed is he that cometh in the Name of the Lord; Hosanna in the highest.

¶ *Then may the Congregation kneel.*

¶ *The Minister standing before the Altar, and facing it, shall say the Prayer of Thanksgiving.*

THE PRAYER OF THANKSGIVING

HOLY art thou, Almighty and Merciful God. Holy art thou, and great is the Majesty of thy glory.
Thou didst so love the world as to give thine only-begotten Son, that whosoever believeth in him might not perish, but have everlasting life; Who, having come into the world to fulfill for us thy holy will and to accomplish all things for our salvation, IN THE NIGHT IN WHICH HE WAS BETRAYED, ªTOOK BREAD; AND, WHEN HE HAD GIVEN THANKS, HE BRAKE IT AND GAVE IT TO HIS DISCIPLES, SAYING, TAKE, EAT; THIS IS MY BODY, WHICH IS GIVEN FOR YOU; THIS DO IN REMEMBRANCE OF ME.   *(a) Here he shall take the BREAD in his hand.*
AFTER THE SAME MANNER ALSO, HE ᵇTOOK THE CUP, WHEN HE HAD SUPPED, AND, WHEN HE HAD GIVEN THANKS, HE GAVE IT TO THEM, SAYING, DRINK YE ALL OF IT; THIS CUP IS THE NEW TESTAMENT IN MY BLOOD, WHICH IS SHED FOR YOU, AND FOR MANY, FOR THE REMISSION OF SINS; THIS DO, AS OFT AS YE DRINK IT, IN REMEMBRANCE OF ME.   *(b) Here he shall take the CUP in his hand.*
Remembering, therefore, his salutary precept, his life-giving Passion and Death, his glorious Resurrection and Ascension and the promise of his coming again, we give thanks to thee, O Lord God Almighty, not as we ought, but as we are able; and we beseech thee mercifully to accept our praise and thanksgiving, and with thy Word and Holy Spirit to bless us, thy servants, and these thine own gifts of bread and wine, so that we and all who partake thereof may be filled with heavenly benediction and grace, and, receiving the remission of sins, be sanctified in soul and body, and have our portion with all thy saints.
And unto thee, O God, Father, Son, and Holy Spirit, be all honor and glory in thy holy Church, world without end. Amen.

11

The Service

¶ *Then shall the Minister sing or say:*

OUR Father, who art in heaven, Hallowed be thy Name, Thy kingdom come, Thy will be done, on earth as it is in heaven. Give us this day our daily bread; And forgive us our trespasses, as we forgive those who trespass against us; And lead us not into temptation, But deliver us from evil.

¶ *The Congregation shall sing or say:*

FOR thine is the kingdom, and the power, and the glory, for ever and ever. Amen.

¶ *Or, instead of the above Prayer of Thanksgiving, "Holy art thou, Almighty and Merciful God," the Minister may say the Words of Institution, followed by the Lord's Prayer.*

THE WORDS OF INSTITUTION

OUR LORD JESUS CHRIST, IN THE NIGHT IN WHICH HE WAS BETRAYED, ªTOOK BREAD; AND, WHEN HE HAD GIVEN THANKS, HE BRAKE IT AND GAVE IT TO HIS DISCIPLES, SAYING, TAKE, EAT; THIS IS MY BODY, WHICH IS GIVEN FOR YOU; THIS DO IN REMEMBRANCE OF ME.   *(a) Here he shall take the BREAD in his hand.*
AFTER THE SAME MANNER ALSO, HE ᵇTOOK THE CUP, WHEN HE HAD SUPPED, AND, WHEN HE HAD GIVEN THANKS, HE GAVE IT TO THEM, SAYING, DRINK YE ALL OF IT; THIS CUP IS THE NEW TESTAMENT IN MY BLOOD, WHICH IS SHED FOR YOU, AND FOR MANY, FOR THE REMISSION OF SINS; THIS DO, AS OFT AS YE DRINK IT, IN REMEMBRANCE OF ME.   *(b) Here he shall take the CUP in his hand.*

THE LORD'S PRAYER

OUR Father, who art in heaven, . . .

¶ *Then shall the Minister turn to the Congregation and sing or say:*
The peace of the Lord be with you alway.

¶ *The Congregation shall sing or say:*
And with thy spirit.

¶ *Then, the Congregation standing, shall be sung or said the Agnus Dei.*

AGNUS DEI

O CHRIST, thou Lamb of God, that takest away the sin of the world, have mercy upon us.
O Christ, thou Lamb of God, that takest away the sin of the world, have mercy upon us.
O Christ, thou Lamb of God, that takest away the sin of the world, grant us thy peace. Amen.

12

---

235. One significant change in the 1958 *Service Book and Hymnal* was the introduction of a complete eucharistic prayer which could be used instead of the words of instruction alone. (*Service Book and Hymnal* [1958], pp. 11–12)

churches in the United States produced an unusual number of liturgical books. The Episcopal Church's *Book of Common Prayer*, first approved for use in the United States in 1789, was revised in 1892 and again in 1928. The Episcopal Church also revised its hymnal twice during the first half of the twentieth century: *The New Hymnal* (1916–18) and the *Hymnal* (1940). The former was the first musical edition of an Episcopal hymnal authorized by a general convention, and the latter became one of the most celebrated English hymnals of the century.

Various Lutheran churches in the United States often produced a combined hymnal and prayer book. The first of these produced in English was John Christopher Kunze's (d. 1807) *A Hymnal and Prayer-Book* (1795). Throughout the eighteenth and nineteenth centuries, many others were published, such as the *Church Book*, initially prepared for the 1868 convention of the General Council, and which later went through many subsequent editions. In 1917, three groups—the General Council, the General Synod, and the United Synod South—produced a single worship book and hymnal. The publication of this *Common Service Book* played an important role in the merger of these three synods into the United Lutheran Church in America in 1918 [quotation 341]. Another notable joint venture was the *Service Book and Hymnal* (1958) [illustration 235], produced by eight different church bodies. This hymnal also contributed to the merger of four of these—the American Lutheran Church, the Evangelical Lutheran Church in America, the United Evangelical Lutheran Church, and the Lutheran Free Church—into the American Lutheran Church in 1961. The remaining four—the Augustana Lutheran Church, the American Evangelical Lutheran Church, the Finnish Evangelical Lutheran Church, and the United Lutheran Church in America—formed the Lutheran Church in America in 1962.

Other significant collaborative efforts in the twentieth century include the work of three Methodist churches. In anticipation of their union in 1939, the Methodist Episcopal Church, the Methodist Episcopal Church-South and the Methodist Protestant Church jointly published *The Methodist Hymnal*. After their union, the new Methodist Church published a *Book of Worship* (1944). A second *Hymnal* and *Book of Worship* were approved in 1964.

Although not a joint venture, the 1906, 1932, and 1946 editions of the *Book of Common Worship*, published by the Presbyterian Church in the U.S.A. (North), eventually were approved by the Presbyterian Church in the U.S.A. (South). These ventures contributed to the joint publication of *The Hymnbook* (1955) and *The Worshipbook* (1970), foreshadowing the 1983 union of these two churches.

Twentieth-century American Protestantism has demonstrated that liturgical books are not simply neutral ritual objects. They em-

Quotation 341: *When the music edition of the Common Service Book came from the press in 1917, it was hailed as one of the most significant events of the quadricentennial observance of the Protestant Reformation. But it also had far-reaching practical results. The spirit of fellowship engendered by 33 years of joint liturgical and hymnological studies on the part of the three general bodies was undoubtedly one of the most potent factors which led to their organic union in 1918 as the United Lutheran Church in America. (Ernest Ryden, in Stulken, Hymnal Companion to the Lutheran Book of Worship, p. 100)*

ORDO MISSÆ

THE ORDINARY
OF THE MASS

1. *After the celebrant has made the required reverence to the altar, he signs himself with the sign of the cross, saying in an appropriate tone of voice:*

In the name of the Father, and of the Son, and of the Holy Spirit. Amen.

Then, with his hands joined, he adds:
℣. I will go to the altar of God.
℟. To God who gives joy to my youth.

2. *And he continues immediately:*
℣. Our help is in the name of the Lord.
℟. Who made heaven and earth.

Next, bowing deeply, he makes the following confession:
I confess to almighty God, to blessed Mary ever Virgin, to blessed Michael the Archangel, to blessed John the Baptist, to the holy apostles Peter and Paul, to all the saints, and to you, brethren, that I have sinned exceedingly in thought, word and deed; (*he strikes his breast three times, saying:*) through my fault, through my fault, through my most grievous fault. Therefore I beseech blessed Mary ever Virgin, blessed Michael the Archangel, blessed John the Baptist, the holy apoſtles Peter and Paul, all the saints, and you, brethren, to pray to the Lord our God for me.

The ministers or those present respond:
May almighty God have mercy on you, forgive you your sins, and bring you to life everlasting.

The celebrant says: Amen, and stands erect. Next the ministers or those present make the confession. Where the celebrant has said to you, brethren, *and you, brethren, they say to* you, father *and you, father.*

1. *Celebrans, facta altari debita reverentia, signans se signo crucis, congrua voce dicit:*

In nómine Patris, et Fílii, et Spíritus Sancti. Amen.

Deinde, iunctis manibus, subiungit:
℣. Introíbo ad altáre Dei.
℟. Ad Deum qui lætíficat iuventútem meam.

2. *Et statim addit:*
℣. Adiutórium nostrum in nómine Dómini.
℟. Qui fecit cælum et terram.

Deinde, profunde inclinatus, facit confessionem:
Confíteor Deo omnipoténti, beátæ Maríæ semper Vírgini, beáto Michaéli Archángelo, beáto Ioánni Baptístæ, sanctis Apóstolis Petro et Paulo, ómnibus Sanctis, et vobis, fratres: quia peccávi nimis cogitatióne, verbo et ópere: (*percutit sibi pectus ter, dicens:*) mea culpa, mea culpa, mea máxima culpa. Ideo precor beátam Maríam semper Vírginem, beátum Micháelem Archángelum, beátum Ioánnem Baptístam, sanctos Apóstolos Petrum et Paulum, omnes Sanctos, et vos, fratres, oráre pro me ad Dóminum Deum nostrum.

Ministri vel circumstantes respondent:
Misereátur tui omnípotens Deus, et, dimíssis peccátis tuis, perdúcat te ad vitam ætérnam.

Sacerdos dicit: Amen et erigit se. Deinde ministri vel circumstantes faciunt confessionem: et ubi a celebrante dicebatur vobis, fratres, *et* vos fratres, *ab eis dicitur tibi, pater, et* te, pater.

563

236. The English-Latin Sacramentary for the United States of America (1966), showing the hybrid state of the eucharistic liturgy immediately after the Second Vatican Council with a partially revised ritual in English and Latin. (Benzinger Edition, 1966)

body belief and thus, in some situations, serve as instruments for unity. Ordinary worshipers were part of this experience because the changes occurred in the books they used week after week. While approved by recognized ecclesiastical bodies, such books were not simply books of the liturgical specialists; they were the people's books, especially the hymnals.

Liturgical Books after Vatican II

In a series of deceptively simple statements, Vatican II decreed the reform of virtually every liturgical book in the Roman Catholic

Quotation 342:

- *The rite of the Mass is to be revised. [no. 50]*
- *Both rites for the Baptism of adults are to be revised. [no. 66]*
- *The rite for the Baptism of infants is to be revised. [no. 67]*
- *The rite of confirmation is also to be revised. [no. 71]*
- *The rite and formulas of Penance are to be revised. [no. 72]*
- *In addition to the separate rites for anointing of the sick and for Viaticum, a continuous rite must be prepared. [no. 74]*
- *Both the ceremonies and texts of the ordination rites are to be revised. [no. 76]*
- *The marriage rite . . . is to be revised. [no. 77]*
- *The sacramentals are to be revised. [no. 79]*
- *The rite of the consecration to a life of virginity . . . is to be subjected to review. [no. 80]*
- *Funeral rites should express more clearly the paschal character of Christian death. [no. 81]*
- *In the revision of the office these norms are to be observed . . . [no. 89]*

(Constitution on the Sacred Liturgy)

Quotation 343: *Provided that the substantial unity of the Roman Rite is preserved, provision shall be made when revising the liturgical books, for legitimate variations and adaptations to different groups, regions and peoples, especially in mission countries. This should be borne in mind when drawing up the rites and rubrics. (Constitution on the Sacred Liturgy, no. 38)*

Church [quotation 342]. Like those at the Council of Trent, the bishops at Vatican II did not attempt the work of revision themselves. This was given to a series of commissions, special committees, and Roman congregations that continue the work today.

Aided by modern technologies, new liturgical books for the Roman Catholic Church appeared very quickly. The books published in the years immediately following the council were hybrid publications, often in both Latin and the vernacular, reflecting a preliminary stage of the reform [illustration 236]. Eventually, a series of standard editions for the universal church (each called an *editio typica* in Latin) was promulgated by Rome. These, in turn, were published in vernacular translations approved by national conferences of bishops and confirmed by Rome. Thus, for example, an *editio typica* of the Roman Missal was issued in 1970, and an approved English translation appeared in 1973.

A third step in the adaptation of Roman Catholic books, as presumed by Vatican II, is their adaptation to various cultures [quotation 343]. For example, after the *editio typica* of the *Order of Funerals* was issued in Latin (1969), an approved English translation appeared (1970). A revised version, prepared by the International Commission on English in the Liturgy (ICEL), approved by the Roman Catholic Bishops of the United States, and confirmed by Rome, then appeared (1989).

With the promulgation of the various standard editions of the rites, the post–Vatican II Roman Catholic Church experienced a liturgical uniformity it had never before known. Even the Council of Trent had allowed all liturgical traditions over two hundred years old to continue. Vatican II eliminated all such rites [illustration 237]. That council did presume, however, that the rites would be adapted. The amount of official adaptation to date has been modest. While many after the council imagined the birth of new rites—such as an African American rite, or even ecumenical union through the recognition of Lutheranism, for example, as a distinctive rite—only the Zairean-Congolese adaptation of the Roman Rite has been approved, which Rome does not recognize as an independent liturgical rite.

As further corroboration of Nathan Mitchell's suggestion that 1984 was a benchmark for a shift in postconciliar reforms (see p. 303), since the mid-1980s there has been increased debate within the Roman Catholic community about the translation of liturgical books. In the U.S. this debate came to a head in the 1990s when permissions for previously approved texts were withdrawn. For example, in 1994 the Vatican withdrew its 1992 permission to employ the New Revised Standard Version of the Bible for liturgical use. At the same time, Rome denied permission to use the Psalter from the

Ordo Missae

Sacerdos, quando celebraturus accesserit ad medium altaris, facta profunda inclinatione, stans muniat se signo Crucis, dicens clara et intelligibili voce :

N nómine Patris, et Fílii, et Spíritus Sancti. Amen.

Deinde eadem voce : ℣. Confitémini Dómino quóniam bonus.

Ministri ℟. Quóniam in sǽculum misericórdia ejus.

Postea inclinatus profunde, dicat :

Confíteor Deo omnipoténti, et beátæ Maríæ semper Vírgini, et beáto Domínico Patri nostro, et ómnibus Sanctis, et vobis Fratres, quia peccávi nimis cogitatióne, locutióne, ópere, et omissióne, mea culpa : precor vos oráre pro me.

Ministri ℟. Misereátur tui, etc.

Deinde Confessionem repetant, et ubi Sacerdos dicebat vobis Fratres, et vos; dicant ipsi tibi Pater, et te.

Quibus dictis, Sacerdos dicat :

Misereátur vestri omnípotens Deus, et dimíttat vobis ómnia peccáta vestra : líberet vos ab omni malo,

salvet, et confírmet in omni ópere bono, et perdúcat vos ad vitam ætérnam.

M. ℟. Amen.

Absolutiónem, et remissiónem ómnium peccatórum vestrórum tríbuat vobis omnípotens et miséricors Dóminus.

M. ℟. Amen.

Confessione facta, et absolutióne, se erigat Sacerdos, et dicat :

Adjutórium nostrum in nómine Dómini.

M. ℟. Qui fecit cælum et terram.

Et appropians ad altare, rursus profunde inclinatus dicat Orationem :

Aufer a nobis, Dómine, cunctas iniquitátes nostras : ut ad Sancta sanctórum puris mereámur méntibus introíre. Per Christum Dóminum nostrum. Amen.

Hac Oratione dicta, osculetur altare, signando illud prius in medio pollice dextero : et erectus muniat se signo Crucis, et accedens ad librum junctis manibus ante pectus, incipiat Missæ

237. Opening of the Order of Mass from a twentieth-century edition of the Dominican Rite, eliminated by Vatican II. (*Missale Ordinis Praedicatorum*, Rome, 1939)

Revised New American Bible for liturgical use, approved by the U.S. Roman Catholic bishops in 1991. The result was rejection of the lectionary that the U.S. bishops had submitted in 1992 and that was reliant upon these translations. In 1997 the ordination rite that the U.S. bishops had approved and submitted in 1996 was rejected because of what Rome considered a flawed English translation. In 2001 Rome published a new set of translation guidelines that not only replaced the previously published guidelines of 1969 but radically reversed the principles for translation [quotation 344].

The publication of a new *editio typica* of the Roman Missal in 2002 has led to further debate about the translation of central texts of the Roman Catholic Mass. In 2006 the U.S. Roman Catholic bishops approved a new translation that changed some of the most

Quotation 344: *The prayer of the Church is always the prayer of some actual community, assembled here and now. It is not sufficient that a formula handed down from some other time or region be translated verbatim, even if accurately, for liturgical use. The formula translated must become the genuine prayer of the congregation and in it each of its members should be able to find and express himself or herself. (On The Translation Of Liturgical Texts For Celebrations With A Congregation* [French, *Comme le prévoit*], 1969, no. 20)

(continued . . .)

Among the separate elements are those which are essential and others which are secondary and subsidiary. The essential elements, so far as is possible, should be preserved in translation, sometimes intact, sometimes in equivalent terms. The general structure of the Roman prayers can be retained unchanged: the divine title, the motive of the petition, the petition itself, the conclusion. Others cannot be retained: the oratorical cursus, rhetorical-prose cadence. (Ibid., no. 28)

(compared to)

The Latin liturgical texts of the Roman Rite, while drawing on centuries of ecclesial experience in transmitting the faith of the Church received from the Fathers, are themselves the fruit of the liturgical renewal, just recently brought forth. In order that such a rich patrimony may be preserved and passed on through the centuries, it is to be kept in mind from the beginning that the translation of the liturgical texts of the Roman Liturgy is not so much a work of creative innovation as it is of rendering the original texts faithfully and accurately into the vernacular language. While it is permissible to arrange the wording, the syntax and the style in such a way as to prepare a flowing vernacular text suitable to the rhythm of popular prayer, the original text, insofar as possible, must be translated integrally and in the most exact manner, without omissions or additions in terms of their content, and without paraphrases or glosses. Any adaptation to the characteristics or the nature of the various vernacular languages is to be sober and discreet. (On the Use of Vernacular Languages in the Publication of the Books of the Roman Liturgy [Latin, Liturgiam Authenticam], 2001, no. 20)

familiar liturgical texts for English-speaking Roman Catholics. For example, the response to "The Lord be with you" is no longer "and also with you," but now the more literal "and with your Spirit." The issue of translation, especially in cultures where there is heightened gender awareness and sensitivity, will be one of the enduring challenges of a universal church whose official language is Latin, but whose people have embraced the vernaculars of the world.

The explosion of liturgical books after Vatican II in the Roman Catholic Church was matched by similar activities in Protestant churches. The Episcopal Church, for example, revised virtually all of its rites and the Psalter as *The Book of Common Prayer and Administration of the Sacraments and Other Rites and Ceremonies of the Church together with the Psalter or Psalms of David* (1979). This volume includes newly revised rites, a lectionary based on the Roman lectionary, an expanded liturgical calendar, and four new eucharistic prayers. Furthermore, the new configuration of the rites—placing baptism, confirmation, marriage, and burial rites in the context of Eucharist—downplays the traditionally more important rites of Morning and Evening Prayer. The Eucharist is central in this revision [quotation 345]. The Episcopal Church also issued a new hymnal in 1982. In 2000 the Church of England published a new experimental liturgical book, *Common Worship*, combining traditional elements of the *Book of Common Prayer* with newer forms of worship.

During the year after the end of Vatican II, an Inter-Lutheran Commission on Worship began a twelve-year project that culminated in the publication of *The Lutheran Book of Worship* (LBW). Proposed as a joint publication of the Lutheran Church in America, the American Lutheran Church, the Evangelical Lutheran Church of Canada, and the Lutheran Church-Missouri Synod, this volume led to further unions. Although the Lutheran Church-Missouri Synod withdrew from the project and produced its own volume, *Lutheran Worship* (1982), the LBW nonetheless became one more vehicle to unity in the American Lutheran community. The Lutheran Church in America, the American Lutheran Church, and the Association of Evangelical Lutheran Churches together formed the Evangelical Lutheran Church in America in 1988. The LBW is its official worship book. It contains the richest liturgical calendar in a Lutheran publication since the Reformation. It also adopts the Roman lectionary with its three-year cycle of readings and includes four musical settings of the eucharistic rite together with three forms of the eucharistic prayer. The *Lutheran Book of Worship: Minister's Desk Edition* (1978) contains three more eucharistic prayers [illustration 238]. This builds on the tradition of the 1958 *Service Book*, which introduced a full eucharistic prayer as an alternative to the preface, *Sanctus*, and words of institution traditionally used in Lutheran churches [illustration 235]. More recently, the Evangelical Lutheran Church embarked

III

P You are indeed holy,
almighty and merciful God;
you are most holy,
and great is the majesty
of your glory.

You so loved the world
that you gave your only Son,
that whoever believed in him
may not perish
but have eternal life.

Having come into the world,
he fulfilled for us your holy will
and accomplished our salvation.

In the night
in which he was betrayed,
our Lord Jesus took bread,
and gave thanks; broke it,
and gave it to his disciples,
saying: Take and eat;
this is my body, given for you.

Do this for the remembrance of me.

Again, after supper,
he took the cup, gave thanks,
and gave it for all to drink,
saying: This cup is
the new covenant in my blood,
shed for you and for all people
for the forgiveness of sin.

Do this for the remembrance of me.

Remembering, therefore,
his salutary command,

his life-giving Passion and death,
his glorious resurrection
and ascension,
and his promise to come again,
we give thanks to you,
Lord God Almighty,
not as we ought,
but as we are able;
and we implore you
mercifully to accept
our praise and thanksgiving,
and, with your Word
and Holy Spirit,
to bless us, your servants,
and these your own gifts
of bread and wine;
that we and all who share
in the body and blood
of your Son
may be filled
with heavenly peace and joy,
and, receiving the forgiveness
of sin,
may be sanctified
in soul and body,
and have our portion
with all your saints.
All honor and glory are yours,
O God, Father, Son,
and Holy Spirit,
in your holy Church,
now and forever.

C Amen

238. Eucharistic Prayer 3 from the *Lutheran Book of Worship: Minister's Desk Edition* (p. 297).

upon a revision process of hymnal and liturgical resources. In response to new generational and cultural trends, they published a supplement to the LBW (*With One Voice*, 1995), a Spanish-language resource (*Libro de Liturgia y Cántico*, 1998), and an African American resource (*This Far by Faith*, 1999). In 2006 they published the comprehensive *Evangelical Lutheran Worship*, the first work of such magnitude to be published simultaneously in print and digital form.

The newly formed United Methodist Church—created through a merger of the Methodist Church with the Evangelical United Brethren Church in 1968—established a commission in 1970 to revise its worship and books. As was also true of Episcopalians and Lutherans, the work of this body first resulted in a series of individual rites published in the *Supplemental Worship Resources* series. These revisions culminated in *The United Methodist Hymnal* (1989), a

Quotation 345: *Baptism, confirmation, marriage and burial all appeared, not as they had been in the context of choir offices, but in specialized forms of the proanaphora. The rest of the Eucharist can, and usually does, follow. So, too, is the case with special rites for Ash Wednesday and Palm Sunday. Although extensive space is devoted to the daily offices, the new* American Prayer Book *is eucharistically centered.* (Boone Porter, in Senn, *New Eucharistic Prayers*, p. 64)

single volume of worship and song. Most significant in these revisions was the use of the three-year *Common Lectionary* (revised in 1994), widely shared among Protestant churches today, and with a greatly expanded calendar. The large number of eucharistic prayers—twenty-four in the 1987 publication for use of the minister entitled *Holy Communion*, for example—is also notable. Subsequently, the United Methodists published a new book of liturgy, prayer, services, and service music entitled *The United Methodist Book of Worship* (1992), and more recently the hymnal supplement *The Faith We Sing* (2000). Similarly, Presbyterians published a new hymnal in 1990 (*The Presbyterian Hymnal*) and a comprehensive worship book in 1993 honoring "the reformed approach to worship, freedom within order" (*Book of Common Worship*, p. 6).

Summary

In these many revisions of liturgical books, often accompanied by long periods of consultation and study, there has been considerable cross-fertilization. Protestant churches have sometimes adopted the Roman lectionary, and Roman Catholics are learning about vernacular liturgy, even to the point of borrowing vernacular texts from other traditions [quotation 346]. One enduring difference is that in most Protestant churches, the revised book is the people's book. This is especially true when churches publish a combined service book and hymnal. These belong to the assembly, and it is not unusual for members of the congregation to have a personal copy of such a book. Roman Catholics, however, revise books mainly for the liturgical specialists. There is no official book for the congregation. With the rise of vernacular liturgy, the unofficial "missals" of the 1940s and 1950s have become largely obsolete. Their replacements range from newsprint missalettes and paperback songbooks to finely crafted hymnals and even modern daily missals. In view of the expensive sanctuary books used by the priest and other ministers, the range of these replacements communicates something of a mixed message about the role of the assembly in worship.

Quotation 346: *In sure and certain hope of the resurrection to eternal life through our Lord Jesus Christ we commend to almighty God our brother/sister N., and we commit his/her body to the ground; earth to earth, ashes to ashes, dust to dust. The Lord bless him/her and keep him/her, the Lord make his face to shine upon him/her and be gracious to him/her, the Lord lift up his countenance upon him/her and give him/her peace.* (Prayer of Committal from The Book of Common Prayer [1979] employed in the Roman Catholic Order of Christian Funerals [1989])

VESSELS

Changes in twentieth-century worship vessels have been less dramatic than those that occurred, for example, in the worship spaces or music. Unlike the evolution of liturgical music in this era, there was no organization comparable to the Society of St. Cecilia to champion a restoration of cups or plates parallel to the restoration of Gregorian chant. Furthermore, unlike the revision of liturgical books in the same period, changes in the materials, styles, and shapes of liturgical vessels seldom were achieved at the request of some church board or Roman congregation. Nonetheless, the metamorphosis of worship vessels—certainly as much as that of spaces, music, or books—symbolizes the desire to rediscover the power of blessing God through sharing simple gifts of bread and wine in the spirit of early Christian worship. This especially was true of the Roman Catholic community, whose Eucharist after Trent had so little in common with that of the domestic church.

Stylistic Changes

As already noted, some Protestant churches introduced domestic vessels into their worship early in the reform. For those who rejected a place for artistry in the liturgy, such as the followers of Zwingli [quotation 347], simple domestic ware was most appropriate for celebrating the Lord's Supper. Similar styles continued within these traditions. For others, however, domestic wineglasses and serving trays were only an interim solution after the purge of "popish" vessels. The sacramental revivals of the nineteenth century prompted the displacement of domestic ware by more specialized vessels in some Protestant churches. Forged from precious metals by professional artisans, the vessels of many Protestant churches during the nineteenth and twentieth centuries often had little in common with those used in the home. For these Protestant churches, as well as for the Roman Catholic Church, the early twentieth century was a time of essentially stylistic changes in worship vessels. These changes were brought about by two influences: the acceptance of the principles of functionalism and the tendency to mass-produce such vessels.

Functionalism

We have often noted the strong correlation between the architecture of a worship space and the style of shape of the vessels used in that space. Thus, it is not surprising that the early twentieth-century tendency to reject ornamentation and artificiality in architecture affected the design of eucharistic vessels as well. Although this approach affected vessels much later than it did church architecture, the mid-twentieth century eventually saw the emergence of eucharistic vessels with little or no ornamentation. The results were often sleek, contemporary works of art. Sometimes this was achieved with traditional materials of silver and gold. Other times, however, new alloys such as stainless steel were the preferred materials [illustration 239].

Quotation 347: *Zwingli believed that "it is clear and indisputable that no external element or action can purify the soul" and was completely consistent to discount the use of physical objects and actions in worship. A sense of the sign value of things in conveying God's grace is altogether lacking. This disjuncture between the physical and spiritual sets Zwingli apart from Luther and Calvin. Essentially it is a matter of piety. If the physical cannot lead one to God, one has to draw a circle around much of the traditional Christian cultus and mark it for destruction.* (White, *Protestant Worship,* p. 61)

239. Monstrance of stainless steel with 24-karat gold pyx by Alexander Schaffner. (*Liturgical Arts*, 39 [1971]: p. 77)

CHALICES
(ORNAMENTAL YET INEXPENSIVE)

No. A296/30.
A nice low priced style 8⅝ inches high.
Free Import
Cup and Paten silver, all gold plated........$22.50
Solid silver, all gold plated......................$30.00
Ciborium to Match.
Diameter of cup, 4 inches.
Silver Cup, all gold-plated......................$22.50
Solid silver, all gold-plated....................$30.00

No. 274/30.
Free Import
Three mat silver medallions on base, 9½ inch, silver
cup and paten, all gold plated..............$47.50
All silver, gold plated $62.50

No. A290/30.
Three medallions in silver on base. Crucifixion,
Blessed Virgin and St. Joseph, 9 inches high.
Free Import
Cup and paten silver, all gold-plated........ $ 75.00
Solid silver, all gold plated.................. $ 95.00
Ciborium to Match.
Diameter of cup, 4¼ inches.
Silver cup, all gold-plated................... $ 75.00
Solid silver, gold-plated $100.00

No. A293/30.
Three silver medallions on base, the Crucifixion,
Annunciation and Nativity; six medallions on cup,
three of the Doctors of the Church and Sacred Heart
of Jesus, Mater Dolorosa and St. Joseph. The knob
has the name of Jesus.
9¾ inches high.
Free Import
Cup and paten, silver, all gold-plated........$120.00
Solid silver, all gold-plated..................$145.00
Ciborium to Match.
Cup 4⅜ in. diameter.
Free import
Cup, silver, all gold-plated..................$120.00
Solid silver, gold-plated....................$155.00

No. A294/30.
Grape design, chased, column in enamel, knob
open work.
9 inches high.
Free Import
Cup and paten, silver, all gold-plated........$110.00
All silver, gold-plated $140.00

No. A298/30.
Six apostles on base and six on cup in enamel
9¾ inches high.
Free Import
Cup and paten, silver, all gold-plated........$260.00
Solid silver, all gold-plated..................$300.00
Ciborium to Match
Cup 4¾ inches diameter
Silver cup, all gold-plated..................$260.00
Solid silver, all gold-plated.................$330.00

240. Page from the 1930 catalog of the John P. Daleiden Company, Chicago.

Mass Production

The principles of functionalism contributed to the creation of some truly artistic vessels. The twentieth-century propensity for mass production, however, generally had the opposite effect. Although liturgical books had been mass-produced since the advent of the printing press in the fifteenth century, vessels were not manufactured in this way until the invention of the assembly line at the turn of the twentieth century. Originally conceived for the production of heavy equipment—for example, the automobile—assembly-line techniques eventually were adapted to a variety of products. By the 1930s, this included the mass production of eucharistic vessels. The result of this technological advance, apparent especially in the U.S., was an approach to the production, marketing, and acquisition of eucharistic vessels similar to that used for other mass-produced commodities. Catalogs of vessels and other church goods emerged [illustration 240]. Although available in various styles and materials, these vessels had to appeal to a broad market. Consequently, they often were manufactured according to uninspiring standards of design and artistry. Through these catalogs, the revivalist tendencies apparent in nineteenth- and early twentieth-century architecture and music persisted in liturgical vessels. Pseudo-Gothic and pseudo-baroque chalices were produced by the thousands. Reproductions of classic designs from the past became available to the consumer. Such mass-produced vessels continue to proliferate today.

The Symbolic Revolution

Like the parallel changes in music and architecture during the early part of the twentieth century, the changes in eucharistic vessels brought about by the principles of functionalism and the advent of mass production were essentially stylistic. A more profound change would occur in the middle of the century, when the shift in liturgical and sacramental thought would place renewed stress on the symbolic nature of the liturgy [quotation 348].

During the nineteenth century, a symbolists' movement in the visual arts and literature—epitomized in the writing of Paul Verlaine (d. 1896)—swept across Europe. During the twentieth century, philosophers such as Ernst Cassirer (d. 1945), Susanne Langer (d. 1985), and Paul Ricoeur (d. 2005) advanced symbolic theory, while anthropologists such as Victor Turner (d. 1983) and Clifford Geertz (d. 2006) explored the ritual symbolism of traditional societies and gave rise to that school of anthropology known as "symbolic anthropology." The work of these and other philosophers and social scientists provided a framework for theologians searching for more satisfying

Quotation 348: *Theologians began to turn their thoughts in quite a different direction after the Second World War. [Between 1949 and 1960] a different question was already preoccupying most theologians—that of the relationship between the metaphysical approach and the sacramentality of the Eucharist. The tendency to approach the Eucharist, not ontologically and via the philosophy of nature, but anthropologically, became increasingly prevalent at this time. . . . Emphasis could again be given in post-war theology to the fact that sacraments are first and foremost symbolic acts or activity as signs—"sacramentum est in genere signi." (Schillebeeckx, The Eucharist, pp. 96–97)*

Quotation 349:
• *In this renewal, both texts and rites should be ordered so as to express more clearly the holy things which they signify.* [no. 21]
• *It is from the scriptures . . . that actions and signs derive their meaning.* [no. 24]
• *The visible signs which the sacred liturgy uses to signify invisible divine things have been chosen by Christ or the church N.* [no. 33]

(*Constitution on the Sacred Liturgy*)

Quotation 350: *The term "sign," once suspect, is again recognized as a positive term for speaking of Christ's presence in the sacrament. For, though symbols and symbolic actions are used, the Lord's supper is an effective sign: It communicates what it promises . . . the action of the church becomes the effective means whereby God in Christ acts and Christ is present with his people.* (*The Eucharist: A Lutheran-Roman Catholic Statement,* 2.1)

Quotation 351: *The bread for the celebration of the Eucharist . . . must be made solely of wheat and, in accordance with the tradition proper to the Latin Church, it must be unleavened. By reason of the sign, the matter of the eucharistic celebration "should appear as actual food." This is to be understood as linked to the consistency of the bread and not to its form, which remains the traditional one. No other ingredients are to be added to the wheaten flour and water.* (John Paul II, *On Certain Norms Concerning Worship of the Eucharistic Mystery,* 1980)

241. Eucharistic bread and appropriately enlarged paten for the reformed liturgy. (*Liturgical Arts,* 1971)

explanations of sacraments than those afforded by medieval theologies, which emphasized intention and abstraction rather than perception or experience. Thus, theologians such as Edward Schillebeeckx (b. 1914) reasserted the primary place of symbols in understanding and celebrating Christian liturgy. Vatican II affirmed such thinking in the *Constitution on the Sacred Liturgy* [quotation 349], which has also become part of the ecumenical consensus on worship since the council [quotation 350]. This symbolic movement has not been without its critics, however. In some ways, the movement away from more symbolic or "dynamic" translations to a more literal approach by Rome [quotation 344] is symptomatic of this critique.

Bread and Its Vessels

The reassertion of the primacy of symbols accompanied a return to fuller, richer symbols in worship, such as bread that could be perceived as bread. This, in turn, resulted in vessels shaped to hold more natural forms of bread. Many Protestant churches that had continued the Western practice of employing unleavened wafer-bread have returned to the ancient practice of a single loaf of leavened bread. In the Roman Catholic community, the *General Instruction of the Roman Missal* of 1970 and all subsequent editions decreed that bread has to appear as real food. This spurred the practice in some communities of homemade bread for the Eucharist and contributed to changes in the size and shape of bread vessels [illustration 241]. Ironically, Pope John Paul II (d. 2005) decreed in 1980 that although the bread was to appear as real food, it could not contain anything other than wheat flour and water [quotation 351]. On the one hand, this directive could be perceived as a reaffirmation of a concern about the purity of the elements used for Eucharist, evident since the Carolingian period, which restricts any additives other than flour and water [quotation 220]. It is also possible, however, to interpret such a directive as a critique of the types of cultural adaptation occurring in the celebration of Roman Catholic Eucharist around the world. Wheat bread, like grape wine, is not indigenous to many parts of the world and must be imported at great cost. Some communities have experimented with local produce, for example, eucharistic elements made from rice or other local grains. These continue to be forbidden by the Roman Catholic Church.

A more recent challenge to shaping bread for eucharistic celebrations has been the discovery of celiac disease, which causes a dangerous reaction of the immune system when a person with this disease is exposed to gluten in the wheat. In 2003 the University of Chicago Hospitals released a study indicating that this disease is much more common than usually recognized and 1 out of 133 in the U.S. suffers from it, though only 1 in 4,700 has been diagnosed.

In response, the Vatican has given permission for the use of "low-gluten hosts" but decreed that hosts that are completely gluten-free are "invalid matter" for the celebration of the Eucharist (Joseph Ratzinger, Congregation for Doctrine of the Faith, 2003).

Wine and Its Vessels

The sharing of the cup within the richer symbolic framework of the late twentieth century suggested that wine should be drunk by all from a common vessel. The Protestant churches had returned the chalice to the laity at the Reformation, but some abandoned the common cup, which so clearly symbolizes the unity of the community [illustration 203]. The *Constitution on the Sacred Liturgy* approved in principle the return of the cup to the laity within the Roman tradition [quotation 352]. Since 1970, Roman Catholics in the U.S. have been allowed to receive communion from the cup on weekdays; in 1978, this permission was extended to all eucharistic celebrations. The return of the cup to the community meant a change in the design of the chalice. It no longer could hold only a sip of wine for the priest but, rather, was to be large enough to be used for the communion of the assembly [illustration 242].

Another consequence of returning the cup to the laity was the introduction of the flagon into the Roman Catholic Eucharist. Because the symbolism of a single cup does not allow more than one chalice on the table, the rest of the wine was to be held in another vessel, such as the flagon, until it is poured into other cups during the fraction rite before communion [illustration 243]. In 2004, however, the Vatican issued the statement *Redemptionis Sacramentum* (Latin, "Sacrament of Redemption"), which addressed what were perceived as "abuses" within Roman Catholic eucharistic practice. One of the practices disallowed by this document was pouring wine after it was consecrated [quotation 353]. This decree in effect diluted the fraction rite in the Roman Catholic Mass, which now only consisted of the breaking of the bread, and created a second fraction rite at the preparation of the gifts, where wine was now to be poured into communion cups. That document also reiterated Rome's position that the only wine allowed is that "from the fruit of the grape, pure and incorrupt, not mixed with other substances" (*Redemptionis Sacramentum*, no. 50).

Parallel to the problems in receiving communion faced by those who suffer from celiac disease are those confronting alcoholics. Recognized as a disease by the American Medical Association in 1956, the U.S. Department of Health and Human Services suggests that between 7 and 8 percent of all adults in the U.S. meet the diagnostic criteria for alcoholism. It is often estimated that the percentage of clergy who meet that criteria is considerably higher. In response,

242. Bronze and gold chalice by William Frederick.

Quotation 352: *The dogmatic principles about communion of the faithful which were laid down by the Council of Trent are confirmed, yet communion under both kinds may be granted when the bishops think fit, not only to clerics and religious but also to the laity, in cases to be determined by the Apostolic See. (Constitution on the Sacred Liturgy, no. 55)*

Quotation 353: *However, the pouring of the Blood of Christ after the consecration from one vessel to another is completely to be avoided, lest anything should happen that would be to the detriment of so great a mystery. Never to be used for containing the Blood of the Lord are flagons, bowls, or other vessels that are not fully in accord with the established norms. (Redemptionis Sacramentum [2004], no. 106)*

243. Participation cups on a tray, and flagon with wine.

many communities have chosen to use grape juice instead of wine, so as to make communion accessible to all, from children to those suffering from alcoholism. Given the long tradition for using mustum (grape juice), the Roman Catholic Church continues to allow the use of mustum, but only with special permission and only for the presiding priest.

Materials for Vessels

The move toward more authentic symbols also effected a change in the materials for the eucharistic vessels during the late twentieth century. Although gold and silver continued to be employed, precious metals were often replaced by glass, pottery, and wood. Even wicker baskets, reminiscent of primitive Christian worship, were used again in some places to hold the eucharistic bread. For the Roman Catholic Church, this required a change in laws prescribing that patens and chalices would be made of gold or silver. In 1962, for example, permission was given to modify only slightly the design of a chalice [quotation 354]. Only seven years later the new *General Instruction of the Roman Missal* removed virtually every specific requirement for the fabrication of eucharistic vessels. Yet, the previously noted shifting perspectives within the Roman Catholic community after 1984 soon gave way to new directives. In 2004 Rome decreed that earthenware, glass, and clay as well as any vessels that break easily were now "reprobated" [quotation 355].

Summary

One of the hallmarks of the twentieth-century liturgical movement has been a renewed belief in the centrality of the assembly in public worship. This belief manifested itself in various ways. One manifestation was the acknowledgment in ritual and music, architecture and vessels that the intention of the presider or even the assembly at Eucharist is insufficient for the fullness of the sacramental act. Liturgy is an action that requires the use of perceivable symbols to bring about its hoped-for meaning. The evolution of eucharistic vessels and of the material gifts of bread and wine that they hold attests to the churches' growing awareness of the importance of symbols. Vessels are not sacred because of the beauty of their design or the preciousness of their materials. Rather, they are sacred because they mediate presence to the assembly. And it is in the hands of the assembly that they belong. Thus, it is primarily the hand of the assembly, rather than the hand of the artist or priest or theologian, that should craft these vessels of grace. Recent restrictions on eucharistic vessels in the Roman Catholic Church also underscore the

Quotation 354: *The Reverend Romuald Bissonnette, Rector of the Pontifical Canadian College, in the name of his eminence, the ordinary of Montreal, asked this Sacred Congregation whether chalices without a node below the cup may be consecrated. Reply: The Sacred Congregation of Rites, after mature consideration of everything; replied: it suffices that the priest can satisfactorily hold the chalice with his thumb and index finger joined.* (Private Response of the Sacred Congregation of Rites [1962], cited in Seasoltz, *The New Liturgy,* p. 462)

symbolic power of such vessels. The deliberate move away from anything ordinary or domestic could be considered an attempt to emphasize the transcendent in worship and interpret sacrality according to a certain aesthetic rather than according to the dynamics of functionalism. It also could signal a more deliberate attempt to regulate the local and moderate the flows of inculturation. Given the complementary tension between the local and global—whether that be in industry or religion—it is clear that the church's eucharistic vessels and worship will continue to evolve.

EUCHARISTIC THEOLOGY

While there may be little agreement as to the appropriate shape, performance, or theology of liturgy in the current era, it seems that there is a broad consensus that liturgy is once again a central theological concern. Public worship has always been a critical pastoral issue, and the various church bodies invested with this responsibility seldom shirked from regulating public prayer and challenging abuses. Much of this, however, was done in what could be considered a "theory → practice" approach, in which the theory or theology about worship was determinative, and prayer practices needed to conform to such theology. In terms of the ancient Christian maxim from Prosper of Aquitaine (d. after 455)—*legem credendi lex statuat suplicandi* (Latin, "the law of praying establishes the law of believing"), sometimes shortened to *lex orandi, lex credendi* (literally, "law of praying, law of believing")—this could be considered an approach that emphasized the *lex credendi* over the actual practice of *lex orandi*.

Conversely, during the twentieth century there was an increasing recognition that the actual performance of the liturgy was *prima theologia* (Latin, "first theology"), a clear rejection of neo-Scholastic instincts to privilege church teaching above all else. This perspective was embedded in the *Constitution on the Sacred Liturgy*, which not only recognized the centrality of worship as theology [quotation 322] but unambiguously emphasized liturgy as an action [quotation 356] rather than a text, rubrics, or some dogmatic teaching. In a sense, liturgy became a "verb" again. Certain theologians interpreted this shift as one that ceded the weight of authority to worship, symbolized as *lex orandi → lex credendi*. From this perspective, the liturgical rites dictate doctrine. There is a broader consensus, however, that the prayer of the church and the belief of the church are in a mutually critical relationship, symbolized as *lex orandi ↔ lex credendi*.

This relationship of mutual critique between prayer and belief, between worship and doctrine, has fueled dynamic developments in

Quotation 355:
- *Vessels should be made from materials that are solid and that in the particular region are regarded as noble.* [no. 290]
- *Chalices and other vessels that serve as receptacles for the blood of the Lord are to have a cup of nonabsorbent material. The base may be of any other solid and worthy material.* [no. 291]
- *The artist may fashion the sacred vessels in a shape that is in keeping with the culture of each region, provided each type of vessel is suited to the intended liturgical use.* [no. 295]

(General Instruction of the Roman Missal [1971])

(compared to)

Sacred vessels for containing the Body and Blood of the Lord must be made in strict conformity with the norms of tradition and of the liturgical books. The Bishops' Conferences have the faculty to decide whether it is appropriate, once their decisions have been given the recognitio by the Apostolic See, for sacred vessels to be made of other solid materials as well. It is strictly required, however, that such materials be truly noble in the common estimation within a given region, so that honor will be given to the Lord by their use, and all risk of diminishing the doctrine of the Real Presence of Christ in the Eucharistic species in the eyes of the faithful will be avoided. Reprobated, therefore, is any practice of using for the celebration of Mass common vessels, or others lacking in quality, or devoid of all artistic merit or which are mere containers, as also other vessels made from glass, earthenware, clay, or other materials that break easily. This norm is to be applied even as regards metals and other materials that easily rust or deteriorate. (Redemptionis Sacramentum, no. 117)

Quotation 356: *From this it follows that every liturgical celebration, because it is an action of Christ the priest and of his body, which is the church, is a preeminently sacred action. No other action of the church equals its effectiveness by the same title nor to the same degree. (Constitution on the Sacred Liturgy, no. 7, emphasis added)*

theology and simultaneously generated enormous tensions. We will explore this dynamic tension in terms of three polarities: local ↔ universal, immanent ↔ transcendent, and ethics ↔ holiness.

Local ↔ Universal

Christian theology in general, and theologies of worship in particular —similar to the phenomenon of glocalization in culture, commerce, and politics—live in a dynamic between the local and the global. If the "law of praying" and the "law of believing" are in a mutually critical relationship, then one needs to ask "whose praying and whose believing" we are considering. Beliefs are ordinarily defined by a church. Often the more historical, structured, and hierarchical the church, the more those beliefs are specified and circumscribed. Thus the Roman Catholic Church, for example, not only has clearly defined liturgical doctrines, but a universal code of law that regulates worship, a universal catechism with official explanations of its worship, and also a universal Roman Rite that prescribes this worship. While this universal rite is translated into various languages and can be adapted, all translations and adaptations must be approved by Rome and cannot in any way challenge the "substantial unity of the Roman rite" [quotation 357], of which Rome is the final arbiter.

Worship, on the other hand, is always a local event. Through insights from the critical philosophers of the twentieth century, we have come to understand that as an action or event, there is no such thing as some kind of generalized Eucharist, but only Eucharist in a particular time and place celebrated by a specific community with its ministers [quotation 358]. Every worship event is a contextualized, unrepeatable action. It occurs within the particular cultural environment and history of a local community. The challenge for members of churches who have official rites is negotiating the terrain between the local and universal. One symbol of this struggle within the Roman Catholic community is the previously noted tension between the legal requirements that Eucharist must be celebrated with bread made from wheat and wine from grapes, when these products are not indigenous to many areas of the world.

The liturgical movement of the early twentieth century contributed to increased emphasis on the local, the need for the vernacular, and the importance of the cultural context for shaping worship. The *Constitution on the Sacred Liturgy* recognized this need and included a celebrated section on "Norms for Adapting the Liturgy to the Temperament and Traditions of Peoples" [quotation 359]. At the same time, that constitution could be considered a product of the Enlightenment, insofar as it presumed the possibility of a generalized,

Quotation 357: *The process of inculturation should maintain the substantial unity of the Roman rite. This unity is currently expressed in the typical editions of liturgical books, published by authority of the supreme pontiff and in the liturgical books approved by the episcopal conferences for their areas and confirmed by the Apostolic See. The work of inculturation does not foresee the creation of new families of rites; inculturation responds to the needs of a particular culture and leads to adaptations which still remain part of the Roman rite.* (Inculturation and the Roman Liturgy, no. 36)

Quotation 358: *Let us consider the existential factor. Theologians and church officials speak freely of baptism and of Eucharist. Baptism, they say, is this or that. Eucharist, they say, is this or that. However, baptism is not a replication, a verbal phrase emphasizing an action, nor is baptism a replicated clone, a substantive phrase emphasizing a thing. Each baptism is not a duplication of a rote activity, nor is each baptism the enfleshing of a duplicative reality. Rather, each baptism is an existential event, an existential action. . . . Each baptism is an individualized, historically discrete, temporally unrepeatable moment in the life of an individual, of a particular community of Christians, and of the temporal-historical presence of an active God. There is no such thing as generic baptism, just as there is no such thing as generic Eucharist.* (Osborne, Christian Sacraments in a Postmodern World, p. 58)

shared, and universally accessible theology of worship. That vision is coupled with a strong centralized presumption for leadership and control. Despite its recognition of "competent territorial ecclesiastical authority" and some significant movement toward decentralization and collegiality, there is ultimately one center for approving all decisions for Roman Catholic liturgy, and that is Rome.

The decades following the Second Vatican Council were a time of considerable experimentation—some of it with official approval, and much of it without. It could be considered a time when the local was gaining ascendancy in global churches like Roman Catholicism, and the particularity of languages, peoples, and even local communities were affirmed. For various reasons, however, that trajectory—at least in the Roman Catholic Church—began to change. As we have noted, since the mid-1980s there was a slowing of the centrifugal and collegial, eclipsed by a centripetal turn that currently seems to emphasize the universal, with a new stress on ritual uniformity. *Lex credendi*, at least as officially prescribed in the Roman Catholic Church, currently seems to supersede the *lex orandi* in all of its particularity. One can understand this as an appropriate corrective or reaction in this postconciliar period, as the principles and vision of Vatican II continue to be debated and interpreted.

It is difficult to predict how long this trajectory will hold ascendancy. Given the dynamics of the new modernity, however, it is improbable that it will continue unabated. Glocalization in the economy, politics, culture, and worship is a tug-of-war, in which tides will shift and the liturgical seas will not remain tranquil. A new synthesis awaits us.

Quotation 359: *Even in the liturgy the church does not wish to impose a rigid uniformity in matters which do not affect the faith or the well-being of the entire community. Rather does it cultivate and foster the qualities and talents of the various races and nations. Anything in people's way of life which is not indissolubly bound up with superstition and error the church studies with sympathy, and, if possible, preserves intact. It sometimes even admits such things into the liturgy itself, provided they harmonize with its true and authentic spirit. (Constitution on the Sacred Liturgy [1963] no. 37)*

Immanent ↔ Transcendent

A parallel polarity to the local ↔ universal is that of the immanent ↔ transcendent. In Christianity immanence refers to God's perceptible action and presence in our world and history. For Christians the supreme act of divine immanence is the incarnation of Christ, in which Christ embraced humanity in a new act of creation, and proclaimed it—like the original act of creation—to be good. The complementary doctrine is transcendence, which admits the total otherness of God, who is a mystery beyond creation and human understanding. In Christ, completely human and divine, these two doctrines perfectly intersect and harmoniously exist in total mutuality without critique.

While these mysteries find absolute harmony in Christ, Christian liturgy is not capable of providing such perfection, for while liturgy is a God act, it is also a human endeavor, as symbolized in the very

Quotation 360:

• *This work of human redemption and perfect glorification of God, foreshadowed by the wonders which God performed among the people of the Old Testament . . .* [no. 5]

• *Christ, indeed, always associates the church with himself in this great work in which* God is perfectly glorified and men and women are sanctified. [no. 7]

• *From the liturgy, therefore, and especially from the Eucharist, grace is poured forth upon us as from a fountain, and* our sanctification in Christ and the glorification of God *to which all other activities of the church are directed . . . are achieved . . .* [no. 10]

• *There is scarcely any proper use of material things which cannot thus be directed toward* people's sanctification and the praise of God. [no. 61]

• *. . . the purpose of sacred music, which is* the glory of God and the sanctification of the faithful . . . [no. 112]

(*The Constitution on the Sacred Liturgy,* emphasis added)

etymology of the word (Greek *leiturgia* from *laos* + *ergon* = "people + work" or "the work of the people"). The challenge of Christian liturgy is to attend appropriately to the mysteries of immanence and transcendence in a manner that is both doctrinally sound and pastorally appropriate. One of the ways that the *Constitution on the Sacred Liturgy* addressed this polarity of the immanent and transcendent was through its repeated assertion that the purpose of liturgy is both the sanctification of people and the glorification of God [quotation 360].

What may be surprising is that, in the majority of these formulations, the sanctification of the people is mentioned before the glorification of God. When considered in the context of the liturgical movement that prepared the way for this constitution, and the stress within this document on the active participation of the people, one could suggest that Vatican II was reintroducing the balance of immanence to the church's liturgy, whose Tridentine Rite clearly emphasized the transcendent.

How one achieves the balance in a liturgy that appropriately respects the mystery and total otherness of God and God's self-revelation in the world—especially through the incarnation—has been a point of significant debate. One enduring symbol of this debate concerns the role of the arts in worship. Those wishing to emphasize worship as an experience of the transcendent sometimes opt for artistic expressions that are removed from the common and the accessible. Symptomatic of this tendency is a preference for ancient languages over the vernacular, chant or "serious composition" rather than popular sounds of contemporary media, vessels far removed from any domestic standard, and the use of the term "sacred" rather than "liturgical" in describing such arts. In some ways, the post-1984 trends in official Roman Catholic views toward worship are following such a trajectory of re-sacralizing liturgy, which some fear was becoming too common, manifesting too many traits of popular entertainment and losing its connections with the treasury of the church's sacred arts.

Another symbol of this refreshed dynamic between the immanent and transcendent is manifest in the styles of theology used for reflecting upon the liturgy. Earlier we noted (p. 180) that at the turn of the first millennium there developed a style of theology that appeared more as a theology *about* the liturgy than a type of theologizing that was grounded *in* the event of worship and people's experiences of those events. We called this a turn to "sacramental theology." During the twentieth century, two significant developments reshaped sacramental theology with a different trajectory. First was a move by some Roman Catholic theologians to challenge the seemingly essential linkage between a neo-Scholastic vision of philosophy and theology. In an attempt to forge a new theology that respected the "turn to the subject," characteristic of both contemporary philosophy as well as the new social sciences, visionaries such as Edward Schillebeeckx (b. 1914) employed phenomenology, anthropology, and new critical philosophies in their sacramental reflections. In so doing, Schillebeeckx and Karl Rahner (d. 1984)—both of whom served as *periti* (Latin, "experts" or "advisers") at Vatican II—helped shift our understanding of sacraments from "nouns" to "verbs," from "things" to "encounters." This view is epitomized in the title of Edward Schillebeeckx's revolutionary work *Christ, the Sacrament of the Encounter with God* (1963). This approach, which considered human experience as an essential element within the sacramental enterprise, contributed to a second major development: the move back to theologizing *from* rather than simply *about* the liturgical event itself.

This renewed style of theologizing stressed the importance of the *lex orandi*, which means taking seriously the ritual texts, structures, environment, and actions as a theological source. This type of theologizing is often described as liturgical theology. While there are many ways to do liturgical theology, authentic forms of liturgical theology take seriously the liturgy as a theological source, even *theologia prima*. Because of this, liturgical theologies—often in dialogue with social sciences such as anthropology—methodologically presume attending to the immanent aspects of worship more than sacramental theologies, especially those whose primary dialogue partner is philosophy. While liturgical theology was in ascendancy after Vatican II, there is a notable leaning in some quarters today toward a more abstract, sacramental form of theology in dialogue with philosophy rather than anthropology, methodologically prone to stressing the transcendent rather than the immanent in worship. How one develops a proper balance between the immanent and transcendent, between liturgical and sacramental theology, continues to be an unresolved issue.

Ethics ↔ Holiness

A final polarity that marks the theological ferment around worship today concerns the dynamic between the call to personal holiness and the commitment to social change. For many Christians, the spiritual life—as well as the worship that nourishes and sustains that life—is focused on a call to personal holiness. This is not to suggest that Christianity is or has been unconcerned about the social order. One of the great forces in nineteenth- and twentieth-century Protestantism, for example, was the social gospel movement and its com-

Quotation 361: *The great ends of the church are the proclamation of the gospel for the salvation of humankind; the shelter, nurture, and spiritual fellowship of the children of God; the maintenance of divine worship; the preservation of truth; the promotion of social righteousness; and the exhibition of the Kingdom of Heaven to the world.* (Mission statement [1910] of the United Presbyterian Church in North America)

Quotation 362: *We prayed that Pentecost might come to the city of Los Angeles. We wanted it to start in the First Methodist Church, but God did not start it there. I bless God that he did not start it in any church in this city, but in a barn, so that we might all come and take part in it. If it had started in a fine church, poor colored people and Spanish people would not have got it, but praise God it started here.* (Los Angeles, *Apostolic Faith Newspaper* [1906])

Quotation 363: *It is no wonder then that the culture of our day is characterized as being the very opposite pole of any genuine Catholic culture. Its general aim is material prosperity through the amassing of national wealth. Only that is good which furthers this aim, all is bad that hinders it, and ethics has no say in the matter. . . .*
The liturgy is the ordinary school of the development of the true Christian and the very qualities and outlook it develops in him are also those that make for the best realization of a genuine Christian culture. (Virgil Michel, *Orate Fratres*, p. 299)

mitment to social justice [quotation 361]. While such forces are often at work in the churches, they are not always intimately wed to worship.

The twentieth century, however, spawned a series of movements in which this linkage was more apparent and vital. The rise of Pentecostalism in the U.S., for example, was closely related to the issues of segregation and racial equality: concerns already apparent in the work of William Seymour and the worship expressions of the Azusa Street revival [quotation 362]. Apostles of the social gospel movement understood the importance of linking prayer and Christian action. In that spirit Walter Rauschenbusch (d. 1918) published *For God and the People: Prayers for the Social Awakening* (1910). According to James White, he was one of a growing number of prominent, mainstream Protestant leaders reuniting worship and justice. In the 1950s the social gospel movement found new vigor in its reincarnation through the civil rights movement. Born and nurtured in the sanctuaries of black churches across the U.S., the civil rights movement forged new linkages between altar calls and civil rights marches, preaching and politics, communion and equality.

The liturgical movement for Roman Catholics also had social justice roots. Lambert Beauduin, sometimes considered the father of the modern liturgical movement, was deeply influenced by the social teachings of Leo XIII (d. 1903) and spent some years working as a labor chaplain in Belgium, supporting workers in their struggle for a just wage. As Keith Pecklers reminds us in *Unread Vision* (p. 22), Beauduin was an important influence on Virgil Michel (d. 1938). This Benedictine from Saint John's in Collegeville was a founding force in the U.S. liturgical movement. For him, as well, liturgy and social justice were intimately wed [quotation 363]. Like Michel, other pioneers in the liturgical movement in the U.S.—such as H. A. Reinhold (d. 1968) and Reynold Hillenbrand (d. 1979)—were strongly influenced by the social teachings of Leo XIII and committed to the belief that Christians who possessed an authentic liturgical spirituality would also be committed to fair labor practices and racial equality.

Two other major theological flows in the second half of the twentieth century contributed to a newly forged link between liturgy and justice. First were the theologies of liberation, originating in Latin America. An early and enduring voice in these theologies that placed the economic plight of the world's poor at the heart of the theological agenda has been the Peruvian theologian Gustavo Gutiérrez (b. 1928). In his seminal 1971 work *Teologia de la liberación* (Spanish, "A Theology of Liberation"), Gutiérrez asserted that, as revealed in the table ministry of Jesus, "communion with God and others presupposes the abolition of all injustice and exploitation" (p. 263).

Related to theologies of liberation are the feminist theologies that emerged in the 1960s as a theological outgrowth of the women's movement. Women constitute the majority of the members of the Christian churches, but their perspectives have seldom been at the center of our theologies. Thus, theologians such as Mary Collins (b. 1935) and Gail Ramshaw (b. 1947) have voiced significant concerns that Christian worship, with its male-dominated language and leadership, is a potential source of oppression for large numbers of Christians. If liturgy and liturgical theology are to take people's experience seriously, where is women's experience a source for our rituals and theologies?

These various religious movements and theological flows have contributed to a renewed linkage between liturgy and life, and led theologians such as Kevin Irwin (b. 1946) to expand the *lex orandi*, *lex credendi* paradigm to include *lex vivendi* (Latin, "the law of living"). Few voices have been more articulate in the English-speaking world about the linkage between liturgy and ethics than Don Saliers (b. 1937), who adds *lex agendi* (Latin, "the law of doing") to Prosper of Aquitaine's maxim in order to stress the critical relationship between liturgy and ethical action [quotation 364].

While there is a growing awareness of the inextricable connection between Christian living and worship, especially in that central action of communion between the human and divine known as Eucharist, this theory has not always translated into credible praxis. Often the moral imperatives celebrated at the heart of Eucharist—the dignity of all human life, the lifting up of the poor and lowly, the vision of Christ's peace—are overlooked or ignored. This is increasingly true in a consumer society such as the U.S., where individual choice rather than the common good has come to dominate. United States Christians in large numbers support the death penalty, economic polices that create a widening divide between the rich and the poor, and the expenditure of vast sums of money in wars that inflict an appalling human cost—despite the fact that, for example, the leadership of the World Council of Churches as well as that of the Roman Catholic Church have condemned these.

Christians of this and every age certainly strive for personal holiness and their own salvation. The growing attention to issues of eucharistic justice and liturgical ethics, however, has also highlighted the sometimes bifurcated vision of Christians whose personal beliefs and worship contexts often privilege individual need over the common good at the dawn of Christianity's third millennium. While certainly distinctive, sometimes the call to personal holiness and ethical social action may become separated. How we weave them together with integrity and respect is our ongoing task. It is, however, also our legacy.

Quotation 364: *The mutually critical correlation of liturgy and ethics is part of the critical reciprocity between the lex orandi [pattern of prayer] and the lex credendi [pattern of belief]. But these issue in the lex agendi [pattern of intention-action] of the church. Hence we may say that true doxology issues in fitting orthodoxy as reflective faith, and both in orthopraxy of the church's servanthood in the social order in which it is placed. I have sought to trace the reciprocity of liturgy and the moral life through affections and virtues formed and ritually enacted ["rehearsed"] in various modes of liturgical prayer. By reflecting on the ethics of character rather than into theories of obligation, we are in a better position to connect the ethical force of authentic Christian liturgy to notions of sanctification. . . . Various Christians traditions will have different accents to sound in this matter. But it does imply that the classical definition of liturgy as the glorification of God and the sanctification of all that is human—to which I would add, "all that is creaturely"—has more bearing upon ethics than most theologians have seen. (Don Saliers, Worship as Theology, p. 187)*

Summary

Reviewing these theological reflections on eucharistic theology in the present era, you might be struck by the fact that such reflections are less focused on issues proper to eucharistic theology (e.g., real presence) or the design of the ritual, and more focused on what could be considered "spirituality." Sandra Schneiders speaks of Christian spirituality as reflection on "lived Christian faith" (p. 1). Maybe the move away from narrowly debated issues—exactly when the consecration takes place, how Christ is present in the Eucharist, whether the consecrated wine should be poured from one vessel to another—is symbolic of a truly reformed vision of worship: less about arcane doctrines or highly regulated liturgy than about what it means to be church, or how we are to be on mission, or what is just living in an ever-compressing world and ever-expanding universe. These, of course, are not new ideas, but they are sometimes forgotten ones. So we end where Christian eucharistic practice began, in the somewhat idealized but always compelling image of Luke reminding us that the early community was continually devoting themselves to the apostles' teaching and to fellowship, to the breaking of bread, and to prayers. We are likewise called.

HATTIE JOHNSON

"Blessed assurance, Jesus is mine! O what a fore-taste of glory divine!" As the entrance procession moved down the center aisle, the choir and congregation sang with gusto, urged on by an insistent pianist with a heavy left hand. Jessica Brown carried the cross high, followed by her brother Freddie and Adrian Washington carrying tall white candles. The choir, red robes accentuating rich brown skin, marched after them in hesitation step to the music, singing at full volume, "This is my story, this is my song." Then came old Mrs. Williams, leaning on her cane but walking proudly with the lectionary tucked under her arm. Deacon Tim and Father Charles, dressed in matching vestments of red, black, and green, brought up the rear of the procession.

Hattie Johnson's was not the strongest voice in the assembly, but she certainly was one of the most earnest. "Perfect submission, perfect delight, visions of rapture now burst on my sight." Who would have guessed that she would be singing the songs of her grandmother in the Catholic Church? Grandma had belonged to Christ First Pentecostal Church in the old neighborhood. Hattie's mother never let her go to the tiny church with Grandma. Instead, she took Hattie to Mass at the Catholic Church—what Grandma used to call "the white man's church." Sunday afternoons after services, though, Grandma would hold Hattie in her lap and tell her all about the worship at First Pentecostal: the preaching, the gifts of the Spirit manifest that morning, and especially the music. Oh, how Hattie loved the songs that Grandma sang to her! And no one is more astounded than she that fifty years later they would be singing some of those same songs in a Catholic Church.

Here at St. Michael's a lot of things have changed besides the music. One of the best changes, from Hattie's point of view, is that there were now white faces and yellow faces and brown faces in the pews, and the faces in the sanctuary mirrored the same rainbow. St. Michael's is certainly no white man's church, she thought to herself. Hattie knew it wasn't like this everywhere in Chicago, and there still were plenty of churches around where all the faces in the sanctuary and in the pews were white. Those will change in time, she thought. And besides, I don't

need those places. St. Michael's is my church and it suits me just fine. The idea brought a smile to her lips as she and the rest of the congregation sat down for the readings.

Old Mrs. Perez sure knew how to read the prophets. The years of raising a family in the projects and fighting for a decent wage must have accounted for some of the conviction in her voice. The prophet's call for justice was just a little more believable coming from the lips of someone like Maria Perez. Father Charles's preaching also was more convincing than most of the preaching Hattie had heard over the years. And she didn't think it was just because he was African American. She had heard other African American preachers, but they didn't have the power of Father Charles. Maybe it was the fact that here at St. Michael's, African Americans and Hispanics and Filipinos all felt at home, and it was Father Charles who, more than anyone else, helped make this their home. When he preached or talked to the congregation, some people talked right on back—and not just "Amen" or "Preach it, pastor." Sometimes people disagreed with him or added another example or gave their own witness. And he just let them do it. Hattie was convinced that Grandma would have liked Father Charles.

A lot of other people also made St. Michael's feel like home to Hattie: Clara and Bobby Mundo, who baked the bread for Mass; Rodney Harris and his son Jimmy, who took up the collection; Adele Marcos, whose sweet voice made the responsorial psalm a real prayer; and whoever was standing close enough to take Hattie's hand while they sang the Our Father. Hattie especially liked that part. She remembered when she was a little girl, how she had to kneel or stand or sit real quiet and not talk or even look at the other people during Mass. From what she remembered, it was a pretty barren experience. How shocked that old congregation would be if they could see the people at St. Michael's today during the sign of peace. As little Michelle Eugene once said during the peace, "There's some serious huggin' going on here."

The communion song today was one of Hattie's favorites, "Pan de vida." Darrel the pianist played it slowly and rhythmically, almost like a quiet dance, as members of the congregation stepped forward to receive the bread from the beautiful copper bowls and drink from one of the thick crystal goblets offered to them by the ministers of communion. Hattie found herself keeping step with the music as she walked back to her place. Sitting down, she let the sounds of the baby grand and the choir wash over her. After communion there always were a lot of announcements. Luckily, most of the important ones were also in the bulletin. Otherwise, Hattie surely would have forgotten them all.

After the last announcement, the congregation stood for the closing prayer and Father Charles's blessing. Then Darrel dug his left hand into the keyboard as the choir began to sing "Go ye therefore and teach all nations, go, go, go." The congregation joined in on the second phrase as Jessica raised the cross and led the ministers down the center aisle. "Baptizing them in the name of the Father and Son and Holy Ghost. Go, go, go." As Hattie joined the informal procession, making its way toward the coffee and rolls in the back of church, she thought again of Grandma and the Christ First Pentecostal Church in the old neighborhood. Maybe if Grandma were alive today she might feel at home at St. Michael's too.

Acknowledgments

Chapter One

Image 3. Used with permission of CNG coins (http://www.cngcoins.com).

Image 6. White, L. Michael *Building God's House in the Roman World: Architectural Adaptation among Pagans, Jews, and Christians.* P. 63. © The Johns Hopkins University Press, 1990. Reprinted with permission of The Johns Hopkins University Press.

Image 18. LXX Psalm 50, 17-20, P.Duk.inv.661V. Used with permission of Duke University Rare Book, Manuscript, and Special Collections Library.

Image 21. Papyrus Fragment of Saint John's Gospel, third century. MS Gen 1026/13. Used with permission of Glasgow University Library, Special Collections.

Image 23. Galavaris, George. *Bread and the Liturgy.* P. 27. © 1970 by the Regents of the University of Wisconsin System. Reprinted with permission of the University of Wisconsin Press.

Image 24. Used with permission of EdgarLOwen.com.

Image 25. Used with permission of Israel Antiquities Authority.

Chapter Two

Image 30. Gilbert, Martin. *The Routledge Atlas of Jewish History.* Sixth edition. © 2003 Routledge/Taylor & Francis Books. Reproduced by permission of Taylor & Francis Books, UK.

Image 32. Used with permission of Dr. Jean-Paul Rodrigue, Hofstra University.

Image 34. Foss, Pedar W. "Kitchens and Dining Rooms at Pompeii: The spatial and social relationship of cooking to eating in the Roman household," Ph.D. thesis, University of Michigan, 1994. Used with permission of Dr. Pedar W. Foss, DePauw University.

Image 36. Used with permission of Dr. L. Michael White, The University of Texas at Austin.

Image 37. Photo by Erich Lessing/Art Resource, NY. Used with permission of Art Resource, Inc.

Image 44. West, M. L. *Ancient Greek Music.* Pp. 324–325. New York: Oxford University Press, 1992 [Clarendon Press 1994]. Used by permission of Oxford University Press.

Image 46. © British Library Board. All Rights Reserved. British Library Add. MS 43725, f.247. Used with permission.

Image 47. Used with permission of OCP.

Image 51. Used with permission of Kelsey Museum of Archaeology, University of Michigan.

Image 55. Used with permission of The Barakat Gallery.

Image 56. Photo by Scala/Art Resource, NY. Used with permission of Art Resource, Inc.

Image 59. Used with permission of A. Longo Editore.

Chapter Three

Image 63. Used with permission of CNG Coins (http://www.cngcoins.com).

Image 78. Used with permission of A. Longo Editore.

Image 80. Mathews, Thomas F. *The Early Christian Churches of Constantinople: Architecture and Liturgy.* P. 70, figure 56. University Park: Pennsylvania State University Press, 1971. Used with permission of Thomas F. Mathews.

Image 90. Excerpts from *The Order of Prayer in the Liturgy of the Hours and Celebration of the Eucharist 2008*, complied by Rev. Peter D. Rocca, C.S.C., Paulist Press ORDO. Copyright © 2007 by Paulist Press, Inc., New York/Mahwah, NJ. Reprinted by permission of Paulist Press, Inc. www.paulistpress.com.

Image 94. Used with permission of A. Longo Editore.

Chapter Four

Image 125. Used with permission of Cambridge University Press.

Image 126. Used with permission of Saint Benedict Abbey, Still River, Massachusetts.

Image 129. Used with permission of OCP.

Chapter Five

Image 142. Gabinetto Fotografico. Used with permission of Soprintendenza Speciale per il Polo Museale Fiorentino.

Image 145. Rare Book Department, Free Library of Philadelphia. Used with permission.

Image 156. Rosenwald manuscript 10, Library of Congress. Used with permission.

Image 169. Used with permission of Miri Rubin and the University of Pennsylvania Press.

Chapter Six

Image 173. White, James. *Protestant Worship: Traditions in Transition.* P. 23. Louisville: Westminster/John Knox Press, 1989. Used with permission of Westminster/John Knox Press.

Image 179. Koerner, Joseph Leo. *The Reformation of the Image.* P. 258. Chicago: University of Chicago Press, 2004. Used with permission of University of Chicago Press.

Image 183. Used with permission of Dr. Irving Hexham, University of Calgary.

Image 184. Used with permission of Alfred Molon Photo Galleries.

Image 190. © British Library Board. All Rights Reserved. British Library C.9d3. Used with permission.

Chapter Seven

Image 217. Photo by Satoshi Asakawa. Used with permission of Kengo Kuma & Associates.

Image 224b. Used with permission of Marvin Herman Associates, Inc. Architects.

Image 225. Photo by Scott Frances, ESTO Photographics. Used with permission of ESTO.

Image 231. Scholtes, Peter. "And They'll Know We Are Christians By Our Love." © F.E.L. Publications 1966. Assigned 1991 to The Lorenz Corporation. All rights reserved. International copyright secured. Used with permission of The Lorenz Corporation.

Image 233. South African hymn. "We Are Marching in the Light of God." Text and music © 1984, Utryck. Agent: Walton Music Corp. Used with permission of Walton Music Corp.

We have made every attempt to obtain permission to reprint all images in this volume. We will gratefully acknowledge in future editions or upon reprint those copyright holders we were unable to reach or hear back from at the time of first printing.

Bibliography

General Bibliography

(Works in the general bibliography appear throughout the volume, while those specific to individual chapters are cited following the general bibliography.)

Anson, Peter F. *Churches: Their Plan and Furnishing.* Edited and revised by Thomas F. Croft-Fraser and H. A. Reinhold. Milwaukee: Bruce Publishing Company, 1948.

Arnold, Denis, ed. *New Oxford Companion to Music.* 2 vols. New York: Oxford University Press, 1983.

Atz, Karl. *Die Christliche Kunst in Wort und Bild.* Regensburg: Nationale Verlagsanstalt, 1899.

Biéler, André. *Architecture in Worship: The Christian Place of Worship.* Edinburgh-London: Oliver & Boyd, 1965.

Braun, Joseph. *Der Christliche Altar in seiner geschichtlichen Entwicklung.* Munich: Guenther Koch & Co., 1924.

———. *Das Christliche Altargerät in seinem Sein und in seiner Entwichlung.* Munich: Max Hueber, 1932.

Brinkhoff, Lukas, et al. *Liturgisch Woordenboek.* 9 vols. Roermond: J. J. Romen and Sons, 1958–1962.

Cabié, Robert. *L'Eucharistie.* Vol. 2 of *L'Église in Prière.* Edited by A. G. Martimort. Paris: Desclée, 1983.

Callewaert, C. *Liturgicae Institutiones.* Vol. 3, *De Missalis Romani Liturgia.* Brugge: Car. Beyaert, 1937.

Cange, Charles Dufresne du. *Glossarium ad Scriptores Mediae et Infirmae Latinitatis.* Edited by L. Favre. 10 vols. Niort, 1883–1887.

Cavanaugh, William Thomas. *The Reservation of the Blessed Sacrament.* The Catholic University of America Canon Law Studies 40. Washington, DC: The Catholic University of America, 1927.

Chupungco, Anscar, ed. *Handbook for Liturgical Studies.* 5 vols. Collegeville, MN: Liturgical Press, 1997–2000.

Conant, Kenneth John. *Carolingian and Romanesque Architecture, 800–1200.* 2nd ed. The Pelican History of Art. Harmondsworth, PA and New York: Penguin Books, 1966.

Corbin, Solange. *L'Église à la Conquête de sa Musique.* Pour la Musique. Edited by Roland-Manuel. Paris: Gallimard, 1960.

Davidson, Archibald, and Willi Apel. *Historical Anthology of Music.* 2 vols. Rev. ed. Cambridge: Harvard University Press, 1949.

Denzinger, Henry. *The Sources of Catholic Dogma.* Translated by Roy Deferrari. St. Louis: B. Herder, 1957.

Foley, Edward, ed. *Worship Music: A Concise Dictionary.* Collegeville, MN: Liturgical Press, 2000.

Frazer, Margaret English. *Medieval Church Treasures.* New York: Metropolitan Museum of Art, 1986.

Gardner, Helen. *Art Through the Ages.* 8th ed. Revised by Horst de la Croix and Richard Tansey. San Diego: Harcourt, Brace, Jovanovich, 1986.

Heales, Alfred. *History and Law of Church Seats or Pews.* 2 vols. London: Butterworths, 1872.

The Holy Bible, New Revised Standard Version. New York: Oxford University Press, 1989.

Jacob, H. E. *Six Thousand Years of Bread.* Translated by Richard and Clara Winston. Westport, CT: Greenwood Press, 1944.

Jasper, R. C. D., and G. J. Cuming. *Prayers of the Eucharist, Early and Reformed.* 2nd ed. New York: Oxford University Press, 1980.

Jedin, Hubert, and John Dolan, eds. *History of the Church.* 10 vols. New York: Crossroad, 1980–1981.

Jones, Cheslyn, et al. *The Study of Liturgy.* Rev. ed. New York: Oxford University Press, 1992.

Jounel, Pierre. "Places of Christian Assembly: the First Millennium." In *The Environment for Worship*, 15–27. Washington, DC: United States Catholic Conference, 1980.

Jungmann, Josef. *The Early Liturgy to the Time of Gregory the Great*. Translated by Francis Brunner. Notre Dame: University of Notre Dame Press, 1959.

————. *The Mass of the Roman Rite: Its Origins and Development*. Translated by Francis Brunner. 2 vols. New York: Benziger Brothers, Inc., 1950.

————. *Pastoral Liturgy*. New York: Herder and Herder, 1962.

Klauser, Theodor. *A Short History of the Western Liturgy*. Translated by John Halliburton. London: Oxford University Press, 1979.

Kostof, Spiro. *A History of Architecture: Settings and Rituals*. New York: Oxford University Press, 1985.

Kraus, Franz Xavier. *Geschichte der Christlichen Kunst*. 2 vols. Freiburg: Herder, 1896.

Krautheimer, Richard. *Early Christian and Byzantine Architecture*. 4th ed. Pelikan History of Art 24. Harmondsworth, PA: Penguin Books, 1986.

Lampe, G. W. H. *A Patristic Greek Lexicon*. New York: Clarendon, 1961.

Leonard, John, and Nathan Mitchell. *The Postures of the Assembly during the Eucharistic Prayer*. Chicago: Liturgy Training Publications, 1994.

Macy, Gary. *Banquet's Wisdom*. 2nd ed. Akron, OH: OSL Publications, 2005.

Mansi, J. D., ed. *Sacrorum Conciliorum Nova et Amplissima Collectio*. 31 vols. Florence-Venice: 1757–1798. Reprinted and expanded to 53 vols. by L. Petit and J. B. Martin. Paris: 1889–1927.

Mathews, Thomas. *The Early Churches of Constantinople: Architecture and Liturgy*. University Park, PA: Pennsylvania State University Press, 1971.

Mazza, Enrico. *The Celebration of the Eucharist: The Origin of the Rite and the Development of Its Interpretation*. Translated by Matthew O'Connell. Collegeville, MN: Liturgical Press, 1999.

McKay, A. G. *Houses, Villas, and Palaces in the Roman World*. Ithaca, NY: Cornell University Press, 1975.

McKinnon, James, ed. *Music in Early Christian Literature*. Cambridge Studies in Music. Cambridge: University Press, 1987.

Meer, F. van der, and Christine Mohrmann. *Atlas of the Early Christian World*. Translated and edited by Mary F. Hedlund and H. H. Rowley. London: Thomas Nelson and Sons Ltd., 1958.

Migne, Jacques Paul, ed. *Patrologia Graeca*. 162 vols. Paris, 1857–1866.

————. *Patrologia Latina*. 221 vols. Paris, 1844–1864.

Mitchell, Nathan. *Cult and Controversy: The Worship of the Eucharist Outside Mass*. New York: Pueblo Publishing, 1982.

Neale, John Mason. *History of Pues*. Cambridge: The Camden Society, 1841.

Norberg-Schulz, Christian. *Meaning in Western Architecture*. New York: Praeger Publishers, 1975.

O'Connell, J. B. *Church Building and Furnishing: A Study in Liturgical Law*. Liturgical Studies. Notre Dame, IN: University of Notre Dame Press, 1955.

Palazzo, Eric. *A History of Liturgical Books from the Beginning to the Thirteenth Century*. Translated by Madeleine Beaumont. Collegeville, MN: Liturgical Press, 1998.

Placzek, Adolf K., ed. *McMillan Encyclopedia of Architects*. 4 vols. New York: The Free Press, 1982.

Power, David. *The Eucharistic Mystery: Revitalizing the Tradition*. New York: Crossroad, 1992.

Randel, Don Michael, ed. *The New Harvard Dictionary of Music*. Cambridge: Belknap Press, 1986.

Righetti, Mario. *Manuale di Storia Liturgica*. 4 vols. Milan: Ancora, 1945–1953.

Sadie, Stanley, ed. *New Grove Dictionary of Music and Musicians*. New York: W. W. Norton, 1988.

Schulte, A. J. "Host." *Catholic Encyclopedia* (1910) 7: 489–97.

Stulken, Mary Kay. *Hymnal Companion to the Lutheran Book of Worship*. Philadelphia: Fortress Press, 1981.

Taft, Robert. *The Liturgy of the Hours in East and West*. Collegeville, MN: Liturgical Press, 1986.

Vogel, Cyrille. *Medieval Liturgy: An Introduction to the Sources.* Translated and revised by William Storey and Niels Rasmussen. Washington, DC: Pastoral Press, 1986.

White, James. *A Brief History of Christian Worship.* Nashville: Abingdon Press, 1993.

White, L. Michael. *The Social Origins of Christian Architecture.* Vol. 1: *Building God's House in the Roman World: Architectural adaptation among Pagans, Jews and Christians.* Baltimore: The Johns Hopkins University Press, 1990. Vol. 2: *Texts and Monuments for the Christian Domus Ecclesiae in its Environment.* Harvard Theological Studies 42. Valley Forge, PA: Trinity Press International, 1997.

Wienandt, Elwyn A., ed. *Opinions on Church Music.* Waco, TX: Baylor University Press, 1974.

Wilken, Robert. *The Myth of Christian Beginnings.* Notre Dame, IN: University of Notre Dame Press, 1981.

Bibliography for Chapter One

The Babylonian Talmud. Edited by Isidore Epstein. 34 vols. London: Soncino Press, 1935–1959.

Berger, Teresa. *Women's Ways of Worship: Gender Analysis and Liturgical History.* Collegeville, MN: Liturgical Press, 1999.

Birnbaum, Philip. *The Passover Haggadah.* New York: Hebrew Publishing Company, 1953.

Brooten, Bernadette. *Women Leaders in the Ancient Synagogue: Inscriptional Evidence and Background Issues.* Brown Judaic Studies 36. Chico, CA: Scholars Press, 1982.

Brown, Raymond E. *The Churches the Apostles Left Behind.* New York: Paulist Press, 1984.

Brown, Raymond E., Joseph Fitzmyer, Roland Murphy, eds. *The New Jerome Biblical Commentary.* Englewood Cliffs, NJ: Prentice-Hall Inc., 1990.

Charles, R. H., ed. *The Book of Jubilees or The Little Genesis.* London: A. and C. Black, 1902.

Chiat, Marilyn. "Form and Function in the Early Synagogue and Church." *Worship* 69, no. 5 (1995): 406–26.

———. *Handbook of Synagogue Architecture.* Chico, CA: Scholars Press, 1982.

Chrysostom, John. *Eight Homilies against the Jews.* http://www.fordham.edu/halsall/source/chrysostom-jews6.html.

Crossan, John Dominic. *The Historical Jesus: The Life of a Mediterranean Jewish Peasant.* San Francisco: HarperSanFrancisco, 1991.

Crowe, Frederick E. *Theology of the Christian Word: A Study in History.* New York: Paulist Press, 1978.

Daly, Robert. *The Origins of the Christian Doctrine of Sacrifice.* Philadelphia: Fortress Press, 1978.

Deichgräber, Reinhard. *Gotteshymnus und Christushymnus in der frühen Christenheit.* Göttingen: Vandenhoeck and Ruprecht, 1967.

Foley, Edward. "The Cantor in Historical Perspective." *Worship* 56 (1982): 194–213.

———. *Foundations of Christian Music: The Music of Pre-Constantinian Christianity.* American Essays in Liturgy. Collegeville, MN: Liturgical Press, 1996.

———. "The Question of Cultic Singing in the Christian Community of the First Century." Unpublished thesis, University of Notre Dame, 1980.

Gelineau, Joseph. "Music and Singing in the Liturgy." *The Study of Liturgy.* 440–49. See general bibliography above, Cheslyn Jones, et al. *The Study of Liturgy.* Rev. ed. New York: Oxford University Press, 1992.

Gutmann, Joseph. "Synagogue Origins: Theories and Facts." In *Ancient Synagogues: The State of Research,* edited by Jacob Neusner, et al, 1–6. Brown Judaic Studies 22. Chico, CA: Scholars Press, 1981.

Hahn, Ferdinand. *The Worship of the Early Church.* Philadelphia: Fortress Press, 1973.

Heinemann, Joseph. *Prayer in the Talmud: Forms and Patterns.* Studia Judaica 9. Berlin-New York: Walter de Gruyter, 1977.

Hoffman, Lawrence. *The Canonization of the Synagogue Service.* Notre Dame–London: University of Notre Dame Press, 1979.

———. *The Sh'ma and Its Blessings.* Vol. 1, *My People's Prayer Book: Traditional Prayers, Modern Commentaries.* Woodstock, VT: Jewish Lights Publishing, 1997.

Hoppe, Leslie. *The Synagogues and Churches of Ancient Palestine.* Collegeville, MN: Liturgical Press, 1993.

Idelsohn, A. Z. *Jewish Music in its Historical Development.* New York: Schocken Books, 1967 [1929].

Jeremias, Joachim. *The Eucharistic Words of Jesus.* Translated by Norman Perrin. Philadelphia: Fortress Press, 1977.

Josephus, Flavius. *The Works of Flavius Josephus.* Translated by William Whiston. Auburn and Buffalo: John E. Beardsley, 1895.

LaVerdiere, Eugene. *Dining in the Kingdom of God.* Chicago: Liturgy Training Publications, 1994.

Malit, Jesus M. "From *Berakah* to *Misa Ng Bayang Pilipino*: Exploring the Depths of a Filipino Eucharistic Spirituality through the *Philipino* Rite." D. Min. thesis-project, Catholic Theological Union, Chicago, 2001.

Martin, Ralph. *Worship in the Early Church.* Rev. ed. Grand Rapids: Wm. B. Eerdmans, 1975.

Maxwell, C. Mervyn. "Chrysostom's Homilies Against the Jews: An English Translation." Ph.D. diss., University of Chicago, 1967.

Meeks, Wayne A. *The First Urban Christians: The Social World of the Apostle Paul.* New Haven: Yale University Press, 1983.

The Mishnah: A New Translation. Edited and translated by Jacob Neusner. New Haven: Yale University Press, 1988.

Murphy-O'Connor, Jerome. "The Corinth that Saint Paul Saw." *Biblical Archaeologist* 47, no. 3 (1984): 147–59.

Nattiez, Jean-Jacques. *Music and Discourse: Toward a Semiology of Music.* Translated by Carolyn Abbate. Princeton: Princeton University Press, 1990.

Neusner, Jacob. *The Way of Torah.* 3rd ed. North Scituate, MA: Duxbury Press, 1979.

Overman, J. Andrew. "Who were the First Urban Christians? Urbanization in Galilee in the First Century." In *SBL Seminar Papers 1988*, edited by David J. Lull, 160–68. Atlanta: Scholars Press, 1988.

Past Worlds. The Times Atlas of Archaeology. London: Times Books Ltd., 1988.

Perelmuter, Hayim Goren. *Siblings: Rabbinic Judaism and Early Christianity at their Beginnings.* New York: Paulist Press, 1989.

Perrin, Norman, and Dennis C. Duling. *The New Testament: An Introduction.* 2nd ed. New York: Harcourt, Brace, Jovanovich, 1982.

Petuchowski, Jakob J., and Michael Brocke, eds. *The Lord's Prayer and Jewish Liturgy.* New York: Seabury Press, 1978.

Reif, Stefan. *Judaism and Hebrew Prayer: New Perspectives on Jewish Liturgical History.* Cambridge: Cambridge University Press, 1993.

Rowley, H. H. *Worship in Ancient Israel: Its Forms and Meaning.* London: SPCK, 1967.

Seager, Andrew. "Ancient Synagogue Architecture: An Overview." In *Ancient Synagogues: The State of Research*, edited by Jacob Neusner, et al., 39–47. Brown Judaic Studies 22. Chico, CA: Scholars Press, 1981.

The Song of the Sabbath Sacrifice. Transcription and translation by Carol Newsom. http://www.ibiblio.org/expo/deadsea.scrolls.exhibit/Library/songs.html.

Stuhlmueller, Carroll. *Psalms 1 & 2.* 2 vols. Old Testament Message 21 & 22. Wilmington, DE: Michael Glazier, 1983.

Vaux, Roland de. *Ancient Israel.* 2 vols. New York: McGraw-Hill, 1965.

Walbank, Frank W. "Alexander." *The New Encyclopaedia Britannica.* 15th ed. Chicago: Encyclopaedia Britannica Inc., 1974. Macropaedia I:468–473.

Werblowsky, R. J. Zwi, and Geoffrey Wigoder, eds. *The Oxford Dictionary of the Jewish Religion.* New York: Oxford University Press, 1997.

Werner, Eric. *The Sacred Bridge.* Vol. 1. New York: Columbia University Press, 1959.

———. *The Sacred Bridge.* Vol. 2. New York: Ktav Publishing House, 1984.

Wigoder, Geoffrey. *The Story of the Synagogue.* San Francisco: Harper & Row, 1986.

Bibliography for Chapter Two

Acta Pauli. Edited and translated by Wilhelm Schubert and Carl Schmidt. Hamburg: J. J. Austin, 1936.

Audet, Jean-Paul. *La Didachè, Instructions des Apôtres.* Etude Bibliques. Paris: J. Gabalda, 1958.

Baldovin, John. "Hippolytus and the Apostolic Tradition: Recent Research and Commentary." *Theological Studies* 64 (2003): 520–42.

Bergant, Dianne. "Come Let Us Go up to the Mountain of the Lord." In *Developmental Disabilities and Sacramental Access: New Paradigms for Sacramental Encounters,* edited by Edward Foley. Collegeville, MN: Liturgical Press, 1994, 13–32.

Berger, Teresa. *Women's Ways of Worship: Gender Analysis and Liturgical History.* Collegeville, MN: Liturgical Press, 1999.

The Book of Pontiffs (Liber Pontificalis). Edited and translated by Raymond Davis. Rev. ed. Translated Texts for Historians 6. Liverpool: Liverpool University Press, 2000.

Bradshaw, Paul. "Ancient Church Orders." In *Fountain of Life,* edited by Gerard Austin, 3–22. Washington, DC: The Pastoral Press, 1991.

Chadwick, Henry. *The Early Church.* Pelican History of the Church 1. Harmondsworth, PA: Penguin Books, 1967.

Charlesworth, James, ed. and trans. *The Odes of Solomon: The Syriac Texts.* Texts and Translations 13, Pseudepigrapha Series 7. Missoula, MT: Scholars Press, 1977.

Clement of Alexandria. Edited by Alexander Roberts and James Donaldson. Hymns translated by W. L. Alexander in *Ante-Nicene Fathers.* Vol. 2. New York: Charles Scribner's Sons, 1926 (296).

Connolly, R. H., ed. and trans. *Didascalia Apostolorum.* Oxford: Oxford University Press, 1929.

Sancti Cypriani Episcopi Opera. *Corpus Christianorum, Series Latina.* 5 vols. Edited by R. Weber, et al. Turnhout: Brepols, 1972.

Daly, Robert. *The Origins of the Christian Doctrine of Sacrifice.* Philadelphia: Fortress Press, 1978.

Danielou, Jean. *The Bible and the Liturgy.* Ann Arbor: Servant Books, 1979 [1956].

Duchesne, Louis. *Le Liber Pontificalis.* 3 vols. Bibliothèque des Ecoles Francaises d'Athenes et de Rome. Paris: E. de Boccard, 1981.

Epiphanius. *The Panarion of St. Epiphanius, Bishop of Salamis.* Translated by Philip Amidon. New York: Oxford University Press, 1990.

Eusebio di Cesarea. *Sulla vita di Costantino.* Edited and translated by Luigi Tartaglia. Napoli: M. D'Auria, 1984.

Eusebius. *The History of the Church.* Translated by G. A. Williamson. Harmondsworth, PA: Penguin Books, 1965.

Fitzmyer, Joseph. "The Languages of Palestine in the First Century A.D." In *A Wandering Aramean: Collected Aramaic Essays,* 29–56. Chico, CA: Scholars Press, 1979.

Funk, F. X., ed. *Didascalia et Constitutiones Apostolorum.* 2 vols. Paderborn: F. Schoeningh, 1905.

Gesta apud Zenophilum. Edited by Carolus Ziwsa. Corpus Scriptorum Ecclesiasticorum Latinorum 26. Vienna: F. Tempsky, 1893 (185–197).

Hennecke, Edgar. *New Testament Apocrypha.* 2 vols. Edited by Wilhelm Schneemelcher. Translated by Robert McLachlan Wilson. Philadelphia: Westminster Press, 1963–1965.

Idelsohn, A. Z. *Jewish Music in Its Historical Development.* New York: Schocken Books, 1967 [1929].

Ignatius of Antioch. *The Apostolic Fathers.* Edited and translated by Kirsop Lake. The Loeb Classical Library 24. London: W. Heinemann, 1930.

Irénée de Lyon. *Contre les hérésies, Livre IV-1.* Edited by Adelin Rousseau. Sources chrétiennes no. 100. Paris: Éditions du Cerf, 1965.

Kraeling, C. H. *Excavation at Dura Europos. Final Report 8, Part 2: The Christian Building.* New Haven: Yale University Press, 1967.

Macaulay, David. *City: The Story of Roman Planning and Construction.* Boston: Houghton Mifflin Company, 1974.

Magie, David, ed. and trans. *Scriptores Historiae Augustae.* 3 vols. Loeb Classical Library 139, 140, and 263. Cambridge: Harvard University Press, 1967.

Malone, Edward. *The Monk and the Martyr: The Monk as the Successor of the Martyr.* Washington, DC: Catholic University of America Press, 1950.

McGowan, Andrew Brian. *Ascetic Eucharists: Food and Drink in Early Christian Ritual Meals.* Oxford: Clarendon Press, 1999.

McKinnon, James. *The Advent Project: The Later-Seventh-Century Creation of the Roman Mass Proper.* Berkeley: University of California Press, 2000.

————. "The Meaning of the Patristic Polemic against Musical Instruments." *Current Musicology* 1 (1985): 69–82.

Mohrmann, Christine. "*Le latin commun et le latin des chrétiens.*" *Vigiliae Christianae* 1, no. 1 (1947): 1–12.

Neusner, Jacob. *There We Sat Down: Talmudic Judaism in the Making.* New York: Ktav Publishing House, 1978.

Perelmuter, Hayim Goren. *Siblings: Rabbinic Judaism and Early Christianity at their Beginnings.* New York: Paulist Press, 1989.

Pliny. "Letter to the Emperor Trajan." *Pliny: Letters and Panegyricus.* Translated by Betty Radice. Loeb Classical Library 59. Cambridge: Harvard University Press, 1969.

Roberts, Colin, and T. C. Skeat. *The Birth of the Codex.* London: Oxford University Press, 1983.

Routley, Erik. *The Music of Christian Hymns.* Chicago: GIA Publications Inc., 1981.

Russell, James. *The Germanization of Early Medieval Christianity: A Sociohistorical Approach to Religious Transformation.* New York–Oxford: Oxford University Press, 1994.

Tacitus. *Annals: Books 13–15.* Translated by John Jackson. Loeb Classical Library 322. London: William Heinemann Ltd., 1937.

Taft, Robert. "Mass without the Consecration?" *Worship* 77 (2003): 482–509.

Tertullian. *Corpus Christianorum, Series Latina.* 2 vols. Edited by Eligius Dekkers. Turnhout: Brepols, 1953.

Bibliography for Chapter Three

Acta Sanctorum. Société des Bollandistes. 3rd ed. 68 vols. Paris: Victor Palmé, 1863–1940.

Amalarii episcopi Opera liturgica omnia. Edited by Ioanne Michaele Hanssens. Studi e testi, 138–140.

Città del Vaticano: Biblioteca Apostolica Vaticana, 1948–1950.

Ambrose. *Des Sacrements. Des Mystères.* Edited and translated by Bernard Botte. Source chrétiennes 25 bis. Paris: Cerf, 1961.

Andrieu, Michel. *Les Ordines Romani du Haut Moyen Âge.* 5 vols. Spicilegium sacrum Lovaniense 11, 23–24, 28–29. Louvain, 1960.

Apel, Willi. *Gregorian Chant.* Bloomington: Indiana University Press, 1958.

The Confessions and Letters of St. Augustine. Edited by Philip Schaff. Nicene and Post-Nicene Fathers, 1. New York: Christian Literature Company, 1892.

Baldovin, John. "Kyrie Eleison and the Entrance Rite of the Roman Eucharist." *Worship* 60 (1986): 334–47.

Bergere, Thea and Richard. *The Story of St. Peter's.* New York: Dodd, Mead & Company, 1966.

Book of Pontiffs, The (Liber Pontificalis). Edited and translated by Raymond Davis. Rev. ed. Translated texts for Historians 6. Liverpool: Liverpool University Press, 2000.

Bouley, Allan. *From Freedom to Formula: The Evolution of the Eucharistic Prayer from Oral Improvisation to Written Texts.* The Catholic University of America Studies in Christian Antiquity, 21. Washington, DC: The Catholic University of America Press, 1981.

Bradshaw, Paul. *The Search for the Origins of Christian Worship.* 2nd ed. New York: Oxford University Press, 2002.

Callam, Daniel. "The Frequency of the Mass in the Latin Church, ca. 400." *Theological Studies* 45 (1985): 615–26.

Chrysostom, John. "Second Baptismal Instruction." Translated by Paul Harkins. *Ancient Christian Writers* 31. Westminster, MD: Newman Press, 1963.

Daly, Robert. *The Origins of the Christian Doctrine of Sacrifice.* Philadelphia: Fortress Press, 1978.

Denis-Boulet, Noele M. *The Christian Calendar.* Translated by P. Hepburne-Scott. The Twentieth Century Encyclopedia of Catholicism 113. New York: Hawthorn Books, 1960.

Dubois, Jacques. *Les martyrologes du moyen âge latin.* Typologie des sources du moyen âge occidental 26. Turnhout: Brepols, 1978.

Duchesne, Louis. *Liber Pontificalis.* 3 vols. Bibliothèque des Ecoles Francaises d'Athènes et de Rome. Paris: E. de Boccard, 1981.

Epistles of St. Clement of Rome and St. Ignatius of Antioch, The. Edited and translated by James Kleist. Ancient Christian Writers 1. Ramsey, NJ: Newman Press, 1946.

Eusebius. *The History of the Church.* Translated by G. A. Williamson. Harmondsworth, PA: Penguin Books, 1965.

Farley, Edward. *Theologia: The Fragmentation and Unity of Theological Education.* Philadelphia: Fortress Press, 1983.

Foley, Edward. "The Song of the Assembly in Medieval Eucharist." In *Medieval Liturgy,* edited by Lizette Larson-Miller, 203–34. Garland Medieval Casebooks, 18. New York-London: Garland Publishing, 1997.

Funk, F. X., ed. *Didascalia et Constitutiones Apostolorum.* 2 vols. Paderborn: F. Schoeningh, 1905.

Galavaris, George. *Bread and the Liturgy: The Symbolism of Early Christian and Byzantine Bread Stamps.* Madison: University of Wisconsin Press, 1970.

Gennadius. *De viris illustribus.* Edited by Ernest Cushing Richardson. Leipzig: J.C. Hinrichs, 1896.

Graduale Sacrosanctae Romanae Ecclesiae de Tempre et de Sanctis. Solemne: 1979.

Grégoire le Grand. *Dialogues.* 3 vols. Edited by Adalbert de Vogüé, translated by Paul Antin, Sources chrétiennes nos. 251, 260, 265. Paris: Éditions du Cerf, 1978–1980.

Gregory, Wilton. "The Lector–Minister of the Word: An Historical and Liturgical Study of the Office of the Lector in the Western Church." 2 vols. Ph.D. diss., The Pontifical Liturgical Institute, 1980.

Hoppin, Richard H. *Medieval Music.* New York: W. W. Norton, 1978.

Irenaeus of Lyon. *Contre les Hérésies, livre iv.* Edited by Adelin Rousseau, et al. Source chrétiennes 100. Paris: Cert, 1965.

Irwin, Kevin. *Context and Text: Method in Liturgical Theology.* Collegeville, MN: Liturgical Press, 1994.

Isidori Hispalensis Episcopi. *Etymologiarvm sive originvm libri XX.* 2 vols. Edited by W.M. Lindsay. Oxford: Clarendon Press, 1962.

Jeffery, Peter. "The Introduction of Psalmody into the Roman Mass by Pope Celestine I (422–32)." *Archiv für Liturgiewissenschaft* 26 (1984): 147–65.

Jungmann, Josef. *Pastoral Liturgy.* New York: Herder and Herder, 1962.

Leo the Great. *Sermons of Leo The Great.* Translated by C. L. Feltoe. Library of Nicene and Post Nicene Fathers. 2nd Series, vol. 12. New York: Christian Literature Company, 1895.

Life of Basil, c.vi. in *Acta Sanctoum,* June, vol. III = *Acta Sanctorum, editio novissima.* Paris: V. Palme, 1863.

Martimort, Aimé-Georges. *Les Lectures liturgiques et leurs Livres.* Typologie des sources du moyen âge occidental 64. Turnhout: Brepols, 1992.

———. *Les "Ordines", les Ordinaires et les Cérémoniaux.* Typologie des sources du moyen âge occidental 56. Turnhout: Brepols, 1991.

Mathews, Thomas F. *The Clash of Gods: A Reinterpretation of Early Christian Art.* Princeton: Princeton University Press, 1993.

———. "An Early Roman Chancel Arrangement and Its Liturgical Function." *Revista di Archeologia Cristiana* 38 (1962): 73–95.

McKinnon, James. *The Advent Project: The Later-Seventh-Century Creation of the Roman Mass Proper.* Berkeley, CA: University of California Press, 2000.

Mohlberg, Leo Cunibert, ed. *Sacramentarium Veronense.* Rerum Ecclesiasticarum Documenta: Series maior, fontes 1. Rome: Herder, 1966.

Osborne, Kenan. *Priesthood: A History of the Ordained Ministry in the Roman Catholic Church.* New York: Paulist Press, 1988.

Poems of Prudentius, The. Translated by M. Clement Eagan. Washington, DC: The Catholic University of America Press, 1962.

Quasten, Johannes. *Music and Worship in Pagan and Christian Antiquity.* Translated by Boniface Ramsey. Washington, DC: National Association of Pastoral Musicians, 1983.

Roberti, Mario Mirabella. *Grado*. 3rd ed. Trieste. n.d.

Schaefer, Francis J. "The Tabernacle: Its History, Structure and Custody." *The Ecclesiastical Review* 87 (1935): 449–68.

Sheerin, Daniel. *The Eucharist*. Messages of the Fathers of the Church 7. Wilmington, DE: Michael Glazier, 1986.

Spinks, Brian. "The Jewish Sources for the Sanctus." *The Heythrop Journal* 21 (1980): 168–79.

Taft, Robert. *Beyond East and West: Problems in Liturgical Understanding*. 2nd revised and enlarged ed. Rome: Pontifical Oriental Institute, 1997.

Toynbee, Jocelyn, and John Ward Perkins. *The Shrine of St. Peter and the Vatican Excavations*. London: Longmans, Green and Co., 1956.

Wilkinson, John. *Egeria's Travels to the Holy Land*. Rev. ed. Jerusalem and Warminster, England: Ariel, 1981.

Willis, G. G. "The Consecration of Churches Down to the Ninth Century." In *Further Essays in Early Roman Liturgy*, 133–73. Alcuin Club 50. London: SPCK, 1968.

Yarnold, Edward. *The Awe-Inspiring Rites of Initiation*. Slough, England: St. Paul Publications, 1977.

Bibliography for Chapter Four

Andrieu, Michel. *Les Ordines Romani du Haut Moyen Âge*. 5 vols. Spicilegium Sacrum Lovaniense. Louvain, 1960.

Baldovin, John. *The Urban Character of Christian Worship: The Origins, Development and Meaning of Stational Liturgy*. Orientalia Christiana analecta 228. Rome: Pont. Institutum Studiorum Orientalium, 1987.

Bede. *A History of the English Church and People*. Translated by Leo Sherley-Price. Rev. ed. Middlesex: Penguin Books, 1968.

Chavasse, Antoine. "L'Organisation stationnale du carême romain, avant le VIIIe siècle: une organisational 'pastorale.'" *Revue des Sciences Religieuses* 56, no. 1 (1982): 17–32.

Chupungco, Anscar. *Cultural Adaptation of the Liturgy*. New York: Paulist Press, 1982.

Clement, Richard W. "A Survey of Antique, Medieval, and Renaissance Book Production." In *Art into Life: Collected Papers from the Kresge Art Museum Medieval Symposia*, edited by Carol Garrett Fisher and Kathleen Scott, 9–47. East Lansing: Michigan State University Press, 1995.

Crook, John. *The Architectural Setting of the Cult of Saints in the Early Christian West, c. 300–c. 1200*. Oxford historical monographs. Oxford: Clarendon Press, 2000.

Eucharistic Vessels of the Middle Ages. n. p.: Garland Publishing, 1975.

Farley, Edward. *Theologia: The Fragmentation and Unity of Theological Education*. Philadelphia: Fortress Press, 1983.

Gregory the Great. "Letter to Bishop Palladius of Santes." In *S. Gregorii Magni Opera: Registrum Epistularum Libri I–VII*, edited by Dag Norberg. Corpus Christianorum, Series Latina. Turnholt: Brepols, 1982.

Gy, Pierre-Marie. "Typologie et ecclésiologie des livres liturgiques médiévaux." In *Liturgie dans l'histoire*, 75–89. Paris: Le Cerf, 1990.

Haüssling, Angelus Albert. *Mönchskonvent und Eucharistiefeier*. Liturgiewissenschaaftliche Quellen und Forschungen 58. Münster: Aschendorff, 1973.

Hucke, Helmut. "Toward a New Historical View of Gregorian Chant." *Journal of the American Musicological Society* 33 (1980): 437–67.

Kandler, K.–H. "Wann werden die Azyma das Brotelement in der Eucharistie im Abendland?" *Zeitschrift für Kirchengeschichte* 75 (1964): 153–55.

Lehmann, Edgar. "Die Anordnung der Altäre in der Karolingischen Kosterkirche zu Centula." In *Karl Der Grosse: Lebenswerk und Nachleben*, edited by Wolfgang Braunsfels and Hermann Schnitzler, 374–83. Dusseldorf, 1966.

Macy, Gary. *Theologies of the Eucharist in the Early Scholastic Period*. Cambridge: Cambridge University Press, 1984.

Madigan, Kevin. "The Parish in the Year 1000." *Chicago Studies* 37, no. 3 (1998): 233–44.

Manion, M. Francis. "Stipends and Eucharistic Praxis." *Worship* 57 (1983): 194–214.

McCracken, George, ed. *Early Medieval Theology.* Library of Christian Classics 9. London: SCM Press, 1957.

McKinnon, James. *The Advent Project: The Later-Seventh-Century Creation of the Roman Mass Proper.* Berkeley: University of California Press, 2000.

McMillan, Sharon. "How the Presbyter Becomes a Priest." In *Studia Liturgica Diversa,* edited by Maxwell Johnson and L. Edward Phillips, 163–75. Portland: Pastoral Press, 2004.

McNeill, John, and Helena Gamer. *Medieval Handbooks of Penance.* New York: Octagon Books, 1965.

McSherry, Patrick. *Wine as Sacramental Matter and the Use of Mustum.* Washington, DC: National Clergy Council on Alcoholism, 1986.

Mirgeler, Arthur. *Mutations of Western Christianity.* Notre Dame: University of Notre Dame Press, 1968 [1961].

Mohlberg, Leo C., ed. *Liber Sacramentorum Romanae Aeclesiae Ordinis Anni Circuli.* Rerum Ecclesiasticarum Documenta: Series maior, fontes 4. Rome: Herder, 1960.

———. *Missale Francorum.* Rerum Ecclesiasticarum Documenta: Series maior, fontes 2. Rome: Herder, 1957.

———. *Missale Gallicanum Vetus.* Rerum Ecclesiasticarum Documenta: Series maior, fontes 3. Rome: Herder, 1958.

———. *Missale Gothicum.* Rerum Ecclesiasticarum Documenta: Series maior, fontes 2. Rome: Herder, 1961.

Monastic Constitutions of Lanfranc, The. Edited and translated by David Knowles. Rev. ed. Christopher Brooke. Oxford: Clarendon Press, 2002.

Nelson, Lynn Harry. *Lectures in Medieval History.* An E-Book. Historical Text Archive Edition, 2004.

Pelikan, Jaroslav. *The Christian Tradition: A History of the Development of Doctrine.* Vol. 3: *The Growth of Medieval Theology (600–1300).* Chicago–London: The University of Chicago Press, 1978.

Poinard, M. Robert. *Tournus: Abbaye Saint-Philibert.* Tournus: Presbytère de Tournus, n.d.

Pounds, Norman J. G. *A History of the English Parish: The Culture of Religion from Augustine to Victoria.* Cambridge–New York: Cambridge University Press, 2000.

Rasmussen, Niels Krogh. *Les Pontificaux du haut Moyen Âge.* Spicilegium Sacrum Lovaniense 49. Leuven: Spicilegium Sacrum Lovaniense, 1998.

Ruff, Anthony. "A Millennium of Congregational Song." *Pastoral Music* (February–March, 1997): 11–15.

Russell, James. *The Germanization of Early Medieval Christianity: A Sociohistorical Approach to Religious Transformation.* New York–Oxford: Oxford University Press, 1994.

Rutherford, Richard. *The Death of a Christian: The Rite of Funerals.* Collegeville, MN: Liturgical Press, 1980.

Ryan, Michael. *Early Irish Communion Vessels: Church Treasures of the Golden Age.* Dublin: National Museum of Ireland, 1985.

Sheerin, Daniel. *The Eucharist.* Messages of the Fathers of the Church 7. Wilmington, DE: Michael Glazier, 1986.

Tertullian. *Corpus Christianorum, Series Latina.* 2 vols. Edited by Eligius Dekkers. Turnhout: Brepols, 1953.

Vogel, Cyrille. "Orientation dans les Ordines Romani." *La Maison Dieu* 70 (1962): 67–99.

———. "La Multiplication des Messes Solitaires au Moyen Âge: Essai de Statistique." *Revue des Sciences Religieuse* 55 (1981): 206–13.

Willis, G. G. *Further Essays in Early Roman Liturgy.* Alcuin Club Collections 50. London: SPCK, 1968.

Bibliography for Chapter Five

Andrieu, Michel. "Aux origines du culte du Saint-Sacrement. Reliquaires et monstrances eucharistiques." *Analecta Bollandiana* 68 (1950): 397–418.

Aquinas, Thomas. *Summa Theologica.* Translated by Fathers of the English Dominican Province. 3 vols. New York: Benzinger Brothers, 1948.

Architecture of Marcus Vitruvius Pollio, The. Translated by Joseph Gwilt. London: Priestley and Weale, 1826.

Armstrong, Regis, J. A. Wayne Hellmann, William Short, eds. *Francis of Assisi: Early Documents.* Vol. 1, The Saint. New York: New City Press, 1999.

Browe, Peter. *Die Verehrung der Eucharistie im Mittelalter.* Rome: Herder, 1967 [1932].

Bynum, Caroline Walker. *Holy Feast and Fast: The Religious Significance of Food to Medieval Women.* Berkeley, CA: University of California Press, 1987.

Cassirer, Ernst. *The Philosophy of the Enlightenment.* Boston: Beacon Press, 1955.

Crecelius, W. "Crailsheimer Schulordnung von 1480 mit deutschen geistlichen Liedern." *Alemannia* 3 (1875): 251–52.

Dijk, S. J. P. van, and J. Hazelden Walker. *The Origins of the Modern Roman Liturgy.* London: Darton, Longman and Todd, 1960.

Duffy, Eamonn. *The Stripping of the Altars: Traditional Religion in England 1400–1580.* New Haven: Yale University Press, 1992.

Eisenstein, Elizabeth. *The Printing Revolution in Early Modern Europe.* Cambridge: Cambridge University Press, 1993.

Engen, John van. *Devotio Moderna: Basic Writings.* New York: Paulist Press, 1988.

Fagan, Brian. *The Little Ice Age: How Climate Made History, 1300–1850.* New York: Basic Books, 2000.

Foley, Edward. *The First Ordinary of the Royal Abbey of St.-Denis in France.* Spicilegium Friburgense 32. Fribourg: The University Press, 1990.

Fortescue, Adrian. *The Mass: A Study of the Roman Liturgy.* London: Longmans, Green & Co., 1912.

Froude, J. A. *Life and Letters of Erasmus.* New York: Charles Scribner's Sons, 1895.

Gleason, Harold, ed. *Examples of Music before 1400.* New York: Appleton-Century-Crofts Inc., 1942.

Guillelmi Duranti Rationale Divinorum Officiorum I-IV. Edited by Anselme Davril and Timothy Thibodeau. Corpus Christianorum, Continuatio Mediaevalis 140. Turnhout: Brepols, 1995.

Harthan, John. *The Book of Hours.* New York: Park Lane, 1977.

Henderson, Ernest F. *Select Historical Documents of the Middle Ages.* London: George Bell and Sons, 1910.

Herbert, Christopher. "Permanent Easter Sepulchres: a Victorian Re-creation?" *Church Archaeology* 7/8/9 (2006): 7–19.

Hoppin, Richard H. *Medieval Music.* New York: W. W. Norton, 1978.

Jungmann, Josef. *Pastoral Liturgy.* New York: Herder and Herder, 1962.

Kennedy, V. L. "The Moment of Consecration and the Elevation of the Host." *Medieval Studies* 6 (1944): 121–50.

King, Ross. *Brunelleschi's Dome.* New York: Penguin Books, 2001.

Kreis, Steve. "Renaissance Humanism." http://www.historyguide.org/intellect/humanism.html (15.xii.05).

Lay Folks Mass Book, The. Edited by Thomas Frederick Simmons. Early English Text Society, Original Series 71. London: Oxford University Press, 1968 [1879].

Lubac, Henri de. *Corpus Mysticum: L'Eucharistie et l'église au Moyen-Âge.* Paris: Aubier, 1944.

Macy, Gary. *Treasures from the Storeroom: Medieval Religion and the Eucharist.* Collegeville, MN: Liturgical Press, 1999.

Marienwerder, Johannes von. *The Life of Dorothea von Montau: A Fourteenth-Century Recluse.* Translated by Ute Stargardt. Studies in Women and Religion, 39. Lewiston, NY: Edwin Mellen Press, 1997.

Ordinarium juxta ritum sacri Ordinis Fratru Fraedicatorum. Edited by Francis Guerrini. Rome: Collegium Angelicum, 1921.

Ostdiek, Gilbert. "The Threefold Fruits of the Mass: Notes and Reflections on Scotus' Quodlibetal Questions, q. 20." In *Essays Honoring Allan B. Wolter,* edited by William A. Frank and Girard Etzkorn, 203–19. St. Bonaventure, NY: Franciscan Institute, 1985.

Panofsky, Erwin. *Gothic Architecture and Scholasticism.* Cleveland, OH: The World Publishing Company, 1957.

Quinn, Patrick. "The Architectural Implications of the Choir in the Worshipping Community." *Liturgical Arts* 34 (1966): 38–46.

Regularis Concordia. Translated and edited by Thomas Symons. London: Thomas Nelson and Sons, 1953.

Reese, Gustave. *Music in the Middle Ages.* New York: W. W. Norton & Company, 1940.

———. *Music in the Renaissance.* Rev. ed. New York: W. W. Norton & Company, 1959.

Rubin, Miri. *Corpus Christi: The Eucharist in Late Medieval Culture*. Cambridge: Cambridge University Press, 1991.

———. *Gentile Tales: The Narrative Assault on Late Medieval Jews*. New Haven, CT: Yale University Press, 1999.

Ruff, Anthony. "Integration and Inconsistencies: The Thesaurus Musicae Sacrae in the Reformed Roman Eucharistic Liturgy." Th.D. diss., Karl-Franzens-Universität, Graz, 1998.

———. "A Millennium of Congregation Song." *Pastoral Music* (February–March, 1997): 11–15.

Simson, Otto von. *The Gothic Cathedra: Origins of Gothic Architecture and the Medieval Concept of Order*. 3rd ed. Bollingen Series 48. Princeton, NJ: Princeton University Press, 1988.

Southern, R. W. *Western Society and the Church in the Middle Ages*. Harmondsworth, PA: Penguin Books, 1970.

Unger, Richard W. *Beer in the Middle Ages and the Renaissance*. Philadelphia: University of Pennsylvania Press, 2004.

Vauchez, André. *The Laity in the Middle Ages: Religious Beliefs and Devotional Practices*. Edited by Daniel Bornstein. Translated by Margaret Schneider. Notre Dame, IN: University of Notre Dame Press, 1993.

Wiora, Walter. "The Origins of German Spiritual Folk Song: Comparative Methods in a Historical Study." *Ethnomusicology* 8 (1964): 1–13.

Bibliography for Chapter Six

Addleshaw, G. W. O., and F. Etchells. *The Architectural Setting of Anglican Worship*. London: Faber and Faber, 1948.

Berthier, J. *A Compendium of Theology*. 4 vols. Translated by Sidney A. Raemers. St. Louis–London: B. Herder, 1932.

Bett, Henry. *Nicholas of Cusa*. Merrick, NY: Richwood Publishing Co., 1976 [1932].

Boston Museum of Fine Arts. *American Church Silver of the Seventeenth and Eighteenth Centuries*. Boston: 1911.

Brilioth, Yngve. *Eucharistic Faith and Practice: Evangelical and Catholic*. Translated by A. G. Herbert. London: SPCK, 1930.

Calvin, John. *Institutes of the Christian Religion*. Edited by John McNeill. Translated by Ford Battles. 2 vols. The Library of Christian Classics, 20–21. Philadelphia: Westminster Press, 1960.

Canons and Decrees of the Council of Trent. Translated by H. J. Schroeder. St. Louis–London: B. Herder, 1941.

Catalogue of Silver Treasures from English Churches. London: Christies, 1955.

China in Transition, 1517–1911. Edited by Dun J. Li. New York: Van Nostrand Reinhold Company, 1969.

Concilium Tridentinum. Edited by Societas Goerresiana. Vol. 8. Freiburg-Bresgau: Herder, 1964 [1919].

Creytens, Raymond. "L'Ordinaire des Frères Prêcheurs au Moyen Âge." *Archivum Fratrum Praedicatorum* 24 (1954): 108–88.

del Río de la Hoz, Isabel. *The Cathedral and City of Toledo*. London: Scala, 2001.

Duffy, Eamon. *The Voices of Morebath: Reformation and Rebellion in an English Village*. New Haven, CT: Yale University Press, 2001.

Ellis, John Tracy. *Perspectives in American Catholicism*. Benedictine Studies 5. Baltimore, MD: Helicon, 1963.

Fiorenza, Francis Schüssler, and John Galvin, eds. *Systematic Theology: A Roman Catholic Perspective*. 2 vols. Minneapolis, MN: Fortress Press, 1991.

The First and Second Prayer Books of Edward VI. Introduction by Douglas Harrison. London: J. M. Dent & Sons, 1975 [1910].

Gardner, Samuel. *A Guide to English Gothic Architecture*. Cambridge: Cambridge University Press, 1922.

Grout, Donald J., and Claude V. Palisca. *A History of Western Music*. 4th ed. New York: W. W. Norton & Company, 1988.

Koerner, Joseph Leo. *The Reformation of the Image*. Chicago: University of Chicago Press, 2004.

Kreis, Steve. "Renaissance Humanism." http://www.historyguide.org/intellect/humanism.html (15.xii.05).

Lippe, Robert, ed. *Missale Romanum, Mediolani 1474.* 2 vols. Henry Bradshaw Society, 17 and 33. London: Harrison and Sons, 1899 and 1907.

Luther, Martin. *Luther's Works.* Edited by Jaroslav Pelikan and Helmut T. Lehman. St. Louis, MO: Concordia; Philadelphia: Fortress Press, 1955–1976.

Martimort, A. G. *Les sacrements.* Vol. 3 of *L'Église in Prière.* Edited by A. G. Martimort. Paris: Desclée, 1984.

McCool, Gerald A. *Catholic Theology in the Nineteenth Century.* New York: Seabury Press, 1977.

McLuhan, Marshall. *The Gutenberg Galaxy: The Making of Typographic Man.* Toronto: University of Toronto Press, 1962.

O'Connell, J. B. *Church Building and Furnishing: The Church's Way: A Study in Liturgical Law.* Notre Dame, IN: University of Notre Dame Press, 1955.

Pahl, Imgaard. *Coena Domini.* Vol. 1. Spicilegium Friburgense 29. Freiburg: 1983.

Peacock, E. *English Church Furniture, Ornaments and Decorations at the Period of the Reformation as Exhibited in a List of the Goods Destroyed in Certain Lincolnshire Churches, 1566.* London: 1866.

Pelikan, Jaroslav. *Bach among the Theologians.* Philadelphia: Fortress Press, 1985.

———. *The Christian Tradition: A History of the Development of Doctrine.* Vol. 4, *Reformation of Church and Dogma (1300–1700).* Chicago–London: The University of Chicago Press, 1984.

Psautier de Geneve 1562–1865, Le. Genève: Bibliothèque Publique et Universitaire, 1986.

Power, David. *The Sacrifice We Offer: The Tridentine Dogma and Its Reinterpretation.* New York: Crossroad, 1987.

Reese, Gustave. *Music in the Renaissance.* Rev. ed. New York: W. W. Norton & Company, 1959.

Reformatio: 400 Jahre Evangelishces Leben im Rheinland. Cologne: Walter Müller, 1965.

Sack, Daniel. *Whitebread Protestants: Food and Religion in American Culture.* New York: Palgrave, 2001

Sehling, Emil. *Die evangelischen Kirchenordnungen des 16 Jahrhunderts.* Leipzig: O. R. Reisland, 1902–1913.

Shepherd, Massey. *At All Times and in All Places.* 3rd rev. ed. New York: Seabury Press, 1965.

"Statuta Synodi Baltimorensis Anno 1791 Celebratae." *Concilia Provincialia Baltimori habita ab anno 1829 usque ad annum 1849, Editio altera.* Baltimore, MD: John Murphy and Co., 1851.

Stevens, Denis. *Tudor Church Music.* Rev. ed. New York: W. W. Norton and Company, 1966.

Stevenson, Robert. *Music in Aztec and Inca Territory.* Berkeley: University of California, 1968.

Stiller, Günther. *Johann Sebastian Bach and Liturgical Life in Leipzig.* Translated by Herbert Bouman, et al. Edited by Robin Leaver. St. Louis, MO: Concordia, 1984.

Swidler, Leonard. *Aufklärung Catholicism, 1780–1850: Liturgical and Other Reforms in the Catholic Aufklärung.* Missoula: Scholars Press, 1978.

Thompson, Bard. *Liturgies of the Western Church.* Cleveland: Collins and World Publishing Co., 1962.

United States Bishops' Committee on the Liturgy, *Environment and Art in Catholic Worship.* Washington, DC: USCC, 1978.

Visser, John de, and Harold Kalman. *Pioneer Churches.* New York: W. W. Norton, 1976.

Voelker, Carole. "Charles Borromeo's Instructiones Fabricae Et Supellectilis Ecclesiasticae, 1577: A Translation With Commentary and Analysis." Ph.D. diss., Syracuse University, 1977.

Watts, W. W. *Catalogue of Chalices and Other Communion Vessels.* London: Victoria and Albert Museum Department of Metalwork, 1922.

Weber, Francis J. "America's First Vernacular Missal." *America's Catholic Heritage, Some Bicentennial Reflections (1776–1976).* St. Paul Editions, 1976.

White, James. *Protestant Worship and Church Architecture.* New York: Oxford University Press, 1964.

———. *Protestant Worship: Traditions in Transition.* Louisville: Westminster John Knox Press, 1989.

———. *Roman Catholic Worship: Trent to Today.* Collegeville, MN: Liturgical Press, 2003.

Bibliography for Chapter Seven

ArchNewsNow. "Rome: White concrete 'sails' soar into a Roman neighborhood." October 23, 2003. http://www.archnewsnow.com/features/Feature 123.htm.

Baptism, Eucharist, and Mininstry. Faith and Order Paper no. 111. Geneva: World Council of Churches, 1982.

Barz, Gregory. *Performing Religion: Negotiating Past and Present in Kwaya Music of Tanzania.* Church and Theology in Context 42. Amsterdam–New York: Rodopi, 2003.

Blacking, John. *How Musical is Man?* Seattle, WA: University of Washington Press, 1973.

Botte, Bernard. *From Silence to Participation.* Translated by John Sullivan. Washington, DC: The Pastoral Press, 1988.

Collins, Peter. *Concrete: The Vision of a New Architecture, A Study of Auguste Perret and His Precursors.* London: Faber and Faber, 1959.

Common Lectionary. New York: The Church Hymnal Corporation, 1983.

Congregation for Divine Worship and the Discipline of the Sacraments. *Inculturation and the Roman Liturgy: Fourth Instruction for the Right Application of the Conciliar Constitution on,* 1994.

———. *Redemptionis Sacramentum,* 2004.

Cope, Gilbert, ed. *Making the Building Serve the Liturgy: Studies in the Re-Ordering of Churches.* London: A. R. Mowbray & Co., 1962.

Debuyst, Frédéric. "Architectural Setting (Modern) and the Liturgical Movement." In *The New Westminster Dictionary of Liturgy and Worship,* edited by J. G. Davies, 36–48. Philadelphia: Westminster Press, 1986.

Deri, Otto. *Exploring Twentieth-Century Music.* New York: Holt, Rinehart and Winston, Inc., 1968.

Empie, Paul, and T. Austin Murphy, eds. *Lutherans and Catholics in Dialogue I–III.* Minneapolis: Augsburg Publishing, 1965.

Fasano, Alessio. "Prevalence of Celiac Disease in At-Risk and Not-At-Risk Groups in the United States." *Archives of Internal Medicine* 163, no. 3 (2003): 286–92.

Ferguson, Harvie. *Modernity and Subjectivity: Body, Soul, Spirit.* Charlottesville, VA: University Press of Virginia, 2000.

Flannery, Austin, ed. *Vatican Council II: The Basic Sixteen Documents: A Completely Revised Translation in Inclusive Language.* Northport, NY: Costello Publishing Co., 1996.

Foley, Edward. "When American Roman Catholics Sing." *Worship* 63 (1989): 98–112.

Gilroy, Paul. *The Black Atlantic: Modernity and Double Consciousness.* Cambridge, MA: Harvard University Press, 1993.

Glover, Raymond. *Perspectives on the New Edition.* Hymnal Studies 1. New York: The Church Hymnal Corporation, 1981.

Grout, Donald J., and Claude V. Palisca. *A History of Western Music.* 4th ed. New York: W. W. Norton & Company, 1988.

Gutiérrez, Gustavo. *A Theology of Liberation.* Translated and edited by Caridad Inda and John Eagleson. Maryknoll, NY: Orbis, 1973.

Halgren Kilde, Jeanne. *When Church Became Theatre: The Transformation of Evangelical Church Architecture and Worship in Nineteenth-Century America.* Oxford: Oxford University Press, 2005.

Hammond, Peter. *Liturgy and Architecture.* London: Barrie and Rockliff, 1960.

Hollenweger, Walter. *Pentecostalism: Origins and Developments Worldwide.* Peabody, MA: Hendrickson, 1997.

Krader, Barbara. "Ethnomusicology." In *New Grove Dictionary of Music and Musicians,* vol. 6, edited by Stanley Sadie, 275–82. London: Oxford University Press, 1980.

Krumpelman, Frances. "The Laity's Books for Prayer and Worship: A Graced Tradition." *Liturgy 90* 23, no. 4 (1992): 8–11; and, 23, no. 5 (1992): 4–7.

Kyriale. Boston: McLaughlin and Reilly Co., 1937.

Liess, Andreas. *Carl Orff: Idee und Werk.* Rev. ed. Zürich-Freiburg im Bresgau: Atlantis, 1977.

Mauck, Marchita. "Architectural Setting (Modern)." In *The New Westminster Dictionary of Liturgy and Worship,* edited by Paul Bradshaw, 21–25. Louisville, KY: Westminster John Knox Press, 2002.

Michel, Virgil. "Christian Culture." *Orate Fratres* 13 (1939): 296–304.

Mitchell, Nathan. "Amen Corner." *Worship* 77, no. 1 (2003): 56–69.

O'Meara, Thomas. "Leaving the Baroque: The Fallacy of Restoration in the Post-Conciliar Era." *America* (3 February 1996): 10–14, 25–28.

Osborne, Kenan. *Christian Sacraments in a Postmodern World: A Theology for the Third Millennium.* New York: Paulist Press, 1999.

Our Lady of the Height Ronchamp. Schnell Art Guide 818. 17th English edition. Munich-Zurich: Verlag Schnell & Steiner, 1986.

Pecklers, Keith. *Dynamic Equivalence: The Living Language of Christian Worship.* Collegeville, MN: Liturgical Press, 2003.

———. *The Unread Vision: The Liturgical Movement in the United States of America, 1926–1955.* Collegeville, MN: Liturgical Press, 1998.

Pugin, Augustus. *The True Principles of Pointed or Christian Architecture.* New York: St. Martin's Press, 1973 [1841].

Robertson, Roland. "Glocalization: Time-Space and Homogeneity-Heterogeneity." In *Global Modernities,* edited by Mike Featherstone, Scott Lash, and Roland Robertson, 25–44. London: Sage, 1995.

Routley, Erik. *A Panorama of Christian Hymnody.* Collegeville, MN: Liturgical Press, 1979.

Saliers, Don. *Worship as Theology: Foretaste of Glory Divine.* Nashville: Abingdon Press, 1994.

Schattauer, Thomas. "Sunday Worship at Neuendettelsau under Wilhelm Löhe." *Worship* 59 (1985): 370–84.

Schillebeeckx, Edward. *The Eucharist.* Translated by N. D. Smith. New York: Sheed and Ward, 1968.

Schneiders, Sandra. "The Study of Christian Spirituality: Contours and Dynamics of a Discipline." *Christian Spirituality Bulletin* 6, no. 1 (1998): 1, 3–12.

Schreiter, Robert. *The New Catholicity: Theology between the Global and the Local.* Maryknoll, NY: Orbis, 1997.

Seasoltz, R. Kevin. *The New Liturgy: A Documentation, 1903–1965.* New York: Herder and Herder, 1966.

Senn, Frank, ed. *New Eucharistic Prayers.* New York: Paulist Press, 1987.

Sheppard, Lancelot, ed. *The People Worship: A History of the Liturgical Movement.* New York: Hawthorn Books, Inc., 1967.

Skelton, Geoffrey. *Paul Hindemith: The Man Behind the Music.* London: Victor Gollancz Ltd., 1975.

Smith, Norris Kelly. *Frank Lloyd Wright: A Study in Architectural Content.* Englewood Cliffs, NJ: Prentice-Hall Inc., 1966.

Southern, R. W. *Western Society and the Church in the Middle Ages.* Harmondsworth, PA: Penguin Books, 1970.

Sövik, E. A. *Architecture for Worship.* Minneapolis, MN: Augsburg Publishing House, 1973.

United States Bishops' Committee on the Liturgy, *Environment and Art in Catholic Worship.* Washington, DC: USCC, 1978.

United States Council of Catholic Bishops, *Economic Justice for All: Pastoral Letter on Catholic Social Teaching and the U.S. Economy.* Washington, DC: USCCB Publishing, 1986.

United States Council of Catholic Bishops, *The Eucharist: A Lutheran-Roman Catholic Statement,* 2.1. http:www.usccb.org/seia/luthrc_eucharist_1968.shtml (section 1.c.).

Weaver, F. Ellen. "Liturgy for the Laity: The Jansenist Case for Popular Participation in Worship in the Seventeenth and Eighteenth Centuries." *Studia Liturgica* 19, no. 1 (1989): 47–59.

White, James. *Protestant Worship: Traditions in Transition.* Louisville, KY: Westminster John Knox Press, 1989.

———. "Sources for the Study of Protestant Worship in America." *Worship* 61 (1987): 516–33.

Willett, John. *The Theatre of Bertolt Brecht.* New York: New Directions, 1968.

Wright, Frank Lloyd. *The Living City.* New York: Horizon Press, 1958.

Index